The Right Thing to Do

Basic Readings in Moral Philosophy

FIFTH EDITION

Edited by

JAMES RACHELS

and

STUART RACHELS

 **Higher Education**

Boston   Burr Ridge, IL   Dubuque, IA   New York   San Francisco   St. Louis
Bangkok   Bogotá   Caracas   Kuala Lumpur   Lisbon   London   Madrid   Mexico City
Milan   Montreal   New Delhi   Santiago   Seoul   Singapore   Sydney   Taipei   Toronto

Higher Education

Published by McGraw-Hill, an imprint of The McGraw-Hill Companies, Inc., 1221 Avenue of the Americas, New York, NY 10020. Copyright © 2010, 2007, 2003, 1999, 1989. All rights reserved. No part of this publication may be reproduced or distributed in any form or by any means, or stored in a database or retrieval system, without the prior written consent of The McGraw-Hill Companies, Inc., including, but not limited to, in any network or other electronic storage or transmission, or broadcast for distance learning.

This book is printed on acid-free paper.

2 3 4 5 6 7 8 9 0 DOC/DOC 0 9

ISBN: 978-0-07-340740-1
MHID: 0-07-340740-2

Editor in Chief: *Michael Ryan*
Editorial Director: *Beth Mejia*
Sponsoring Editor: *Mark Georgiev*
Marketing Manager: *Pamela Cooper*
Managing Editor: *Nicole Bridge*
Production Editor: *David Blatty*
Design Manager: *Margarite Reynolds*
Production Supervisor: *Louis Swaim*
Composition: *11/12 Baskerville by Laserwords*
Printing: *R. R. Donnelley & Sons*

Cover Art: Aleksandr Rodchenko. (1891–1956). Non-Objective Painting no. 80 (Black on Black). 1918. Oil on canvas, 32 1/4" × 31 1/4". Gift of the artist, through Jay Leyda. (114. 1936). Digital Image © The Museum of Modern Art/Licensed by Scala/Art Resource, NY. © Aleksandr Rodchenko/RAO, Moscow/VAGA, New York.

Library of Congress Cataloging-in-Publication Data

The right thing to do:basic readings in moral philosophy.—5th ed./[edited by] Stuart Rachels.
    p. cm.
  Includes bibliographical references and index.
  ISBN-13: 978-0-07-340740-1 (alk. paper)
  ISBN-10: 0-07-340740-2 (alk. paper)
 1. Ethics—Textbooks. I. Rachels, Stuart, 1969-
BJ1012.R5 2010
170—dc22   2009000732

The Internet addresses listed in the text were accurate at the time of publication. The inclusion of a Web site does not indicate an endorsement by the authors or McGraw-Hill, and McGraw-Hill does not guarantee the accuracy of the information presented at these sites.

www.mhhe.com

Contents

iii

STARVATION

WAR, TERRORISM, AND TORTURE

THE DEATH PENALTY

SEX AND DRUGS

RACE

BIOETHICS

Preface

Moral philosophy is the study of how one should live. This anthology is an introduction to that great subject. The readings cover the main moral theories and present a wealth of ideas about various practical matters.

This book is a companion to *The Elements of Moral Philosophy*, which was also written by James Rachels and revised by Stuart Rachels. These two books complement each other and may be read together. However, nothing in either book presupposes knowledge of the other.

To select the pieces for this volume, I read about 150 essays. I was looking for articles on serious moral topics that are deftly argued; that are pleasant to read; that lend themselves to lively discussion; and that the average college student can grasp. I believe that the selections chosen are not merely good articles on suitable topics; they are first-rate essays on compelling issues. Students who read this book will want to read more, unless the subject is simply not for them.

This edition contains fourteen new essays, and nine were eliminated. So, there is now more material to choose from. Two topics account for half of the expansion: war and sexuality. The morality of war has become increasingly important as the conflicts in Iraq and Afghanistan continue. And I wanted greater coverage of sexual morality because, well, sex is a riveting subject. Thus, there are now essays in the book on monogamy, date rape, terrorism, torture, and the atomic bombings of Japan.

Two selections have been retained but improved: I replaced the 1974 version of Peter Singer's "All Animals Are Equal" with the 1990 version, and Michael Huemer was good enough to revise some of the statistics in his essay, "America's Unjust Drug War."

I eliminated some articles because they felt dated. Other articles got cut because they weren't being used enough. Instructors who regret the departure of Hobbes and Hume should consider assigning

Jonathan Bennett's "translations" of their work, available for free at www.earlymoderntexts.com. Bennett has rewritten many of the philosophical classics in order to make them easier to understand.

For their help, I thank Mahesh Ananth, Samuel Barnett, David Blatty, Nicole Bridge, Phil Butcher, Heather Elliott, Susan Gouijnstook, Dan Haggerty, Michael Huemer, Douglas Husak, Kevin Kukla, Nathan Nobis, Vida Pavesich, Carol Rachels, Shane Schauf, Patricia Steck, and the anonymous reviewers commissioned by McGraw-Hill Publishers.

To learn more about James Rachels, visit www.jamesrachels.org.

I describe the revisions to this book in greater detail on my website: www.jamesrachels.org/stuart. If you have suggestions for the next edition, please let me know: srachels@bama.ua.edu.

—Stuart Rachels

About the Authors

JAMES RACHELS (1941–2003) wrote *The End of Life: Euthanasia and Morality* (1986), *Created from Animals: The Moral Implications of Darwinism* (1990), *Can Ethics Provide Answers? And Other Essays in Moral Philosophy* (1997), *The Elements of Moral Philosophy* (editions 1–4), *Problems from Philosophy* (first edition, 2005), and *The Legacy of Socrates: Essays in Moral Philosophy* (2007). His website is www.jamesrachels.org.

STUART RACHELS is Associate Professor of Philosophy at the University of Alabama. He has revised several of James Rachels' books, including *The Elements of Moral Philosophy* (sixth edition, 2010) and *Problems from Philosophy* (second edition, 2009). Stuart won the United States Chess Championship in 1989, at the age of 20, and he is a Bronze Life Master at bridge. His website is www.jamesrachels.org/stuart.

CHAPTER 1

A Short Introduction to Moral Philosophy

James Rachels

An ancient legend tells the story of Gyges, a poor shepherd who found a magic ring in a fissure opened by an earthquake. The ring would make its wearer invisible, so he could go anywhere and do anything undetected. Gyges was an unscrupulous fellow, and he quickly realized that the ring could be put to good advantage. We are told that he used its power to gain entry to the royal palace where he seduced the queen, murdered the king, and seized the throne. (It is not explained how invisibility helped him to seduce the queen—but let that pass.) In no time at all, he went from being a poor shepherd to being king of all the land.

This story is recounted in Book II of Plato's *Republic*. Like all of Plato's works, the *Republic* is written in the form of a dialogue between Socrates and his companions. Glaucon, who is having an argument with Socrates, uses the story of Gyges's ring to make a point.

Glaucon asks us to imagine that there are two such rings, one given to a man of virtue and the other given to a rogue. How might we expect them to behave? The rogue, of course, will do anything necessary to increase his own wealth and power. Since the cloak of invisibility will protect him from discovery, he can do anything he pleases without fear of being caught. Therefore, he will recognize no moral constraints on his conduct, and there will be no end to the mischief he will do.

But how will the so-called virtuous man behave? Glaucon suggests that he will do no better than the rogue:

> No one, it is commonly believed, would have such iron strength of mind as to stand fast in doing right or keep his hands off other men's goods, when he could go to the market-place and fearlessly

1

help himself to anything he wanted, enter houses and sleep with any woman he chose, set prisoners free and kill men at his pleasure, and in a word go about among men with the powers of a god. He would behave no better than the other; both would take the same course.

Moreover, Glaucon asks, why shouldn't he? Once he is freed from the fear of reprisal, why shouldn't a person simply do what he pleases, or what he thinks is best for himself? Why should he care at all about "morality"?

The *Republic*, written over 2300 years ago, was one of the first great works of moral philosophy in Western history. Since then, philosophers have formulated theories to explain what morality is, why it is important, and why it has the peculiar hold on us that it does. What, if anything, justifies us in believing that we *morally ought* to act in one way rather than another?

Relativism

Perhaps the oldest philosophical theory about morality is that right and wrong are relative to the customs of one's society—on this view, there is nothing behind the demands of morality except social convention. Herodotus, the first of the great Greek historians, lived at about the time of Socrates. His *History* is full of wonderful anecdotes that illustrate his belief that "right" and "wrong" are little more than names for social conventions. Of the Massagetae, a tribe in Central Asia, he writes:

> The following are some of their customs—Each man has but one wife, yet all the wives are held in common. . . . Human life does not come to its natural close with these people; but when a man grows very old, all his kinsfolk collect together and offer him up in sacrifice; offering at the same time some cattle also. After the sacrifice they boil the flesh and feast on it; and those who thus end their days are reckoned the happiest. If a man dies of disease they do not eat him, but bury him in the ground, bewailing his ill-fortune that he did not come to be sacrificed. They sow no grain, but live on their herds, and on fish, of which there is great plenty in the Araxes. Milk is what they chiefly drink. The only god they worship is the sun, and to him they offer the horse in sacrifice, under the notion of giving the swiftest of the gods the swiftest of all mortal creatures.

Herodotus did not think the Massagetae were to be criticized for such practices. Their customs were neither better nor worse than those of other peoples; they were merely different. The Greeks, who considered themselves more "civilized," may have thought that their customs were superior, but, Herodotus says, that is only because everyone believes the customs of his own society to be the best. The "truth" depends on one's point of view—that is, on the society in which one happens to have been raised.

Relativists think that Herodotus was obviously on to something and that those who believe in "objective" right and wrong are merely naïve. Critics, however, object to the theory on a number of grounds. First, it is exceedingly conservative, in that the theory endorses whatever moral views happen to be current in a society. Consider our own society. Many people believe that our society's moral code is mistaken, at least on some points—for example, they may disagree with the dominant social view regarding capital punishment, or homosexuality, or the treatment of nonhuman animals. Must we conclude that these would-be reformers are wrong, merely because they oppose the majority view? Why must the majority always be right?

But there is a deeper problem with Relativism, emphasized by Socrates. Some social customs are, indeed, merely arbitrary, and when these customs are at issue it is fruitless to insist that one society's practices are better than another's. Funerary practices are a good example. The Greeks burned their dead, while the Callatians ate their dead, but neither practice is better than the other. However, it does not follow from this that *all* social practices are arbitrary in the same way. Some are, and some are not. The Greeks and the Callatians were free to accept whatever funerary practices they liked because no objective reason could be given why one practice was superior to the other. In the case of other practices, however, there may be good reasons why some are superior. It is not hard, for example, to explain why honesty and respect for human life are socially desirable, and similarly it is not hard to explain why slavery and racism are undesirable. Because we can support our judgments about these matters with rational arguments, we do not have to regard those judgments as "merely" the expression of our particular society's moral code.

Divine Commands

A second ancient idea, also familiar to Socrates, was that moral living consists in obedience to divine commands. If this were true, then we could easily answer the challenge of Gyges's ring—even if we had the power of invisibility, we would still be subject to divine retribution, so ultimately we could not "get away with" doing whatever we wanted.

But Socrates did not believe that right living could consist merely in trying to please the gods. In the *Euthyphro,* another of Plato's dialogues, Socrates is shown considering at some length whether "right" can be the same as "what the gods command." Now we may notice, to begin with, that there are considerable practical difficulties with this as a general theory of ethics. How, for example, are we supposed to *know* what the gods command? There are, of course, those who claim to have spoken with God about the matter and who therefore claim to be in a position to pass on his instructions to the rest of us. But people who claim to speak for God are not the most trustworthy folks—hearing voices can be a sign of schizophrenia or a megalomania just as easily as an instance of divine communication. Others, more modestly, rely on scripture or church tradition for guidance. But those sources are notoriously ambiguous—they give vague and often contradictory instructions—so, when people consult these authorities, they typically rely on whatever elements of scripture or church tradition support the moral views they are already inclined to agree with. Moreover, because scripture and church tradition have been handed down from earlier times, they provide little direct help in addressing distinctively contemporary problems: the problem of environmental preservation, for example, or the problem of how much of our resources should be allocated to AIDS research as opposed to other worthy endeavors.

Still, it may be thought that God's commands provide the ultimate *authority* for ethics, and that is the issue Socrates addressed. Socrates accepted that the gods exist and that they may issue instructions. But he showed that this cannot be the ultimate basis of ethics. He points out that we have to distinguish two possibilities: Either the gods have some reason for the instructions they issue, or they do not. If they do not, then their commands are merely arbitrary—the gods are like petty tyrants who demand that we act in this way and that, even though there is no good reason for it. But this is an impious view that religious people will not want to accept. On the other hand, if we say that the gods do have good reasons for their instructions, then we have admitted that there is a standard of rightness independent of their commands—namely, the standard to which the gods themselves refer in deciding what to require of us.

It follows, then, that even if one accepts a religious picture of the world, the rightness or wrongness of actions cannot be understood merely in terms of their conformity to divine prescriptions. We may always ask why the gods command what they do, and the answer to *that* question will reveal why right actions are right and why wrong actions are wrong.

Aristotle

Although Relativism and the Divine Command Theory have always had supporters, they have never been popular among serious students of moral philosophy. The first extended, systematic treatise on moral philosophy, produced two generations after Socrates, was Aristotle's *Nicomachean Ethics* (ca. 330 B.C.), and Aristotle wasted no time on such notions. Instead, Aristotle offered a detailed account of the virtues—the qualities of character that people need to do well in life. The virtues include courage, prudence, generosity, honesty, and many more; Aristotle sought to explain what each one is and why it is important. His answer to the question of Gyges's ring was that virtue is necessary for human beings to achieve happiness; therefore, the man of virtue is ultimately better off *because* he is virtuous.

Aristotle's view of the virtuous life was connected with his overall way of understanding the world and our place in it. Aristotle's conception of what the world is like was enormously influential; it dominated Western thinking for over 1700 years. A central feature of this conception was that *everything in nature exists for a purpose.* "Nature," Aristotle said, "belongs to the class of causes which act for the sake of something."

It seems obvious that artifacts such as knives and chariots have purposes, because we have their purposes in mind when we make them. But what about natural objects that we do not make? Do they have purposes too? Aristotle thought so. One of his examples was that we have teeth so that we can chew. Such biological examples are quite persuasive; the parts of our bodies do seem, intuitively, to have particular purposes—eyes are for seeing, the heart is for pumping blood, and so on. But Aristotle's thesis was not limited to organic beings. According to him, *everything* in nature has a purpose. He also thought, to take a different sort of example, that rain falls so that plants can grow. As odd as it may seem to a modern reader, Aristotle was perfectly serious about this. He considered other alternatives, such as that the rain falls "of necessity" and that this helps the plants only "by coincidence," and rejected them. His considered view was that plants and animals are what they are, and that the rain falls as it does, "because it is better so."

The world, therefore, is an orderly, rational system, with each thing having its own proper place and serving its own special purpose. There is a neat hierarchy: The rain exists for the sake of the plants, the plants exist for the sake of the animals, and the animals exist—of course—for the sake of people, whose well-being is the point of the whole arrangement. In the *Politics* Aristotle wrote:

> [W]e must believe, first that plants exist for the sake of animals, second that all other animals exist for the sake of man, tame animals for the use he can make of them as well as for the food they provide; and as for wild animals, most though not all of these can be used for food or are useful in other ways; clothing and instruments can be made out of them. If then we are right in believing that nature makes nothing without some end in view, nothing to no purpose, it must be that nature has made all things specifically for the sake of man.

It was a stunningly anthropocentric view. Aristotle may be forgiven, however, when we consider that virtually every important thinker in our history has entertained some such thought. Humans are a remarkably vain species.

Natural Law

The Christian thinkers who came later found Aristotle's view of the world to be congenial. There was only one thing missing: The addition of God was required to make the picture complete. (Aristotle had denied that God was a necessary part of the picture. For him, the worldview we have outlined was not religious; it was simply a description of how things are.) Thus, the Christian thinkers said that the rain falls to help the plants because *that is what the Creator intended,* and the animals are for human use because *that is what God made them for.* Values and purposes were, therefore, conceived to be a fundamental part of the nature of things, because the world was believed to have been created according to a divine plan.

This view of the world had a number of consequences for ethics. On the most general level, it affirmed the supreme value of human life, and it explained why humans are entitled to do whatever they please with the rest of nature. The basic moral arrangement—human beings, whose lives are sacred, dominating a world made for their benefit—was enshrined as the Natural Order of Things.

At a more detailed level, a corollary of this outlook was that the "laws of nature" specify how things *ought to be,* as well as describing how things *are*. In turn, knowing how things ought to be enables us to evaluate states of affairs as objectively good or bad. Things are as they ought to be when they are serving their natural purposes; when they do not or cannot serve those purposes, things have gone wrong. Thus, teeth that have decayed and cannot be used for chewing are defective; and drought, which deprives plants of the rain they need, is a natural, objective evil.

There are also implications for human action: On this view, moral rules are one type of law of nature. The key idea here is that some forms of human behavior are "natural" while others are not; and "unnatural" acts are said to be wrong. Beneficence, for example, is natural for us because God has made us as social creatures. We want and need the friendship of other people, and we have natural affections for them; hence, behaving brutishly toward them is unnatural. Or to take a different sort of example, the purpose of the sex organs is procreation. Thus, any use of them for other purposes is "contrary to nature"—which is why the Christian church has traditionally regarded any form of sexual activity that does not result in pregnancy, such as masturbation, gay sex, or the use of contraceptives, as impermissible.

This combination of ideas, together with others like them, formed the core of an outlook known as natural-law ethics. The Theory of Natural Law was developed most fully by Saint Thomas Aquinas (1225–1274), who lived at a time when the Aristotelian worldview was unchallenged. Aquinas was the foremost thinker among traditional Catholic theologians. Today natural-law theory still has adherents inside the Catholic Church, but few outside. The reason is that the Aristotelian worldview, on which natural-law ethics depended, has been replaced by the outlook of modern science.

Galileo, Newton, Darwin, and others developed ways of understanding natural phenomena that made no use of evaluative notions. In their way of thinking, the rain has no purpose. It does not fall in order to help the plants grow. Plants typically get the amount of water they need because each species has evolved, by natural selection, in the environment in which that amount of water is available. Natural selection produces an orderly arrangement that *appears* to have been designed, but that is only an illusion. To explain nature there is no need to assume purpose-involving principles, neither Aristotle's "final causes" nor the Christians' God. This changed outlook was by far the most insidious feature of the new science; it is little wonder that the church's first response was to condemn it.

Modern science transformed people's view of what the world is like. But part of the transformation, inseparable from the rest, was an altered view of the nature of ethics. Right and wrong could no longer be deduced from the nature of things, for on the new view the natural world does not, in and of itself, manifest value and purpose. The *inhabitants* of the world may have needs and desires that generate values special to them, but that is all. The world apart from those inhabitants knows and cares nothing for their values, and it has no values of its own. A hundred and fifty years before Nietzsche declared, "There are no moral facts," the Scottish philosopher David Hume had come to the same conclusion. Hume summed up the moral implications of the new worldview in his *Treatise of Human Nature* (1739) when he wrote:

> Take any action allow'd to be vicious: Willful murder, for instance. Examine it in all lights, and see if you can find that matter of fact, or real existence, which you call *vice*. In whichever way you take it, you find only certain passions, motives, volitions and thoughts. There is no other matter of fact in the case.

To Aristotle's idea that "nature has made all things for the sake of man," Hume replied: "The life of a man is of no greater importance to the universe than that of an oyster."

The Social Contract

If there are no moral facts and no God, what becomes of morality? Ethics must somehow be understood as a purely human phenomenon—as the product of human needs, interests, and desires—and nothing else. Figuring out how to do this has been the basic project of moral philosophy from the 17th century on.

Thomas Hobbes, the foremost English philosopher of the 17th century, suggested one way in which ethics might be understood in purely human terms. Hobbes assumed that "good" and "bad" are just names we give to things we like and dislike. Thus, because we may like different things, we may disagree about what is good or bad. However, Hobbes said, in our fundamental psychological makeup we are all very much alike. We are all basically self-interested creatures who want to live and to live as well as possible. This is the key to understanding ethics. Ethics arises when people realize *what they must do* to live well.

Hobbes was the first important modern thinker to provide a secular, naturalistic basis for ethics. He pointed out that each of us is enormously better off living in a mutually cooperative society than we would be if we tried to make it on our own. The benefits of social living go far beyond companionship: Social cooperation makes possible schools, hospitals, and highways; houses with electricity and central heating; airplanes and telephones; newspapers and books; movies, opera, and bingo; science and agriculture. Without social cooperation we would lose these benefits and more. Therefore, it is to the advantage of each of us to do whatever is necessary to establish and maintain a cooperative society.

But it turns out that a mutually cooperative society can exist only if we adopt certain rules of behavior—rules that require telling the truth, keeping our promises, respecting one another's lives and property, and so on:

- Without the presumption that people will tell the truth, there would be no reason for people to pay any attention to what other people say. Communication would be impossible. And without communication among its members, society would collapse.
- Without the requirement that people keep their promises, there could be no division of labor—workers could not count on getting paid, retailers could not rely on their agreements with suppliers, and so on—and the economy would collapse. There could be no business, no building, no agriculture, no medicine.
- Without assurances against assault, murder, and theft, no one could feel secure; everyone would have to be constantly on guard against everyone else, and social cooperation would be impossible.

Thus, to obtain the benefits of social living, we must strike a bargain with one another, with each of us agreeing to obey these rules, provided others do likewise. We must also establish mechanisms for enforcing these rules—such as legal sanctions and other, less formal methods of enforcement—so that we can *count on* one another to obey them. This "social contract" is the basis of morality. Indeed, morality can be defined as nothing more or less than *the set of rules that rational people will agree to obey, for their mutual benefit, provided that other people will obey them as well.*

This way of understanding morality has a number of appealing features. First, it takes the mystery out of ethics and makes it a practical, down-to-earth business. Living morally is not a matter of blind obedience to the mysterious dictates of a supernatural being; nor is it a matter of fidelity to lofty but pointless abstract rules. Instead, it is a matter of doing what it takes to make social living possible.

Second, this theory makes it clear how morality can be rational and objective even if there are no moral facts. It is not merely a matter of opinion that the rule against murder must be a part of any workable social scheme or that rational people, to secure their own welfare, must agree to adopt such a rule. Nor is it merely a matter of opinion that rules requiring truthfulness and promise keeping are needed for people to flourish in a social setting. Even if there are no moral facts, the reasoning that leads to such conclusions is perfectly objective.

Third, the Social Contract Theory explains why we should *care* about ethics—it offers at least a partial response to the problem of Gyges's ring. If there is no God to punish us, why should we bother to do what is "right," especially when it is not to our advantage? The answer is that it *is* to our advantage to live in a society where people behave morally—thus, it is rational for us to accept moral restrictions on our conduct as part of a bargain we make with other people. We benefit directly from the ethical conduct of others, and our own compliance with the moral rules is the price we pay to secure their compliance.

Fourth, the Social Contract approach gives us a sensible and mature way of determining what our ethical duties really are. When "morality" is mentioned, the first thing that pops into many people's minds is an attempt to restrict their sex lives. It is unfortunate that the word *morals* has come to have such a connotation. The whole purpose of having a system of morality, according to Social Contract Theory, is to make it possible for people to live their individual lives in a setting of social cooperation. Its purpose is *not* to tell people what kinds of lives they should live (except insofar as it is necessary to restrict conduct in the interests of maintaining social cooperation). Therefore, an ethic based on the Social Contract would have little interest in what people do in their bedrooms.

Finally, we may note again that Social Contract Theory assumes relatively little about human nature. It treats human beings as self-interested creatures and does not assume that they are naturally altruistic, even to the slightest degree. One of the theory's charms is that it can reach the conclusion that we ought, often, to *behave* altruistically, without assuming that we *are* naturally altruistic. We want to live as well as possible, and moral obligations are created as we band together with other people to form the cooperative societies that are necessary for us to achieve this fundamentally self-interested goal.

Altruism and Self-Interest

Are people essentially self-interested? Although the Social Contract Theory continues to attract supporters, not many philosophers and psychologists today would accept Hobbes's egoistic view of human nature. It seems evident that humans have at least *some* altruistic feelings, if only for their family and friends. We have evolved as social creatures just as surely as we have evolved as creatures with legs—caring for our kin and members of our local group is as natural for us as walking.

If humans do have some degree of natural altruism, does this have any significance for morals? Hume thought so. Hume agreed with Hobbes that our moral opinions are expressions of our feelings. In 1739, when he invited his readers to consider "willful murder" and see if they could find that "matter of fact" called "vice," Hume concluded:

> You can never find it, till you turn your reflexion into your own breast, and find a sentiment of disapproval, which arises in you, towards this action. Here is a matter of fact; but 'tis the object of feeling. . . . It lies in yourself, not in the object. So that when you pronounce any action or character to be vicious, you mean nothing, but that from the constitution of your nature you have a feeling or sentiment of blame from the contemplation of it.

And what, exactly, is "the constitution of our nature"? Of course, it is part of our nature to care about ourselves and our own welfare. But Hume added that we also have "*social* sentiments"—feelings that connect us with other people and make us concerned about their welfare. That is why, Hume said, we measure right and wrong by "the true interests of mankind":

> In all determinations of morality, this circumstance of public utility is ever principally in view; and wherever disputes arise, either in philosophy or common life, concerning the bounds of duty, the question cannot, by any means, be decided with greater certainty than by ascertaining, on any side, the true interests of mankind.

This view came to be known as Utilitarianism. In modern moral philosophy, it is the chief alternative to the Theory of the Social Contract.

Utilitarianism

Utilitarians hold that there is one principle that sums up all our moral duties. The ultimate moral principle is that *we should always do whatever will produce the greatest possible balance of happiness over unhappiness for everyone who will be affected by our action.* This "principle of utility" is deceptively simple. It is actually a combination of three ideas: First, in determining what to do, we should be guided by the expected consequences of our actions—we should do whatever will have the best consequences. Second, in determining which consequences are best, we should give the greatest possible weight to the happiness or unhappiness that would be caused—we should do whatever will cause the most happiness or the least unhappiness. And finally, the principle of utility assumes that each individual's happiness is equally as important as anyone else's.

Although Hume expressed the basic idea of Utilitarianism, two other philosophers elaborated it in greater detail. Jeremy Bentham, an Englishman who lived in the late 18th and early 19th centuries, was the leader of a group of philosophical radicals who aimed to reform the laws of Britain along utilitarian lines. This group was remarkably successful in advancing such causes as prison reform and restrictions on the use of child labor. John Stuart Mill, the son of one of Bentham's original followers, gave the theory its most popular and influential defense in his book *Utilitarianism,* published in 1861.

The utilitarian movement attracted critics from the outset. It was an easy target because it ignored conventional religious notions. The point of morality, according to the Utilitarians, had nothing to do with obeying God or gaining credit in Heaven. Rather, the point was just to make life in this world as comfortable and happy as possible. So some critics condemned Utilitarianism as a godless doctrine. To this Mill replied:

> [T]he question depends upon what idea we have formed of the moral character of the Deity. If it be a true belief that God desires, above all things, the happiness of his creatures, and that this was his purpose in their creation, utility is not only not a godless doctrine, but more profoundly religious than any other.

Utilitarianism was also an easy target because it was (and still is) a *subversive* theory, in that it turned many traditional moral ideas upside down. Bentham argued, for example, that the purpose of the criminal justice system cannot be understood in the traditional way as "paying back" wrongdoers for their wicked deeds—that only piles misery upon misery. Instead, the social response to crime should be threefold: to identify and deal with the causes of criminal behavior; where possible, to reform individual lawbreakers and make them into productive citizens; and to "punish" people only insofar as it is necessary to deter others from committing similar crimes. Or, to take a different example, by insisting that everyone's happiness is equally important, the Utilitarians offended various elitist notions of group superiority. According to the Utilitarian standard, neither race, sex, nor social class makes a difference to one's moral status. Mill himself wrote a book on *The Subjection of Women* that became a classic of the 19th-century suffragist movement.

Finally, Utilitarianism was controversial because it had no use for "absolute" moral rules. The Utilitarians regarded the traditional rules—against killing, lying, breaking one's promises, and so on—as "rules of thumb," useful because following them will generally be for the best. But they are not absolute—whenever breaking such a rule will have better results for everyone concerned, the rule should be broken. The rule against killing, for example, might be suspended in the case of voluntary euthanasia for someone dying of a painful illness. Moreover, the Utilitarians regarded some traditional rules as dubious, even as rules of thumb. For example, Christian moralists had traditionally said that masturbation is evil because it violates the Natural Law; but from the point of view of the Principle of Utility, it appears to be harmless. A more serious matter is the traditional religious condemnation of homosexuality, which has resulted in misery for countless people. Utilitarianism implies that if an activity makes people happy, without anyone being harmed, it cannot be wrong.

But it is one thing to describe a moral view; it is another thing to justify it. Utilitarianism says that our moral duty is to "promote the general happiness." Why should we do that? How can the challenge of Gyges's ring be answered? As Mill puts it:

> I feel that I am bound not to rob or murder, betray or deceive; but why am I bound to promote the general happiness? If my own happiness lies in something else, why may I not give that the preference?

Aside from the "external sanctions" of law and public opinion, Mill thinks there is only one possible reason for accepting this or any other moral standard. The "internal sanction" of morality must always be "a feeling in our minds," regardless of what sort of ethic this feeling endorses:

> The ultimate sanction, therefore, of all morality (external motives apart) being a subjective feeling in our own minds, I see nothing embarrassing to those whose standard is utility in the question, What is the sanction of that particular standard? We may answer, the same as all other moral standards—the conscientious feelings of mankind. Undoubtedly this sanction has no binding efficacy on those who do not possess the feelings it appeals to; but neither will these persons be more obedient to any other moral principle than the utilitarian one.

The kind of morality we accept will, therefore, depend on the nature of our feelings: If human beings have "social feelings," then Mill says that utilitarian morality will be the natural standard for them:

> The firm foundation [of utilitarian morality] is that of the social feelings of mankind—the desire to be in unity with our fellow creatures, which is already a powerful principle in human nature, and happily one of those which tend to become stronger, even without express inculcation, from the influences of advancing civilization.

Impartiality

Utilitarianism, as we have seen, has implications that are at odds with traditional morality. Much the same could be said about the Social Contract Theory. In most of the practical matters that have been mentioned—punishment, racial discrimination, women's rights, euthanasia, homosexuality—the two theories have similar implications. But there is one matter on which they differ dramatically. Utilitarians believe that we have a very extensive moral duty to help other people. Social Contract theorists deny this.

Suppose, for example, you are thinking of spending $1000 for a new living room carpet. Should you do this? What are the alternatives? One alternative is to give the money to an agency such as the United Nations Children's Fund. Each year between 10 and 20 million third-world children die of easily preventable diseases, because there isn't enough money to provide the vitamin-A capsules, antibiotics, and oral rehydration treatments they need. By giving the money to UNICEF, and making do a while longer with your old carpet, you could provide much-needed medical care for dozens of children. From the point of view of utility—seeking the best overall outcome for everyone concerned—there is no doubt you should give the money to UNICEF. Obviously, the medicine will help the kids a lot more than the new rug will help you.

But from the point of view of the Social Contract, things look very different. If morality rests on an agreement between people—remember, an agreement they enter into *to promote their own interests*—what would the agreement say about helping other people? Certainly, we would want the contract to impose a duty not to harm other people, even strangers. Each of us would obviously benefit from that. And it might be in our best interests to accept a mutual obligation to provide aid to others when it is easy and convenient to do so. But would rational people accept a general duty to provide virtually unlimited aid to strangers, even at great cost to themselves? From the standpoint of self-interest, that sounds crazy. Jan Narveson, a contract theorist who teaches philosophy at the University of Waterloo in Canada, writes in his book *Moral Matters* (1993):

> [M]orals, if they are to be rational, must amount to agreements among people—people of all kinds, each pursuing his or her own interests, which are various and do not necessarily include much concern for others and their interests. But people have minds, and apply information gleaned from observing the world around them to the task of promoting their interests, and they have a broad repertoire of powers including some that can make them exceedingly dangerous, as well as others that can make them very helpful. This gives us reason to agree with each other that we will refrain from harming others in the pursuit of our interests, to respect each other's property and grant extensive civil rights, but not necessarily to go very far out of our way to be very helpful to those we don't know and may not particularly care for. . . .
>
> It is reasonable, then, to arrive at a general understanding that we shall be ready to help when help is urgent and when giving it is not very onerous to us. But a general understanding that we shall help everyone as if they were our spouses or dearest friends is quite another matter.

Unlike many philosophers who prefer to keep things abstract, Narveson is good about spelling out the implications of his view in a way that leaves no room for misunderstanding:

> What about parting with the means for making your sweet little daughter's birthday party a memorable one, in order to keep a

dozen strangers alive on the other side of the world? Is this something you are morally required to do? Indeed not. She may well
matter to you more than they. This illustrates again the fact that
people do *not* "count equally" for most of us. Normal people care
more about some people than others, and build their very lives
around those carings.

Which view is correct? Do we have a moral duty to provide
extensive aid to strangers, or not? Both views appeal ultimately to our
emotions. A striking feature of Narveson's argument is its appeal to
the fact that we *care more* for some people than others. This is certainly true: As he says, we care more for our own children than for
"strangers on the other side of the world." But does this really mean
that I may choose some trivial benefit for my children over the very
lives of the strangers? Suppose there are two buttons on my desk at
this moment, and by pressing button A, I can provide my son with a
nice party; by pressing B, I can save the lives of a dozen strangers. Is
it really all right for me to press A, just because I "care more" for my
son? Mill agrees that the issue must be decided on the basis of feelings (how else could it be?), but for him it is not these small-scale personal feelings that have the final say. Instead, it is one's "conscientious
feelings"—the feelings that prevail after everything has been thought
through—that finally determine one's obligations. Mill assumes that
we cannot, when we are thoughtful and reflective, approve of ourselves pushing button A.

However, some contemporary Utilitarians have argued that the
matter need not be left to the vicissitudes of individual feeling. It may
be true, they say, that we all care more for ourselves, our family, and
our friends than we care for strangers. But we have rational capacities
as well as feelings, and if we think objectively about the matter, we
will realize that other people are no different. Others, even strangers, also care about themselves, their families, and their friends, in
the same way that we do. Their needs and interests are comparable
to our own. In fact, *there is nothing of this general sort that makes anyone
different from anyone else*—and if we are in all relevant respects similar
to one another, then there is no justification for anyone taking his
or her own interests to be more important. Peter Singer, a utilitarian
philosopher, writes in his book *How Are We to Live?* (1995):

> Reason makes it possible for us to see ourselves in this way. . . .
> I am able to see that I am just one being among others, with
> interests and desires like others. I have a personal perspective on
> the world, from which my interests are at the front and centre of

the stage, the interests of my family and friends are close behind, and the interests of strangers are pushed to the back and sides. But reason enables me to see that others have similarly subjective perspectives, and that from "the point of view of the universe" my perspective is no more privileged than theirs. Thus my ability to reason shows me the possibility of detaching myself from my own perspective, and shows me what the universe might look like if I had no personal perspective.

So, from an objective viewpoint, each of us must acknowledge that our own perspective—our own particular set of needs, interests, likes, and dislikes—is only one among many and has no special status.

Kant

The idea of impartiality is also central to the third major alternative in modern moral philosophy, the system of ethical ideas devised by the great German philosopher Immanuel Kant (1724–1804). Like the Social Contract theorists and the Utilitarians, Kant sought to explain ethics without appealing to divine commands or "moral facts." Kant's solution was to see morality as a product of "pure reason." Just as we must do some things because of our *desires*—for example, because I desire to go to a concert, I must buy a ticket—the moral law is binding on us because of our *reason.*

Like the Utilitarians, Kant believed that morality can be summed up in one ultimate principle, from which all our duties and obligations are derived. But his version of the "ultimate moral principle" was very different from the Principle of Utility, because Kant did not emphasize the outcomes of actions. What was important for him was "doing one's duty," and he held that a person's duty is not determined by calculating consequences.

Kant called his ultimate moral principle the "Categorical Imperative." But he gave this principle two very different formulations. The first version of the Categorical Imperative, as expressed in his *Fundamental Principles of the Metaphysics of Morals* (1785), goes like this:

> Act only according to that maxim by which you can at the same time will that it should become a universal law.

Stated in this way, Kant's principle summarizes a procedure for deciding whether an act is morally permissible. When you are contemplating a particular action, you are to ask what rule you would be following if you were to do it. (This will be the "maxim" of the act.)

Then you are to ask whether you would be willing for that rule to be followed by everyone all the time. (That would make it a "universal law" in the relevant sense.) If so, the rule may be followed, and the act is permissible. However, if you would not be willing for everyone to follow the rule, then you may not follow it, and the act is morally impermissible.

This explains why the Moral Law is binding on us simply by virtue of our rationality. The first requirement of rationality is that we be consistent, and it would not be consistent to act on a maxim that we could not want others to adopt as well. Kant believed, in addition, that consistency requires us to interpret moral rules as having no exceptions. For this reason, he endorsed a whole range of absolute prohibitions, covering everything from lying to suicide.

However, Kant also gave another formulation of the Categorical Imperative. Later in the same book, he said that the ultimate moral principle may be understood as saying:

> So act that you treat humanity, whether in your own person or in
> that of another, always as an end and never as means only.

What does it mean to say that persons are to be treated as "ends" and never as "means"? Kant gives this example: Suppose you need money, and so you want a "loan," but you know you could not repay it. In desperation, you consider making a false promise (to repay) in order to trick a friend into giving you the money. May you do this? Perhaps you need the money for a good purpose—so good, in fact, that you might convince yourself the lie would be justified. Nevertheless, if you lied to your friend, you would merely be manipulating him and using him "as a means."

On the other hand, what would it be like to treat your friend "as an end"? Suppose you told the truth—that you need the money for a certain purpose but could not repay it. Then your friend could make up his own mind about whether to let you have it. He could exercise his own powers of reason, consulting his own values and wishes, and make a free, autonomous choice. If he did decide to give the money for this purpose, he would be choosing to make that purpose his own. Thus, you would not merely be using him as a means to achieving your goal.

Conclusion

Our purpose here is not to reach any firm conclusion about which of these approaches, if any, is correct. But we may end with an observation about how that project might be undertaken.

Philosophical ideas are often very abstract, and it is difficult to see what sort of evidence counts for or against them. It is easy enough to appreciate, intuitively, the ideas behind each of these theories, but how do we determine which, if any, is correct? It is a daunting question. Faced with this problem, people are tempted to accept or reject philosophical ideas on the basis of their intuitive appeal—if an idea sounds good, one may embrace it; or if it rubs one the wrong way, it may be discarded. But this is hardly a satisfactory way to proceed if we want to discover the truth. How an idea strikes us is not a reliable guide, for our "intuitions" may be mistaken.

Happily, there is an alternative. An idea is no better than the arguments that support it. So, to evaluate a philosophical idea, we may examine the reasoning behind it. The great philosophers knew this very well: They did not simply announce their philosophical opinions; instead, they presented arguments in support of their views. The leading idea, from the time of Socrates to the present, has been that truth is discovered by considering the reasons for and against the various alternatives. The "correct" theory is the one that has the best arguments on its side. Thus, philosophical thinking consists, to a large extent, in formulating and assessing arguments. This is not the whole of philosophy, but it is a big part of it. It is what makes philosophy a rational enterprise.

CHAPTER 2

Some Basic Points about Arguments

James Rachels

Philosophy without argument would be a lifeless exercise. What good would it be to produce a theory, if there were no reasons for thinking it correct? And of what interest is the rejection of a theory, if there are no good reasons for thinking it incorrect? A philosophical idea is exactly as good as the arguments in its support.

Therefore, if we want to think clearly about philosophical matters, we have to learn something about the evaluation of arguments. We have to learn to distinguish the sound ones from the unsound ones. This can be a tedious business, but it is indispensable if we want to come within shouting distance of the truth.

Arguments

In ordinary English, the word *argument* often means a fight, and there is a hint of unpleasantness in the word. That is not the way the word is used here. In the logician's sense, an argument is a chain of reasoning designed to prove something. It consists of one or more *premises* and a *conclusion,* together with the claim that the conclusion *follows from* the premises. Here is a simple argument. This example is not particularly interesting in itself, but it is short and clear, and it will help us grasp the main points we need to understand.

(1) All men are mortal.

Socrates is a man.

Therefore, Socrates is mortal.

The first two statements are the premises; the third statement is the conclusion; and it is claimed that the conclusion follows from the premises.

20

What does it mean to say that the conclusion "follows from" the premises? It means that a certain logical relation exists between the premises and the conclusion, namely, that *if* the premises are true, then the conclusion must be true also. (Another way to put the same point is: The conclusion follows from the premises if and only if it is impossible for the premises to be true, and the conclusion false, at the same time.) In example (1), we can see that the conclusion does follow from the premises. If it is true that all men are mortal, and Socrates is a man, then it must be true that Socrates is mortal. (Or, it is impossible for it to be true that all men are mortal, and for Socrates to be a man, and yet false that Socrates is mortal.)

In example (1), the conclusion follows from the premises, *and* the premises are in fact true. However, the conclusion of an argument may follow from the premises even if the premises are not actually true. Consider this argument:

(2) All people from Georgia are famous.

Jimmy Carter is from Georgia.

Therefore, Jimmy Carter is famous.

Clearly, the conclusion of this argument does follow from the premises: *If* it were true that all Georgians were famous, and Jimmy Carter was from Georgia, then it follows that Jimmy Carter would be famous. This logical relation holds between the premises and conclusion even though one of the premises is in fact false.

At this point, logicians customarily introduce a bit of terminology. They say that an argument is *valid* just in case its conclusion follows from its premises. Both the examples given above are valid arguments, in this technical sense.

In order to be a *sound* argument, however, two things are necessary: The argument must be valid, *and* its premises must be true. Thus, the argument about Socrates is a sound argument, but the argument about Jimmy Carter is not sound, because even though it is valid, its premises are not all true.

It is important to notice that an argument may be unsound even though its premises and conclusion are both true. Consider the following silly example:

(3) The earth has one moon.

John F. Kennedy was assassinated.

Therefore, snow is white.

The premises of this "argument" are both true, and the conclusion is true as well. Yet it is obviously a bad argument, because it is not valid—the conclusion does not follow from the premises. The point is that *when we ask whether an argument is valid, we are not asking whether the premises actually are true, or whether the conclusion actually is true. We are only asking whether, if the premises were true, the conclusion would really follow from them.*

So far, our examples have all been trivial. I have used these trivial examples because they permit us to make the essential logical points clearly and uncontroversially. But these points are applicable to the analysis of any argument, trivial or not. To illustrate, let us consider how these points can be used in analyzing a more important and controversial issue. We will look at the arguments for Moral Skepticism in some detail.

Moral Skepticism

Moral Skepticism is the idea that *there is no such thing as objective moral truth.* It is not merely the idea that we cannot *know* the truth about right and wrong. It is the more radical idea that, where ethics is concerned, "truth" does not exist. The essential point may be put in several different ways. It may be said that:

- Morality is subjective; it is a matter of how we feel about things, not a matter of how things *are*.
- Morality is only a matter of opinion, and one person's opinion is just as good as another's.
- Values exist only in our minds, not in the world outside us.

However the point is put, the underlying thought is the same: The idea of "objective moral truth" is only a fiction; in reality, there is no such thing.

We want to know whether Moral Skepticism is correct. Is the idea of moral "truth" only an illusion? What arguments can be given in favor of this idea? In order to determine whether it is correct, we need to ask what arguments can be given for it and whether those arguments are sound.

The Cultural Differences Argument. One argument for Moral Skepticism might be based on the observation that in different cultures people have different ideas concerning right and wrong. For example, in traditional Eskimo society, infanticide was thought to be morally acceptable—if a family already had too many children, a new baby might have been left to die in the snow. In our own society, however, this would be considered wrong. There are many other examples of the same kind. Different cultures have different moral codes.

Reflecting on such facts, many people have concluded that there is no such thing as objective right and wrong. Thus, they advance the following argument:

(4) In some societies, such as among the Eskimos, infanticide is thought to be morally acceptable.

In other societies, such as our own, infanticide is thought to be morally odious.

Therefore, infanticide is neither objectively right nor objectively wrong; it is merely a matter of opinion that varies from culture to culture.

We may call this the "Cultural Differences Argument." This kind of argument has been tremendously influential; it has persuaded many people to be skeptical of the whole idea of "moral truth." But is it a *sound* argument? We may ask two questions about it: First, are the premises true, and second, does the conclusion really follow from them? If the answer to either question is no, then the argument must be rejected. In this case, the premises seem to be correct—there have been many cultures in which infanticide was accepted. Therefore, our attention must focus on the second matter: Is the argument *valid?*

To figure this out, we may begin by noting that the premises concern *what people believe.* In some societies, people think infanticide is all right. In others, people believe it is immoral. The conclusion, however, concerns not what people believe, but whether infanticide *really is* immoral. The problem is that this sort of conclusion does not follow from those sorts of premises. It does not follow, from the mere fact that people have different beliefs about something, that there is no "truth" in the matter. Therefore, the Cultural Differences Argument is not valid.

To make the point clearer, consider this analogous argument:

(5) In some societies, the world is thought to be flat.

In other societies, the world is thought to be round.

Therefore, objectively speaking, the world is neither flat nor round. It is merely a matter of opinion that varies from culture to culture.

Clearly, *this* argument is not valid. We cannot conclude that the world is shapeless simply because not everyone agrees what shape it has. But exactly the same can be said about the Cultural Differences Argument: We cannot validly move from premises about what people *believe* to a conclusion about what is so, because people—even whole societies—may be wrong. The world has a definite shape, and those who think it is flat are mistaken. Similarly, infanticide might be objectively wrong (or not wrong), and those who think differently might be mistaken. Therefore, the Cultural Differences Argument is not valid, and so it provides no legitimate support for the idea that "moral truth" is only an illusion.

There are two common reactions to this analysis. These reactions illustrate traps that people often fall into.

1. The first reaction goes like this: Many people find the conclusion of the Cultural Differences Argument very appealing. This makes it hard for them to believe that the argument is invalid—when it is pointed out that the argument is fallacious, they tend to respond: "But right and wrong really *are* only matters of opinion!" They make the mistake of thinking that, if we reject an argument, we are somehow impugning the truth of its conclusion. But that is not so. Remember example (3) above; it illustrates how an argument may have a true conclusion and still be a bad argument. If an argument is unsound, then it fails to provide any reason for thinking the conclusion is true. The conclusion may still be true—that remains an open question—but the point is just that the unsound argument gives it no support.

2. It may be objected that it is unfair to compare morality with an obviously objective matter like the shape of the earth, because we can prove what shape the earth has by scientific methods. Therefore, we know that the flat-earthers are simply wrong. But morality is different. There is no way to prove that a moral opinion is true or false.

This objection misses the point. The Cultural Differences Argument tries to derive the skeptical conclusion about morality *from a certain set of facts,* namely, the facts about cultural disagreements. This objection suggests that the conclusion might be derived from a *different* set of facts, namely, facts about what is and what is not provable. It suggests, in effect, a different argument, which might be formulated like this:

> **(6)** If infanticide (or anything else, for that matter) is objectively right or wrong, then it should be possible to *prove* it right or wrong.
>
> But it is not possible to prove infanticide right or wrong.

Therefore, infanticide is neither objectively right nor objectively wrong. It is merely a matter of opinion that varies from culture to culture.

This argument is fundamentally different from the Cultural Differences Argument, even though the two arguments have the same conclusion. They are different because they appeal to different considerations in trying to prove that conclusion—in other words, they have different premises. Therefore, the question of whether argument (6) is sound is separate from the question of whether the Cultural Differences Argument is sound. The Cultural Differences Argument is not valid, for the reason given above.

We should emphasize the importance of *keeping arguments separate*. It is easy to slide from one argument to another without realizing what one is doing. It is easy to think that, if moral judgments are "unprovable," then the Cultural Differences Argument is strengthened. But it is not. Argument (6) merely introduces a different set of issues. It is important to pin down an argument and evaluate *it* as carefully as possible, before moving on to different considerations.

The Provability Argument. Now let us consider in more detail the question of whether it is possible to prove a moral judgment true or false. The following argument, which we might call the "Provability Argument," is a more general form of argument (6):

(7) If there were any such thing as objective truth in ethics, we should be able to prove that some moral opinions are true and others false.

But in fact we cannot prove which moral opinions are true and which are false.

Therefore, there is no such thing as objective truth in ethics.

Once again, we have an argument with a certain superficial appeal. But are the premises true? And does the conclusion really follow from them? It seems that the conclusion does follow. Therefore, the crucial question will be whether the premises are in fact true.

The general claim that moral judgments can't be proven *sounds* right: Anyone who has ever argued about a matter like abortion knows how frustrating it can be to try to "prove" that one's point of view is correct. However, if we inspect this claim more closely, it turns out to be questionable.

Suppose we consider a matter that is simpler than abortion. A student says that a test given by a teacher was unfair. This is clearly a moral judgment—fairness is a basic moral value. Can the student prove the test was unfair? She might point out that the test was so long that not even the best students could complete it in the time allowed (and the test was to be graded on the assumption that it should be completed). Moreover, the test covered trivial matters while ignoring matters the teacher had stressed as important. And finally, the test included questions about some matters that were not covered in either the assigned readings or the class discussions.

Suppose all this is true. And further suppose that the teacher, when asked to explain, has no defense to offer. (In fact, the teacher seems confused about the whole thing and doesn't seem to have had any idea what he was doing.) Now, hasn't the student proved the test was unfair? What more in the way of proof could we possibly want?

It is easy to think of other examples that make the same point:

- *Jones is a bad man.* To prove this, one might point out that Jones is a habitual liar; he manipulates people; he cheats when he thinks he can get away with it; he is cruel to other people; and so on.
- *Dr. Smith is irresponsible.* She bases her diagnoses on superficial considerations; she drinks Budweiser before performing delicate surgery; she refuses to listen to other doctors' advice; and so on.
- *A certain used-car salesman is unethical.* He conceals defects in his cars; he takes advantage of poor people by pressuring them into paying high prices for cars he knows to be defective; he runs false advertisements in any newspaper that will carry them; and so on.

The point is that we can, and often do, back up our ethical judgments with good reasons. Thus, it does not seem right to say that they are all unprovable, as though they were nothing more than "mere opinions." If a person has good reasons for his judgments, then he is not *merely* giving "his opinion." On the contrary, he may be making a judgment which any reasonable person would have to agree with.

If we can sometimes give good reasons for our moral judgments, what accounts for the persistent impression that they are "unprovable"? There are two reasons why the Provability Argument appears better than it is.

First, there is a tendency to focus attention only on the most difficult moral issues. The question of abortion, for example, is an enormously difficult and complicated matter. If we think only of questions like *this,* it is easy to believe that "proof" in ethics is impossible. The same could be said of the sciences. There are many complicated matters that physicists cannot agree on; if we focused our attention entirely on *them,* we might conclude that there is no "proof" in physics. But, of course, there are many simpler matters in physics that can be proven and about which all competent physicists agree. Similarly, in ethics, there are many matters far simpler than abortion, about which all reasonable people must agree.

Second, it is easy to confuse two matters that are really very different:

1. Proving an opinion to be correct
2. Persuading someone to accept your proof

Suppose you are discussing a moral issue with someone, and you have perfectly cogent reasons in support of your position, while they have no good reasons on their side. Still, they refuse to accept your logic and continue to insist they are right. This is a common, if frustrating, experience. You may be tempted to conclude that it is impossible to prove you are right. But this would be a mistake. Your proof may be impeccable; the trouble may be that the other person is being stubborn. (Of course, that is not the *only* possible explanation of what is going on, but it is one possible explanation.) The same thing can happen in any sort of discussion. You may be arguing about intelligent design versus evolution, and the other person may be unreasonable. But that does not necessarily mean there is something wrong with your arguments. There may be something wrong with the other person.

Conclusion

We have examined two of the most important arguments in support of Moral Skepticism and seen that these arguments are no good. Moral Skepticism might still turn out to be true, but if so, then other, better arguments will have to be found. Provisionally, at least, we have to conclude that Moral Skepticism is not nearly as plausible as we might have thought.

The purpose of this exercise, however, was to illustrate the process of evaluating philosophical arguments. We may summarize what we have learned about evaluating arguments like this:

1. Arguments are offered to provide support for a theory or idea; a philosophical theory may be regarded as acceptable only if there are sound arguments in its favor.

2. An argument is sound only if its premises are true and the conclusion follows logically from them.
   (a) A conclusion "follows from" the premises just in case the following is so: *If* the premises were true, then the conclusion would have to be true also. (An alternative way of saying the same thing: A conclusion follows from the premises just in case it is impossible for the premises to be true and the conclusion false at the same time.)
   (b) A conclusion can follow from premises even if those premises are in fact false.
   (c) A conclusion can be true and yet not follow from a given set of premises.
3. Therefore, in evaluating an argument, we ask two *separate* questions: Are the premises true? And, does the conclusion follow from them?
4. It is important to avoid two common mistakes. We should be careful to keep arguments separate, and not slide from one to the other, thereby confusing different issues. And, we should not think an argument stronger than it is simply because we happen to agree with its conclusion. Moreover, we should remember that, if an argument is unsound, that does not mean the conclusion must be false—it only means that *this* argument does nothing to show it is true.

CHAPTER 3

*U*tilitarianism

John Stuart Mill

In the history of moral philosophy, the name of John Stuart Mill (1806–1873) is inevitably linked with that of Jeremy Bentham (1748–1832). Few philosophers have combined theory and practice as successfully as Bentham. A wealthy Londoner, he studied law but never practiced, instead devoting himself to writing and working for social reform. He became the leader of a group of philosophical radicals known as the Benthamites, who campaigned for causes like prison reform and restrictions on the use of child labor. Bentham was an effective member of the British establishment, and almost all the Benthamites' legislative proposals eventually became law.

Bentham was convinced that both law and morals must be based on a realistic, nonsupernatural conception of human beings. The first sentence of his greatest work, *The Principles of Morals and Legislation,* declares: "Nature has placed mankind under the governance of two sovereign masters, *pain* and *pleasure.*" Some things give us pleasure, and others cause us pain. This fundamental fact explains why we behave as we do—we seek pleasure and avoid pain—and it explains why we judge some things to be good and other things to be evil. Therefore, he reasoned, morality must consist in trying to bring about as much pleasure as possible, while striving to minimize pain. This ultimate moral principle, the Principle of Utility, requires us to always choose the action or social policy that provides the most happiness for all.

One of Bentham's followers was James Mill, a distinguished Scottish philosopher, historian, and economist. James Mill's son, John Stuart, would become the leading advocate of utilitarian moral theory for the next generation. James Mill, in fact, educated his son with this in mind. He had the boy studying Greek and Latin at age 3, and by the time

---

From John Stuart Mill, *Utilitarianism* (1861).

he entered his teens, John Stuart was already mastering the blend of subjects that the British call "political economy." He was 26 when Bentham died, and he knew the older man well. He was not, however, merely a follower of the master. Mill became more accomplished than Bentham, contributing to subjects that Bentham barely knew, such as the philosophy of science and the foundations of mathematical knowledge.

Unlike Bentham, the Mills were not wealthy, and John Stuart earned his living in the office of the East India Company, as had his father. In 1830, he met and fell in love with Harriet Taylor, who, alas, was married with three children. Harriet was faithful to her husband until he died in 1849. Two years later, she and Mill married. With Harriet as his partner, Mill became a leader in the women's rights movement and published *The Subjection of Women* in 1869.

The following excerpts are from Mill's book *Utilitarianism*, in which he develops some of the basic ideas of utilitarian moral theory.

II. What Utilitarianism Is

. . . The creed which accepts as the foundation of morals, Utility, or the Greatest Happiness Principle, holds that actions are right in proportion as they tend to promote happiness, wrong as they tend to produce the reverse of happiness. By happiness is intended pleasure, and the absence of pain; by unhappiness, pain, and the privation of pleasure. To give a clear view of the moral standard set up by the theory, much more requires to be said; in particular, what things it includes in the ideas of pain and pleasure; and to what extent this is left an open question. But these supplementary explanations do not affect the theory of life on which this theory of morality is grounded—namely, that pleasure, and freedom from pain, are the only things desirable as ends; and that all desirable things (which are as numerous in the utilitarian as in any other scheme) are desirable either for the pleasure inherent in themselves, or as means to the promotion of pleasure and the prevention of pain.

Now, such a theory of life excites in many minds, and among them in some of the most estimable in feeling and purpose, inveterate dislike. To suppose that life has (as they express it) no higher end than pleasure—no better and nobler object of desire and pursuit—they designate as utterly mean and grovelling; as a doctrine worthy only of swine, to whom the followers of Epicurus were, at a very early period, contemptuously likened; and modern holders of the doctrine are occasionally made the subject of equally polite comparisons by its German, French, and English assailants.

When thus attacked, the Epicureans have always answered, that it is not they, but their accusers, who represent human nature in a degrading light; since the accusation supposes human beings to be capable of no pleasures except those of which swine are capable. If this supposition were true, the charge could not be gainsaid, but would then be no longer an imputation; for if the sources of pleasure were precisely the same to human beings and to swine, the rule of life which is good enough for the one would be good enough for the other. The comparison of the Epicurean life to that of beasts is felt as degrading, precisely because a beast's pleasures do not satisfy a human being's conceptions of happiness. Human beings have faculties more elevated than the animal appetites, and when once made conscious of them, do not regard anything as happiness which does not include their gratification. I do not, indeed, consider the Epicureans to have been by any means faultless in drawing out their scheme of consequences from the utilitarian principle. To do this in any sufficient manner, many Stoic, as well as Christian elements require to be included. But there is no known Epicurean theory of life which does not assign to the pleasures of the intellect, of the feelings and imagination, and of the moral sentiments, a much higher value as pleasures than to those of mere sensation. It must be admitted, however, that utilitarian writers in general have placed the superiority of mental over bodily pleasures chiefly in the greater permanency, safety, uncostliness, etc. of the former—that is, in their circumstantial advantages rather than in their intrinsic nature. And on all these points utilitarians have fully proved their case; but they might have taken the other, and, as it may be called, higher ground, with entire consistency. It is quite compatible with the principle of utility to recognise the fact, that some *kinds* of pleasure are more desirable and more valuable than others. It would be absurd that while, in estimating all other things, quality is considered as well as quantity, the estimation of pleasures should be supposed to depend on quantity alone.

If I am asked, what I mean by difference of quality in pleasures, or what makes one pleasure more valuable than another, merely as a pleasure, except its being greater in amount, there is but one possible answer. Of two pleasures, if there be one to which all or almost all who have experience of both give a decided preference, irrespective of any feeling of moral obligation to prefer it, that is the more desirable pleasure. If one of the two is, by those who are competently acquainted with both, placed so far above the other that they prefer it, even though knowing it to be attended with a greater amount of discontent, and would not resign it for any quantity of the other pleasure which their nature is capable of, we are justified in ascribing to the preferred enjoyment a superiority in quality, so far outweighing quantity as to render it, in comparison, of small account.

Now it is an unquestionable fact that those who are equally acquainted with, and equally capable of appreciating and enjoying, both, do give a most marked preference to the manner of existence which employs their higher faculties. Few human creatures would consent to be changed into any of the lower animals, for a promise of the fullest allowance of a beast's pleasures; no intelligent human being would consent to be a fool, no instructed person would be an ignoramus, no person of feeling and conscience would be selfish and base, even though they should be persuaded that the fool, the dunce, or the rascal is better satisfied with his lot than they are with theirs. They would not resign what they possess more than he, for the most complete satisfaction of all the desires which they have in common with him. If they ever fancy they would, it is only in cases of unhappiness so extreme, that to escape from it they would exchange their lot for almost any other, however undesirable in their own eyes. A being of higher faculties requires more to make him happy, is capable probably of more acute suffering, and is certainly accessible to it at more points, than one of an inferior type; but in spite of these liabilities, he can never really wish to sink into what he feels to be a lower grade of existence. We may give what explanation we please of this unwillingness; we may attribute it to pride, a name which is given indiscriminately to some of the most and to some of the least estimable feelings of which mankind are capable; we may refer it to the love of liberty and personal independence, an appeal to which was with the Stoics one of the most effective means for the inculcation of it; to the love of power, or to the love of excitement, both of which do really enter into and contribute to it: but its most appropriate appellation is a sense of dignity, which all human beings possess in one form or other, and in some, though by no means in exact, proportion to their higher faculties, and which is so essential a part of the happiness of those in whom it is strong, that nothing which conflicts with it could be, otherwise than momentarily, an object of desire to them. Whoever supposes that this preference takes place at a sacrifice of happiness—that the superior being, in anything like the equal circumstances, is not happier than the inferior—confounds the two very different ideas, of happiness, and content. It is indisputable that the being whose capacities of enjoyment are low, has the greatest chance of having them fully satisfied; and a highly-endowed being will always feel that any happiness which he can look for, as the world is constituted, is imperfect. But he can learn to bear its imperfections, if they are at all bearable; and they will not make him envy the being who is indeed unconscious of the imperfections, but only because he feels not at all the good which those imperfections qualify. It is better to be a human being dissatisfied than a pig satisfied; better to be Socrates dissatisfied than a fool satisfied. And if the fool, or the pig, is of a different opinion, it is because they only know their own side of the question. The other party to the comparison knows both sides.

It may be objected, that many who are capable of the higher pleasures, occasionally, under the influence of temptation, postpone them to the lower. But this is quite compatible with a full appreciation of the intrinsic superiority of the higher. Men often, from infirmity of character, make their election for the nearer good, though they know it to be the less valuable; and this no less when the choice is between two bodily pleasures, than when it is between bodily and mental. They pursue sensual indulgences to the injury of health, though perfectly aware that health is the greater good. It may be further objected, that many who begin with youthful enthusiasm for everything noble, as they advance in years sink into indolence and selfishness. But I do not believe that those who undergo this very common change, voluntarily choose the lower description of pleasures in preference to the higher. I believe that before they devote themselves exclusively to the one, they have already become incapable of the other. Capacity for the nobler feelings is in most natures a very tender plant, easily killed, not only by hostile influences, but by mere want of sustenance; and in the majority of young persons it speedily dies away if the occupations to which their position in life has devoted them, and the society into which it has thrown them, are not favourable to keeping that higher capacity in exercise. Men lose their high aspirations as they lose their intellectual tastes, because they have not time or opportunity for indulging them; and they addict themselves to inferior pleasures, not because they deliberately prefer them, but because they are either the only ones to which they have access, or the only ones which they are any longer capable of enjoying. It may be questioned whether any one who has remained equally susceptible to both classes of pleasures, ever knowingly and calmly preferred the lower, though many, in all ages, have broken down in an ineffectual attempt to combine both.

From this verdict of the only competent judges, I apprehend there can be no appeal. On a question which is the best worth having of two pleasures, or which of two modes of existence is the most grateful to the feelings, apart from its moral attributes and from its consequences, the judgment of those who are qualified by knowledge of both, or, if they differ, that of the majority among them, must be admitted as final. And there needs be the less hesitation to accept this judgment respecting the quality of pleasures, since there is no other tribunal to be referred to even on the question of quantity. What means are there of determining which is the acutest of two pains, or the intensest of two pleasurable sensations, except the general suffrage of those who are familiar with both? Neither pains nor pleasures are homogeneous, and pain is always heterogeneous with pleasure. What is there to decide whether a particular pleasure is worth purchasing at the cost of a particular pain, except the feelings and judgment of the experienced? When, therefore, those feelings and judgment declare the pleasures derived from the higher faculties to be preferable *in kind*, apart from the question of intensity, to those of which the animal nature, disjoined from the higher faculties, is susceptible, they are entitled on this subject to the same regard.

I have dwelt on this point, as being a necessary part of a perfectly just conception of Utility or Happiness, considered as the directive rule of human conduct. But it is by no means an indispensable condition to the acceptance of the utilitarian standard; for that standard is not the agent's own greatest happiness, but the greatest amount of happiness altogether; and if it may possibly be doubted whether a noble character is always the happier for its nobleness, there can be no doubt that it makes other people happier, and that the world in general is immensely a gainer by it. Utilitarianism, therefore, could only attain its end by the general cultivation of nobleness of character, even if each individual were only benefitted by the nobleness of others, and his own, so far as happiness is concerned, were a sheer deduction from the benefit. But the bare enunciation of such an absurdity as this last, renders refutation superfluous.

According to the Greatest Happiness Principle, as above explained, the ultimate end, with reference to and for the sake of which all other things are desirable (whether we are considering our own good or that of other people), is an existence exempt as far as possible from pain, and as rich as possible in enjoyments, both in point of quantity and quality; the test of quality, and the rule for measuring it against quantity, being the preference felt by those who, in their opportunities of experience, to which must be added their habits of self-consciousness and self-observation, are best furnished with the means of comparison. This, being, according to the utilitarian opinion, the end of human action, is necessarily also the standard of morality; which may accordingly be defined, the rules and precepts for human conduct, by the observance of which an existence such as has been described might be, to the greatest extent possible, secured to all mankind; and not to them only, but, so far as the nature of things admits, to the whole sentient creation. . . .

I must again repeat, what the assailants of utilitarianism seldom have the justice to acknowledge, that the happiness which forms the utilitarian standard of what is right in conduct, is not the agent's own happiness, but that of all concerned. As between his own happiness and that of others, utilitarianism requires him to be as strictly impartial as a disinterested and benevolent spectator. In the golden rule of Jesus of Nazareth, we read the complete spirit of the ethics of utility. To do as one would be done by, and to love one's neighbour as oneself, constitute the ideal perfection of utilitarian morality. As the means of making the nearest approach to this ideal, utility would enjoin, first, that laws and social arrangements should place the happiness, or (as speaking practically it may be called) the interest, of every individual, as nearly as possible in harmony with the interest of the whole; and secondly, that education and opinion, which have so vast a power over human character, should so use that power as to establish in the mind of every individual an indissoluble association between his own happiness and the good of the whole; especially between his own happiness and the practice of such modes of conduct, negative and positive, as regard for the universal happiness prescribes: so that not only he may be unable to conceive the possibility of happiness to himself, consistently with conduct opposed to the general good, but also that a direct impulse to promote the general good may be in every individual one of the habitual motives of action, and the sentiments connected therewith may fill a large and prominent place in every human being's sentient existence. If the impugners of the utilitarian morality represented it to their own minds in this its true character, I know not what recommendation possessed by any other morality they could possibly affirm to be wanting to it: what more beautiful or more exalted developments of human nature any other ethical system can be supposed to foster, or what springs of action, not accessible to the utilitarian, such systems rely on for giving effect to their mandates. . . .

IV. Of What Sort of Proof the Principle of Utility Is Susceptible

It has already been remarked, that questions of ultimate ends do not admit of proof, in the ordinary acceptation of the term. To be incapable of proof by reasoning is common to all first principles; to the first premises of our knowledge, as well as to those of our conduct. But the former, being matters of fact, may be the subject of a direct appeal to the faculties which judge of fact—namely, our senses, and our internal consciousness. Can an appeal be made to the same faculties on questions of practical ends? Or by what other faculty is cognizance taken of them?

Questions about ends are, in other words, questions about what things are desirable. The utilitarian doctrine is, that happiness is desirable, and the only thing desirable, as an end; all other things being only desirable as means to that end. What ought to be required of this doctrine—what conditions is it requisite that the doctrine should fulfill—to make good its claim to be believed?

The only proof capable of being given that an object is visible, is that people actually see it. The only proof that a sound is audible, is that people hear it: and so of the other sources of our experience. In like manner, I apprehend, the sole evidence it is possible to produce that anything is desirable, is that people do actually desire it. If the end which the utilitarian doctrine proposes to itself were not, in theory and in practice, acknowledged to be an end, nothing could ever convince any person that it was so. No reason can be given why the general happiness is desirable, except that each person, so far as he believes it to be attainable, desires his own happiness. This, however, being a fact, we have not only all the proof which the case admits of, but all which it is possible to require, that happiness is a good: that each person's happiness is a good to that person, and the general happiness, therefore, a good to the aggregate of all persons. Happiness has made out its title as *one* of the ends of conduct, and consequently one of the criteria of morality.

But it has not, by this alone, proved itself to be the sole criterion. To do that, it would seem, by the same rule, necessary to show, not only that people desire happiness, but that they never desire anything else. Now it is palpable that they do desire things which, in common language, are decidedly distinguished from happiness. They desire, for example, virtue, and the absence of vice, no less really than pleasure and the absence of pain. The desire of virtue is not as universal, but it is as authentic a fact, as the desire of happiness. And hence the opponents of the utilitarian standard deem that they have a right to infer that there are other ends of human action besides happiness, and that happiness is not the standard of approbation and disapprobation.

But does the utilitarian doctrine deny that people desire virtue, or maintain that virtue is not a thing to be desired? The very reverse. It maintains not only that virtue is to be desired, but that it is to be desired disinterestedly, for itself. Whatever may be the opinion of utilitarian moralists as to the original conditions by which virtue is made virtue; however they may believe (as they do) that actions and dispositions are only virtuous because they promote another end than virtue; yet this being granted, and it having been decided, from considerations of this description, what *is* virtuous, they not only place virtue at the very head of the things which are good as means to the ultimate end, but they also recognise as a psychological fact the possibility of its being, to the individual, a good in itself, without looking to any end beyond it; and hold, that the mind is not in a right state, not in a state comfortable to Utility, not in the state most conducive to the general happiness, unless it does love virtue in this manner—as a thing desirable in itself, even although, in the individual instance, it should not produce those other desirable consequences which it tends to produce, and on account of which it is held to be virtue. This opinion is not, in the smallest degree, a departure from the Happiness principle. The ingredients of happiness are very various, and each of them is desirable in itself, and not merely when considered as swelling an aggregate. The principle of utility does not mean that any given pleasure, as music, for instance, or any given exemption from pain, as for example health, are to be looked upon as a means to a collective something termed happiness, and to be desired on that account. They are desired and desirable in and for themselves; besides being means, they are a part of the end. Virtue, according to the utilitarian doctrine, is not naturally and originally part of the end, but it is capable of becoming so; and in those who love it disinterestedly it has become so, and is desired and cherished, not as a means to happiness, but as a part of their happiness.

To illustrate this farther, we may remember that virtue is not the only thing, originally a means, and which if it were not a means to anything else, would be and remain indifferent, but which by association with what it is a means to, comes to be desired for itself, and that too with the utmost intensity. What, for example, shall we say of the love of money? There is nothing originally more desirable about money than about any heap of glittering pebbles. Its worth is solely that of the things which it will buy; the desires for other things than itself, which it is a means of gratifying. Yet the love of money is not only one of the strongest moving forces of human life, but money is, in many cases, desired in and for itself; the desire to possess it is often stronger than the desire to use it, and goes on increasing when all the desires which point to ends beyond it, to be encompassed by it, are falling off. It may be then said truly, that money is desired not for the sake of an end, but as part of the end. From being a means to happiness, it has come to be itself a principal ingredient of the individual's conception of happiness. The same may be said of the majority of the great objects of human life—power, for example, or fame; except that to each of these there is a certain amount of immediate pleasure annexed, which has at least the semblance of being naturally inherent in them; a thing which cannot be said of money. Still, however, the strongest natural attraction, both of power and of fame, is the immense aid they give to the attainment of our other wishes; and it is the strong association thus generated between them and all our objects of desire, which gives to the direct desire of them the intensity it often assumes, so as in some characters to surpass in strength all other desires. In these cases the means have become a part of the end, and a more important part of it than any of the things which they are means to. What was once desired as an instrument for the attainment of happiness, has come to be desired for its own sake. In being desired for its own sake it is, however, desired as *part* of happiness. The person is made, or thinks he would be made, happy by its mere possession; and is made unhappy by failure to obtain it. The desire of it is not a different thing from the desire of happiness, any more than the love of music, or the desire of health. They are included in happiness. They are some of the elements of which the desire of happiness is made up. Happiness is not an abstract idea, but a concrete whole; and these are some of its parts. And the utilitarian standard sanctions and approves their being so. Life would be a poor thing, very ill provided with sources of happiness, if there were not this provision of nature, by which things originally indifferent, but conducive to, or otherwise associated with, the satisfaction of our primitive desires, become in themselves sources of pleasure more valuable than the primitive pleasures, both in permanency, in the space of human existence that they are capable of covering, and even in intensity.

Virtue, according to the utilitarian conception, is a good of this description. There was no original desire of it, or motive to it, save its conduciveness to pleasure, and especially to protection from pain. But through the association thus formed, it may be felt a good in itself, and desired as such with as great intensity as any other good; and with this difference between it and the love of money, of power, or of fame, that all of these may, and often do, render the individual noxious to the other members of the society to which he belongs, whereas there is nothing which makes him so much a blessing to them as the cultivation of the disinterested love of virtue. And consequently, the utilitarian standard, while it tolerates and approves those other acquired desires, up to the point beyond which they would be more injurious to the general happiness than promotive of it, enjoins and requires the cultivation of the love of virtue up to the greatest strength possible, as being above all things important to the general happiness.

It results from the preceding considerations, that there is in reality nothing desired except happiness. Whatever is desired otherwise than as a means to some end beyond itself, and ultimately to happiness, is desired as itself a part of happiness, and is not desired for itself until it has become so.

CHAPTER 4

Utilitarianism and Integrity

Bernard Williams

Utilitarianism is the theory that we should always try to bring about as much happiness as possible. It is hard to argue against the value of being happy, but critics are quick to point out that we value many other things as well.

Sir Bernard Williams (1929–2003), one of the great critics of Utilitarianism, held professorships at both Cambridge University and Oxford University. In this selection, he considers two difficult test cases for the utilitarian theory.

(1) George, who has just taken his Ph.D. in chemistry, finds it extremely difficult to get a job. He is not very robust in health, which cuts down the number of jobs he might be able to do satisfactorily. His wife has to go out to work to support them, which itself causes a great deal of strain, since they have small children and there are severe problems about looking after them. The results of all this, especially on the children, are damaging. An older chemist, who knows about this situation, says that he can get George a decently paid job in a certain laboratory, which pursues research into chemical and biological warfare. George says that he cannot accept this, since he is opposed to chemical and biological warfare. The older man replies that he is not too keen on it himself, come to that, but after all George's refusal is not going to make the job or the laboratory go away; what is more, he happens to know that if George refuses the job, it will certainly go to

Excerpted from Bernard Williams, "A Critique of Utilitarianism," *Utilitarianism: For and Against,* Cambridge University Press, 1973. Reprinted by permission of Cambridge University Press.

a contemporary of George's who is not inhibited by any such scruples and is likely if appointed to push along the research with greater zeal than George would. Indeed, it is not merely concern for George and his family, but (to speak frankly and in confidence) some alarm about this other man's excess of zeal, which has led the older man to offer to use his influence to get George the job. . . . George's wife, to whom he is deeply attached, has views (the details of which need not concern us) from which it follows that at least there is nothing particularly wrong with research into CBW. What should he do?

(2) Jim finds himself in the central square of a small South American town. Tied up against the wall are a row of twenty Indians, most terrified, a few defiant, in front of them several armed men in uniform. A heavy man in a sweat-stained khaki shirt turns out to be the captain in charge and, after a good deal of questioning of Jim which establishes that he got there by accident while on a botanical expedition, explains that the Indians are a random group of the inhabitants who, after recent acts of protest against the government, are just about to be killed to remind other possible protestors of the advantages of not protesting. However, since Jim is an honoured visitor from another land, the captain is happy to offer him a guest's privilege of killing one of the Indians himself. If Jim accepts, then as a special mark of the occasion, the other Indians will be let off. Of course, if Jim refuses, then there is no special occasion, and Pedro here will do what he was about to do when Jim arrived, and kill them all. Jim, with some desperate recollection of schoolboy fiction, wonders whether if he got hold of a gun, he could hold the captain, Pedro and the rest of the soldiers to threat, but it is quite clear from the set-up that nothing of that kind is going to work: any attempt at that sort of thing will mean that all the Indians will be killed, and himself. The men against the wall, and the other villagers, understand the situation, and are obviously begging him to accept. What should he do?

To these dilemmas, it seems to me that utilitarianism replies, in the first case, that George should accept the job, and in the second, that Jim should kill the Indian. Not only does utilitarianism give these answers but, if the situations are essentially as described and there are no further special factors, it regards them, it seems to me, as *obviously* the right answers. But many of us would certainly wonder whether, in (1), that could possibly be the right answer at all; and in the case of (2), even one who came to think that perhaps that was the answer, might well wonder whether it was obviously the answer. Nor is it just a question of the rightness or obviousness of these answers. It is also a question of what sort of considerations come into finding the answer. A feature of utilitarianism is that it cuts out a kind of consideration which for some others makes a difference to what they feel about such cases: a consideration involving the idea, as we might first and very simply put it, that each of us is specially responsible for what *he* does, rather than for what other people do. This is an idea closely connected with the value of integrity. It is often suspected that utilitarianism, at least in its direct forms, makes integrity as a value more or less unintelligible. I shall try to show that this suspicion is correct. Of course, even if that is correct, it would not necessarily follow that we should reject utilitarianism; perhaps, as utilitarians sometimes suggest, we should just forget about integrity, in favour of such things as a concern for the general good. However, if I am right, we cannot merely do that, since the reason why utilitarianism cannot understand integrity is that it cannot coherently describe the relations between a man's projects and his actions.

Two Kinds of Remoter Effect

A lot of what we have to say about this question will be about the relations between my projects and other people's projects. But before we get on to that, we should first ask whether we are assuming too hastily what the utilitarian answers to the dilemmas will be. In terms of more direct effects of the possible decisions, there does not indeed seem much doubt about the answer in either case; but it might be said that in terms of more remote or less evident effects counterweights might be found to enter the utilitarian scales. Thus the effect on George of a decision to take the job might be invoked, or its effect on others who might know of his decision. The possibility of there being more beneficent labours in the future from which he might be barred or disqualified, might be mentioned; and so forth. Such effects—in particular, possible effects on the agent's character, and effects on the public at large—are often invoked by utilitarian writers dealing with problems about lying or promise-breaking, and some similar considerations might be invoked here.

There is one very general remark that is worth making about arguments of this sort. The certainty that attaches to these hypotheses about possible effects is usually pretty low; in some cases, indeed, the hypothesis invoked is so implausible that it would scarcely pass if it were not being used to deliver the respectable moral answer, as in the standard fantasy that one of the effects of one's telling a particular lie is to weaken the disposition of the world at large to tell the truth. The demands on the certainty or probability of these beliefs as beliefs about particular actions are much milder than they would be on beliefs favouring the unconventional course. It may be said that this is as it should be, since the presumption must be in favour of the conventional course: but that scarcely seems a *utilitarian* answer, unless utilitarianism has already taken off in the direction of not applying the consequences to the particular act at all.

Leaving aside that very general point, I want to consider now two types of effect that are often invoked by utilitarians, and which might be invoked in connexion with these imaginary cases. The attitude or tone involved in invoking these effects may sometimes seem peculiar; but that sort of peculiarity soon becomes familiar in utilitarian discussions, and indeed it can be something of an achievement to retain a sense of it.

First, there is the psychological effect on the agent. Our descriptions of these situations have not so far taken account of how George or Jim will be after they have taken the one course or the other; and it might be said that if they take the course which seemed at first the utilitarian one, the effects on them will be in fact bad enough and extensive enough to cancel out the initial utilitarian advantages of that course. Now there is one version of this effect in which, for a utilitarian, some confusion must be involved, namely that in which the agent feels bad, his subsequent conduct and relations are crippled and so on, *because he thinks that he has done the wrong thing*—for if the balance of outcomes was as it appeared to be *before* invoking this effect, then he has not (from the utilitarian point of view) done the wrong thing. So that version of the effect, for a rational and utilitarian agent, could not possibly make any difference to the assessment of right and wrong. However, perhaps he is not a thoroughly rational agent, and is disposed to have bad feelings, whichever he decided to do. Now such feelings, which are from a strictly utilitarian point of view irrational—nothing, a utilitarian can point out, is advanced by having them—cannot, consistently, have any great weight in a utilitarian calculation. I shall consider in a moment an argument to suggest that they should have no weight at all in it. But short of that, the utilitarian could reasonably say that such feelings should not be encouraged, even if we accept their existence, and that to give them a lot of weight is to encourage them. Or, at the very best, even if they are straightforwardly and without any discount to be put into the calculation, their weight must be small: they are after all (and at best) one man's feelings.

That consideration might seem to have particular force in Jim's case. In George's case, his feelings represent a larger proportion of what is to be weighed, and are more commensurate in character with other items in the calculation. In Jim's case, however, his feelings might seem to be of very little weight compared with other things that are at stake. There is a powerful and recognizable appeal that can be made on this point: as that a refusal by Jim to do what he has been invited to do would be a kind of self-indulgent squeamishness. That is an appeal which can be made by other than utilitarians—indeed, there are some uses of it which cannot be consistently made by utilitarians, as when it essentially involves the idea that there is something dishonourable about such self-indulgence. But in some versions it is a familiar, and it must be said a powerful, weapon of utilitarianism. One must be clear, though, about what it can and cannot accomplish. The most it can do, so far as I can see, is to invite one to consider how seriously, and for what reasons, one feels that what one is invited to do is (in these circumstances) wrong, and in particular, to consider that question from the utilitarian point of view. When the agent is not seeing the situation from a utilitarian point of view, the appeal cannot force him to do so; and if he does come round to seeing it from a utilitarian point of view, there is virtually nothing left for the appeal to do. If he does not see it from a utilitarian point of view, he will not see his resistance to the invitation, and the unpleasant feelings he associates with accepting it, *just* as disagreeable experiences of his; they figure rather as emotional expressions of a thought that to accept would be wrong. He may be asked, as by the appeal, to consider whether he is right, and indeed whether he is fully serious, in thinking that. But the assertion of the appeal, that he is being self-indulgently squeamish, will not itself answer that question, or even help to answer it, since it essentially tells him to regard his feelings just as unpleasant experiences of his, and he cannot, by doing that, answer the question they pose when they are precisely not so regarded, but are regarded as indications of what he thinks is right and wrong. If he does come round fully to the utilitarian point of view then of course he will regard these feelings just as unpleasant experiences of his. And once Jim—at least—has come to see them in that light, there is nothing left for the appeal to do, since *of course* his feelings, so regarded, are of virtually no weight at all in relation to the other things at stake. The "squeamishness" appeal is not an argument which adds in a hitherto neglected consideration. Rather, it is an invitation to consider the situation, and one's own feelings, from a utilitarian point of view.

The reason why the squeamishness appeal can be very unsettling, and one can be unnerved by the suggestion of self-indulgence in going against utilitarian considerations, is not that we are utilitarians who are uncertain what utilitarian value to attach to our moral feelings, but that we are partially at least not utilitarians, and cannot regard our moral feelings merely as objects of utilitarian value. Because our moral relation to the world is partly given by such feelings, and by a sense of what we can or cannot "live with," to come to regard those feelings from a purely utilitarian point of view, that is to say, as happenings outside one's moral self, is to lose a sense of one's moral identity; to lose, in the most literal way, one's integrity. . . .

CHAPTER 5

The Experience Machine

Robert Nozick

Robert Nozick (1938–2002) was Joseph Pellegrino University Professor of Philosophy at Harvard University. The following selection is from his book *Anarchy, State, and Utopia,* a brilliant and entertaining defense of minimal government. In this excerpt, Nozick uses a thought-experiment to explore questions about what matters to us *other than what our experiences are like.* How we answer these questions will cast light on the ethics of drug use, television watching, and perhaps even sleeping late.

. . . Suppose there were an experience machine that would give you any experience you desired. Superduper neuropsychologists could stimulate your brain so that you would think and feel you were writing a great novel, or making a friend, or reading an interesting book. All the time you would be floating in a tank, with electrodes attached to your brain. Should you plug into this machine for life, preprogramming your life's experiences? If you are worried about missing out on desirable experiences, we can suppose that business enterprises have researched thoroughly the lives of many others. You can pick and choose from their large library or smorgasbord of such experiences, selecting your life's experiences for, say, the next two years. After two years have passed, you will have ten minutes or ten hours out of the tank, to select the experiences of your *next* two years. Of course, while in the tank you won't know that you're there; you'll think it's all actually happening. Others can also plug in to have the experiences they want, so there's no need to stay unplugged to serve them. (Ignore

Excerpted from Robert Nozick, *Anarchy, State, and Utopia* (1974). Reprinted by permission of Basic Books, a member of Perseus Books, L.L.C.

problems such as who will service the machines if everyone plugs in.) Would you plug in? *What else can matter to us, other than how our lives feel from the inside?* Nor should you refrain because of the few moments of distress between the moment you've decided and the moment you're plugged. What's a few moments of distress compared to a lifetime of bliss (if that's what you choose), and why feel any distress at all if your decision *is* the best one?

What does matter to us in addition to our experiences? First, we want to *do* certain things, and not just have the experience of doing them. In the case of certain experiences, it is only because first we want to do the actions that we want the experiences of doing them or thinking we've done them. (But *why* do we want to do the activities rather than merely to experience them?) A second reason for not plugging in is that we want to *be* a certain way, to be a certain sort of person. Someone floating in a tank is an indeterminate blob. There is no answer to the question of what a person is like who has long been in the tank. Is he courageous, kind, intelligent, witty, loving? It's not merely that it's difficult to tell; there's no way he is. Plugging into the machine is a kind of suicide. It will seem to some, trapped by a picture, that nothing about what we are like can matter except as it gets reflected in our experiences. But should it be surprising that what *we are* is important to us? Why should we be concerned only with how our time is filled, but not with what we are?

Thirdly, plugging into an experience machine limits us to a man-made reality, to a world no deeper or more important than that which people can construct. There is no *actual* contact with any deeper reality, though the experience of it can be simulated. Many persons desire to leave themselves open to such contact and to a plumbing of deeper significance. This clarifies the intensity of the conflict over psychoactive drugs, which some view as mere local experience machines, and others view as avenues to a deeper reality; what some view as equivalent to surrender to the experience machine, others view as following one of the reasons *not* to surrender!

We learn that something matters to us in addition to experience by imagining an experience machine and then realizing that we would not use it. We can continue to imagine a sequence of machines each designed to fill lacks suggested for the earlier machines. For example, since the experience machine doesn't meet our desire to *be* a certain way, imagine a transformation machine which transforms us into whatever sort of person we'd like to be (compatible with our staying us). Surely one would not use the transformation machine to become as one would wish, and thereupon plug into the experience machine! So something matters in addition to one's experiences *and* what one is like. Nor is the reason merely that one's experiences are unconnected with what one is like. For the experience machine might be limited to provide only experiences possible to the sort of person plugged in. Is it that we want to make a difference in the world? Consider then the result machine, which produces in the world any result you would produce and injects your vector input into any joint activity. We shall not pursue here the fascinating details of these or other machines. What is most disturbing about them is their living of our lives for us. Is it misguided to search for *particular* additional functions beyond the competence of machines to do for us? Perhaps what we desire is to live (an active verb) ourselves, in contact with reality. (And this, machines cannot do *for* us.) Without elaborating on the implications of this, which I believe connect surprisingly with issues about free will and causal accounts of knowledge, we need merely note the intricacy of the question of what matters *for people* other than their experiences. . . .

CHAPTER 6

The Subjectivity of Values

J. L. Mackie

Everyone agrees that ethics is subjective in the sense that people have their own personal moral beliefs. But in this selection, John L. Mackie contends that ethics is subjective in a much more radical sense—that, really, there is no right or wrong.

Consider this analogy: The earth is spherical, and not flat, because there is this thing—the earth—that has the property of being spherical. But when someone says abortion is wrong, according to Mackie, there can be no property of wrongness that inheres in abortion as spherical-ness adheres in the earth; there is just the feeling, or belief, that abortion is wrong.

In Mackie's view, the belief that Abraham Lincoln is morally better than John Wilkes Booth is similar to Homer Simpson's belief that syrup is better than jelly. Homer Simpson might like syrup more than jelly, but he's not "right" in feeling that way. Similarly, Mackie thinks, you might approve of the president who emancipated the slaves more than you approve of the man who shot him, but you are not "right" in feeling that way. It's just how you feel.

John L. Mackie (1917–1981) was born in Australia and taught at the University of Oxford during his last 14 years. This selection is from his book *Ethics: Inventing Right and Wrong* (1977).

Moral Scepticism

There are no objective values. This is a bald statement of the thesis of this chapter, but before arguing for it I shall try to clarify and restrict it in ways that may meet some objections and prevent some misunderstanding.

Excerpted from J. L. Mackie, *Ethics: Inventing Right and Wrong*, Penguin, 1977, pp. 15–17, 25–28, 29–31, 34–35, 35–39, 40, 41. Reproduced by permission of Penguin Books, Ltd.

The statement of this thesis is liable to provoke one of three very different reactions. Some will think it not merely false but pernicious; they will see it as a threat to morality and to everything else that is worthwhile, and they will find the presenting of such a thesis in what purports to be a book on ethics paradoxical or even outrageous. Others will regard it as a trivial truth, almost too obvious to be worth mentioning, and certainly too plain to be worth much argument. Others again will say that it is meaningless or empty, that no real issue is raised by the question whether values are or are not part of the fabric of the world. But, precisely because there can be these three different reactions, much more needs to be said.

The claim that values are not objective, are not part of the fabric of the world, is meant to include not only moral goodness, which might be most naturally equated with moral value, but also other things that could be more loosely called moral values or disvalues— rightness and wrongness, duty, obligation, an action's being rotten and contemptible, and so on. It also includes non-moral values, notably aesthetic ones, beauty and various kinds of artistic merit. I shall not discuss these explicitly, but clearly much the same considerations apply to aesthetic and to moral values, and there would be at least some initial implausibility in a view that gave the one a different status from the other.

Since it is with moral values that I am primarily concerned, the view I am adopting may be called moral scepticism. But this name is likely to be misunderstood: "moral scepticism" might also be used as a name for either of two first order views, or perhaps for an incoherent mixture of the two. A moral sceptic might be the sort of person who says "All this talk of morality is tripe," who rejects morality and will take no notice of it. Such a person may be literally rejecting all moral judgements; he is more likely to be making moral judgements of his own, expressing a positive moral condemnation of all that conventionally passes for morality; or he may be confusing these two logically incompatible views, and saying that he rejects all morality, while he is in fact rejecting only a particular morality that is current in the society in which he has grown up. But I am not at present concerned with the merits or faults of such a position. These are first order moral views, positive or negative: the person who adopts either of them is taking a certain practical, normative, stand. By contrast, what I am discussing is a second order view, a view about the status of moral values and the nature of moral valuing, about where and how they fit into the world. These first and second order views are not merely distinct but completely independent: one could be a second order moral sceptic without being a first order one, or again the other way round. A man could hold strong moral views, and indeed ones whose content was thoroughly conventional, while believing that they were simply attitudes and policies with regard to conduct that he and other people held. Conversely, a man could reject all established morality while believing it to be an objective truth that it was evil or corrupt.

With another sort of misunderstanding moral scepticism would seem not so much pernicious as absurd. How could anyone deny that there is a difference between a kind action and a cruel one, or that a coward and a brave man behave differently in the face of danger? Of course, this is undeniable; but it is not to the point. The kinds of behaviour to which moral values and disvalues are ascribed are indeed part of the furniture of the world, and so are the natural, descriptive, differences between them; but not, perhaps, their differences in value. It is a hard fact that cruel actions differ from kind ones, and hence that we can learn, as in fact we all do, to distinguish them fairly well in practice, and to use the words "cruel" and "kind" with fairly clear descriptive meanings; but is it an equally hard fact that actions which are cruel in such a descriptive sense are to be condemned? The present issue is with regard to the objectivity specifically of value, not with regard to the objectivity of those natural, factual, differences on the basis of which differing values are assigned. . . .

Standards of Evaluation

One way of stating the thesis that there are no objective values is to say that value statements cannot be either true or false. But this formulation, too, lends itself to misinterpretation. For there are certain kinds of value statements which undoubtedly can be true or false, even if, in the sense I intend, there are no objective values. Evaluations of many sorts are commonly made in relation to agreed and assumed standards. The classing of wool, the grading of apples, the awarding of prizes at sheepdog trials, flower shows, skating and diving championships, and even the marking of examination papers are carried out in relation to standards of quality or merit which are peculiar to each particular subject-matter or type of contest, which may be explicitly laid down but which, even if they are nowhere explicitly stated, are fairly well understood and agreed upon by those who are recognized as judges or experts in each particular field. Given any sufficiently determinate standards, it will be an objective issue, a matter of truth and falsehood, how well any particular specimen measures up to those standards. Comparative judgements in particular will be capable of truth and falsehood: it will be a factual question whether this sheep-dog has performed better than that one.

The subjectivist about values, then, is not denying that there can be objective evaluations relative to standards, and these are as possible in the aesthetic and moral fields as in any of those just mentioned. More than this, there is an objective distinction which applies in many such fields, and yet would itself be regarded as a peculiarly moral one: the distinction between justice and injustice. In one important sense of the word it is a paradigm case of injustice if a court declares someone to be guilty of an offence of which it knows him to be innocent. More generally, a finding is unjust if it is at variance with what the relevant law and the facts together require, and particularly if it is known by the court to be so. More generally still, any award of marks, prizes, or the like is unjust if it is at variance with the agreed standards for the contest in question: if one diver's performance in fact measures up better to the accepted standards for diving than another's, it will be unjust if the latter is awarded higher marks or the prize. In this way the justice or injustice of decisions relative to standards can be a thoroughly objective matter, though there may still be a subjective element in the interpretation or application of standards. But the statement that a certain decision is thus just or unjust will not be objectively prescriptive: in so far as it can be simply true it leaves open the question whether there is any objective requirement to do what is just and to refrain from what is unjust, and equally leaves open the practical decision to act in either way.

Recognizing the objectivity of justice in relation to standards, and of evaluative judgements relative to standards, then, merely shifts the question of the objectivity of values back to the standards themselves. The subjectivist may try to make his point by insisting that there is no objective validity about the choice of standards. Yet he would clearly be wrong if he said that the choice of even the most basic standards in any field was completely arbitrary. The standards used in sheepdog trials clearly bear some relation to the work that sheepdogs are kept to do, the standards for grading apples bear some relation to what people generally want in or like about apples, and so on. On the other hand, standards are not as a rule strictly validated by such purposes. The appropriateness of standards is neither fully determinate nor totally indeterminate in relation to independently specifiable aims or desires. But however determinate it is, the objective appropriateness of standards in relation to aims or desires is no more of a threat to the denial of objective values than is the objectivity of evaluation relative to standards. In fact it is logically no different from the objectivity of goodness relative to desires. Something may be called good simply in so far as it satisfies or is such as to satisfy a certain desire; but the objectivity of such relations of satisfaction does not constitute in our sense an objective value.

Hypothetical and Categorical Imperatives

We may make this issue clearer by referring to Kant's distinction between hypothetical and categorical imperatives, though what he called imperatives are more naturally expressed as "ought" statements than in the imperative mood. "If you want X, do Y" (or "You ought to do Y") will be a hypothetical imperative if it is based on the supposed fact that Y is, in the circumstances, the only (or the best) available means to X, that is, on a causal relation between Y and X. The reason for doing Y lies in its causal connection with the desired end, X; the oughtness is contingent upon the desire. But "You ought to do Y" will be a categorical imperative if you ought to do Y irrespective of any such desire for any end to which Y would contribute, if the oughtness is not thus contingent upon any desire.

A categorical imperative, then, would express a reason for acting which was unconditional in the sense of not being contingent upon any present desire of the agent to whose satisfaction the recommended action would contribute as a means—or more directly: "You ought to dance," if the implied reason is just that you want to dance or like dancing, is still a hypothetical imperative. Now Kant himself held that moral judgements are categorical imperatives, or perhaps are all applications of one categorical imperative, and it can plausibly be maintained at least that many moral judgements contain a categorically imperative element. So far as ethics is concerned, my thesis that there are no objective values is specifically the denial that any such categorically imperative element is objectively valid. The objective values which I am denying would be action-directing absolutely, not contingently (in the way indicated) upon the agent's desires and inclinations.

Another way of trying to clarify this issue is to refer to moral reasoning or moral arguments. In practice, of course, such reasoning is seldom fully explicit: but let us suppose that we could make explicit the reasoning that supports some evaluative conclusion, where this conclusion has some action-guiding force that is not contingent upon desires or purposes or chosen ends. Then what I am saying is that somewhere in the input to this argument—perhaps in one or more of the premisses, perhaps in some part of the form of the argument—there will be something which cannot be objectively validated—some premiss which is not capable of being simply true, or some form of argument which is not valid as a matter of general logic, whose authority or cogency is not objective, but is constituted by our choosing or deciding to think in a certain way.

The Claim to Objectivity

If I have succeeded in specifying precisely enough the moral values whose objectivity I am denying, my thesis may now seem to be trivially true. Of course, some will say, valuing, preferring, choosing, recommending, rejecting, condemning, and so on, are human activities, and there is no need to look for values that are prior to and logically independent of all such activities. There may be widespread agreement in valuing, and particular value-judgements are not in general arbitrary or isolated: they typically cohere with others, or can be criticized if they do not, reasons can be given for them, and so on: but if all that the subjectivist is maintaining is that desires, ends, purposes, and the like figure somewhere in the system of reasons, and that no ends or purposes are objective as opposed to being merely intersubjective, then this may be conceded without much fuss.

But I do not think that this should be conceded so easily. As I have said, the main tradition of European moral philosophy includes the contrary claim, that there are objective values of just the sort I have denied. . . . Kant in particular holds that the categorical imperative is not only categorical and imperative but objectively so: though a rational being gives the moral law to himself, the law that he thus makes is determinate and necessary. Aristotle begins the *Nicomachean Ethics* by saying that the good is that at which all things aim, and that ethics is part of a science which he calls "politics," whose goal is not knowledge but practice; yet he does not doubt that there can be *knowledge* of what is the good for man, nor, once he has identified this as well-being or happiness, *eudaimonia,* that it can be known, rationally determined, in what happiness consists; and it is plain that he thinks that this happiness is intrinsically desirable, not good simply because it is desired. . . . Even the sentimentalist Hutcheson defines moral goodness as "some quality apprehended in actions, which procures approbation, . . ."

while saying that the moral sense by which we perceive virtue and vice has been given to us (by the Author of nature) to direct our actions. Hume indeed was on the other side, but he is still a witness to the dominance of the objectivist tradition, since he claims that when we "see that the distinction of vice and virtue is not founded merely on the relations of objects, nor is perceiv'd by reason," this "wou'd subvert all the vulgar systems of morality." . . .

The prevalence of this tendency to objectify values—and not only moral ones—is confirmed by a pattern of thinking that we find in existentialists and those influenced by them. The denial of objective values can carry with it an extreme emotional reaction, a feeling that nothing matters at all, that life has lost its purpose. Of course this does not follow; the lack of objective values is not a good reason for abandoning subjective concern or for ceasing to want anything. But the abandonment of a belief in objective values can cause, at least temporarily, a decay of subjective concern and sense of purpose. That it does so is evidence that the people in whom this reaction occurs have been tending to objectify their concerns and purposes, have been giving them a fictitious external authority. A claim to objectivity has been so strongly associated with their subjective concerns and purposes that the collapse of the former seems to undermine the latter as well.

This view, that conceptual analysis would reveal a claim to objectivity, is sometimes dramatically confirmed by philosophers who are officially on the other side. Bertrand Russell, for example, says that "ethical propositions should be expressed [as desires]"; he defends himself effectively against the charge of inconsistency in both holding ultimate ethical valuations to be subjective and expressing emphatic opinions on ethical questions. Yet at the end he admits:

> Certainly there *seems* to be something more. Suppose, for example, that someone were to advocate the introduction of bullfighting in this country. In opposing the proposal, I should *feel*, not only that I was expressing my desires, but that my desires in the matter are *right*, whatever that may mean. As a matter of argument, I can, I think, show that I am not guilty of any logical inconsistency in holding to the above interpretation of ethics and at the same time expressing strong ethical preferences. But in feeling I am not satisfied.

But he concludes, reasonably enough, with the remark: "I can only say that, while my own opinions as to ethics do not satisfy me, other people's satisfy me still less."

I conclude, then, that ordinary moral judgements include a claim to objectivity, an assumption that there are objective values in just the sense in which I am concerned to deny this. And I do not think it is going too far to say that this assumption has been incorporated in the basic, conventional, meanings of moral terms. Any analysis of the meanings of moral terms which omits this claim to objective, intrinsic, prescriptivity is to that extent incomplete. . . .

If second order ethics were confined, then, to linguistic and conceptual analysis, it ought to conclude that moral values at least are objective: that they are so is part of what our ordinary moral statements mean: the traditional moral concepts of the ordinary man as well as of the main line of western philosophers are concepts of objective value. But it is precisely for this reason that linguistic and conceptual analysis is not enough. The claim to objectivity, however ingrained in our language and thought, is not self-validating. It can and should be questioned. But the denial of objective values will have to be put forward not as the result of an analytic approach, but as an "error theory," a theory that although most people in making moral judgements implicitly claim, among other things, to be pointing to something objectively prescriptive, these claims are all false. It is this that makes the name "moral scepticism" appropriate.

But since this is an error theory, since it goes against assumptions ingrained in our thought and built into some of the ways in which language is used, since it conflicts with what is sometimes called common sense, it needs very solid support. It is not something we can accept lightly or casually and then quietly pass on. If we are to adopt this view, we must argue explicitly for it. Traditionally it has been supported by arguments of two main kinds, which I shall call the argument from relativity and the argument from queerness, but these can, as I shall show, be supplemented in several ways.

The Argument from Relativity

The argument from relativity has as its premiss the well-known variation in moral codes from one society to another and from one period to another, and also the differences in moral beliefs between different groups and classes within a complex community. Such variation is in itself merely a truth of descriptive morality, a fact of anthropology which entails neither first order nor second order ethical views. Yet it may indirectly support second order subjectivism: radical differences between first order moral judgements make it difficult to treat those judgements as apprehensions of objective truths. But it is not the mere occurrence of disagreements that tells against the objectivity of values. Disagreement on questions in history or biology or cosmology does not show that there are no objective issues in these fields for investigators to disagree about. But such scientific disagreement results from speculative inferences or explanatory hypotheses based on inadequate evidence, and it is hardly plausible to interpret moral disagreement in the same way. Disagreement about moral codes seems to reflect people's adherence to and participation in different ways of life. The causal connection seems to be mainly that way round: it is that people approve of monogamy because they participate in a monogamous way of life rather than that they participate in a monogamous way of life because they approve of monogamy. Of course, the standards may be an idealization of the way of life from which they arise: the monogamy in which people participate may be less complete, less rigid, than that of which it leads them to approve. This is not to say that moral judgements are purely conventional. Of course there have been and are moral heretics and moral reformers, people who have turned against the established rules and practices of their own communities for moral reasons, and often for moral reasons that we would endorse. But this can usually be understood as the extension, in ways which, though new and unconventional, seemed to them to be required for consistency, of rules to which they already adhered as arising out of an existing way of life. In short, the argument from relativity has some force simply because the actual variations in the moral codes are more readily explained by the hypothesis that they reflect ways of life than by the hypothesis that they express perceptions, most of them seriously inadequate and badly distorted, of objective values.

But there is a well-known counter to this argument from relativity; namely to say that the items for which objective validity is in the first place to be claimed are not specific moral rules or codes but very general basic principles which are recognized at least implicitly to some extent in all society—such principles as provide the foundations of what Sidgwick has called different methods of ethics: the principle of universalizability, perhaps, or the rule that one ought to conform to the specific rules of any way of life in which one takes part, from which one profits, and on which one relies, or some utilitarian principle of doing what tends, or seems likely, to promote the general happiness. It is easy to show that such general principles, married with differing concrete circumstances, different existing social patterns or different preferences, will beget different specific moral rules; and there is some plausibility in the claim that the specific rules thus generated will vary from community to community or from group to group in close agreement with the actual variations in accepted codes.

The argument from relativity can be only partly countered in this way. To take this line the moral objectivist has to say that it is only in these principles that the objective moral character attaches immediately to its descriptively specified ground or subject: other moral judgements are objectively valid or true, but only derivatively and contingently—if things had been otherwise, quite different sorts of actions would have been right. And despite the prominence in recent philosophical ethics of universalization, utilitarian principles, and the like, these are very far from constituting the whole of what is actually affirmed as basic in ordinary moral thought. Much of this is concerned rather with what Hare calls "ideals" or, less kindly, "fanaticism." That is, people judge that some things are good or right, and others are bad or wrong, not because—or at any rate not only because—they exemplify some general principle for which widespread implicit acceptance could be claimed, but because something about those things arouses certain responses immediately in them, though they would arouse radically and irresolvably different responses in others. "Moral sense" or "intuition" is an initially more plausible description of what supplies many of our basic moral judgements than "reason." With regard to all these starting points of moral thinking the argument from relativity remains in full force.

The Argument from Queerness

Even more important, however, and certainly more generally applicable, is the argument from queerness. This has two parts, one metaphysical, the other epistemological. If there were objective values, then they would be entities or qualities or relations of a very strange sort, utterly different from anything else in the universe. Correspondingly, if we were aware of them, it would have to be by some special faculty of moral perception or intuition, utterly different from our ordinary ways of knowing everything else. These points were recognized by Moore when he spoke of non-natural qualities, and by the intuitionists in their talk about a "faculty of moral intuition." Intuitionism has long been out of favour, and it is indeed easy to point out its implausibilities. What is not so often stressed, but is more important, is that the central thesis of intuitionism is one to which any objectivist view of values is in the end committed: intuitionism merely makes unpalatably plain what other forms of objectivism wrap up. Of course the suggestion that moral judgements are made or moral problems solved by just sitting down and having an ethical intuition is a travesty of actual moral thinking. But, however complex the real process, it will require (if it is to yield authoritatively prescriptive conclusions) some input of this distinctive sort, either premises or forms of argument or both. When we ask the awkward question, how we can be aware of this authoritative prescriptivity, of the truth of these distinctively ethical premises or of the cogency of this distinctively ethical pattern of reasoning, none of our ordinary accounts of sensory perception or introspection or the framing and confirming of explanatory hypotheses or inference or logical construction or conceptual analysis, or any combination of these, will provide a satisfactory answer; "a special sort of intuition" is a lame answer, but it is the one to which the clearheaded objectivist is compelled to resort.

Indeed, the best move for the moral objectivist is not to evade this issue, but to look for companions in guilt. For example, Richard Price argues that it is not moral knowledge alone that such an empiricism as those of Locke and Hume is unable to account for, but also our knowledge and even our ideas of essence, number, identity, diversity, solidity, inertia, substance, the necessary existence and infinite extension of time and space, necessity and possibility in general, power, and causation. If the understanding, which Price defines as the faculty within us that discerns truth, is also a source of new simple ideas of so many other sorts, may it not also be a power of immediately perceiving right and wrong, which yet are real characters of actions?

This is an important counter to the argument from queerness. The only adequate reply to it would be to show how, on empiricist foundations, we can construct an account of the ideas and beliefs and knowledge that we have of all these matters. I cannot even begin to do that here, though I have undertaken some parts of the task elsewhere. I can only state my belief that satisfactory accounts of most of these can be given in empirical terms. If some supposed metaphysical necessities or essences resist such treatment, then they too should be included, along with objective values, among the targets of the argument from queerness. . . .

Plato's Forms give a dramatic picture of what objective values would have to be. The Form of the Good is such that knowledge of it provides the knower with both a direction and an overriding motive; something's being good both tells the person who knows this to pursue it and makes him pursue it. An objective good would be sought by anyone who was acquainted with it, not because of any contingent fact that this person, or every person, is so constituted that he desires this end, but just because the end has to-be-pursuedness somehow built into it. Similarly, if there were objective principles of right and wrong, any wrong (possible) course of action would have not-to-be-doneness somehow built into it. Or we should have something like Clarke's necessary relations of fitness between situations and actions, so that a situation would have a demand for such-and-such an action somehow built into it. . . .

Another way of bringing out this queerness is to ask, about anything that is supposed to have some objective moral quality, how this is linked with its natural features. What is the connection between the natural fact that an action is a piece of deliberate cruelty—say, causing pain just for fun—and the moral fact that it is wrong? It cannot be an entailment, a logical or semantic necessity. Yet it is not merely that the two features occur together. The wrongness must somehow be "consequential" or "supervenient"; it is wrong because it is a piece of deliberate cruelty. But just what *in the world* is signified by this "because"? And how do we know the relation that it signifies, if this is something more than such actions being socially condemned, and condemned by us too, perhaps through our having absorbed attitudes from our social environment? It is not even sufficient to postulate a faculty which "sees" the wrongness: something must be postulated which can see at once the natural features that constitute the cruelty, and the wrongness, and the mysterious consequential link between the two. Alternatively, the intuition required might be the perception that wrongness is a higher order property belonging to certain natural properties; but what is this belonging of properties to other properties, and how can we discern it? How much simpler and more comprehensible the situation would be if we could replace the moral quality with some sort of subjective response which could be causally related to the detection of the natural features on which the supposed quality is said to be consequential. . . .

CHAPTER 7

The Categorical Imperative

Immanuel Kant

Immanuel Kant, whom many regard as the greatest modern philosopher, led an uneventful life. He never traveled more than a few miles from Königsberg, East Prussia, where he was born in 1724. He was a professor in the local university, popular with students, and a much-sought-after dinner guest. He was also known for his regular habits: A bachelor, he arose each morning at 4 A.M., prepared his lectures, taught from 7 A.M. until noon, read until 4 P.M., took a walk, had dinner, and wrote until bedtime. He repeated this routine every day for years. Yet despite his quiet habits, on the day he was buried in 1804, thousands of people followed his coffin down the street, and the bells of all the churches tolled.

Kant's unorthodox views on religion did cause some controversy. However, Kant was not an atheist. He was from a family of Pietists, who distrusted organized religion. In his later years, when he was rector of the university, it was his duty to lead the faculty procession to the university chapel for religious services; and he would, but, upon reaching the chapel, he would stand aside and not enter. In 1786, having become the most famous philosopher in Germany, and having argued that God's existence cannot be proven, Kant was ordered to publish nothing more on the subject.

Today, "Kant scholarship" is an academic specialty unto itself; many scholars spend their whole lives trying to understand what Kant wrote, and every year new books appear defending new interpretations of his philosophy. The multitude of interpretations is partly due

Excerpted from Immanuel Kant, "Foundations of the Metaphysics of Morals" (1785), in *The Critique of Practical Reason and Other Writings in Moral Philosophy,* trans. Lewis White Beck (Chicago: University of Chicago Press, 1949), pp. 73–74, 80–83, 86–87. Reprinted by permission of the Estate of Lewis White Beck.

to the richness of Kant's thought and to the difficulty of the topics
he discussed. But it is also due to the fact that he was an exceedingly
obscure writer.

Kant believed that morality can be summed up in one ultimate
principle, the Categorical Imperative. According to the Categorical
Imperative, to act morally is to act from motives that everyone, everywhere could live by.

The following selection is from Kant's *Foundations of the Metaphysics of Morals,* the most accessible presentation of his ethical theory.

All imperatives command either hypothetically or categorically. The former present the practical necessity of a possible action as a means to
achieving something else which one desires (or which one may possibly
desire). The categorical imperative would be one which presented an
action as of itself objectively necessary, without regard to any other end.

Since every practical law presents a possible action as good and
thus as necessary for a subject practically determinable by reason, all
imperatives are formulas of the determination of action which is necessary by the principle of a will which is in any way good. If the action
is good only as a means to something else, the imperative is hypothetical; but if it is thought of as good in itself, and hence as necessary in a
will which of itself conforms to reason as the principle of this will, the
imperative is categorical.

The imperative thus says what action possible to me would be
good, and it presents the practical rule in relation to a will which
does not forthwith perform an action simply because it is good, in
part because the subject does not always know that the action is good
and in part (when he does know it) because his maxims can still be
opposed to the objective principles of practical reason.

The hypothetical imperative, therefore, says only that the action
is good to some purpose, possible or actual. In the former case it
is a problematical, in the latter an assertorical, practical principle.
The categorical imperative, which declares the action to be of itself
objectively necessary without making any reference to a purpose,
i.e., without having any other end, holds as an apodictical (practical)
principle. . . .

If I think of a hypothetical imperative as such, I do not know what
it will contain until the condition is stated [under which it is an

imperative]. But if I think of a categorical imperative, I know immediately what it contains. For since the imperative contains besides the law only the necessity of the maxim of acting in accordance with this law, while the law contains no condition to which it is restricted, there is nothing remaining in it except the universality of law as such to which the maxim of the action should conform; and in effect this conformity alone is represented as necessary by the imperative.

There is, therefore, only one categorical imperative. It is: Act only according to that maxim by which you can at the same time will that it should become a universal law.

Now if all imperatives of duty can be derived from this one imperative as a principle, we can at least show what we understand by the concept of duty and what it means, even though it remain undecided whether that which is called duty is an empty concept or not.

The universality of law according to which effects are produced constitutes what is properly called nature in the most general sense (as to form), i.e., the existence of things so far as it is determined by universal laws. [By analogy], then, the universal imperative of duty can be expressed as follows: Act as though the maxim of your action were by your will to become a universal law of nature.

We shall now enumerate some duties, adopting the usual division of them into duties to ourselves and to others and into perfect and imperfect duties.

1. A man who is reduced to despair by a series of evils feels a weariness with life but is still in possession of his reason sufficiently to ask whether it would not be contrary to his duty to himself to take his own life. Now he asks whether the maxim of his action could become a universal law of nature. His maxim, however, is: For love of myself, I make it my principle to shorten my life when by a longer duration it threatens more evil than satisfaction. But it is questionable whether this principle of self-love could become a universal law of nature. One immediately sees a contradiction in a system of nature, whose law would be to destroy life by the feeling whose special office is to impel the improvement of life. In this case it would not exist as nature; hence that maxim cannot obtain as a law of nature, and thus it wholly contradicts the supreme principle of all duty.

2. Another man finds himself forced by need to borrow money. He well knows that he will not be able to repay it, but he also sees that nothing will be loaned him if he does not firmly promise to repay it at a certain time. He desires to make such a promise, but he has enough conscience to ask himself whether it is not improper and opposed

to duty to relieve his distress in such a way. Now, assuming he does decide to do so, the maxim of his action would be as follows: When I believe myself to be in need of money, I will borrow money and promise to repay it, although I know I shall never do so. Now this principle of self-love or of his own benefit may very well be compatible with his whole future welfare, but the question is whether it is right. He changes the pretension of self-love into a universal law and then puts the question: How would it be if my maxim became a universal law? He immediately sees that it could never hold as a universal law of nature and be consistent with itself; rather it must necessarily contradict itself. For the universality of a law which says that anyone who believes himself to be in need could promise what he pleased with the intention of not fulfilling it would make the promise itself and the end to be accomplished by it impossible; no one would believe what was promised to him but would only laugh at any such assertion as vain pretense.

   3. A third finds in himself a talent which could, by means of some cultivation, make him in many respects a useful man. But he finds himself in comfortable circumstances and prefers indulgence in pleasure to troubling himself with broadening and improving his fortunate natural gifts. Now, however, let him ask whether his maxim of neglecting his gifts, besides agreeing with his propensity to idle amusement, agrees also with what is called duty. He sees that a system of nature could indeed exist in accordance with such a law, even though man (like the inhabitants of the South Sea Islands) should let his talents rust and resolve to devote his life merely to idleness, indulgence, and propagation—in a word, to pleasure. But he cannot possibly will that this should become a universal law of nature or that it should be implanted in us by a natural instinct. For, as a rational being, he necessarily wills that all his faculties should be developed, inasmuch as they are given to him for all sorts of possible purposes.

   4. A fourth man, for whom things are going well, sees that others (whom he could help) have to struggle with great hardships, and he asks, "What concern of mine is it? Let each one be as happy as heaven wills, or as he can make himself; I will not take anything from him or even envy him; but to his welfare or to his assistance in time of need I have no desire to contribute." If such a way of thinking were a universal law of nature, certainly the human race could exist, and without doubt even better than in a state where everyone talks of sympathy and good will or even exerts himself occasionally to practice them while, on the other hand, he cheats when he can and betrays

or otherwise violates the rights of man. Now although it is possible that a universal law of nature according to that maxim could exist, it is nevertheless impossible to will that such a principle should hold everywhere as a law of nature. For a will which resolved this would conflict with itself, since instances can often arise in which he would need the love and sympathy of others, and in which he would have robbed himself, by such a law of nature springing from his own will, of all hope of the aid he desires.

The foregoing are a few of the many actual duties, or at least of duties we hold to be actual, whose derivation from the one stated principle is clear. We must be able to will that a maxim of our action become a universal law; this is the canon of the moral estimation of our action generally. Some actions are of such a nature that their maxim cannot even be *thought* as a universal law of nature without contradiction, far from it being possible that one could will that it should be such. In others this internal impossibility is not found though it is still impossible to *will* that their maxim should be raised to the universality of a law of nature, because such a will would contradict itself. We easily see that the former maxim conflicts with the stricter or narrower (imprescriptable) duty, the latter with broader (meritorious) duty. Thus all duties, so far as the kind of obligation (not the object of their action) is concerned, have been completely exhibited by these examples in their dependence on the one principle. . . .

Now, I say, man and, in general, every rational being exists as an end in himself and not merely as a means to be arbitrarily used by this or that will. In all his actions, whether they are directed to himself or to other rational beings, he must always be regarded at the same time as an end. All objects of inclinations have only a conditional worth, for if the inclinations and the needs founded on them did not exist, their object would be without worth. The inclinations themselves as the sources of needs, however, are so lacking in absolute worth that the universal wish of every rational being must be indeed to free himself completely from them. Therefore, the worth of any objects to be obtained by our actions is at all times conditional. Beings whose existence does not depend on our will but on nature, if they are not rational beings, have only a relative worth as means and are therefore called "things"; on the other hand, rational beings are designated "persons," because their nature indicates that they are ends in themselves, i.e., things which may not be used merely as means. Such a being is thus an object of respect and, so far, restricts all [arbitrary] choice. Such beings are not merely subjective ends whose existence as a result of our action has a worth for us but are objective ends, i.e., beings whose existence in itself is an end. Such an end is one for which no other end can be substituted, to which these beings should serve merely as means. For, without them, nothing of absolute worth could be found, and if all worth is conditional and thus contingent, no supreme practical principle for reason could be found anywhere.

Thus if there is to be a supreme practical principle and a categorical imperative for the human will, it must be one that forms an objective principle of the will from the conception of that which is necessarily an end for everyone because it is an end in itself. Hence this objective principle can serve as a universal practical law. The ground of this principle is: rational nature exists as an end in itself. Man necessarily thinks of his own existence in this way; thus far it is a subjective principle of human actions. Also every other rational being thinks of his existence by means of the same rational ground which holds also for myself; thus it is at the same time an objective principle from which, as a supreme practical ground, it must be possible to derive all laws of the will. The practical imperative, therefore, is the following: Act so that you treat humanity, whether in your own person or in that of another, always as an end and never as a means only.

CHAPTER 8

*T*he Virtues

Aristotle

Aristotle (384–322 B.C.) may be the most influential thinker of all time. His theory of physics reigned for a thousand years; his system of logic was dominant until the 19th century; Charles Darwin called him "the greatest biologist of all time"; and his theory of ethics still has many followers.

Aristotle was born in Stagira in northern Greece and moved to Athens when he was 17. There he became a pupil of Plato. Aristotle left Athens after Plato's death in 347 B.C.; four years later, he became tutor to the young boy who was to become Alexander the Great. From 334 B.C. until his death, Aristotle headed his own school in Athens.

The following selection, from Books I and II of Aristotle's *Nicomachean Ethics,* discusses two central themes in his moral philosophy: the nature of the good life, and what it means to be virtuous.

But what is happiness? If we consider what the function of man is, we find that happiness is a virtuous activity of the soul

But presumably to say that happiness is the supreme good seems a platitude, and some more distinctive account of it is still required. This might perhaps be achieved by grasping what is the function of man. If we take a flautist or a sculptor or any artist—or in general any class of men who have a specific function or activity—his goodness and proficiency is considered to lie in the performance of that

---

Excerpted from *The Ethics of Aristotle,* trans. J. A. K. Thomson (London: Penguin Books, 1976), bks. 1, 2, pp. 75–80, 84, 91–92, 94, 100–102. Reprinted by permission of Taylor & Francis Books UK.

function; and the same will be true of man, assuming that man has a function. But is it likely that whereas joiners and shoemakers have certain functions or activities, man as such has none, but has been left by nature a functionless being? Just as we can see that eye and hand and foot and every one of our members has some function, should we not assume that in like manner a human being has a function over and above these particular functions? What, then, can this possibly be? Clearly life is a thing shared also by plants, and we are looking for man's *proper* function; so we must exclude from our definition the life that consists in nutrition and growth. Next in order would be a sort of sentient life; but this too we see is shared by horses and cattle and animals of all kinds. There remains, then, a practical life of the rational part. (This has two aspects: one amenable to reason, the other possessing it and initiating thought.) As this life also has two meanings, we must lay down that we intend here life determined by activity, because this is accepted as the stricter sense. Now if the function of man is an activity of the soul in accordance with, or implying, a rational principle; and if we hold that the function of an individual and of a good individual of the same kind—e.g. of a harpist and of a good harpist, and so on generally—is generically the same, the latter's distinctive excellence being attached to the name of the function (because the function of the harpist is to play the harp, but that of the good harpist is to play it well); and if we assume that the function of man is a kind of life, viz., an activity or series of actions of the soul, implying a rational principle; and if the function of a good man is to perform these well and rightly; and if every function is performed well when performed in accordance with its proper excellence: if all this is so, the conclusion is that the good for man is an activity of soul in accordance with virtue, or if there are more kinds of virtue than one, in accordance with the best and most perfect kind.

There is a further qualification: in a complete lifetime. One swallow does not make a summer; neither does one day. Similarly neither can one day, or a brief space of time, make a man blessed and happy. . . .

Our view of happiness is supported by popular beliefs

viii. We must examine our principle not only as reached logically, from a conclusion and premises, but also in the light of what is commonly said about it; because if a statement is true all the data are in harmony with it, while if it is false they soon reveal a discrepancy.

Now goods have been classified under three heads, as (*a*) external, (*b*) of the soul, and (*c*) of the body. Of these we say that goods of the soul are good in the strictest and fullest sense, and we rank actions and activities of soul as goods of the soul; so that according to this view, which is of long standing and accepted by philosophers, our definition will be correct. We are right, too, in saying that the end consists in certain actions or activities, because this puts it among goods of the soul and not among external goods. Our definition is also supported by the belief that the happy man lives and fares well; because what we have described is virtually a kind of good life or prosperity. Again, our definition seems to include all the required constituents of happiness; for some think that it is virtue, others prudence, and others wisdom; others that it is these, or one of these, with the addition of pleasure, or not in total separation from it; and others further include favourable external conditions. Some of these views are popular beliefs of long standing; others are those of a few distinguished men. It is reasonable to suppose that neither group is entirely mistaken, but is right in some respect, or even in most.

Now our definition is in harmony with those who say that happiness is virtue, or a particular virtue; because an activity in accordance with virtue implies virtue. But presumably it makes no little difference whether we think of the supreme good as consisting in the *possession* or in the *exercise* of virtue: in a state of mind or in an activity. For it is possible for the *state* to be present in a person without effecting any good result (e.g. if he is asleep or quiescent in some other way), but not for the *activity:* he will necessarily act, and act well. Just as at the Olympic Games it is not the best-looking or the strongest men present that are crowned with wreaths, but the competitors (because it is from them that the winners come), so it is those who *act* that rightly win the honours and rewards in life.

Moreover, the life of such people is in itself pleasant. For pleasure is an experience of the soul, and each individual finds pleasure in that of which he is said to be fond. For example, a horse gives pleasure to one who is fond of horses, and a spectacle to one who is fond of sight-seeing. In the same way just acts give pleasure to a lover of justice, and virtuous conduct generally to the lover of virtue. Now most people find that the things which give them pleasure conflict, because they are not pleasant by nature; but lovers of beauty find pleasure in things that are pleasant by nature, and virtuous actions are of this kind, so that they are pleasant not only to this type of person but also in themselves. So their life does not need to have pleasure attached to it as a sort of accessory, but contains its own pleasure in itself. Indeed, we may go further and assert that anyone who does not delight in fine actions is not even a good man; for nobody would say that a man is just unless he enjoys acting justly, nor liberal unless he enjoys liberal actions, and similarly in all the other cases. If this is so, virtuous actions must be pleasurable in themselves. What is more, they are both good and fine, and each in the highest degree, assuming that the good man is right in his judgement of them; and his judgement is as we have described. So happiness is the best, the finest, the most pleasurable thing of all; and these qualities are not separated as the inscription at Delos suggests:

> Justice is loveliest, and health is best,
> But sweetest to obtain is heart's desire.

All these attributes belong to the best activities; and it is these, or the one that is best of them, that we identify with happiness.

Nevertheless it seems clear that happiness needs the addition of external goods, as we have said; for it is difficult if not impossible to do fine deeds without any resources. Many can only be done by the help of friends, or wealth, or political influence. There are also certain advantages, such as good ancestry or good children, or personal beauty, the lack of which mars our felicity; for a man is scarcely happy if he is very ugly to look at, or of low birth, or solitary and childless; and presumably even less so if he has children or friends who are quite worthless, or if he had good ones who are now dead. So, as we said, happiness seems to require this sort of prosperity too; which is why some identify it with good fortune, although others identify it with virtue. . . .

We are now in a position to define the happy man as "one who is active in accordance with complete virtue, and who is adequately furnished with external goods, and that not for some unspecified period but throughout a complete life." And probably we should add "destined both to live in this way and to die accordingly"; because the future is obscure to us, and happiness we maintain to be an *end* in every way utterly final and complete. . . .

Moral virtues, like crafts, are acquired by practice and habituation

i. Virtue, then, is of two kinds, intellectual and moral. Intellectual virtue owes both its inception and its growth chiefly to instruction, and for this very reason needs time and experience. Moral goodness, on the other hand, is the result of habit, from which it has actually got its name, being a slight modification of the word *ethos*. This fact makes it obvious that none of the moral virtues is engendered in us by nature, since nothing that is what it is by nature can be made to behave differently by habituation. For instance, a stone, which has a natural tendency downwards, cannot be habituated to rise, however often you try to train it by throwing it into the air; nor can you train fire to burn downwards; nor can anything else that has any other natural tendency be trained to depart from it. The moral virtues, then, are engendered in us neither *by* nor *contrary to* nature; we are constituted by nature to receive them, but their full development in us is due to habit.

Again, of all those faculties with which nature endows us we first acquire the potentialities, and only later effect their actualization. (This is evident in the case of the senses. It was not from repeated acts of seeing or hearing that we acquired the senses but the other way round: we had these senses before we used them; we did not acquire them as the result of using them.) But the virtues we do acquire by first exercising them, just as happens in the arts. Anything that we have to learn to do we learn by the actual doing of it: people become builders by building and instrumentalists by playing instruments. Similarly we become just by performing just acts, temperate by performing temperate ones, brave by performing brave ones. This view is supported by what happens in city-states. Legislators make their citizens good by habituation; this is the intention of every legislator, and those who do not carry it out fail of their object. This is what makes the difference between a good constitution and a bad one.

Again, the causes or means that bring about any form of excellence are the same as those that destroy it, and similarly with art; for it is as a result of playing the harp that people become good and bad harpists. The same principle applies to builders and all other craftsmen. Men will become good builders as a result of building well, and bad ones as a result of building badly. Otherwise there would be no need of anyone to teach them: they would all be *born* either good or bad. Now this holds good also of the virtues. It is the way that we behave in our dealings with other people that makes us just or unjust, and the way that we behave in the face of danger, accustoming ourselves to be timid or confident, that makes us brave or cowardly. Similarly with situations involving desires and angry feelings: some people become temperate and patient from one kind of conduct in such situations, others licentious and choleric from another. In a word, then, like activities produce like dispositions. Hence we must give our activities a certain quality, because it is their characteristics that determine the resulting dispositions. So it is a matter of no little importance what sort of habits we form from the earliest age—it makes a vast difference, or rather all the difference in the world. . . .

A cardinal rule: right conduct is incompatible with excess
or deficiency in feelings and actions

First, then, we must consider this fact: that it is in the nature of moral qualities that they are destroyed by deficiency and excess, just as we can see (since we have to use the evidence of visible facts to throw light on those that are invisible) in the case of bodily health and strength. For both excessive and insufficient exercise destroy one's strength, and both eating and drinking too much or too little destroy health, whereas the right quantity produces, increases and preserves it. So it is the same with temperance, courage and the other virtues. The man who shuns and fears everything and stands up to nothing becomes a coward; the man who is afraid of nothing at all, but marches up to every danger, becomes foolhardy. Similarly the man who indulges in every pleasure and refrains from none becomes licentious; but if a man behaves like a boor and turns his back on every pleasure, he is a case of insensibility. Thus temperance and courage are destroyed by excess and deficiency and preserved by the mean. . . .

If, then, every science performs its function well only when it observes the mean and refers its products to it (which is why it is customary to say of well-executed works that nothing can be added to them or taken away, the implication being that excess and deficiency alike destroy perfection, while the mean preserves it)—if good craftsmen, as we hold, work with the mean in view; and if virtue, like nature, is more exact and more efficient than any art, it follows that virtue aims to hit the mean. By virtue I mean moral virtue since it is this that is concerned with feelings and actions, and these involve excess, deficiency and a mean. It is possible, for example, to feel fear, confidence, desire, anger, pity, and pleasure and pain generally, too much or too little; and both of these are wrong. But to have these feelings at the right times on the right grounds towards the right people for the right motive and in the right way is to feel them to an intermediate, that is to the best, degree; and this is the mark of virtue. Similarly there are excess and deficiency and a mean in the case of actions. But it is in the field of actions and feelings that virtue operates; and in them excess and deficiency are failings, whereas the mean is praised and recognized as a success: and these are both marks of virtue. Virtue, then, is a mean condition, inasmuch as it aims at hitting the mean.

Again, failure is possible in many ways (for evil, as the Pythagoreans represented it, is a form of the Unlimited, and good of the Limited), but success is only possible in one way. That is why the one is easy and the other difficult; it is easy to miss the target and difficult to hit it. Here, then, is another reason why excess and deficiency fall under evil, and the mean state under good:

> For men are bad in countless ways, but good in only one.

A provisional definition of virtue

So virtue is a purposive disposition, lying in a mean that is relative to us and determined by a rational principle, and by that which a prudent man would use to determine it. It is a mean between two kinds of vice, one of excess and the other of deficiency; and also for this reason, that whereas these vices fall short of or exceed the right measure in both feelings and actions, virtue discovers the mean and chooses it. Thus from the point of view of its essence and the definition of its real nature, virtue is a mean; but in respect of what is right and best, it is an extreme.

CHAPTER 9

Master Morality and Slave Morality

Friedrich Nietzsche

The German philosopher Friedrich Nietzsche (1844–1900) is one of the most controversial figures in intellectual history. He expressed himself in angry, flamboyant prose, and he despised women. After he went insane and died, apparently from syphilis, his sister used his work to further her own dark agenda. Under her influence, Nietzsche became the favorite philosopher of the Nazis, including Adolph Hitler, who was once photographed contemplating a bust of the philosopher. However, Nietzsche was not an anti-Semite; he called the Jews "the strongest, toughest, and purest race" living in Europe. Nietzsche's sister Elisabeth was the Nazi.

In this selection, Nietzsche contrasts "Master Morality" with "Slave Morality," and there is no doubt which he prefers. Master morality is the morality of the proud and the strong; slave morality is the morality of the weak. Nietzsche regards "slave values" as pathetic. For good or for ill, Nietzsche was consistent: his books contain sections with titles such as "Why I Am So Clever" and "Why I Write Such Good Books." Nietzsche exemplified the values he praised.

Wandering through the many subtler and coarser moralities which have so far been prevalent on earth, or still are prevalent, I found that certain features recurred regularly together and were closely associated—until I finally discovered two basic types and one basic difference.

Excerpted from *Beyond Good and Evil*, trans. Walter Kaufmann (New York: Vintage Books, 1966), pp. 204–207.

There are *master morality* and *slave morality*—I add immediately that in all the higher and more mixed cultures there also appear attempts at mediation between these two moralities, and yet more often the interpenetration and mutual misunderstanding of both, and at times they occur directly alongside each other—even in the same human being, within a *single* soul. The moral discrimination of values has originated either among a ruling group whose consciousness of its difference from the ruled group was accompanied by delight—or among the ruled, the slaves and dependents of every degree.

In the first case, when the ruling group determines what is "good," the exalted, proud states of the soul are experienced as conferring distinction and determining the order of rank. The noble human being separates from himself those in whom the opposite of such exalted, proud states finds expression: he despises them. It should be noted immediately that in this first type of morality the opposition of "good" and *"bad"* means approximately the same as "noble" and "contemptible." (The opposition of "good" and *"evil"* has a different origin.) One feels contempt for the cowardly, the anxious, the petty, those intent on narrow utility; also for the suspicious with their unfree glances, those who humble themselves, the doglike people who allow themselves to be maltreated, the begging flatterers, above all the liars: it is part of the fundamental faith of all aristocrats that the common people lie. "We truthful ones"—thus the nobility of ancient Greece referred to itself.

It is obvious that moral designations were everywhere first applied to *human beings* and only later, derivatively, to actions. Therefore it is a gross mistake when historians of morality start from such questions as: why was the compassionate act praised? The noble type of man experiences *itself* as determining values; it does not need approval; it judges, "what is harmful to me is harmful in itself"; it knows itself to be that which first accords honor to things; it is *value-creating*. Everything it knows as part of itself it honors: such a morality is self-glorification. In the foreground there is the feeling of fullness, of power that seeks to overflow, the happiness of high tension, the consciousness of wealth that would give and bestow: the noble human being, too, helps the unfortunate, but not, or almost not, from pity, but prompted more by an urge begotten by excess of power. The noble human being honors himself as one who is powerful, also as one who has power over himself, who knows how to speak and be silent, who delights in being severe and hard with himself and respects all severity and hardness. "A hard heart Wotan put into my breast," says an old Scandinavian saga: a fitting poetic expression, seeing that it comes from the soul of a proud Viking. Such a type of man is actually proud of the fact that he is *not* made for pity, and the hero of the saga therefore adds as a warning: "If the heart is not hard in youth it will never harden." Noble and courageous human beings who think that way are furthest removed from that morality which finds the distinction of morality precisely in pity, or in acting for others; faith in oneself, pride in oneself, a fundamental hostility and irony against "selflessness" belong just as definitely to noble morality as does a slight disdain and caution regarding compassionate feelings and a "warm heart."

It is the powerful who *understand* how to honor; this is their art, their realm of invention. The profound reverence for age and tradition—all law rests on this double reverence—the faith and prejudice in favor of ancestors and disfavor of those yet to come are typical of the morality of the powerful; and when the men of "modern ideas," conversely, believe almost instinctively in "progress" and "the future" and more and more lack respect for age, this in itself would sufficiently betray the ignoble origin of these "ideas."

A morality of the ruling group, however, is most alien and embarrassing to the present taste in the severity of its principle that one has duties only to one's peers; that against beings of a lower rank, against everything alien, one may behave as one pleases or "as the heart desires," and in any case "beyond good and evil"—here pity and like feelings may find their place. The capacity for, and the duty of, long gratitude and long revenge—both only among one's peers—refinement in repaying, the sophisticated concept of friendship, a certain necessity for having enemies (as it were, as drainage ditches for the affects of envy, quarrelsomeness, exuberance—at bottom, in order to be capable of being good *friends*): all these are typical characteristics of noble morality which, as suggested, is not the morality of "modern ideas" and therefore is hard to empathize with today, also hard to dig up and uncover.

It is different with the second type of morality, *slave morality*. Suppose the violated, oppressed, suffering, unfree, who are uncertain of themselves and weary, moralize: what will their moral valuations have in common? Probably, a pessimistic suspicion about the whole condition of man will find expression, perhaps a condemnation of man along with his condition. The slave's eye is not favorable to the virtues of the powerful: he is skeptical and suspicious, *subtly* suspicious, of all the "good" that is honored there—he would like to persuade himself that even their happiness is not genuine. Conversely, those qualities are brought out and flooded with light which serve to ease existence for those who suffer: here pity, the complaisant and obliging hand, the warm heart, patience, industry, humility, and friendliness are honored—for here these are the most useful qualities and almost the only means for enduring the pressure of existence. Slave morality is essentially a morality of utility.

Here is the place for the origin of that famous opposition of "good" and "evil": into evil one's feelings project power and danger-ousness, a certain terribleness, subtlety, and strength that does not permit contempt to develop. According to slave morality, those who are "evil" thus inspire fear; according to master morality it is precisely those who are "good" that inspire, and wish to inspire, fear, while the "bad" are felt to be contemptible.

The opposition reaches its climax when, as a logical conse-quence of slave morality, a touch of disdain is associated also with the "good" of this morality—this may be slight and benevolent—because the good human being has to be *undangerous* in the slaves' way of thinking: he is good-natured, easy to deceive, a little stupid perhaps. Wherever slave morality becomes preponderant, language tends to bring the words "good" and "stupid" closer together. . . .

CHAPTER 10

Caring Relations and Principles of Justice

Virginia Held

Historically, men have dominated public life, and in the public sphere, relationships are often impersonal and contractual. Businessmen nego-tiate; they bargain and make deals. Moreover, public figures may make decisions that affect large numbers of people, and so they may need to calculate which decision would have the best overall outcome. Small wonder, then, that men's moral theories emphasize duty, contracts, and the calculation of costs and benefits.

A moral theory tailored to the traditional concerns of women would look very different. In the small-scale world of friends and fam-ily, bargaining and calculating play a much smaller role, while love and caring dominate. According to Virginia Held, the values of care are no less important than the values of justice.

Virginia Held is Professor Emerita at the City University of New York. She wrote *The Ethics of Care: Personal, Political, and Global* (2005).

The Controversy

The question of whether impartial, universal, and rational moral principles must always be given priority over other possible grounds for moral motivation continues to provoke extensive debate. David Velleman has recently added his defense of Kantian ethics. . . .

Velleman concentrates on the case that Bernard Williams dis-cusses . . . of whether a man may justifiably save his wife rather than

From *Controversies in Feminism*, edited by James P. Sterba (Lanham, MD: Rowman & Lit-tlefield, 2001), pp. 67–81. Reprinted by permission of Rowman & Littlefield Publishers.

a stranger, if he can save only one. Williams suggests that if the man stops to think about whether universal principles could permit him to give special consideration to his wife rather than treating both persons impartially, the man is having "one thought too many.". . .

Williams's arguments are presented from the point of view of a man with a set of projects, the sorts of projects that make life worth living for this man. The image, like its Kantian alternative, is still that of an individual deliberator. Williams pits the individual's particular goals—to live life with his wife or, in another case, to be a painter—against the individual's rational and impartial moral principles, and he doubts that the latter should always have priority. Williams disputes the view that our particular projects must always be constrained by universal principles requiring that we should only pursue what universal principles permit. If a man's life would be worth living only if he put, for example, his art ahead of his universalizable moral obligations to his family, Williams is not willing to give priority to his moral obligations. In the example of the man and the drowning others, the man's wife may be his project, but the dilemma is posed in terms of an individual's own particular goals versus his universal moral obligations. At a formal level it remains within the traditional paradigm of egoism versus universalism. Williams is unwilling to yield the claims of the ego, especially those that enable it to continue to be the person it is, to the requirements of universalization. But he does not reject the traditional way of conceptualizing the alternatives. . . . The problem is seen as pitting the claims of an individual ego against those of impartial rules.

The feminist challenge to Kantian moralities does require a change in this paradigm. It does not pit an individual ego against universal principles, but considers a particular relationship between persons, a caring relationship, and questions whether it should always yield to universal principles of justice. . . . When universal principles conflict with the claims of relationships, the feminist challenge disputes that the principles should always have priority. The feminist critique . . . gives us reason to doubt that . . . justice should always have priority over care. . . .

Differences among Feminists

. . . The feminist critique of liberalism . . . is the more fundamental one that turning everyone into a complete liberal individual leaves no one adequately attentive to relationships between persons. . . . It is possible for two strangers to have a so-called "relation" of equality between them, with nothing at all to bind them together into a friendship or a community. Liberal equality doesn't itself provide or concern itself with the more substantial components of relationship. It is in evaluating and making recommendations for the latter that an ethic of care is most appropriate. As many feminists argue, the issues for moral theory are less a matter of justice versus care than of how to appropriately integrate justice and care, or care and justice if we are wary of the traditional downgrading and marginalizing of care. And it is not satisfactory to think of care, as it is conceptualized by liberal individualism, as a mere personal preference an individual may choose or not. Neither is it satisfactory to think of caring relationships as merely what rational individuals may choose to care about as long as they give priority to universal, and impartial, moral principles.

Marilyn Friedman calls attention to when partiality is or is not morally valuable. "Personal relationships," she writes, "vary widely in their moral value. The quality of a particular relationship is profoundly important in determining the moral worth of any partiality which is necessary for sustaining that relationship." Partiality toward other white supremacists on the part of a white supremacist, for instance, does not have moral worth. When relationships cause harm, or are based on such wrongful relations as that of master and slave, we should not be partial toward them. But when a relationship has moral worth, such as a caring relationship between parents and children, or a relation of trust between friends and lovers clearly may have, the question of the priority, or not, of impartiality can arise. And as moralities of impartial rules so easily forget, and as Friedman makes clear, "close relationships call . . . for personal concern, loyalty, interest, passion, and responsiveness to the uniqueness of loved ones, to their specific needs, interests, history, and so on. In a word, personal relationships call for attitudes of partiality rather than impartiality."

Evaluating the worth of relationships does not mean that universal norms have priority after all. It means that from the perspective of justice, some relationships are to be judged unjustifiable, often to the point that they should be ended to the extent possible, although this is often a limited extent. (For instance, we will never stop being the sibling of our siblings, or the ex-friend or ex-spouse of the friends or spouse with whom we have broken a relation.) But once a relationship can be deemed to have value, moral issues can arise as to whether the claims of the relationship should or should not be subordinated to the perspective of justice. . . . Moreover, the aspects of a relationship that make it a bad relationship can often be interpreted as failures to appropriately care for particular others, rather than only as violations of impartial moral rules. Certainly, avoiding serious moral wrongs should take priority over avoiding trivial ones, and pursuing highly important moral goods should take priority over pursuing insignificant ones. But this settles nothing about caring relations versus impartial moral rules. . . . Some caring relations are of the utmost importance, . . . while some of the requirements of impartial moral rules are relatively insignificant. And sometimes it is the reverse. . . .

A Look at Some Cases

Let me now try to examine in greater detail what is at issue between an ethic of care and a morality built on impartiality, and why a satisfactory feminist morality should not accept the view that universal, impartial, liberal moral principles of justice and right should always be accorded priority over the concerns of caring relationships, which include considerations of trust, friendship, and loyalty. The argument needs to be examined both at the level of personal relationships and at the level of social policy. Advocates of an ethic of care have argued successfully against the view that care—within the bounds of what is permitted by universal principles—is admirable in personal relations, but that the core value of care is inappropriate for the impersonal relations of strangers and citizens. I will explore issues of both kinds.

Consider, first, the story of Abraham. It has been discussed by a number of defenders of an ethic of care who do not agree with the religious and moral teaching that Abraham made the right decision when be chose to obey the command of God and kill his infant son. . . . From the perspective of an ethic of care, the relationship between child and parent should not always be subordinated to the command of God or of universal moral rules. But let's consider a secular case in which there is a genuine conflict between impartialist rules and the parent-child relation. . . .

Suppose the father of a young child is by profession a teacher with a special skill in helping troubled young children succeed academically. Suppose now that on a utilitarian calculation of how much overall good will be achieved, he determines that, from the point of view of universal utilitarian rules, he ought to devote more time to his work, staying at his school after hours and so on, letting his wife and others care for his own young child. But he also thinks that from the perspective of care, he should build his relationship with his child, developing the trust and mutual consideration of which it is capable.

Even if the universal rules allow him some time for family life, and even if he places appropriate utilitarian value on developing his relationship with his child—the good it will do the child, the pleasure it will give him, the good it will enable the child to do in the future, etc.—the calculation still comes out, let's say, as before: he should devote more time to his students. But the moral demands of care suggest to him that he should spend more time with his child. . . .

The argument for impartiality might go something like this: Reasoning as an abstract agent, I should act on moral rules that all could accept from a perspective of impartiality. Those rules recommend that we treat all persons equally, including our children, with respect to exercising our professional skills, and that when we have special skills we should use them for the benefit of all persons equally. For example, a teacher should not favor his own child if his child happens to be one of his students. And if one has the abilities and has had the social advantages to become a teacher, one should exercise those skills when they are needed, especially when they are seriously needed.

But the father in my example also considers the perspective of care. From this perspective his relationship with his child is of enormous and irreplaceable value. He thinks that out of concern for this particular relationship he should spend more time with his child. He experiences the relationship as one of love and trust and loyalty, and thinks in this case that he should subordinate such other considerations as exercising his professional skills to this relationship. He thinks he should free himself to help his child feel the trust and encouragement his development will require, even if this conflicts with impartial morality.

He reflects on what the motives would be in choosing between the alternatives. For one alternative, the motive would be: because universal moral rules recommend it. For the other, the motive would be: because this is my child and I am the father of this child and the relationship between us is no less important than universal rules. He reflects on whether the latter can be a moral motive and concludes that it can in the sense that he can believe it is the motive he ought to act on. And he can do this without holding that every father ought to act similarly toward his child. He can further conclude that if Kantian and utilitarian moralities deny that such a motive can be moral, then they have mistakenly defined the moral to suit their purposes, and, by arbitrary fiat, excluded whatever might challenge their universalizing requirements. He may have read Annette Baier's discussion of the possible tendency of women to resist subordinating their moral sensitivities to autonomously chosen Kantian rules. Baier writes:

> What did Kant, the great prophet of autonomy, say in his moral theory about women? He said they were incapable of legislation, not fit to vote, that they needed the guidance of more 'rational' males. Autonomy was not for them; it was only for first-class, really rational persons. . . . But where Kant concludes 'so much the worse for women,' we can conclude 'so much the worse for the male fixation on the special skill of drafting legislation, for the bureaucratic mentality of rule-worship, and for the male exaggeration of the importance of independence over mutual interdependence.

The father in my example may think fathers should join mothers in paying more attention to relationships of care and in resisting the demands of impartial rules when they are excessive.

From the perspective of all, or everyone, perhaps particular relationships should be subordinated to universal rules. But from the perspective of particular persons in relationships, it is certainly meaningful to ask: Why must we adopt the perspective of all and everyone when it is a particular relationship that we care about at least as much as "being moral" in the sense required by universal rules? . . . What I am arguing is that in the ethics of care, the moral claims of caring are no less valid than the moral claims of impartial rules. This is not to say that considerations of impartiality are unimportant; it does deny that they should always have priority. This makes care ethics a challenge to liberalism as a moral theory, not a mere supplement. . . .

Models of Morality

At the level of morality, we need to decide which "models" are appropriate for which contexts. . . .

An ethic of care suggests that the priority of justice is at best persuasive for the legal-judicial context. It might also suggest that calculations of general utility are at best appropriate for some choices about public policy. A moral theory is still needed to show us how, within the relatedness that should exist among all persons as fellow human beings, and that does exist in many personal contexts and numerous group ones, we should apply the various possible models. We will then be able to see how we should apply the legal-judicial model of impartiality to given ranges of issues, or the utilitarian model of concern for the general welfare to another range of issues, all the time recognizing other issues, such as those that can be seen most clearly among friends and within families and in cases of group solidarity, for which these models are inappropriate or inadequate. And we will see how the model of caring relations can apply and have priority in some contexts, and how it should not be limited to the personal choices made by individuals after they have met all the requirements of justice. A comprehensive moral theory would show, I believe, how care and its related values are not less important than justice. Whether they are more important remains to be argued, but not in this paper.

CHAPTER 11

Why Abortion Is Immoral

Don Marquis

Abortion was not traditionally treated as a crime in Western law. Under English common law, abortion was tolerated even when performed late in the pregnancy, and in the United States, no laws prohibited it until well into the 19th century. When such laws were enacted, they were motivated by three concerns: a desire to discourage illicit sexual activity, the belief that abortion was an unsafe medical procedure, and the feeling that it is morally wrong to kill an unborn baby.

In the 20th century, every state passed laws forbidding abortion. However, these laws were held unconstitutional by the U.S. Supreme Court in its famous (some would say infamous) decision in *Roe v. Wade* (1973). The Court held that states cannot ban abortion until the fetus is "viable"—that is, until the fetus is mature enough to survive outside the womb. The upshot is that American women can get abortions until they are about six months pregnant.

Today, most Americans support the *Roe v. Wade* decision, and the Supreme Court is unlikely to overturn it so long as Barack Obama remains president. Five Supreme Court justices out of nine currently agree with the decision. If a vacancy arises on the Court, President Obama will almost certainly nominate someone who supports legalized abortion.

When people discuss the morality of abortion, they usually begin by asking, Is the fetus a person, with a right to life? However, Don Marquis of the University of Kansas asks a different question: Do we have the same reasons not to kill a fetus that we have not to kill an adult? Killing adults, he says, is wrong because it deprives them of their future. But in killing a fetus, we are also depriving it of its future. Thus, it seems inconsistent to object to one but not the other.

From *The Journal of Philosophy*, vol. 86 (1989), pp. 183–85, 189–92, 194. Reprinted by permission.

The view that abortion is, with rare exceptions, seriously immoral has received little support in the recent philosophical literature. No doubt most philosophers affiliated with secular institutions of higher education believe that the anti-abortion position is either a symptom of irrational religious dogma or a conclusion generated by seriously confused philosophical argument. The purpose of this essay is to undermine this general belief. This essay sets out an argument that purports to show, as well as any argument in ethics can show, that abortion is, except possibly in rare cases, seriously immoral, that it is in the same moral category as killing an innocent adult human being. . . .

I

A sketch of standard anti-abortion and pro-choice arguments exhibits how those arguments possess certain symmetries that explain why partisans of those positions are so convinced of the correctness of their own positions, why they are not successful in convincing their opponents, and why, to others, this issue seems to be unresolvable. An analysis of the nature of this standoff suggests a strategy for surmounting it.

Consider the way a typical anti-abortionist argues. She will argue or assert that life is present from the moment of conception or that fetuses look like babies or that fetuses possess a characteristic such as a genetic code that is both necessary and sufficient for being human. Anti-abortionists seem to believe that (1) the truth of all of these claims is quite obvious, and (2) establishing any of these claims is sufficient to show that abortion is morally akin to murder.

A standard pro-choice strategy exhibits similarities. The pro-choicer will argue or assert that fetuses are not persons or that fetuses are not rational agents or that fetuses are not social beings. Pro-choicers seem to believe that (1) the truth of any of these claims is quite obvious, and (2) establishing any of these claims is sufficient to show that an abortion is not a wrongful killing.

In fact, both the pro-choice and the anti-abortion claims do seem to be true, although the "it looks like a baby" claim is more difficult to establish the earlier the pregnancy. We seem to have a standoff. How can it be resolved?

As everyone who has taken a bit of logic knows, if any of these arguments concerning abortion is a good argument, it requires not only some claim characterizing fetuses, but also some general moral principle that ties a characteristic of fetuses to having or not having the right to life or to some other moral characteristic that will generate the obligation or the lack of obligation not to end the life of a fetus. Accordingly, the arguments of the anti-abortionist and the pro-choicer need a bit of filling in to be regarded as adequate.

Note what each partisan will say. The anti-abortionist will claim that her position is supported by such generally accepted moral principles as "It is always prima facie seriously wrong to take a human life" or "It is always prima facie seriously wrong to end the life of a baby." Since these are generally accepted moral principles, her position is certainly not obviously wrong. The pro-choicer will claim that her position is supported by such plausible moral principles as "Being a person is what gives an individual intrinsic moral worth" or "It is only seriously prima facie wrong to take the life of a member of the human community." Since these are generally accepted moral principles, the pro-choice position is certainly not obviously wrong. Unfortunately, we have again arrived at a standoff.

Now, how might one deal with this standoff? The standard approach is to try to show how the moral principles of one's opponent lose their plausibility under analysis. It is easy to see how this is possible. On the one hand, the anti-abortionist will defend a moral principle concerning the wrongness of killing which tends to be broad in scope in order that even fetuses at an early stage of pregnancy will fall under it. The problem with broad principles is that they often embrace too much. In this particular instance, the principle "It is always prima facie wrong to take a human life" seems to entail that it is wrong to end the existence of a living human cancer-cell culture, on the grounds that the culture is both living and human. Therefore, it seems that the anti-abortionist's favored principle is too broad.

On the other hand, the pro-choicer wants to find a moral principle concerning the wrongness of killing which tends to be narrow in scope in order that fetuses will *not* fall under it. The problem with narrow principles is that they often do not embrace enough. Hence, the needed principles such as "It is prima facie seriously wrong to kill only persons" or "It is prima facie wrong to kill only rational agents" do not explain why it is wrong to kill infants or young children or the severely retarded or even perhaps the severely mentally ill. Therefore, we seem again to have a standoff. The anti-abortionist charges, not unreasonably, that pro-choice principles concerning killing are too narrow to be acceptable; the pro-choicer charges, not unreasonably, that anti-abortionist principles concerning killing are too broad to be acceptable. . . .

. . . All this suggests that a necessary condition of resolving the abortion controversy is a more theoretical account of the wrongness of killing. After all, if we merely believe, but do not understand, why killing adult human beings such as ourselves is wrong, how could we conceivably show that abortion is either immoral or permissible?

II

In order to develop such an account, we can start from the following unproblematic assumption concerning our own case: it is wrong to kill *us*. Why is it wrong? Some answers can be easily eliminated. It might be said that what makes killing us wrong is that a killing brutalizes the one who kills. But the brutalization consists of being inured to the performance of an act that is hideously immoral; hence, the brutalization does not explain the immorality. It might be said that what makes killing us wrong is the great loss others would experience due to our absence. Although such hubris is understandable, such an explanation does not account for the wrongness of killing hermits, or those whose lives are relatively independent and whose friends find it easy to make new friends.

A more obvious answer is better. What primarily makes killing wrong is neither its effect on the murderer nor its effect on the victim's friends and relatives, but its effect on the victim. The loss of one's life is one of the greatest losses one can suffer. The loss of one's life deprives one of all the experiences, activities, projects, and enjoyments that would otherwise have constituted one's future. Therefore, killing someone is wrong, primarily because the killing inflicts (one of) the greatest possible losses on the victim. To describe this as the loss of life can be misleading, however. The change in my biological state does not by itself make killing me wrong. The effect of the loss of my biological life is the loss to me of all those activities, projects, experiences, and enjoyments which would otherwise have constituted my future personal life. These activities, projects, experiences, and enjoyments are either valuable for their own sakes or are means to something else that is valuable for its own sake. Some parts of my future are not valued by me now, but will come to be valued by me as I grow older and as my values and capacities change. When I am killed, I am deprived both of what I now value which would have been part of my future personal life, but also what I would come to value. Therefore, when I die, I am deprived of all of the value of my future. Inflicting this loss on me is ultimately what makes killing me wrong. This being the case, it would seem that what makes killing *any* adult human being prima facie seriously wrong is the loss of his or her future.[1] . . .

The claim that what makes killing wrong is the loss of the victim's future is directly supported by two considerations. In the first place, this theory explains why we regard killing as one of the worst of crimes. Killing is especially wrong, because it deprives the victim of more than perhaps any other crime. In the second place, people with AIDS or cancer who know they are dying believe, of course, that dying is a very bad thing for them. They believe that the loss of a future to them that they would otherwise have experienced is what makes their premature death a very bad thing for them. A better theory of the wrongness of killing would require a different natural property associated with killing which better fits with the attitudes of the dying. What could it be?

The view that what makes killing wrong is the loss to the victim of the value of the victim's future gains additional support when some of its implications are examined. In the first place, it is incompatible with the view that it is wrong to kill only beings who are biologically human. It is possible that there exists a different species from another planet whose members have a future like ours. Since having a future like that is what makes killing someone wrong, this theory entails that it would be wrong to kill members of such a species. Hence, this theory is opposed to the claim that only life that is biologically human has great moral worth, a claim which many anti-abortionists have seemed to adopt. This opposition, which this theory has in common with personhood theories, seems to be a merit of the theory.

In the second place, the claim that the loss of one's future is the wrong-making feature of one's being killed entails the possibility that the futures of some actual nonhuman mammals on our own planet are sufficiently like ours that it is seriously wrong to kill them also. Whether some animals do have the same right to life as human beings depends on adding to the account of the wrongness of killing some additional account of just what it is about my future or the futures of other adult human beings which makes it wrong to kill us. No such additional account will be offered in this essay. Undoubtedly, the provision of such an account would be a very difficult matter. Undoubtedly, any such account would be quite controversial. Hence, it surely should not reflect badly on this sketch of an elementary theory of the wrongness of killing that it is indeterminate with respect to some very difficult issues regarding animal rights.

In the third place, the claim that the loss of one's future is the wrong-making feature of one's being killed does not entail, as sanctity of human life theories do, that active euthanasia is wrong. Persons who are severely and incurably ill, who face a future of pain and despair, and who wish to die will not have suffered a loss if they are killed. It is, strictly speaking, the value of a human's future which makes killing wrong in this theory. This being so, killing does not necessarily wrong some persons who are sick and dying. Of course, there may be other reasons for a prohibition of active euthanasia, but that is another matter. Sanctity-of-human-life theories seem to hold that active euthanasia is seriously wrong even in an individual case where there seems to be good reason for it independently of public policy considerations. This consequence is most implausible, and it is a plus for the claim that the loss of a future of value is what makes killing wrong that it does not share this consequence.

In the fourth place, the account of the wrongness of killing defended in this essay does straightforwardly entail that it is prima facie seriously wrong to kill children and infants, for we do presume that they have futures of value. Since we do believe that it is wrong to kill defenseless little babies, it is important that a theory of the wrongness of killing easily account for this. Personhood theories of the wrongness of killing, on the other hand, cannot straightforwardly account for the wrongness of killing infants and young children. Hence, such theories must add special ad hoc accounts of the wrongness of killing the young. The plausibility of such ad hoc theories seems to be a function of how desperately one wants such theories to work. The claim that the primary wrong-making feature of a killing is the loss to the victim of the value of its future accounts for the wrongness of killing young children and infants directly; it makes the wrongness of such acts as obvious as we actually think it is. This is a further merit of this theory. Accordingly, it seems that this value of a future-like-ours theory of the wrongness of killing shares strengths of both sanctity-of-life and personhood accounts while avoiding weaknesses of both. In addition, it meshes with a central intuition concerning what makes killing wrong.

The claim that the primary wrong-making feature of a killing is the loss to the victim of the value of its future has obvious consequences for the ethics of abortion. The future of a standard fetus includes a set of experiences, projects, activities, and such which are identical with the futures of adult human beings and are identical with the futures of young children. Since the reason that is sufficient to explain why it is wrong to kill human beings after the time of birth is a reason that also applies to fetuses, it follows that abortion is prima facie seriously morally wrong.

This argument does not rely on the invalid inference that, since it is wrong to kill persons, it is wrong to kill potential persons also. The category that is morally central to this analysis is the category of having a valuable future like ours; it is not the category of personhood. The argument to the conclusion that abortion is prima facie seriously morally wrong proceeded independently of the notion of person or potential person or any equivalent. Someone may wish to start with this analysis in terms of the value of a human future, conclude that abortion is, except perhaps in rare circumstances, seriously morally wrong, infer that fetuses have the right to life, and then call fetuses "persons" as a result of their having the right to life. Clearly, in this case, the category of person is being used to state the *conclusion* of the analysis rather than to generate the *argument* of the analysis. . . .

Of course, this value of a future-like-ours argument, if sound, shows only that abortion is prima facie wrong, not that it is wrong in any and all circumstances. Since the loss of the future to a standard fetus, if killed, is, however, at least as great a loss as the loss of the future to a standard adult human being who is killed, abortion, like ordinary killing, could be justified only by the most compelling reasons. The loss of one's life is almost the greatest misfortune that can happen to one. Presumably abortion could be justified in some circumstances, only if the loss consequent on failing to abort would be at least as great. Accordingly, morally permissible abortions will be rare indeed unless, perhaps, they occur so early in pregnancy that a fetus is not yet definitely an individual. Hence, this argument should be taken as showing that abortion is presumptively very seriously wrong, where the presumption is very strong—as strong as the presumption that killing another adult human being is wrong.

Note

1. I have been most influenced on this matter by Jonathan Glover, *Causing Death and Saving Lives* (New York: Penguin, 1977), ch. 3; and Robert Young, "What Is So Wrong with Killing People?" *Philosophy* I.IV, 210 (1979), 515–28.

CHAPTER 12

A Defense of Abortion

Judith Jarvis Thomson

For the sake of argument, Judith Jarvis Thomson grants that a fetus is a person, with a right to life, from the moment of conception. Can we conclude from that assumption that abortion is immoral? The answer turns out to be surprisingly complicated. Thomson's discussion not only throws light on the abortion issue, but also illuminates the nature of rights.

Readers of this essay who are unfamiliar with Henry Fonda may instead think of Brad Pitt, George Clooney, or Johnny Depp. The philosophical point involving Fonda will be the same.

Judith Jarvis Thomson is Professor Emerita at the Massachusetts Institute of Technology (MIT). Her most recent book is *Normativity* (2009).

Most opposition to abortion relies on the premise that the fetus is a human being, a person, from the moment of conception. . . .

. . . I think that the premise is false, that the fetus is not a person from the moment of conception. A newly fertilized ovum, a newly implanted clump of cells, is no more a person than an acorn is an oak tree. But I shall not discuss any of this. For it seems to me to be of great interest to ask what happens if, for the sake of argument, we allow the premise. How, precisely, are we supposed to get from there to the conclusion that abortion is morally impermissible? Opponents of abortion commonly spend most of their time establishing that the fetus is a person, and hardly any time explaining the step from there to the

From *Philosophy and Public Affairs*, vol. 1, no. 1 (Autumn 1971), pp. 47–66. Reprinted by permission.

impermissibility of abortion. Perhaps they think the step too simple and obvious to require much comment. . . . Whatever the explanation, I suggest that the step they take is neither easy nor obvious, that it calls for closer examination than it is commonly given, and that when we do give it this closer examination we shall feel inclined to reject it.

I propose, then, that we grant that the fetus is a person from the moment of conception. How does the argument go from here? Something like this, I take it. Every person has a right to life. So the fetus has a right to life. No doubt the mother has a right to decide what shall happen in and to her body; everyone would grant that. But surely a person's right to life is stronger and more stringent than the mother's right to decide what happens in and to her body, and so outweighs it. So the fetus may not be killed; an abortion may not be performed.

It sounds plausible. But now let me ask you to imagine this. You wake up in the morning and find yourself back to back in bed with an unconscious violinist. A famous unconscious violinist. He has been found to have a fatal kidney ailment, and the Society of Music Lovers has canvassed all the available medical records and found that you alone have the right blood type to help. They have therefore kidnapped you, and last night the violinist's circulatory system was plugged into yours, so that your kidneys can be used to extract poisons from his blood as well as your own. The director of the hospital now tells you, "Look, we're sorry the Society of Music Lovers did this to you—we would never have permitted it if we had known. But still, they did it, and the violinist now is plugged into you. To unplug you would be to kill him. But never mind, it's only for nine months. By then he will have recovered from his ailment, and can safely be unplugged from you." Is it morally incumbent on you to accede to this situation? No doubt it would be very nice of you if you did, a great kindness. But do you *have* to accede to it? What if it were not nine months, but nine years? Or longer still? What if the director of the hospital says, "Tough luck, I agree, but you've now got to stay in bed, with the violinist plugged into you, for the rest of your life. Because remember this. All persons have a right to life, and violinists are persons. Granted you have a right to decide what happens in and to your body, but a person's right to life outweighs your right to decide what happens in and to your body. So you cannot ever be unplugged from him." I imagine you would regard this as outrageous, which suggests that something really is wrong with that plausible-sounding argument I mentioned a moment ago.

In this case, of course, you were kidnapped; you didn't volunteer for the operation that plugged the violinist into your kidneys. Can those who oppose abortion on the ground I mentioned make an exception for a pregnancy due to rape? Certainly. They can say that persons have a right to life only if they didn't come into existence because of rape; or they can say that all persons have a right to life, but that some have less of a right to life than others, in particular, that those who came into existence because of rape have less. But these statements have a rather unpleasant sound. Surely the question of whether you have a right to life at all, or how much of it you have, shouldn't turn on the question of whether or not you are the product of a rape. And in fact the people who oppose abortion on the ground I mentioned do not make this distinction, and hence do not make an exception in case of rape.

Nor do they make an exception for a case in which the mother has to spend the nine months of her pregnancy in bed. They would agree that would be a great pity, and hard on the mother; but all the same, all persons have a right to life, the fetus is a person, and so on. I suspect, in fact, that they would not make an exception for a case in which, miraculously enough, the pregnancy went on for nine years, or even the rest of the mother's life.

Some won't even make an exception for a case in which continuation of the pregnancy is likely to shorten the mother's life; they regard abortion as impermissible even to save the mother's life. Such cases are nowadays very rare, and many opponents of abortion do not accept this extreme view. All the same, it is a good place to begin: a number of points of interest come out in respect to it.

1. Let us call the view that abortion is impermissible even to save the mother's life "the extreme view." I want to suggest first that it does not issue from the argument I mentioned earlier without the addition of some fairly powerful premises. Suppose a woman has become pregnant, and now learns that she has a cardiac condition such that she will die if she carries the baby to term. What may be done for her? The fetus, being a person, has a right to life, but as the mother is a person too, so has she a right to life. Presumably they have an equal right to life. How is it supposed to come out that an abortion may not be performed? If mother and child have an equal right to life, shouldn't we perhaps flip a coin? Or should we add to the mother's right to life her right to decide what happens in and to her body, which everybody seems to be ready to grant—the sum of her rights now outweighing the fetus' right to life?

The most familiar argument here is the following. We are told that performing the abortion would be directly killing the child, whereas doing nothing would not be killing the mother, but only letting her die. Moreover, in killing the child, one would be killing an innocent person, for the child has committed no crime, and is not aiming at his mother's death. And then there are a variety of ways in which this might be continued. (1) But as directly killing an innocent person is always and absolutely impermissible, an abortion may not be performed. Or, (2) as directly killing an innocent person is murder, and murder is always and absolutely impermissible, an abortion may not be performed. Or, (3) as one's duty to refrain from directly killing an innocent person is more stringent than one's duty to keep a person from dying, an abortion may not be performed. Or, (4) if one's only options are directly killing an innocent person or letting a person die, one must prefer letting the person die, and thus an abortion may not be performed.

Some people seem to have thought that these are not further premises which must be added if the conclusion is to be reached, but that they follow from the very fact that an innocent person has a right to life. But this seems to me to be a mistake, and perhaps the simplest way to show this is to bring out that while we must certainly grant that innocent persons have a right to life, the theses in (1) through (4) are all false. Take (2), for example. If directly killing an innocent person is murder, and thus is impermissible, then the mother's directly killing the innocent person inside her is murder, and thus is impermissible. But it cannot seriously be thought to be murder if the mother performs an abortion on herself to save her life. It cannot seriously be said that she *must* refrain, that she *must* sit passively by and wait for her death. Let us look again at the case of you and the violinist. There you are, in bed with the violinist, and the director of the hospital says to you, "It's all most distressing, and I deeply sympathize, but you see this is putting an additional strain on your kidneys, and you'll be dead within the month. But you *have* to stay where you are all the same. Because unplugging you would be directly killing an innocent violinist, and that's murder, and that's impermissible." If anything in the world is true, it is that you do not commit murder, you do not do what is impermissible, if you reach around to your back and unplug yourself from that violinist to save your life.

The main focus of attention in writings on abortion has been on what a third party may or may not do in answer to a request from a woman for an abortion. This is in a way understandable. Things being as they are, there isn't much a woman can safely do to abort herself. So the question asked is what a third party may do, and what the mother may do, if it is mentioned at all, is deduced, almost as an afterthought, from what it is concluded that third parties may do. But it seems to me that to treat the matter in this way is to refuse to grant to the mother that very status of person which is so firmly insisted on for the fetus. For we cannot simply read off what a person may do from what a third party may do. Suppose you find yourself trapped in a tiny house with a growing child. I mean a very tiny house, and a rapidly growing child—you are already up against the wall of the house and in a few minutes you'll be crushed to death. The child on the other hand won't be crushed to death; if nothing is done to stop him from growing he'll be hurt, but in the end he'll simply burst open the house and walk out a free man. Now I could well understand it if a bystander were to say, "There's nothing we can do for you. We cannot choose between your life and his, we cannot be the ones to decide who is to live, we cannot intervene." But it cannot be concluded that you too can do nothing, that you cannot attack it to save your life. However innocent the child may be, you do not have to wait passively while it crushes you to death. Perhaps a pregnant woman is vaguely felt to have the status of house, to which we don't allow the right of self-defense. But if the woman houses the child, it should be remembered that she is a person who houses it.

I should perhaps stop to say explicitly that I am not claiming that people have a right to do anything whatever to save their lives. I think, rather, that there are drastic limits to the right of self-defense. If someone threatens you with death unless you torture someone else to death, I think you have not the right, even to save your life, to do so. But the case under consideration here is very different. In our case there are only two people involved, one whose life is threatened, and one who threatens it. Both are innocent: the one who is threatened is not threatened because of any fault, the one who threatens does not threaten because of any fault. For this reason we may feel that we bystanders cannot intervene. But the person threatened can.

In sum, a woman surely can defend her life against the threat to it posed by the unborn child, even if doing so involves its death. And this shows not merely that the theses in (1) through (4) are false; it shows also that the extreme view of abortion is false, and so we need not canvass any other possible ways of arriving at it from the argument I mentioned at the outset.

2. The extreme view could of course be weakened to say that while abortion is permissible to save the mother's life, it may not be performed by a third party, but only by the mother herself. But this cannot be right either. For what we have to keep in mind is that the mother and the unborn child are not like two tenants in a small house which has, by an unfortunate mistake, been rented to both: the mother *owns* the house. The fact that she does adds to the offensiveness of deducing that the mother can do nothing from the supposition that third parties can do nothing. But it does more than this: it casts a bright light on the supposition that third parties can do nothing. Certainly it lets us see that a third party who says "I cannot choose between you" is fooling himself if he thinks this is impartiality. If Jones has found and fastened on a certain coat, which he needs to keep him from freezing, but which Smith also needs to keep him from freezing, then it is not impartiality that says "I cannot choose between you" when Smith owns the coat. Women have said again and again "This body is *my* body!" and they have reason to feel angry, reason to feel that it has been like shouting into the wind. Smith, after all, is hardly likely to bless us if we say to him, "Of course it's your coat, anybody would grant that it is. But no one may choose between you and Jones who is to have it.". . .

I suppose that in some views of human life the mother's body is only on loan to her, the loan not being one which gives her any prior claim to it. One who held this view might well think it impartiality to say "I cannot choose." But I shall simply ignore this possibility. My own view is that if a human being has any just, prior claim to anything at all, he has a just, prior claim to his own body. And perhaps this needn't be argued for here anyway, since, as I mentioned, the arguments against abortion we are looking at do grant that the woman has a right to decide what happens in and to her body.

But although they do grant it, I have tried to show that they do not take seriously what is done in granting it. I suggest the same thing will reappear even more clearly when we turn away from cases in which the mother's life is at stake, and attend, as I propose we now do, to the vastly more common cases in which a woman wants an abortion for some less weighty reason than preserving her own life.

3. Where the mother's life is not at stake, the argument I mentioned at the outset seems to have a much stronger pull. "Everyone has a right to life, so the unborn person has a right to life." And isn't the child's right to life weightier than anything other than the mother's own right to life, which she might put forward as ground for an abortion?

This argument treats the right to life as if it were unproblematic. It is not, and this seems to me to be precisely the source of the mistake.

For we should now, at long last, ask what it comes to, to have a right to life. In some views having a right to life includes having a right to be given at least the bare minimum one needs for continued life. But suppose that what in fact *is* the bare minimum a man needs for continued life is something he has no right at all to be given? If I am sick unto death, and the only thing that will save my life is the touch of Henry Fonda's cool hand on my fevered brow, then all the same, I have no right to be given the touch of Henry Fonda's cool hand on my fevered brow. It would be frightfully nice of him to fly in from the West Coast to provide it. It would be less nice, though no doubt well meant, if my friends flew out to the West Coast and carried Henry Fonda back with them. But I have no right at all against anybody that he should do this for me. Or again, to return to the story I told earlier, the fact that for continued life that violinist needs the continued use of your kidneys does not establish that he has a right to be given the continued use of your kidneys. He certainly has no right against you that *you* should give him continued use of your kidneys. For nobody has any right to use your kidneys unless you give him such a right; and nobody has the right against you that you shall give him this right—if you do allow him to go on using your kidneys, this is a kindness on your part, and not something he can claim from you as his due. Nor has he any right against anybody else that *they* should give him continued use of your kidneys. Certainly he had no right against the Society of Music Lovers that they should plug him into you in the first place. And if you now start to unplug yourself, having learned that you will otherwise have to spend nine years in bed with him, there is nobody in the world who must try to prevent you, in order to see to it that he is given something he has a right to be given.

Some people are rather stricter about the right to life. In their view, it does not include the right to be given anything, but amounts to, and only to, the right not to be killed by anybody. But here a related difficulty arises. If everybody is to refrain from killing that violinist, then everybody must refrain from doing a great many different sorts of things. Everybody must refrain from slitting his throat, everybody must refrain from shooting him—and everybody must refrain from unplugging you from him. But does he have a right against everybody that they shall refrain from unplugging you from him? To refrain from doing this is to allow him to continue to use your kidneys. It could be argued that he has a right against us that *we* should allow him to continue to use your kidneys. That is, while he had no right against us that we should give him the use of your kidneys, it might be argued that he anyway has a right against us that we shall not now intervene and deprive him of the use of your kidneys. I shall come back to third-party interventions later. But certainly the violinist has no right against you that *you* shall allow him to continue to use your kidneys. As I said, if you do allow him to use them, it is a kindness on your part, and not something you owe him.

    . . . I would stress that I am not arguing that people do not have a right to life—quite to the contrary, it seems to me that the primary control we must place on the acceptability of an account of rights is that it should turn out in that account to be a truth that all persons have a right to life. I am arguing only that having a right to life does not guarantee having either a right to be given the use of or a right to be allowed continued use of another person's body—even if one needs it for life itself. So the right to life will not serve the opponents of abortion in the very simple and clear way in which they seem to have thought it would.

    4. There is another way to bring out the difficulty. In the most ordinary sort of case, to deprive someone of what he has a right to is to treat him unjustly. Suppose a boy and his small brother are jointly given a box of chocolates for Christmas. If the older boy takes the box and refuses to give his brother any of the chocolates, he is unjust to him, for the brother has been given a right to half of them. But suppose that, having learned that otherwise it means nine years in bed with that violinist, you unplug yourself from him. You surely are not being unjust to him, for you gave him no right to use your kidneys, and no one else can have given him any such right. But we have to notice that in unplugging yourself, you are killing him; and violinists, like everybody else, have a right to life, and thus in the view we were considering just now, the right not to be killed. So here you do what he supposedly has a right you shall not do, but you do not act unjustly to him in doing it.

    The emendation which may be made at this point is this: the right to life consists not in the right not to be killed, but rather in the right not to be killed unjustly. This runs a risk of circularity, but never mind: it would enable us to square the fact that the violinist has a right to life with the fact that you do not act unjustly toward him in unplugging yourself, thereby killing him. For if you do not kill him unjustly, you do not violate his right to life, and so it is no wonder you do him no injustice.

But if this emendation is accepted, the gap in the argument against abortion stares us plainly in the face: it is by no means enough to show that the fetus is a person, and to remind us that all persons have a right to life—we need to be shown also that killing the fetus violates its right to life, i.e., that abortion is unjust killing. And is it?

I suppose we may take it as a datum that in a case of pregnancy due to rape the mother has not given the unborn person a right to the use of her body for food and shelter. Indeed, in what pregnancy could it be supposed that the mother has given the unborn person such a right? It is not as if there were unborn persons drifting about the world, to whom a woman who wants a child says "I invite you in."

But it might be argued that there are other ways one can have acquired a right to the use of another person's body than by having been invited to use it by that person. Suppose a woman voluntarily indulges in intercourse, knowing of the chance it will issue in pregnancy, and then she does become pregnant; is she not in part responsible for the presence, in fact the very existence, of the unborn person inside her? No doubt she did not invite it in. But doesn't her partial responsibility for its being there itself give it a right to the use of her body? If so, then her aborting it would be more like the boy's taking away the chocolates, and less like your unplugging yourself from the violinist—doing so would be depriving it of what it does have a right to, and thus would be doing it an injustice.

And then, too, it might be asked whether or not she can kill it even to save her own life: If she voluntarily called it into existence, how can she now kill it, even in self-defense?

The first thing to be said about this is that it is something new. Opponents of abortion have been so concerned to make out the independence of the fetus, in order to establish that it has a right to life, just as its mother does, that they have tended to overlook the possible support they might gain from making out that the fetus is *dependent* on the mother, in order to establish that she has a special kind of responsibility for it, a responsibility that gives it rights against her which are not possessed by any independent person—such as an ailing violinist who is a stranger to her.

On the other hand, this argument would give the unborn person a right to its mother's body only if her pregnancy resulted from a voluntary act, undertaken in full knowledge of the chance a pregnancy might result from it. It would leave out entirely the unborn person whose existence is due to rape. Pending the availability of some further argument, then, we would be left with the conclusion that unborn persons whose existence is due to rape have no right to the use of their mothers' bodies, and thus that aborting them is not depriving them of anything they have a right to and hence is not unjust killing.

And we should also notice that it is not at all plain that this argument really does go even as far as it purports to. For there are cases and cases, and the details make a difference. If the room is stuffy, and I therefore open a window to air it, and a burglar climbs in, it would be absurd to say, "Ah, now he can stay, she's given him a right to the use of her house—for she is partially responsible for his presence there, having voluntarily done what enabled him to get in, in full knowledge that there are such things as burglars, and that burglars burgle." It would be still more absurd to say this if I had had bars installed outside my windows, precisely to prevent burglars from getting in, and a burglar got in only because of a defect in the bars. It remains equally absurd if we imagine it is not a burglar who climbs in, but an innocent person who blunders or falls in. Again, suppose it were like this: people-seeds drift about in the air like pollen, and if you open your windows, one may drift in and take root in your carpets or upholstery. You don't want children, so you fix up your windows with fine mesh screens, the very best you can buy. As can happen, however, and on very, very rare occasions does happen, one of the screens is defective; and a seed drifts in and takes root. Does the person-plant who now develops have a right to the use of your house? Surely not—despite the fact that you voluntarily opened your windows, you knowingly kept carpets and upholstered furniture, and you knew that screens were sometimes defective. Someone may argue that you are responsible for its rooting, that it does have a right to your house, because after all you *could* have lived out your life with bare floors and furniture, or with sealed windows and doors. But this won't do—for by the same token anyone can avoid a pregnancy due to rape by having a hysterectomy, or anyway by never leaving home without a (reliable!) army.

It seems to me that the argument we are looking at can establish at most that there are *some* cases in which the unborn person has a right to the use of its mother's body, and therefore *some* cases in which abortion is unjust killing. There is room for much discussion and argument as to precisely which, if any. But I think we should sidestep this issue and leave it open, for at any rate the argument certainly does not establish that all abortion is unjust killing.

5. There is room for yet another argument here, however. We surely must all grant that there may be cases in which it would be morally indecent to detach a person from your body at the cost of his life. Suppose you learn that what the violinist needs is not nine years of your life, but only one hour: all you need do to save his life is to spend one hour in that bed with him. Suppose also that letting him use your kidneys for that one hour would not affect your health in the slightest. Admittedly you were kidnapped. Admittedly you did not give anyone permission to plug him into you. Nevertheless it seems to me plain you *ought* to allow him to use your kidneys for that hour—it would be indecent to refuse.

Again, suppose pregnancy lasted only an hour, and constituted no threat to life or health. And suppose that a woman becomes pregnant as a result of rape. Admittedly she did not voluntarily do anything to bring about the existence of a child. Admittedly she did nothing at all which would give the unborn person a right to the use of her body. All the same it might well be said, as in the newly emended violinist story, that she *ought* to allow it to remain for that hour—that it would be indecent in her to refuse.

Now some people are inclined to use the term "right" in such a way that it follows from the fact that you ought to allow a person to use your body for the hour he needs, that he has a right to use your body for the hour he needs, even though he has not been given that right by any person or act. They may say that it follows also that if you refuse, you act unjustly toward him. This use of the term is perhaps so common that it cannot be called wrong; nevertheless it seems to me to be an unfortunate loosening of what we would do better to keep a tight rein on. Suppose that box of chocolates I mentioned earlier had not been given to both boys jointly, but was given only to the older boy. There he sits, stolidly eating his way through the box, his small brother watching enviously. Here we are likely to say "You ought not to be so mean. You ought to give your brother some of those chocolates." My own view is that it just does not follow from the truth of this that the brother has any right to any of the chocolates. If the boy refuses to give his brother any, he is greedy, stingy, callous—but not unjust. I suppose that the people I have in mind will say it does follow that the brother has a right to some of the chocolates, and thus that the boy does act unjustly if he refuses to give his brother any. But the effect of saying this is to obscure what we should keep distinct, namely the difference between the boy's refusal in this case and the boy's refusal in the earlier case, in which the box was given to both boys jointly, and in which the small brother thus had what was from any point of view clear title to half.

A further objection to so using the term "right" that from the fact that A ought to do a thing for B, it follows that B has a right against A that A do it for him, is that it is going to make the question of whether or not a man has a right to a thing turn on how easy it is to provide him with it; and this seems not merely unfortunate, but morally unacceptable. Take the case of Henry Fonda again. I said earlier that I had no right to the touch of his cool hand on my fevered brow, even though I needed it to save my life. I said it would be frightfully nice of him to fly in from the West Coast to provide me with it, but that I had no right against him that he should do so. But suppose he isn't on the West Coast. Suppose he has only to walk across the room, place a hand briefly on my brow—and lo, my life is saved. Then surely he ought to do it, it would be indecent to refuse. Is it to be said "Ah, well, it follows that in this case she has a right to the touch of his hand on her brow, and so it would be an injustice in him to refuse"? So that I have a right to it when it is easy for him to provide it, though no right when it's hard? It's rather a shocking idea that anyone's rights should fade away and disappear as it gets harder and harder to accord them to him.

So my own view is that even though you ought to let the violinist use your kidneys for the one hour he needs, we should not conclude that he has a right to do so—we should say that if you refuse, you are, like the boy who owns all the chocolates and will give none away, self-centered and callous, indecent in fact, but not unjust. And similarly, that even supposing a case in which a woman pregnant due to rape ought to allow the unborn person to use her body for the hour he needs, we should not conclude that he has a right to do so; we should conclude that she is self-centered, callous, indecent, but not unjust, if she refuses. The complaints are no less grave; they are just different. However, there is no need to insist on this point. If anyone does wish to deduce "he has a right" from "you ought," then all the same he must surely grant that there are cases in which it is not morally required of you that you allow that violinist to use your kidneys, and in which he does not have a right to use them, and in which you do not do him an injustice if you refuse. And so also for mother and unborn child. Except in such cases as the unborn person has a right to demand it—and we were leaving open the possibility that there may be such cases—nobody is morally *required* to make large sacrifices, of health, of all other interests and concerns, of all other duties and commitments, for nine years, or even for nine months, in order to keep another person alive.

6. We have in fact to distinguish between two kinds of Samaritan: the Good Samaritan and what we might call the Minimally Decent Samaritan. The story of the Good Samaritan, you will remember, goes like this:

> A certain man went down from Jerusalem to Jericho, and fell among thieves, which stripped him of his raiment, and wounded him, and departed, leaving him half dead.
>
> And by chance there came down a certain priest that way; and when he saw him, he passed by on the other side.
>
> And likewise a Levite, when he was at the place, came and looked on him, and passed by on the other side.
>
> But a certain Samaritan, as he journeyed, came where he was; and when he saw him he had compassion on him.
>
> And went to him, and bound up his wounds, pouring in oil and wine, and set him on his own beast, and brought him to an inn, and took care of him.
>
> And on the morrow, when he departed, he took out two pence, and gave them to the host, and said unto him, "Take care of him; and whatsoever thou spendest more, when I come again, I will repay thee."   (Luke 10:30–35)

The Good Samaritan went out of his way, at some cost to himself, to help one in need of it. We are not told what the options were, that is, whether or not the priest and the Levite could have helped by doing less than the Good Samaritan did, but assuming they could have, then the fact they did nothing at all shows they were not even Minimally Decent Samaritans, not because they were not Samaritans, but because they were not even minimally decent.

These things are a matter of degree, of course, but there is a difference, and it comes out perhaps most clearly in the story of Kitty Genovese, who, as you will remember, was murdered while thirty-eight people watched or listened, and did nothing at all to help her. A Good Samaritan would have rushed out to give direct assistance against the murderer. Or perhaps we had better allow that it would have been a Splendid Samaritan who did this, on the ground that it would have involved a risk of death for himself. But the thirty-eight not only did not do this, they did not even trouble to pick up a phone to call the police. Minimally Decent Samaritanism would call for doing at least that, and their not having done it was monstrous.

After telling the story of the Good Samaritan, Jesus said "Go, and do thou likewise." Perhaps he meant that we are morally required to act as the Good Samaritan did. Perhaps he was urging people to do more than is morally required of them. At all events it seems plain that it was not morally required of any of the thirty-eight that he rush out to give direct assistance at the risk of his own life, and that it is not morally required of anyone that he give long stretches of his life— nine years or nine months—to sustaining the life of a person who has no special right (we were leaving open the possibility of this) to demand it.

Indeed, with one rather striking class of exceptions, no one in any country in the world is *legally* required to do anywhere near as much as this for anyone else. The class of exceptions is obvious. My main concern here is not the state of the law in respect to abortion, but it is worth drawing attention to the fact that in no state in this country is any man compelled by law to be even a Minimally Decent Samaritan to any person; there is no law under which charges could be brought against the thirty-eight who stood by while Kitty Genovese died. By contrast, in most states in this country women are compelled by law to be not merely Minimally Decent Samaritans, but Good Samaritans to unborn persons inside them. This doesn't by itself set- tle anything one way or the other, because it may well be argued that there should be laws in this country—as there are in many European countries—compelling at least Minimally Decent Samaritanism. But it does show that there is a gross injustice in the existing state of the law. And it shows also that the groups currently working against liber- alization of abortion laws, in fact working toward having it declared unconstitutional for a state to permit abortion, had better start work- ing for the adoption of Good Samaritan laws generally, or earn the charge that they are acting in bad faith.

I should think, myself, that Minimally Decent Samaritan laws would be one thing, Good Samaritan laws quite another, and in fact highly improper. But we are not here concerned with the law. What we should ask is not whether anybody should be compelled by law to be a Good Samaritan, but whether we must accede to a situation in which somebody is being compelled—by nature, perhaps—to be a Good Samaritan. We have, in other words, to look now at third-party interventions. I have been arguing that no person is morally required to make large sacrifices to sustain the life of another who has no right to demand them, and this even where the sacrifices do not include life itself; we are not morally required to be Good Samaritans or anyway Very Good Samaritans to one another. But what if a man cannot extricate himself from such a situation? What if he appeals to us to extricate him? It seems to me plain that there are cases in which we can, cases in which a Good Samaritan would extricate him. There you are, you were kidnapped, and nine years in bed with that violinist lie ahead of you. You have your own life to lead. You are sorry, but you simply cannot see giving up so much of your life to the sustaining of his. You cannot extricate yourself, and ask us to do so. I should have thought that—in light of his having no right to the use of your body— it was obvious that we do not have to accede to your being forced to give up so much. We can do what you ask. There is no injustice to the violinist in our doing so.

7. Following the lead of the opponents of abortion, I have throughout been speaking of the fetus merely as a person, and what I have been asking is whether or not the argument we began with, which proceeds only from the fetus' being a person, really does establish its conclusion. I have argued that it does not.

But of course there are arguments and arguments, and it may be said that I have simply fastened on the wrong one. It may be said that what is important is not merely the fact that the fetus is a person, but that it is a person for whom the woman has a special kind of responsibility issuing from the fact that she is its mother. And it might be argued that all my analogies are therefore irrelevant—for you do not have that special kind of responsibility for that violinist, Henry Fonda does not have that special kind of responsibility for me. And our attention might be drawn to the fact that men and women both *are* compelled by law to provide support for their children.

I have in effect dealt (briefly) with this argument in section 4 above; but a (still briefer) recapitulation now may be in order. Surely we do not have any such "special responsibility" for a person unless we have assumed it, explicitly or implicitly. If a set of parents do not try to prevent pregnancy, do not obtain an abortion, and then at the time of birth of the child do not put it out for adoption, but rather take it home with them, then they have assumed responsibility for it, they have given it rights, and they cannot *now* withdraw support from it at the cost of its life because they now find it difficult to go on providing for it. But if they have taken all reasonable precautions against having a child, they do not simply by virtue of their biological relationship to the child who comes into existence have a special responsibility for it. They may wish to assume responsibility for it, or they may not wish to. And I am suggesting that if assuming responsibility for it would require large sacrifices, then they may refuse. A Good Samaritan would not refuse—or anyway, a Splendid Samaritan, if the sacrifices that had to be made were enormous. But then so would a Good Samaritan assume responsibility for that violinist; so would Henry Fonda, if he is a Good Samaritan, fly in from the West Coast and assume responsibility for me.

8. My argument will be found unsatisfactory on two counts by many of those who want to regard abortion as morally permissible. First, while I do argue that abortion is not impermissible, I do not argue that it is always permissible. There may well be cases in which carrying the child to term requires only Minimally Decent Samaritanism of the mother, and this is a standard we must not fall below. I am inclined to think it a merit of my account precisely that it does *not* give a general yes or a general no. It allows for and supports our sense that, for example, a sick and desperately frightened fourteen-year-old schoolgirl, pregnant due to rape, may *of course* choose abortion, and that any law which rules this out is an insane law. And it also allows for and supports our sense that in other cases resort to abortion is even positively indecent. It would be indecent in the woman to request an abortion, and indecent in a doctor to perform it, if she is in her seventh month, and wants the abortion just to avoid the nuisance of postponing a trip abroad. The very fact that the arguments I have been drawing attention to treat all cases of abortion, or even all cases of abortion in which the mother's life is not at stake, as morally on a par ought to have made them suspect at the outset.

Secondly, while I am arguing for the permissibility of abortion in some cases, I am not arguing for the right to secure the death of the unborn child. It is easy to confuse these two things in that up to a certain point in the life of the fetus it is not able to survive outside the mother's body; hence removing it from her body guarantees its death. But they are importantly different. I have argued that you are not morally required to spend nine months in bed, sustaining the life of that violinist; but to say this is by no means to say that if, when you unplug yourself, there is a miracle and he survives, you then have a right to turn around and slit his throat. You may detach yourself even if this costs him his life; you have no right to be guaranteed his death, by some other means, if unplugging yourself does not kill him. There are some people who will feel dissatisfied by this feature of my argument. A woman may be utterly devastated by the thought of a child, a bit of herself, put out for adoption and never seen or heard of again. She may therefore want not merely that the child be detached from her, but more, that it die. Some opponents of abortion are inclined to regard this as beneath contempt—thereby showing insensitivity to what is surely a powerful source of despair. All the same, I agree that the desire for the child's death is not one which anybody may gratify, should it turn out to be possible to detach the child alive.

At this place, however, it should be remembered that we have only been pretending throughout that the fetus is a human being from the moment of conception. A very early abortion is surely not the killing of a person, and so is not dealt with by anything I have said here.

CHAPTER 13

On the Moral and Legal Status of Abortion and Postscript on Infanticide

Mary Anne Warren

Should we consider the human fetus to be a person, with a full-fledged right to life? If so, then abortion can be considered murder; if not, then a more lenient attitude toward abortion may be taken. Mary Anne Warren believes that physical characteristics, such as genes, are never enough to make someone a person. Persons, she says, are defined by their mental capacities, such as self-awareness and the ability to use a language. Fetuses lack such characteristics, so they are not persons. She also rejects the idea that the *potential* of the fetus might outweigh the mother's rights. Warren concludes that abortion is morally acceptable.

Mary Anne Warren was a professor of philosophy for many years at San Francisco State University.

We will be concerned with both the moral status of abortion, which for our purposes we may define as the act which a woman performs in voluntarily terminating, or allowing another person to terminate, her pregnancy, and the legal status which is appropriate for this act. . . . It is possible to show that, on the basis of intuitions which we may expect even the opponents of abortion to share, a fetus is not a person, and hence not the sort of entity to which it is proper to ascribe full moral rights.

From the *Monist*, vol. 57, no. 1 (1973), pp. 43–61; and from *The Problem of Abortion*, edited by Joel Feinberg (Belmont, CA: Wadsworth Publishers), 1984, pp. 116–119.

Of course, while some philosophers would deny the possibility of any such proof, others will deny that there is any need for it, since the moral permissibility of abortion appears to them to be too obvious to require proof. But the inadequacy of this attitude should be evident from the fact that both the friends and the foes of abortion consider their position to be morally self-evident. Because pro-abortionists have never adequately come to grips with the conceptual issues surrounding abortion, most if not all, of the arguments which they advance in opposition to laws restricting access to abortion fail to refute or even weaken the traditional antiabortion argument, namely, that a fetus is a human being, and therefore abortion is murder.

These arguments are typically of one of two sorts. Either they point to the terrible side effects of the restrictive laws, e.g., the deaths due to illegal abortions, and the fact that it is poor women who suffer the most as a result of these laws, or else they state that to deny a woman access to abortion is to deprive her of her right to control her own body. Unfortunately, however, the fact that restricting access to abortion has tragic side effects does not, in itself, show that the restrictions are unjustified, since murder is wrong regardless of the consequences of prohibiting it; and the appeal to the right to control one's body, which is generally construed as a property right, is at best a rather feeble argument for the permissibility of abortion. Mere ownership does not give me the right to kill innocent people whom I find on my property, and indeed I am apt to be held responsible if such people injure themselves while on my property. It is equally unclear that I have any moral right to expel an innocent person from my property when I know that doing so will result in his death. . . .

The question which we must answer in order to produce a satisfactory solution to the problem of the moral status of abortion is this: How are we to define the moral community, the set of beings with full and equal moral rights, such that we can decide whether a human fetus is a member of this community or not? What sort of entity, exactly, has the inalienable rights to life, liberty, and the pursuit of happiness? Jefferson attributed these rights to all *men,* and it may or may not be fair to suggest that he intended to attribute them *only* to men. Perhaps he ought to have attributed them to all human beings. . . .

1. On the Definition of 'Human'

. . . The term 'human' has two distinct, but not often distinguished, senses. This fact results in a slide of meaning, which serves to conceal the fallaciousness of the traditional argument that since (1) it is wrong to kill innocent human beings, and (2) fetuses are innocent human beings, then (3) it is wrong to kill fetuses. For if 'human' is used in the same sense in both (1) and (2) then, whichever of the two senses is meant, one of these premises is question-begging. And if it is used in two different senses then of course the conclusion doesn't follow.

Thus, (1) is a self-evident moral truth, and avoids begging the question about abortion, only if 'human being' is used to mean something like "a full-fledged member of the moral community." (It may or may not also be meant to refer exclusively to members of the species *Homo sapiens*.) We may call this the *moral* sense of 'human'. It is not to be confused with what we will call the *genetic* sense, i.e., the sense in which *any* member of the species is a human being, and no member of any other species could be. If (1) is acceptable only if the moral sense is intended, (2) is non-question-begging only if what is intended is the genetic sense. . . .

2. Defining the Moral Community

Can it be established that genetic humanity is sufficient for moral humanity? I think that there are very good reasons for not defining the moral community in this way. I would like to suggest an alternative way of defining the moral community, which I will argue for only to the extent of explaining why it is, or should be, self-evident. The suggestion is simply that the moral community consists of all and only *people*, rather than all and only human beings; and probably the best way of demonstrating its self-evidence is by considering the concept of personhood, to see what sorts of entity are and are not persons, and what the decision that a being is or is not a person implies about its moral rights.

What characteristics entitle an entity to be considered a person? This is obviously not the place to attempt a complete analysis of the concept of personhood, but we do not need such a fully adequate analysis just to determine whether and why a fetus is or isn't a person. All we need is a rough and approximate list of the most basic criteria of personhood, and some idea of which, or how many, of these an entity must satisfy in order to properly be considered a person.

In searching for such criteria, it is useful to look beyond the set of people with whom we are acquainted, and ask how we would decide whether a totally alien being was a person or not. (For we have no right to assume that genetic humanity is necessary for personhood.) Imagine a space traveler who lands on an unknown planet and encounters a race of beings utterly unlike any he has ever seen or heard of. If he wants to be sure of behaving morally toward these beings, he has to somehow decide whether they are people, and hence have full moral rights, or whether they are the sort of thing which he need not feel guilty about treating as, for example, a source of food.

How should he go about making this decision? If he has some anthropological background, he might look for such things as religion, art, and the manufacturing of tools, weapons, or shelters, since these factors have been used to distinguish our human from our prehuman ancestors, in what seems to be closer to the moral than the genetic sense of 'human'. And no doubt he would be right to consider the presence of such factors as good evidence that the alien beings were people, and morally human. It would, however, be overly anthropocentric of him to take the absence of these things as adequate evidence that they were not, since we can imagine people who have progressed beyond, or evolved without ever developing, these cultural characteristics.

I suggest that the traits which are most central to the concept of personhood, or humanity in the moral sense, are, very roughly, the following:

(1) consciousness (of objects and events external and/or internal to the being), and in particular the capacity to feel pain;

(2) reasoning (the *developed* capacity to solve new and relatively complex problems);

(3) self-motivated activity (activity which is relatively independent of either genetic or direct external control);

(4) the capacity to communicate, by whatever means, messages of an indefinite variety of types, that is, not just with an indefinite number of possible contents, but on indefinitely many possible topics;

(5) the presence of self-concepts, and self-awareness. . . .

Admittedly, there are apt to be a great many problems involved in formulating precise definitions of these criteria, let alone in developing universally valid behavioral criteria for deciding when they apply. But I will assume that both we and our explorer know approximately what (1)–(5) mean, and that he is also able to determine whether or not they apply. How, then, should he use his findings to decide whether or not the alien beings are people? We needn't suppose that an entity must have *all* of these attributes to be properly considered a person; (1) and (2) alone may well be sufficient for personhood, and quite probably (1)–(3) are sufficient. Neither do we need to insist that any one of these criteria is *necessary* for personhood, although once again (1) and (2) look like fairly good candidates for necessary conditions, as does (3), if 'activity' is construed so as to include the activity of reasoning.

All we need to claim, to demonstrate that a fetus is not a person, is that any being which satisfies *none* of (1)–(5) is certainly not a person. I consider this claim to be so obvious that I think anyone who denied it, and claimed that a being which satisfied none of (1)–(5) was a person all the same, would thereby demonstrate that he had no notion at all of what a person is—perhaps because he had confused the concept of a person with that of genetic humanity. If the opponents of abortion were to deny the appropriateness of these five criteria, I do not know what further arguments would convince them. We would probably have to admit that our conceptual schemes were indeed irreconcilably different, and that our dispute could not be settled objectively.

I do not expect this to happen, however, since I think that the concept of a person is one which is very nearly universal (to people), and that it is common to both proabortionists and antiabortionists, even though neither group has fully realized the relevance of this concept to the resolution of their dispute. Furthermore, I think that on reflection even the antiabortionists ought to agree not only that (1)–(5) are central to the concept of personhood, but also that it is a part of this concept that all and only people have full moral rights. The concept of a person is in part a moral concept; once we have admitted that x is a person we have recognized, even if we have not agreed to respect, x's right to be treated as a member of the moral community. It is true that the claim that x is a *human being* is more commonly voiced as part of an appeal to treat x decently than is the claim that x is a person, but this is either because 'human being' is here used in the sense which implies personhood, or because the genetic and moral senses of 'human' have been confused.

Now if (1)–(5) are indeed the primary criteria of personhood, then it is clear that genetic humanity is neither necessary nor sufficient for establishing that an entity is a person. Some human beings are not people, and there may well be people who are not human beings. A man or woman whose consciousness has been permanently obliterated but who remains alive is a human being which is no longer a person; defective human beings, with no appreciable mental capacity, are not and presumably never will be people; and a fetus is a human being which is not yet a person, and which therefore cannot coherently be said to have full moral rights. Citizens of the next century should be prepared to recognize highly advanced, self-aware robots or computers, should such be developed, and intelligent inhabitants of other worlds, should such be found, as people in the fullest sense, and to respect their moral rights. But to ascribe full moral rights to an entity which is not a person is as absurd as to ascribe moral obligations and responsibilities to such an entity.

3. Fetal Development and the Right to Life

. . . It is clear that even though a seven- or eight-month fetus has features which make it apt to arouse in us almost the same powerful protective instinct as is commonly aroused by a small infant, nevertheless it is not significantly more personlike than is a very small embryo. It is *somewhat* more personlike; it can apparently feel and respond to pain, and it may even have a rudimentary form of consciousness, insofar as its brain is quite active. Nevertheless, it seems safe to say that it is not fully conscious, in the way that an infant of a few months is, and that it cannot reason, or communicate messages of indefinitely many sorts, does not engage in self-motivated activity, and has no self-awareness. Thus, in the *relevant* respects, a fetus, even a fully developed one, is considerably less personlike than is the average mature mammal, indeed the average fish. And I think that a rational person must conclude that if the right to life of a fetus is to be based upon its resemblance to a person, then it cannot be said to have any more right to life than, let us say, a newborn guppy (which also seems to be capable of feeling pain), and that a right of that magnitude could never override a woman's right to obtain an abortion, at any stage of her pregnancy. . . .

Thus, since the fact that even a fully developed fetus is not personlike enough to have any significant right to life on the basis of its personlikeness shows that no legal restrictions upon the stage of pregnancy in which an abortion may be performed can be justified on the grounds that we should protect the rights of the older fetus; and since there is no other apparent justification for such restrictions, we may conclude that they are entirely unjustified. . . .

4. Potential Personhood and the Right to Life

We have seen that a fetus does not resemble a person in any way which can support the claim that it has even some of the same rights. But what about its *potential*, the fact that if nurtured and allowed to develop naturally it will very probably become a person? Doesn't that alone give it at least some right to life? It is hard to deny that the fact that an entity is a potential person is a strong prima facie reason for not destroying it; but we need not conclude from this that a potential person has a right to life, by virtue of that potential. It may be that our feeling that it is better, other things being equal, not to destroy a potential person is better explained by the fact that potential people are still (felt to be) an invaluable resource, not to be lightly squandered. Surely, if every speck of dust were a potential person, we would be much less apt to conclude that every potential person has a right to become actual.

Still, we do not need to insist that a potential person has no right to life whatever. There may well be something immoral, and not just imprudent, about wantonly destroying potential people, when doing so isn't necessary to protect anyone's rights. But even if a potential person does have some prima facie right to life, such a right could not possibly outweigh the right of a woman to obtain an abortion, since the rights of any actual person invariably outweigh those of any potential person, whenever the two conflict. Since this may not be immediately obvious in the case of a human fetus, let us look at another case.

Suppose that our space explorer falls into the hands of an alien culture, whose scientists decide to create a few hundred thousand or more human beings, by breaking his body into its component cells, and using these to create fully developed human beings, with, of course, his genetic code. We may imagine that each of these newly created men will have all of the original man's abilities, skills, knowledge, and so on, and also have an individual self-concept, in short that each of them will be a bona fide (though hardly unique) person. Imagine that the whole project will take only seconds, and that its chances of success are extremely high, and that our explorer knows all of this, and also knows that these people will be treated fairly. I maintain that in such a situation he would have every right to escape if he could, and thus to deprive all of these potential people of their potential lives; for his right to life outweighs all of theirs together, in spite of the fact that they are all genetically human, all innocent, and all have a very high probability of becoming people very soon, if only he refrains from acting.

Indeed, I think he would have a right to escape even if it were not his life which the alien scientists planned to take, but only a year of his freedom, or, indeed, only a day. Nor would he be obligated to stay if he had gotten captured (thus bringing all these people-potentials into existence) because of his own carelessness, or even if he had done so deliberately, knowing the consequences. Regardless of how he got captured, he is not morally obligated to remain in captivity for *any* period of time for the sake of permitting any number of potential people to come into actuality, so great is the margin by which one actual person's right to liberty outweighs whatever right to life even a hundred thousand potential people have. And it seems reasonable to conclude that the rights of a woman will outweigh by a similar margin whatever right to life a fetus may have by virtue of its potential personhood.

Thus, neither a fetus's resemblance to a person, nor its potential for becoming a person provides any basis whatever for the claim that it has any significant right to life. Consequently, a woman's right to protect her health, happiness, freedom, and even her life, by terminating an unwanted pregnancy, will always override whatever right to life it may be appropriate to ascribe to a fetus, even a fully developed one. And thus, in the absence of any overwhelming social need for every possible child, the laws which restrict the right to obtain an abortion, or limit the period of pregnancy during which an abortion may be performed, are a wholly unjustified violation of a woman's most basic moral and constitutional rights.

Postscript on Infanticide

One of the most troubling objections to the argument presented in this article is that it may appear to justify not only abortion but infanticide as well. A newborn infant is not a great deal more personlike than a nine-month fetus, and thus it might seem that if late-term abortion is sometimes justified, then infanticide must also be sometimes justified. Yet most people consider that infanticide is a form of murder, and thus never justified.

While it is important to appreciate the emotional force of this objection, its logical force is far less than it may seem at first glance. There are many reasons why infanticide is much more difficult to justify than abortion, even though if my argument is correct neither constitutes the killing of a person. In this country, and in this period of history, the deliberate killing of viable newborns is virtually never justified. This is in part because neonates are so very *close* to being persons that to kill them requires a very strong moral justification—as does the killing of dolphins, whales, chimpanzees, and other highly personlike creatures. It is certainly wrong to kill such beings just for the sake of convenience, or financial profit, or "sport."

Another reason why infanticide is usually wrong, in our society, is that if the newborn's parents do not want it, or are unable to care for it, there are (in most cases) people who are able and eager to adopt it and to provide a good home for it. Many people wait years for the opportunity to adopt a child, and some are unable to do so even though there is every reason to believe that they would be good parents. The needless destruction of a viable infant inevitably deprives some person or persons of a source of great pleasure and satisfaction, perhaps severely impoverishing their lives. Furthermore, even if an infant is considered to be unadoptable (e.g., because of some extremely severe mental or physical handicap) it is still wrong in most cases to kill it. For most of us value the lives of infants, and would prefer to pay taxes to support orphanages and state institutions for the handicapped rather than to allow unwanted infants to be killed. So long as most people feel this way, and so long as our society can afford to provide care for infants which are unwanted or which have special needs that preclude home care, it is wrong to destroy any infant which has a chance of living a reasonably satisfactory life.

If these arguments show that infanticide is wrong, at least in this society, then why don't they also show that late-term abortion is wrong? After all, third trimester fetuses are also highly personlike, and many people value them and would much prefer that they be preserved, even at some cost to themselves. As a potential source of pleasure to some family, a viable fetus is just as valuable as a viable infant. But there is an obvious and crucial difference between the two cases: once the infant is born, its continued life cannot (except, perhaps, in very exceptional cases) pose any serious threat to the woman's life or health, since she is free to put it up for adoption, or, where this is impossible, to place it in a state-supported institution.

While she might prefer that it die, rather than being raised by others, it is not clear that such a preference would constitute a right on her part. True, she may suffer greatly from the knowledge that her child will be thrown into the lottery of the adoption system, and that she will be unable to ensure its well-being, or even to know whether it is healthy, happy, doing well in school, etc.; for the law generally does not permit natural parents to remain in contact with their children, once they are adopted by another family. But there are surely better ways of dealing with these problems than by permitting infanticide in such cases. (It might help, for instance, if the natural parents of adopted children could at least receive some information about their progress, without necessarily being informed of the identity of the adopting family.)

In contrast, a pregnant woman's right to protect her own life and health clearly outweighs other people's desire that the fetus be preserved—just as, when a person's life or limb is threatened by some wild animal, and when the threat cannot be removed without killing the animal, the person's right to self-protection outweighs the desires of those who would prefer that the animal not be harmed. Thus, while the moment of birth may not mark any sharp discontinuity in the degree to which an infant possesses a right to life, it does mark the end of the mother's absolute right to determine its fate. Indeed, if and when a late-term abortion could be safely performed without killing the fetus, she would have no absolute right to insist on its death (e.g., if others wish to adopt it or to pay for its care), for the same reason that she does not have a right to insist that a viable infant be killed.

It remains true that according to my argument neither abortion nor the killing of neonates is properly considered a form of murder. Perhaps it is understandable that the law should classify infanticide as murder or homicide, since there is no other existing legal category which adequately or conveniently expresses the force of our society's disapproval of this action. But the moral distinction remains, and it has several important consequences.

In the first place, it implies that when an infant is born into a society which—unlike ours—is so impoverished that it simply cannot care for it adequately without endangering the survival of existing persons, killing it or allowing it to die is not necessarily wrong—provided that there is no *other* society which is willing and able to provide such care. Most human societies, from those at the hunting and gathering stage of economic development to the highly civilized Greeks and

Romans, have permitted the practice of infanticide under such unfortunate circumstances, and I would argue that it shows a serious lack of understanding to condemn them as morally backward for this reason alone.

In the second place, the argument implies that when an infant is born with such severe physical anomalies that its life would predictably be a very short and/or very miserable one, even with the most heroic of medical treatment, and where its parents do not choose to bear the often crushing emotional, financial and other burdens attendant upon the artificial prolongation of such a tragic life, it is not morally wrong to cease or withhold treatment, thus allowing the infant a painless death. It is wrong (and sometimes a form of murder) to practice involuntary euthanasia on persons, since they have the right to decide for themselves whether or not they wish to continue to live. But terminally ill neonates cannot make this decision for themselves, and thus it is incumbent upon responsible persons to make the decision for them, as best they can. The mistaken belief that infanticide is always tantamount to murder is responsible for a great deal of unnecessary suffering, not just on the part of infants which are made to endure needlessly prolonged and painful deaths, but also on the part of parents, nurses, and other involved persons, who must watch infants suffering needlessly, helpless to end that suffering in the most humane way.

I am well aware that these conclusions, however modest and reasonable they may seem to some people, strike other people as morally monstrous, and that some people might even prefer to abandon their previous support for women's right to abortion rather than accept a theory which leads to such conclusions about infanticide. But all that these facts show is that abortion is not an isolated moral issue; to fully understand the moral status of abortion we may have to reconsider other moral issues as well, issues not just about infanticide and euthanasia, but also about the moral rights of women and of nonhuman animals. It is a philosopher's task to criticize mistaken beliefs which stand in the way of moral understanding, even when—perhaps especially when—those beliefs are popular and widespread. The belief that moral strictures against killing should apply equally to *all* genetically human entities, and *only* to genetically human entities, is such an error. The overcoming of this error will undoubtedly require long and often painful struggle; but it must be done.

CHAPTER 14

All Animals Are Equal

Peter Singer

Peter Singer has taken controversial stands on assisted reproduction, animal rights, infanticide, the environment, and famine relief. Singer's appointment to Princeton University in 1999 created a public uproar reminiscent of 1940, when the City College of New York appointed Bertrand Russell, one of the 20th century's greatest philosophers, to a one-year professorship. In Russell's case, the outcry culminated in a judge's ruling that cancelled the state university's appointment. Commenting on the case, Albert Einstein said, "Great spirits have always found violent opposition from mediocrities." Since Princeton is a private university, Singer's ordeal stayed out of the courts.

The treatment of nonhuman animals has traditionally been regarded as a trivial matter. Until recently, almost every ethicist who wrote on the subject provided some rationale for excluding animals from moral concern. Aristotle said that, in the natural order of things, animals exist to serve human purposes. The Christian tradition added that man alone is made in God's image and that animals do not have souls. Immanuel Kant said that animals are not self-conscious, so we can have no duties to them.

The utilitarians took a different view, holding that we should consider the interests of all beings, human and nonhuman. When Peter Singer (1946–) took up this argument in the mid-1970s, many people thought he was joking.

This selection is taken from the second edition of Singer's book, *Animal Liberation,* which was reprinted in 2009. Today, Professor Singer splits his time between Princeton University in the U.S. and Melbourne University in Australia.

From Peter Singer, *Animal Liberation,* New York Review of Books. Reprinted by permission of Peter Singer.

"Animal Liberation" may sound more like a parody of other liberation movements than a serious objective. The idea of "The Rights of Animals" actually was once used to parody the case for women's rights. When Mary Wollstonecraft, a forerunner of today's feminists, published her *Vindication of the Rights of Woman* in 1792, her views were widely regarded as absurd, and before long an anonymous publication appeared entitled *A Vindication of the Rights of Brutes*. The author of this satirical work (now known to have been Thomas Taylor, a distinguished Cambridge philosopher) tried to refute Mary Wollstonecraft's arguments by showing that they could be carried one stage further. If the argument for equality was sound when applied to women, why should it not be applied to dogs, cats, and horses? The reasoning seemed to hold for these "brutes" too; yet to hold that brutes had rights was manifestly absurd. Therefore the reasoning by which this conclusion had been reached must be unsound, and if unsound when applied to brutes, it must also be unsound when applied to women, since the very same arguments had been used in each case.

In order to explain the basis of the case for the equality of animals, it will be helpful to start with an examination of the case for the equality of women. Let us assume that we wish to defend the case for women's rights against the attack by Thomas Taylor. How should we reply?

One way in which we might reply is by saying that the case for equality between men and women cannot validly be extended to nonhuman animals. Women have a right to vote, for instance, because they are just as capable of making rational decisions about the future as men are; dogs, on the other hand, are incapable of understanding the significance of voting, so they cannot have the right to vote. There are many other obvious ways in which men and women resemble each other closely, while humans and animals differ greatly. So, it might be said, men and women are similar beings and should have similar rights, while humans and nonhumans are different and should not have equal rights.

The reasoning behind this reply to Taylor's analogy is correct up to a point, but it does not go far enough. There are obviously important differences between humans and other animals, and these differences must give rise to some differences in the rights that each have. Recognizing this evident fact, however, is no barrier to the case for extending the basic principle of equality to nonhuman animals. The differences that exist between men and women are equally undeniable, and the supporters of Women's Liberation are aware that these differences may give rise to different rights. Many feminists hold that women have the right to an abortion on request. It does not follow that since these same feminists are campaigning for equality between men and women they must support the right of men to have abortions too. Since a man cannot have an abortion, it is meaningless to talk of his right to have one. Since dogs can't vote, it is meaningless to talk of their right to vote. There is no reason why either Women's Liberation or Animal Liberation should get involved in such nonsense. The extension of the basic principle of equality from one group to another does not imply that we must treat both groups in exactly the same way, or grant exactly the same rights to both groups. Whether we should do so will depend on the nature of the members of the two groups. The basic principle of equality does not require equal or identical *treatment;* it requires equal consideration. Equal consideration for different beings may lead to different treatment and different rights.

So there is a different way of replying to Taylor's attempt to parody the case for women's rights, a way that does not deny the obvious differences between human beings and nonhumans but goes more deeply into the question of equality and concludes by finding nothing absurd in the idea that the basic principle of equality applies to so-called brutes. At this point such a conclusion may appear odd; but if we examine more deeply the basis on which our opposition to discrimination on grounds of race or sex ultimately rests, we will see that we would be on shaky ground if we were to demand equality for blacks, women, and other groups of oppressed humans while denying equal consideration to nonhumans. To make this clear we need to see, first, exactly why racism and sexism are wrong. When we say that all human beings, whatever their race, creed, or sex, are equal, what is it that we are asserting? Those who wish to defend hierarchical, inegalitarian societies have often pointed out that by whatever test we choose it simply is not true that all humans are equal. Like it or not we must face the fact that humans come in different shapes and sizes; they come with different moral capacities, different intellectual abilities, different amounts of benevolent feeling and sensitivity to the needs of others, different abilities to communicate effectively, and different capacities to experience pleasure and pain. In short, if the demand for equality were based on the actual equality of all human beings, we would have to stop demanding equality.

Still, one might cling to the view that the demand for equality among human beings is based on the actual equality of the different races and sexes. Although, it may be said, humans differ as individuals, there are no differences between the races and sexes as such. From the mere fact that a person is black or a woman we cannot infer anything about that person's intellectual or moral capacities. This, it may be said, is why racism and sexism are wrong. The white racist claims that whites are superior to blacks, but this is false; although there are differences among individuals, some blacks are superior to some whites in all of the capacities and abilities that could conceivably be relevant. The opponent of sexism would say the same: a person's sex is no guide to his or her abilities, and this is why it is unjustifiable to discriminate on the basis of sex.

The existence of individual variations that cut across the lines of race or sex, however, provides us with no defense at all against a more sophisticated opponent of equality, one who proposes that, say, the interests of all those with IQ scores below 100 be given less consideration than the interests of those with ratings over 100. Perhaps those scoring below the mark would, in this society, be made the slaves of those scoring higher. Would a hierarchical society of this sort really be so much better than one based on race or sex? I think not. But if we tie the moral principle of equality to the factual equality of the different races or sexes, taken as a whole, our opposition to racism and sexism does not provide us with any basis for objecting to this kind of inegalitarianism.

There is a second important reason why we ought not to base our opposition to racism and sexism on any kind of factual equality, even the limited kind that asserts that variations in capacities and abilities are spread evenly among the different races and between the sexes: we can have no absolute guarantee that these capacities and abilities really are distributed evenly, without regard to race or sex, among human beings. So far as actual abilities are concerned there do seem to be certain measurable differences both among races and between sexes. These differences do not, of course, appear in every case, but only when averages are taken. More important still, we do not yet know how many of these differences are really due to the different genetic endowments of the different races and sexes, and how many are due to poor schools, poor housing, and other factors that are the result of past and continuing discrimination. Perhaps all of the important differences will eventually prove to be environmental rather than genetic. Anyone opposed to racism and sexism will certainly hope that this will be so, for it will make the task of ending discrimination a lot easier; nevertheless, it would be dangerous to rest the case against racism and sexism on the belief that all significant differences are environmental in origin. The opponent of, say, racism who takes this line will be unable to avoid conceding that if differences in ability did after all prove to have some genetic connection with race, racism would in some way be defensible.

Fortunately there is no need to pin the case for equality to one particular outcome of a scientific investigation. The appropriate response to those who claim to have found evidence of genetically based differences in ability among the races or between the sexes is not to stick to the belief that the genetic explanation must be wrong, whatever evidence to the contrary may turn up; instead we should make it quite clear that the claim to equality does not depend on intelligence, moral capacity, physical strength, or similar matters of fact. Equality is a moral idea, not an assertion of fact. There is no logically compelling reason for assuming that a factual difference in ability between two people justifies any difference in the amount of consideration we give to their needs and interests. *The principle of the equality of human beings is not a description of an alleged actual equality among humans: it is a prescription of how we should treat human beings.*

Jeremy Bentham, the founder of the reforming utilitarian school of moral philosophy, incorporated the essential basis of moral equality into his system of ethics by means of the formula: "Each to count for one and none for more than one." In other words, the interests of every being affected by an action are to be taken into account and given the same weight as the like interests of any other being. A later utilitarian, Henry Sidgwick, put the point in this way: "The good of any one individual is of no more importance, from the point of view (if I may say so) of the Universe, than the good of any other." More recently the leading figures in contemporary moral philosophy have shown a great deal of agreement in specifying as a fundamental presupposition of their moral theories some similar requirement that works to give everyone's interests equal consideration—although these writers generally cannot agree on how this requirement is best formulated.

It is an implication of this principle of equality that our concern for others and our readiness to consider their interests ought not to depend on what they are like or on what abilities they may possess. Precisely what our concern or consideration requires us to do may vary according to the characteristics of those affected by what we do: concern for the well-being of children growing up in America would require that we teach them to read; concern for the well-being of pigs may require no more than that we leave them with other pigs in a place where there is adequate food and room to run freely. But the basic element—the taking into account of the interests of the being, whatever those interests may be—must, according to the principle of equality, be extended to all beings, black or white, masculine or femi-nine, human or nonhuman.

Thomas Jefferson, who was responsible for writing the principle of the equality of men into the American Declaration of Indepen-dence, saw this point. It led him to oppose slavery even though he was unable to free himself fully from his slaveholding background. He wrote in a letter to the author of a book that emphasized the notable intellectual achievements of Negroes in order to refute the then com-mon view that they had limited intellectual capacities:

> Be assured that no person living wishes more sincerely than I do, to see a complete refutation of the doubts I myself have enter-tained and expressed on the grade of understanding allotted to them by nature, and to find that they are on a par with our-selves . . . but whatever be their degree of talent it is no measure of their rights. Because Sir Isaac Newton was superior to others in understanding, he was not therefore lord of the property or persons of others.

Similarly, when in the 1850s the call for women's rights was raised in the United States, a remarkable black feminist named Sojourner Truth made the same point in more robust terms at a femi-nist convention:

> They talk about this thing in the head; what do they call it? ["Intellect," whispered someone nearby.] That's it. What's that got to do with women's rights or Negroes' rights? If my cup won't hold but a pint and yours holds a quart, wouldn't you be mean not to let me have my little half-measure full?

It is on this basis that the case against racism and the case against sexism must both ultimately rest; and it is in accordance with this principle that the attitude that we may call "speciesism," by anal-ogy with racism, must also be condemned. Speciesism—the word is not an attractive one, but I can think of no better term—is a prejudice or attitude of bias in favor of the interests of members of one's own species and against those of members of other species. It should be obvious that the fundamental objections to racism and sexism made by Thomas Jefferson and Sojourner Truth apply equally to species-ism. If possessing a higher degree of intelligence does not entitle one human to use another for his or her own ends, how can it entitle humans to exploit nonhumans for the same purpose?

Many philosophers and other writers have proposed the prin-ciple of equal consideration of interests, in some form or other, as a basic moral principle; but not many of them have recognized that this principle applies to members of other species as well as to our own. Jeremy Bentham was one of the few who did realize this. In a forward-looking passage written at a time when black slaves had been freed by the French but in the British dominions were still being treated in the way we now treat animals, Bentham wrote:

> The day *may* come when the rest of the animal creation may acquire those rights which never could have been withholden from them but by the hand of tyranny. The French have already discovered that the blackness of the skin is no reason why a human being should be abandoned without redress to the caprice of a tormentor. It may one day come to be recognized that the number of the legs, the villosity of the skin, or the termination of the *os sacrum* are reasons equally insufficient for abandoning a sensitive being to the same fate. What else is it that should trace the insuperable line? Is it the faculty of reason, or perhaps the faculty of discourse? But a full-grown horse or dog is beyond comparison a more rational, as well as a more conversable animal, than an infant of a day or a week or even a month, old. But suppose they were otherwise, what would it avail? The question is not, Can they *reason?* nor Can they *talk?* but, Can they *suffer?*

In this passage Bentham points to the capacity for suffering as the vital characteristic that gives a being the right to equal consideration. The capacity for suffering—or more strictly, for suffering and/or enjoyment or happiness—is not just another characteristic like the capacity for language or higher mathematics. Bentham is not saying that those who try to mark "the insuperable line" that determines whether the interests of a being should be considered happen to have chosen the wrong characteristic. By saying that we must consider the interests of all beings with the capacity for suffering or enjoyment Bentham does not arbitrarily exclude from consideration any interests at all—as those who draw the line with reference to the possession of reason or language do. The capacity for suffering and enjoyment is *a prerequisite for having interests at all,* a condition that must be satisfied before we can speak of interests in a meaningful way. It would be nonsense to say that it was not in the interests of a stone to be kicked along the road by a schoolboy. A stone does not have interests because it cannot suffer. Nothing that we can do to it could possibly make any difference to its welfare. The capacity for suffering and enjoyment is, however, not only necessary, but also sufficient for us to say that a being has interests—at an absolute minimum, an interest in not suffering. A mouse, for example, does have an interest in not being kicked along the road, because it will suffer if it is.

Although Bentham speaks of "rights" in the passage I have quoted, the argument is really about equality rather than about rights. Indeed, in a different passage, Bentham famously described "natural rights" as "nonsense" and "natural and imprescriptable rights" as "nonsense upon stilts." He talked of moral rights as a shorthand way of referring to protections that people and animals morally ought to have; but the real weight of the moral argument does not rest on the assertion of the existence of the right, for this in turn has to be justified on the basis of the possibilities for suffering and happiness. In this way we can argue for equality for animals without getting embroiled in philosophical controversies about the ultimate nature of rights.

In misguided attempts to refute the arguments of this book, some philosophers have gone to much trouble developing arguments to show that animals do not have rights. They have claimed that to have rights a being must be autonomous, or must be a member of a community, or must have the ability to respect the rights of others, or must possess a sense of justice. These claims are irrelevant to the case for Animal Liberation. The language of rights is a convenient political shorthand. It is even more valuable in the era of thirty-second TV news clips than it was in Bentham's day; but in the argument for a radical change in our attitude to animals, it is in no way necessary.

If a being suffers there can be no moral justification for refusing to take that suffering into consideration. No matter what the nature of the being, the principle of equality requires that its suffering be counted equally with the like suffering—insofar as rough comparisons can be made—of any other being. If a being is not capable of suffering, or of experiencing enjoyment or happiness, there is nothing to be taken into account. So the limit of sentience (using the term as a convenient if not strictly accurate shorthand for the capacity to suffer and/or experience enjoyment) is the only defensible boundary of concern for the interests of others. To mark this boundary by some other characteristic like intelligence or rationality would be to mark it in an arbitrary manner. Why not choose some other characteristic, like skin color?

Racists violate the principle of equality by giving greater weight to the interests of members of their own race when there is a clash between their interests and the interests of those of another race. Sexists violate the principle of equality by favoring the interests of their own sex. Similarly, speciesists allow the interests of their own species to override the greater interests of members of other species. The pattern is identical in each case. . . .

Animals can feel pain. As we saw earlier, there can be no moral justification for regarding the pain (or pleasure) that animals feel as less important than the same amount of pain (or pleasure) felt by humans. But what practical consequences follow from this conclusion? To prevent misunderstanding I shall spell out what I mean a little more fully.

If I give a horse a hard slap across its rump with my open hand, the horse may start, but it presumably feels little pain. Its skin is thick enough to protect it against a mere slap. If I slap a baby in the same way, however, the baby will cry and presumably feel pain, for its skin is more sensitive. So it is worse to slap a baby than a horse, if both slaps are administered with equal force. But there must be some kind of blow—I don't know exactly what it would be, but perhaps a blow with a heavy stick—that would cause the horse as much pain as we cause a baby by slapping it with our hand. That is what I mean by "the same amount of pain," and if we consider it wrong to inflict that much pain on a baby for no good reason then we must, unless we are speciesists, consider it equally wrong to inflict the same amount of pain on a horse for no good reason.

Other differences between humans and animals cause other complications. Normal adult human beings have mental capacities that will, in certain circumstances, lead them to suffer more than animals would in the same circumstances. If, for instance, we decided to perform extremely painful or lethal scientific experiments on normal adult humans, kidnapped at random from public parks for this purpose, adults who enjoy strolling in parks would become fearful that they would be kidnapped. The resultant terror would be a form of suffering additional to the pain of the experiment. The same experiments performed on nonhuman animals would cause less suffering since the animals would not have the anticipatory dread of being kidnapped and experimented upon. This does not mean, of course, that it would be *right* to perform the experiment on animals, but only that there is a reason, which is *not* speciesist, for preferring to use animals rather than normal adult human beings, if the experiment is to be done at all. It should be noted, however, that this same argument gives us a reason for preferring to use human infants—orphans perhaps—or severely retarded human beings for experiments, rather than adults, since infants and retarded humans would also have no idea of what was going to happen to them. So far as this argument is concerned nonhuman animals and infants and retarded humans are in the same category; and if we use this argument to justify experiments on nonhuman animals we have to ask ourselves whether we are also prepared to allow experiments on human infants and retarded adults; and if we make a distinction between animals and these humans, on what basis can we do it, other than a bare-faced—and morally indefensible—preference for members of our own species?

There are many matters in which the superior mental powers of normal adult humans make a difference: anticipation, more detailed memory, greater knowledge of what is happening, and so on. Yet these differences do not all point to greater suffering on the part of the normal human being. Sometimes animals may suffer more because of their more limited understanding. If, for instance, we are taking prisoners in wartime we can explain to them that although they must submit to capture, search, and confinement, they will not otherwise be harmed and will be set free at the conclusion of hostilities. If we capture wild animals, however, we cannot explain that we are not threatening their lives. A wild animal cannot distinguish an attempt to overpower and confine from an attempt to kill; the one causes as much terror as the other.

It may be objected that comparisons of the sufferings of different species are impossible to make and that for this reason when the interests of animals and humans clash the principle of equality gives no guidance. It is probably true that comparisons of suffering between members of different species cannot be made precisely, but precision is not essential. Even if we were to prevent the infliction of suffering on animals only when it is quite certain that the interests of humans will not be affected to anything like the extent that animals are affected, we would be forced to make radical changes in our treatment of animals that would involve our diet, the farming methods we use, experimental procedures in many fields of science, our approach to wildlife and to hunting, trapping and the wearing of furs, and areas of entertainment like circuses, rodeos, and zoos. As a result, a vast amount of suffering would be avoided. . . .

CHAPTER 15

Torturing Puppies and Eating Meat: It's All in Good Taste

Alastair Norcross

Farm animals in America once grazed on open fields beside country roads. Those days, however, are gone. Nowadays, farm animals live in smelly, high-density, automated warehouses. Every independent study has found these places to be inhumane. The cramped conditions are stressful and unnatural for the animals; cows pumped full of food often experience internal abscesses; chickens and turkeys have their beaks cut off, and pigs and cows have their tails severed—all without anesthetic—to avoid the fighting that occurs precisely because the animals are crushed together.

The number of animals that suffer under these conditions is staggering—in the billions, year after year. When people in our culture think of a moral horror, they think of the Holocaust—the campaign of genocide in which Hitler and his Nazi thugs starved, beat, and ultimately murdered six million Jews. They do not think of factory farming. Yet for every human being who suffered under Hitler's tyranny, several thousand animals have suffered in these farms during the past twenty years. The Nobel Laureate Isaac Bashevis Singer wrote, "In relation to [animals], all people are Nazis; for the animals it is an eternal Treblinka."

In this selection, Alastair Norcross asks how we can justify our treatment of chickens when we would never dream of treating puppies in the same way. Despite the seriousness of the topic, Norcross's piece contains humor—some of it directed at my home

From the *Southwest Philosophy Review,* vol. 20, no. 1 (January 2004), pp. 117–123. Reprinted by permission.

state of Alabama, and some directed specifically at the city of Tuscaloosa, where I live. We Alabamians can take the ridicule—even when it's not in good taste.

Alastair Norcross is a professor of philosophy at the University of Colorado at Boulder, where many people play the banjo.

Consider the story of Fred, who receives a visit from the police one day. They have been summoned by Fred's neighbors, who have been disturbed by strange sounds emanating from Fred's basement. When they enter the basement they are confronted by the following scene: Twenty-six small wire cages, each containing a puppy, some whining, some whimpering, some howling. The puppies range in age from newborn to about six months. Many of them show signs of mutilation. Urine and feces cover the bottoms of the cages and the basement floor. Fred explains that he keeps the puppies for twenty-six weeks, and then butchers them while holding them upside-down. During their lives he performs a series of mutilations on them, such as slicing off their noses and their paws with a hot knife, all without any form of anesthesia. Except for the mutilations, the puppies are never allowed out of the cages, which are barely big enough to hold them at twenty-six weeks. The police are horrified, and promptly charge Fred with animal abuse. As details of the case are publicized, the public is outraged. Newspapers are flooded with letters demanding that Fred be severely punished. There are calls for more severe penalties for animal abuse. Fred is denounced as a vile sadist.

Finally, at his trial, Fred explains his behavior, and argues that he is blameless and therefore deserves no punishment. He is, he explains, a great lover of chocolate. A couple of years ago, he was involved in a car accident, which resulted in some head trauma. Upon his release from the hospital, having apparently suffered no lasting ill effects, he visited his favorite restaurant and ordered their famous rich dark chocolate mousse. Imagine his dismay when he discovered that his experience of the mousse was a pale shadow of its former self. The mousse tasted bland, slightly pleasant, but with none of the intense chocolaty flavor he remembered so well. The waiter assured him that the recipe was unchanged from the last time he had tasted it, just the day before his accident. In some consternation, Fred rushed out to buy a bar of his favorite Belgian chocolate. Again, he was dismayed to discover that his experience of the chocolate was barely even pleasurable. Extensive investigation revealed that his experience of other foods remained unaffected, but chocolate, in all its forms, now tasted bland and insipid. Desperate for a solution to his problem, Fred visited a renowned gustatory neurologist, Dr. T. Bud. Extensive tests revealed that the accident had irreparably damaged the godiva gland, which secretes cocoamone, the hormone responsible for the experience of chocolate. Fred urgently requested hormone replacement therapy. Dr. Bud informed him that, until recently, there had been no known source of cocoamone, other than the human godiva gland, and that it was impossible to collect cocoamone from one person to be used by another. However, a chance discovery had altered the situation. A forensic veterinary surgeon, performing an autopsy on a severely abused puppy, had discovered high concentrations of cocoamone in the puppy's brain. It turned out that puppies, who don't normally produce cocoamone, could be stimulated to do so by extended periods of severe stress and suffering. The research that led to this discovery, while gaining tenure for its authors, had not been widely publicized, for fear of antagonizing animal welfare groups. Although this research clearly gave Fred the hope of tasting chocolate again, there were no commercially available sources of puppy-derived cocoamone. Lack of demand, combined with fear of bad publicity, had deterred drug companies from getting into the puppy torturing business. Fred appeals to the court to imagine his anguish, on discovering that a solution to his severe deprivation was possible, but not readily available. But he wasn't inclined to sit around bemoaning his cruel fate. He did what any chocolate lover would do. He read the research, and set up his own cocoamone collection lab in his basement. Six months of intense puppy suffering, followed by a brutal death, produced enough cocoamone to last him a week, hence the twenty-six cages. He isn't a sadist or an animal abuser, he explains. If there were a method of collecting cocoamone without torturing puppies, he would gladly employ it. He derives no pleasure from the suffering of the puppies itself. He sympathizes with those who are horrified by the pain and misery of the animals, but the court must realize that human pleasure is at stake. The puppies, while undeniably cute, are mere animals. He admits that he would be just as healthy without chocolate, if not more so. But this isn't a matter of survival or health. His life would be unacceptably impoverished without the experience of chocolate.

End of story. Clearly, we are horrified by Fred's behavior, and unconvinced by his attempted justification. It is, of course, unfortunate for Fred that he can no longer enjoy the taste of chocolate, but that in no way excuses the imposition of severe suffering on the puppies. I expect near universal agreement with this claim (the exceptions being those who are either inhumanly callous or thinking ahead, and wish to avoid the following conclusion, to which such agreement commits them). No decent person would even contemplate torturing puppies merely to enhance a gustatory experience. However, billions of animals endure intense suffering every year for precisely this end. Most of the chicken, veal, beef, and pork consumed in the U.S. comes from intensive confinement facilities, in which the animals live cramped, stress-filled lives and endure unanaesthetized mutilations. The vast majority of people would suffer no ill health from the elimination of meat from their diets. Quite the reverse. The supposed benefits from this system of factory farming, apart from the profits accruing to agribusiness, are increased levels of gustatory pleasure for those who claim that they couldn't enjoy a meat-free diet as much as their current meat-filled diets. If we are prepared to condemn Fred for torturing puppies merely to enhance his gustatory experiences, shouldn't we similarly condemn the millions who purchase and consume factory-raised meat? Are there any morally significant differences between Fred's behavior and their behavior?

The first difference that might seem to be relevant is that Fred tortures the puppies himself, whereas most Americans consume meat that comes from animals that have been tortured by others. But is this really relevant? What if Fred had been squeamish and had employed someone else to torture the puppies and extract the cocoamone? Would we have thought any better of Fred? Of course not.

Another difference between Fred and many consumers of factory-raised meat is that many, perhaps most, such consumers are unaware of the treatment of the animals, before they appear in neatly wrapped packages on supermarket shelves. Perhaps I should moderate my challenge, then. If we are prepared to condemn Fred for torturing puppies merely to enhance his gustatory experiences, shouldn't we similarly condemn those who purchase and consume factory-raised meat, in full, or even partial, awareness of the suffering endured by the animals? While many consumers are still blissfully ignorant of the appalling treatment meted out to meat, that number is rapidly dwindling, thanks to vigorous publicity campaigns waged by animal welfare groups. Furthermore, any meat-eating readers of this article are now deprived of the excuse of ignorance.

Perhaps a consumer of factory-raised animals could argue as follows: While I agree that Fred's behavior is abominable, mine is crucially different. If Fred did not consume his chocolate, he would not raise and torture puppies (or pay someone else to do so). Therefore Fred could prevent the suffering of the puppies. However, if I did not buy and consume factory-raised meat, no animals would be spared lives of misery. Agribusiness is much too large to respond to the behavior of one consumer. Therefore I cannot prevent the suffering of any animals. I may well regret the suffering inflicted on animals for the sake of human enjoyment. I may even agree that the human enjoyment doesn't justify the suffering. However, since the animals will suffer no matter what I do, I may as well enjoy the taste of their flesh.

There are at least two lines of response to this attempted defense. First, consider an analogous case. You visit a friend in an exotic location, say Alabama. Your friend takes you out to eat at the finest restaurant in Tuscaloosa. For dessert you select the house specialty, "Chocolate Mousse à la Bama," served with a small cup of coffee, which you are instructed to drink before eating the mousse. The mousse is quite simply the most delicious dessert you have ever tasted. Never before has chocolate tasted so rich and satisfying. Tempted to order a second, you ask your friend what makes this mousse so delicious. He informs you that the mousse itself is ordinary, but the coffee contains a concentrated dose of cocoamone, the newly discovered chocolate-enhancing hormone. Researchers at Auburn University have perfected a technique for extracting cocoamone from the brains of freshly slaughtered puppies, who have been subjected to lives of pain and frustration. Each puppy's brain yields four doses, each of which is effective for about fifteen minutes, just long enough to enjoy one serving of mousse. You are, naturally, horrified and disgusted. You will certainly not order another serving, you tell your friend. In fact, you are shocked that your friend, who had always seemed to be a morally decent person, could have both recommended the dessert to you and eaten one himself, in full awareness of the loathsome process necessary for the experience. He agrees that the suffering of the puppies is outrageous, and that the gain in human pleasure in no way justifies the appalling treatment they have to endure. However, neither he nor you can save any puppies by refraining from consuming cocoamone. Cocoamone production is now Alabama's leading industry, surpassing even banjo-making and inbreeding.[1] The industry is much too large to respond to the behavior of one or two consumers. Since the puppies will suffer no matter what either of you does, you may as well enjoy the mousse.

If it is as obvious as it seems that a morally decent person, who is aware of the details of cocoamone production, couldn't order Chocolate Mousse à la Bama, it should be equally obvious that a morally decent person, who is aware of the details of factory farming, can't purchase and consume factory-raised meat. If the attempted excuse of causal impotence is compelling in the latter case, it should be compelling in the former case. But it isn't.

The second response to the claim of causal impotence is to deny it. Consider the case of chickens, the most cruelly treated of all animals raised for human consumption, with the possible exception of veal calves. In 1998, almost 8 billion chickens were slaughtered in the U.S.,[2] almost all of them raised on factory farms. Suppose that there are 250 million chicken eaters in the U.S., and that each one consumes, on average, 25 chickens per year (this leaves a fair number of chickens slaughtered for nonhuman consumption, or for export). Clearly, if only one of those chicken eaters gave up eating chicken, the industry would not respond. Equally clearly, if they all gave up eating chicken, billions of chickens (approximately 6.25 billion per year) would not be bred, tortured, and killed. But there must also be some number of consumers, far short of 250 million, whose renunciation of chicken would cause the industry to reduce the number of chickens bred in factory farms. The industry may not be able to respond to each individual's behavior, but it must respond to the behavior of fairly large numbers. Suppose that the industry is sensitive to a reduction in demand for chicken equivalent to 10,000 people becoming vegetarians. (This seems like a reasonable guess, but I have no idea what the actual numbers are, nor is it important.) For each group of 10,000 who give up chicken, a quarter of a million fewer chickens are bred per year. It appears, then, that if you give up eating chicken, you have only a one in ten thousand chance of making any difference to the lives of chickens, unless it is certain that fewer than 10,000 people will ever give up eating chicken, in which case you have no chance. Isn't a one in ten thousand chance small enough to render your continued consumption of chicken blameless? Not at all. While the chance that your behavior is harmful may be small, the harm that is risked is enormous. The larger the numbers needed to make a difference to chicken production, the larger the difference such numbers would make. A one in ten thousand chance of saving 250,000 chickens per year from excruciating lives is morally and mathematically equivalent to the certainty of saving 25 chickens per year. We commonly accept that even small risks of great harms are unacceptable. That is why we disapprove of parents who fail to secure their children in car seats or with seat belts, who leave their small children unattended at home, or who drink or smoke heavily during pregnancy. Or consider commercial aircraft safety measures. The chances that the oxygen masks, the lifejackets, or the emergency exits on any given plane will be called on to save any lives in a given week, are far smaller than one in ten thousand. And yet we would be outraged to discover that an airline had knowingly allowed a plane to fly for a week with non-functioning emergency exits, oxygen masks, and lifejackets. So, even if it is true that your giving up factory raised chicken has only a tiny chance of preventing suffering, given that the amount of suffering that would be prevented is in inverse proportion to your chance of preventing it, your continued consumption is not thereby excused.

But perhaps it is not even true that your giving up chicken has only a tiny chance of making any difference. Suppose again that the poultry industry only reduces production when a threshold of 10,000 fresh vegetarians is reached. Suppose also, as is almost certainly true, that vegetarianism is growing in popularity in the U.S. (and elsewhere). Then, even if you are not the one, newly converted vegetarian, to reach the next threshold of 10,000, your conversion will reduce the time required before the next threshold is reached. The sooner the threshold is reached, the sooner production, and therefore animal suffering, is reduced. Your behavior, therefore, does make a difference. Furthermore, many people who become vegetarians influence others to become vegetarian, who in turn influence others, and so on. It appears, then, that the claim of causal impotence is mere wishful thinking, on the part of those meat lovers who are morally sensitive enough to realize that human gustatory pleasure does not justify inflicting extreme suffering on animals. . . .

I have been unable to discover any morally relevant differences between the behavior of Fred, the puppy torturer, and the behavior of the millions of people who purchase and consume factory-raised meat, at least those who do so in the knowledge that the animals live lives of suffering and deprivation. Just as morality demands that we not torture puppies merely to enhance our own eating pleasure, morality also demands that we not support factory farming by purchasing factory-raised meat.

Notes

1. I realize that I am playing on stereotypes for comic effect. Banjo-making, of course, has never really been one of Alabama's leading industries.

2. *Livestock Slaughter 1998 Summary,* NASS, USDA (Washington, DC: March 1999), 2; and *Poultry Slaughter,* NASS, USDA (Washington, DC: February 2, 1999), 1f.

CHAPTER 16

Do Animals Have Rights?

Tibor R. Machan

Animals are not moral agents—they are not morally responsible for what they do, nor are they capable of moral goodness. People are moral agents—we are smarter and more valuable than animals. Tibor R. Machan emphasizes ideas like these in this selection. Even though we should treat animals humanely, we should recognize that they have no fundamental right to life, liberty, or property. Animals have no such rights because they cannot make free choices based on their own values.

Tibor R. Machan is the author of *Putting Humans First: Why We Are Nature's Favorite* (2004). Machan is a professor at Chapman University and a research fellow at the Hoover Institute.

Although the idea that animals have rights goes back to the 18th century, at least, it has only recently become something of a *cause celebre* among numerous serious and well-placed intellectuals, including moral and political philosophers. Although Jeremy Bentham seems to have suggested legislation requiring humane treatment of animals, he didn't defend animal rights, per se—not surprisingly, since Bentham himself had not been impressed with the more basic (Lockean) doctrine of natural rights—calling them "nonsense upon stilts." John Locke's idea of individual rights has had enormous influence, and even where it is not respected, it is ultimately invoked as some kind of model for what it would take for something to have rights.

From *Public Affairs Quarterly*, vol. 5, no. 2, April 1991. Reprinted by permission of Public Affairs Quarterly.

In recent years the doctrine of animals rights has found champions in important circles where the general doctrine of rights is itself well respected. For example, Professor Tom Regan, in his important book *The Case for Animal Rights* (UC Press, 1983), finds the idea of natural rights intellectually congenial but then extends this idea to cover animals near humans on the evolutionary scale. The tradition from within which Regan works is clearly Lockean, only he does not agree that human nature is distinctive enough, in relevant respects, to restrict the scope of natural rights to human beings alone.

Following a different tradition, namely, utilitarianism, the idea of animal liberation has emerged. And this idea comes to roughly the same thing, practically speaking. Only the argument is different because for utilitarians what is important is not that someone or something must have a specific sphere of dominion but that they be well off in their lives. So long as the bulk of the relevant creatures enjoy a reasonably high living standard, the moral and political objectives for us will have been met. But if this goal is neglected, moral and political steps are required to improve on the situation. Animal liberation is such a step.

This essay will maintain that animals have no rights and need no liberation. I will argue that to think they do is a category mistake—it is, to be blunt, to unjustifiably anthropomorphize animals, to treat them as if they were what they are not, namely, human beings. Rights and liberty are political concepts applicable to human beings because human beings are moral agents, in need of what Harvard philosopher Robert Nozick calls "moral space," that is, a definite sphere of moral jurisdiction where their authority to act is respected and protected so it is they, not intruders, who govern themselves and either succeed or fail in their moral tasks.

Oddly, it is clearly admitted by most animal rights or liberation theorists that only human beings are moral agents—for example, they never urge animals to behave morally (by, e.g., standing up for their rights, by leading a political revolution). No animal rights theorist proposes that animals be tried for crimes and blamed for moral wrongs.

If it is true that the moral nature of human beings gives rise to the conception of basic rights and liberties, then by this alone animal rights and liberation theorists have made an admission fatal to their case.

Before getting under way I want to note that rights and liberty are certainly not the whole of moral concern to us. There are innumerable other moral issues one can raise, including about the way human beings relate to animals. In particular, there is the question of how people should treat animals. Should they be hunted even when this does not serve any vital human purpose? Should they be utilized in hurtful—indeed, evidently agonizing—fashion even for trivial human purposes? Should their pain and suffering be ignored in the process of being made use of for admittedly vital human purposes?

It is clear that once one has answered the question of whether animals have rights (or ought to be liberated from human beings) in the negative, one has by no means disposed of these other issues. In this essay I will be dealing mostly with the issue of animal rights and liberation. Yet I will also touch briefly on the other moral issues just raised. I will indicate why they may all be answered in the negative without it being the case that animals have rights or should be liberated—i.e., without raising any serious political issues.

Why Might Animals Have Rights?

To have a right amounts to having those around one abstain from intruding on one within a given sphere of jurisdiction. If I have the right to the use of our community swimming pool, no one may prevent me from making the decision as to whether I do or do not use the pool. Someone's having a right is a kind of freedom from the unavoidable interference of moral agents, beings who are capable of choosing whether they will interfere or not interfere with the rights holder.

When a right is considered natural, the freedom involved in having this right is supposed to be justified by reference to the kind of being one is, one's nature as a certain kind of entity. The idea of natural rights was formulated in connection with the issue of the proper relationship between human beings, especially citizens and governments. The idea goes back many centuries . . .

The major political thinker with an influential doctrine of natural rights was John Locke. In his *Second Treatise on Government* he argued that each human being is responsible to follow the Law of Nature, the source of morality. But to do so, each also requires a sphere of personal authority, which is identified by the principle of the natural right to property—including one's person and estate. In other words, to be a morally responsible being in the company of other persons one needs what Robert Nozick has called "moral space," i.e., a sphere of sovereignty or personal jurisdiction so that one can engage in self-government—for better or for worse.

Locke made it a provision of having such a right that there be sufficient and good enough of whatever one may have a right to left for others—i.e., the Lockean proviso against absolute monopoly. For Locke the reason government is necessary is "that though in the state of Nature [every human being] hath such a right [to absolute freedom], yet the enjoyment of it is very uncertain and constantly exposed to the invasion of others."[1] So we establish government to make us secure in the enjoyment of our rights.

Since Locke's time the doctrine of natural rights has undergone a turbulent intellectual history, falling into disrepute at the hands of empiricism and positivism but gaining a revival at the hands of some influential political philosophers of the second half of the 20th century.

Ironically, at a time in recent intellectual history when natural rights theory had not been enjoying much support, the idea that animals might also have rights came under increasing discussion. Most notable among those who proposed such a notion was Thomas Taylor, whose anonymous work, *Vindication of the Rights of Brutes,* was published in 1792 but discussed animal rights only in the context of demeaning human rights. More positive (though brief) was the contribution of Jeremy Bentham, who in his *An Introduction to the Principles of Morals and Legislation* (1789) argued that those animals that can suffer are owed moral consideration, even if those that molest us or those we may make good use of may be killed—but not "tormented."

In the latter part of the 19th century an entire work was devoted to the idea by Henry S. Salt, entitled *Animals' Rights.*[2] And in our time numerous philosophers and social commentators have made the attempt to demonstrate that if we are able to ascribe basic rights to life, liberty and property to human beings, we can do the same for many of the higher animals. In essentials their arguments can be broken down into two parts. First, they subscribe to Darwin's thesis that no difference of kind, only a difference of degree, can be found between other animals and human beings.[3] Second, even if there were a difference in kind between other animals—especially mammals—and human beings, since they both can be shown to have interests (e.g., the avoidance of pain or suffering), for certain moral and legal purposes the difference does not matter, only the similarity does. In connection with both of these arguments the central conclusion is that if human beings can be said to have certain basic rights—e.g., to life, liberty or consideration for their capacity to suffer—then so do (higher) animals.[4]

Now I do not wish to give the impression that no diversity exists among those who defend animal rights. Some do so from the viewpoint of natural rights, treating animals' rights as basic limiting principles which may not be ignored except when it would also make sense to disregard the rights of human beings. Even on this matter there are serious differences among defenders of animal rights—some do not allow any special regard for human beings,[5] some hold that when it comes to a choice between a person and a dog, it is ordinarily the person who should be given protection.[6] But others choose to defend animal rights on utilitarian grounds—to the extent that it amounts to furthering overall pleasure or happiness in the world, animals must be given equal consideration to what human beings receive. Thus only if there really is demonstrable contribution to the overall pleasure or happiness on earth, may an animal capable of experiencing pleasure or happiness be sacrificed for the sake of some human purpose. Barring such demonstrable contribution, animals and humans enjoy equal rights.[7]

At times the argument for animal rights begins with the rather mild point that "reason requires that other animals are as much within the scope of moral concern as are men" but then moves on to the more radical claim that therefore "we must view our entire history as well as all aspects of our daily lives from a new perspective."[8]

Of course, people have generally invoked some moral considerations as they treated animals—I can recall living on a farm in Hungary when I was 11 and getting all kinds of lectures about how I ought to treat the animals, receiving severe rebuke when I mistreated a cat and lots of praise when I took the favorite cow grazing every day and established a close bond with it over time. Hardly anyone can have escaped one or another moral lecture from parents or neighbors concerning the treatment of pets, household animals, or birds. When a young boy once tried out an air gun by shooting a pigeon sitting on a telephone wire before the apartment house in which he lived, I recall that there was no end of rebuke in response to his wanton callousness. Yet none of those who engaged in the moralizing ever entertained the need to "view our entire history as well as all aspects of our daily lives from a new perspective." Rather they seemed to have understood that reckless disregard for the life or well-being of animals shows a defect of character, lack of sensitivity, callousness—realizing, at the same time, that numerous human purposes justify our killing and using animals in the various ways most of us do use them.

And this really is the crux of the matter. But why? Why is it more reasonable to think of animals as available for our sensible use rather than owed the kind of respect and consideration we ought to extend to other human beings? It is one thing to have this as a commonsense conviction, it is another to know it as a sound viewpoint, in terms of which we may confidently conduct ourselves.

Why We May Use Animals

While I will return to the arguments for animal rights, let me first place on record the case for the use of animals for human purposes. Without this case reasonably well established, it will not be possible to critically assess the case for animal rights. After all, this is a comparative matter—which viewpoint makes better sense, which is, in other words, more likely to be true?

One reason for the propriety of our use of animals is that we are more important or valuable than other animals and some of our projects may require animals for them to be successful. Notice that this is different from saying that human beings are "uniquely important," a position avidly ridiculed by Stephen R. L. Clark, who claims that "there seems no decent ground in reason or revelation to suppose that man is uniquely important or significant."[9] If man were uniquely important, that would mean that one could not assign any value to plants or non-human animals apart from their relationship to human beings. That is not the position I am defending. I argue that there is a scale of importance in nature, and among all the various kinds of being, human beings are the most important—even while it is true that some members of the human species may indeed prove themselves to be the most vile and worthless, as well.

How do we establish that we are more important or valuable? By considering whether the idea of lesser or greater importance or value in the nature of things makes clear sense and applying it to an understanding of whether human beings or other animals are more important. If it turns out that ranking things in nature as more or less important makes sense, and if we qualify as more important than other animals, there is at least the beginning of a reason why we may make use of other animals for our purposes.

That there are things of different degrees of value in nature is admitted by animal rights advocates, so there is no great need here to argue about that. When they insist that we treat animals differently from the way we treat, say, rocks or iron ore—so that while we may not use the former as we choose, we may use the latter—they testify, at least by implication, that animals are more important than, say, iron ore. Certainly they invoke some measure of importance or value and place animals higher in line with this measure than they place other aspects of nature. They happen, also, to deny that human beings rank higher than animals, or least they do not admit that human beings' higher ranking warrants their using animals for their purposes. But that is a distinct issue which we can consider later.

Quite independently of the implicit acknowledgment by animal rights advocates of the hierarchy of nature, there simply is evidence through the natural world of the existence of beings of greater complexity and of higher value. For example, while it makes no sense to evaluate as good or bad such things as planets or rocks or pebbles—except as they may relate to human purposes—when it comes to plants and animals the process of evaluation commences very naturally indeed. We can speak of better or worse trees, oaks, redwoods, or zebras, foxes or chimps. While at this point we confine our evaluation to the condition or behavior of such beings without any intimation of their responsibility for being better or worse, when we start discussing human beings our evaluation takes on a moral component. Indeed, none are more ready to testify to this than animal rights advocates who, after all, do not demand any change of behavior on the part of non-human animals and yet insist that human beings conform to certain moral edicts as a matter of their own choice. This means that even animal rights advocates admit outright that to the best of our knowledge it is with human beings that the idea of moral goodness and moral responsibility enters the universe.

Clearly this shows a hierarchical structure in nature: some things do not invite evaluations at all—it is a matter of no significance or of indifference whether they are or are not or what they are or how they behave. Some things invite evaluation but without implying any moral standing with reference to whether they do well or badly. And some things—namely, human beings—invite moral evaluation. The level of importance or value may be noted to move from the inanimate to the animate world, culminating, as far as we now know, with human life. Normal human life involves moral tasks, and that is why we are more important than other beings in nature—we are subject to moral appraisal, it is a matter of our doing whether we succeed or fail in our lives.

Now when it comes to our moral task, namely, to succeed as human beings, we are dependent upon reaching sensible conclusions about what we should do. We can fail to do this and too often do so. But we can also succeed. The process that leads to our success involves learning, among other things, what it is that nature avails us with to achieve our highly varied tasks in life. Clearly among these highly varied tasks could be some that make judicious use of animals—for example, to find out whether some medicine is safe for human use, we might wish to use animals. To do this is the rational thing for us to do, so as to make the best use of nature for our success in living our lives. That does not mean there need be no guidelines involved in how we might make use of animals—any more than there need be no guidelines involved in how we use anything else.

Why Individual Human Rights?

Where do individual *human* rights come into this picture? The rights being talked of in connection with human beings have as their source, as we have noted earlier, the human capacity to make moral choices. We have the right to life, liberty and property—as well as more specialized rights connected with politics, the press, religion—because we have as our central task in life to act morally. And in order to be able to do this throughout the scope of our lives, we require a reasonably clear sphere of personal jurisdiction—a dominion where we are sovereign and can either succeed or fail to live well, to do right, to act properly.

If we did not have rights, we would not have such a sphere of personal jurisdiction and there would be no clear idea as to whether we are acting in our own behalf or those of other persons. No one could be blamed or praised, for we would not know clearly enough whether what the person is doing is in his or her authority to do or in someone else's. This is precisely the problem that arises in communal living and, especially, in totalitarian countries where everything is under forced collective governance. The reason moral distinctions are still possible to make under such circumstances is that in fact—as distinct from law—there is always some sphere of personal jurisdiction wherein people may exhibit courage, prudence, justice, honesty, and other virtues. But where collectivism has been successfully enforced, there is no individual responsibility at play and people's morality and immorality are submerged within the group.

Indeed the main reason for governments has for some time been recognized to be nothing other than that our individual human rights should be protected. In the past—and in many places even today—it was thought that government (or the State) has some kind of leadership role in human communities. This belief followed the view that human beings differ amongst themselves radically, some being lower, some higher class, some possessing divine rights, others lacking them, some having a personal communion with God, others lacking this special advantage.

With such views in place, it made clear enough sense to argue that government should have a patriarchal role in human communities—the view against which John Locke forcefully argued his theory of natural individual human rights.[10]

Where Is There Room for Animal Rights?

We have seen that the most sensible and influential doctrine of human rights rests on the fact that human beings are indeed members of a discernibly different species—the members of which have a moral life to aspire to and must have principles upheld for them in communities that make their aspiration possible. Now there is plainly no valid intellectual place for rights in the non-human world, the world in which moral responsibility is for all practical purposes absent. Some would want to argue that some measure of morality can be found within the world of at least higher animals—e.g., dogs. For example, Rollin holds that "In actual fact, some animals even seem to exhibit behavior that bespeaks something like moral agency or moral agreement."[11] His argument for this is rather anecdotal but it is worth considering:

> Canids, including the domesticated dog, do not attack another when the vanquished bares its throat, showing a sign of submission. Animals typically do not prey upon members of their own species. Elephants and porpoises will and do feed injured members of their species. Porpoises will help humans, even at risk to themselves. Some animals will adopt orphaned young of other species. (Such cross-species "morality" would certainly not be explainable by simple appeal to mechanical evolution, since there is no advantage whatever to one's own species.) Dogs will act "guilty" when they break a rule such as one against stealing food from a table and will, for the most part, learn not to take it.[12]

Animal rights advocates such as Rollin maintain that it is impossible to clearly distinguish between human and non-human animals, including on the grounds of the former's characteristic as a moral agent. Yet what they do to defend this point is to invoke borderline cases, imaginary hypotheses and anecdotes.

In contrast, in his book *The Difference of Man and the Difference It Makes,* Mortimer Adler undertakes the painstaking task of showing that even with the full acknowledgment of the merits of Darwinian and, especially, post-Darwinian evolutionary theory, there is ample reason to uphold the doctrine of species-distinction—a distinction, incidentally, that is actually presupposed within Darwin's own work.[13] Adler shows that although the theistic doctrine of radical species differences is incompatible with current evolutionary theory, the more naturalistic view that species are superficially (but nonnegligibly) different is indeed necessary to it. The fact of occasional borderline cases is simply irrelevant—what is crucial is that the generalization is true that human beings are basically different from other animals— by virtue of "a crucial threshold in a continuum of degrees." As Adler explains:

> Distinct species are genetically isolated populations between which interbreeding is impossible, arising (except in the case of polyploidy) from varieties between which interbreeding was not impossible, but between which it was prevented. Modern theorists, with more assurance than Darwin could manage, treat distinct species as natural kinds, not as man-made class distinctions.[14]

Adler adds that "Without the critical insight provided by the distinction between superficial and radical differences in kind, biologists [as well as animal rights advocates, one should add] might be tempted to follow Darwin in thinking that all differences in kind must be apparent, not real."[15]

Since Locke's admittedly incomplete—sometimes even confusing—theory had gained respect and, especially, practical import (e.g., in British and American political history), it became clear enough that the only justification for the exercise of state power—namely the force of the law—is that the rights of individuals are being or have been violated. But as with all successful doctrines, Locke's idea became corrupted by innumerable efforts to concoct rights that government must protect, rights that were actually disguised special interest objectives— values that some people, perhaps quite legitimately, wanted very badly to have secured for them.

While it is no doubt true that many animal rights advocates sincerely believe that they have found a justification for the actual existence of animal rights, it is equally likely that if the Lockean doctrine of rights had not become so influential, they would now be putting their point differently—in a way, namely, that would secure for them what they, as a special interest group, want: the protection of animals they have such love and sympathy for.

Closing Reflections

As with most issues on the minds of many intelligent people as well as innumerable crackpots, a discussion of whether there are animal rights and how we ought to treat animals cannot be concluded with dogmatic certainty one way or the other. Even though those who defend animal rights are certain almost beyond a shadow of doubt, all I can claim is to being certain beyond a reasonable doubt. Animals are not the sort of beings with basic rights to life, liberty and property, whereas human beings, in the main, are just such beings. Yet we know that animals can feel pain and can enjoy themselves and this must give us pause when we consider using them for our legitimate purposes. We ought to be humane, we ought to kill them and rear them and train them and hunt them in a fashion consistent with such care about them as sentient beings.

In a review of Tom Regan's provocative book already mentioned, *The Case for Animal Rights,* John Hospers makes the following observations that I believe put the matter into the best light we can shed on our topic:

> As one reads page after page of Regan's book, one has the growing impression that his thesis is in an important way "going against nature." It is a fact of nature that living things have to live on other living things in order to stay alive themselves. It is a fact of nature that carnivores must consume, not plants (which they can't digest), but other sentient beings capable of intense pain and suffering, and that they can survive in no other way. It is a fact of nature that animal reproduction is such that far more creatures are born or hatched than can possibly survive. It is a fact of nature that most creatures die slow lingering tortuous deaths, and that few animals in the wild ever reach old age. It is a fact of nature that we cannot take one step in the woods without killing thousands of tiny organisms whose lives we thereby extinguish. This has been the order of nature for millions of years before man came on the scene, and has indeed been the means by which any animal species has survived to the present day; to fight it is like trying to fight an atomic bomb with a dartgun. . . . This is the world as it is, nature in the raw, unlike the animals in Disney cartoons.[16]

Of course, one might then ask, why should human beings make any attempt to behave differently among themselves, why bother with morality at all?

The fact is that with human nature a problem arose in nature that had not been there before—basic choices had to be confronted, which other animals do not have to confront. The question "How should I live?" faces each human being. And that is what makes it unavoidable for human beings to dwell on moral issues as well as to see other human beings as having the same problem to solve, the same question to dwell on. For this reason we are very different from other animals—we also do terrible, horrible, awful things to each other as well as to nature, but we can also do much, much better and achieve incredible feats nothing else in nature can come close to.

Indeed, then, the moral life is the exclusive province of human beings, so far as we can tell for now. Other—lower (!)—animals simply cannot be accorded the kind of treatment that such a moral life demands, namely, respect for and protection of basic rights.

Notes

1. John Locke, *Two Treatises on Government*, Par. 123.

2. Henry S. Salt, *Animals' Rights* (London: George Bell & Sons, Ltd., 1892; Clark Summit, PA: Society for Animal Rights, Inc., 1980). This is perhaps *the* major philosophical effort to defend animals' rights prior to Tom Regan's treatises on the same topic.

3. Charles Darwin, *The Descent of Man*, Chpts. 3 and 4. Reprinted in Tom Regan and Peter Singer, eds., *Animal Rights and Human Obligations* (Englewood Cliffs, NJ: Prentice-Hall, 1976), pp. 72–81.

4. On these points both the deontologically oriented Tom Regan and the utilitarian Peter Singer tend to agree, although they differ considerably in their arguments.

5. Peter Singer holds that "we would be on shaky grounds if we were to demand equality for blacks, women, and other groups of oppressed humans while denying equal consideration to nonhumans." "All Animals Are Equal," op. cit., Regan & Singer, *Animal Rights*, p. 150.

6. Tom Regan contends that "[it] is not to say that practices that involve taking the lives of animals cannot possibly be justified . . . in order to seriously consider approving such a practice [it] would [have to] prevent, reduce, or eliminate a much greater amount of evil . . . there is no other way to bring about these consequences . . . and . . . we have very good

reason to believe that these consequences will obtain." "Do Animals Have a Right to Life?" op. cit., Regan & Singer, *Animal Rights,* pp. 205–6.

7. This is the gist of Singer's thesis.

8. Bernard E. Rollin, *Animal Rights and Human Morality* (Buffalo, NY: Prometheus Books, 1981), p. 4.

9. Stephen R. L. Clark, *The Moral Status of Animals* (Oxford, England: Clarendon Press, 1977), p. 13.

10. John Locke, *Two Treatises.*

11. Rollin, *Animal Rights,* p. 14.

12. Ibid.

13. See a discussion of this in Mortimer Adler, *The Difference of Man and the Difference It Makes* (New York: World Publishing Co., 1968), pp. 73ff.

14. Ibid.

15. Ibid., p. 75.

16. John Hospers, "Review of the Case for Animal Rights," *Reason Papers,* No. 10, p. 123.

CHAPTER 17

9/11 and Starvation

Mylan Engel, Jr.

Regrettable things, even tragic things, happen all the time. Which of these things do we care about? Which of these things do we notice? One fact is that people tend to care more about *concentrated* harms than *diffuse* harms. A traffic wreck involving 20 cars may grab our attention, while 10 separate wrecks, each involving 2 cars, may not. Also, people tend to care more about the striking and unpredictable than about the commonplace and familiar. An outbreak of the West Nile virus makes the news, but nobody notices as 36,000 Americans die each year from the flu.

Mylan Engel, Jr., is a professor of philosophy at Northern Illinois University.

You probably remember many of the tragic events of September 11, 2001. Nineteen terrorists hijacked four commercial airliners, crashing two of them into the World Trade Center towers, one into the Pentagon, and one in a field in Pennsylvania. Two thousand nine hundred and eighty-seven innocent individuals died needlessly. People around the world stared at their televisions in horror and disbelief as the news media aired clips of the attack 'round the clock. The tragedy immediately roused President Bush to declare "War on terrorism." Volunteers from all across America traveled to New York at their own expense to aid in the rescue and clean-up efforts. Charitable contributions poured into the American Red Cross, which in turn wrote checks totaling $143.4 million in emergency aid (averaging $45,837

Excerpted from Mylan Engel, Jr., "Taking Hunger Seriously," *Croatian Journal of Philosophy*, vol. IV, no. 10, 2004. Reprinted by permission.

per family). The U.S. government put together a $5 billion relief package that will provide $1.6 million to each of the victim's families. The U.S. has spent billions more on its military efforts to root out Osama bin Laden and his al-Qaeda terrorist network. As the dust from the 9/11 attacks has finally settled, it is safe to say that Americans are now taking terrorism seriously.

Here are some of the tragic events that took place on 9/11 that you probably don't recall. On that infamous day, over 33,000 innocent children under the age of five died *senseless, needless* deaths—18,000 died from malnutrition and another 15,300 died of untreated poverty-related disease. It must be stressed that almost all of these deaths were *unnecessary*. They could have *easily been prevented*. The U.S. alone grows enough grain and soybeans to feed the world's human population several times over. Given this overabundance of food, the lives of those children who starved to death on 9/11 could have easily been saved, had we only diverted a relatively modest portion of this food to them. As for the disease-related deaths, nineteen percent of the 33,000 children who lost their lives on 9/11 died from the dehydrating effects of chronic diarrhea. Almost all of these 6,350 diarrheal dehydration deaths could have been prevented by administering each child a single packet of oral rehydration salts (cost per packet: 15 cents). Another nineteen percent of these children died from acute respiratory infections, most of whom could have been saved with a course of antibiotics (cost: 25 cents). Most of the 2,300 children who died from measles could have been saved with vitamin A therapy (cost per capsule: less than 10 cents). What makes the deaths of these children particularly tragic is that virtually all of them were readily preventable. They only occurred because otherwise good people did nothing to prevent them.

Despite the fact that the number of innocent children who died needlessly on 9/11 was ten times greater than the number of innocent people who lost their lives in the 9/11 terrorist attack, compassionate conservative President Bush did not declare war on hunger or on poverty. The U.S. Government did not immediately institute a multi-billion-dollar relief package for the world's absolutely poor. People did not make out generous checks to famine relief organizations. The media did not so much as mention the tragedy of so many young innocent lives lost. And, as if 9/11 wasn't enough for us to deal with, on 9/12 another 33,000 innocent children under the age of five died unnecessarily, and another 33,000 on 9/13. In the twenty-two months that have transpired since the 9/11 tragedy, over 22 million innocent children under the age of five have died needlessly. By any objective measure, the tragedy of the 9/11 attack pales in comparison to the tragedy of world hunger and famine-related disease. Each year the latter claims 3,800 times more innocent lives than the 9/11 attack. Despite the magnitude of the tragedy of global hunger and childhood malnutrition, the overwhelming majority of affluent and moderately affluent people, including most philosophers, send no money to famine relief organizations. Of the 4 million people who receive solicitations from UNICEF each year, less than one percent donate anything at all. For most of us, world hunger doesn't even register a blip on our moral radar screens, much less present itself as a serious moral problem requiring action on our part. . . .

CHAPTER 18

The Singer Solution to World Poverty

Peter Singer

In 1972, a young Australian philosopher, Peter Singer, published an article titled "Famine, Affluence, and Morality" in the very first volume of *Philosophy and Public Affairs*. This new journal was part of a movement that changed philosophy. For most of the 20th century, moral philosophers had concentrated on abstract questions of ethical theory; they rarely wrote about practical issues. After 1970, however, "applied ethics" became a lively part of the subject, and Peter Singer became its best-known writer.

In "Famine, Affluence, and Morality," Singer argued that it is indefensible for affluent people to spend money on luxuries while the less fortunate are starving. If we can prevent something bad from happening, he said, without sacrificing anything of comparable moral importance, then we ought to do so. But death by starvation is bad; and we can prevent many people from dying of starvation by sacrificing our luxuries, which are not as important. Therefore, we ought to do so.

This simple argument caused quite a stir. It seems to imply that we in the rich countries are leading immoral lives. Most of us find that hard to believe. The argument seems too demanding; it seems to require too much of us. Yet it is hard to refute.

In 1999, Singer moved to the United States to join the faculty at Princeton University. Conservative groups protested his appointment, and a number of editorials appeared in the national press, attacking him and his work. At the height of the debate, *The New York Times*

From *The New York Times Magazine,* September 5, 1999. Reprinted by permission of the author.

invited Singer to explain his views about our duty to aid others. The article he wrote is presented below.

In the Brazilian film *Central Station,* Dora is a retired schoolteacher who makes ends meet by sitting at the station writing letters for illiterate people. Suddenly she has an opportunity to pocket $1,000. All she has to do is persuade a homeless 9-year-old boy to follow her to an address she has been given. (She is told he will be adopted by wealthy foreigners.) She delivers the boy, gets the money, spends some of it on a television set, and settles down to enjoy her new acquisition. Her neighbor spoils the fun, however, by telling her that the boy was too old to be adopted—he will be killed and his organs sold for transplantation. Perhaps Dora knew this all along, but after her neighbor's plain speaking, she spends a troubled night. In the morning Dora resolves to take the boy back.

Suppose Dora had told her neighbor that it is a tough world, other people have nice new TVs too, and if selling the kid is the only way she can get one, well, he was only a street kid. She would then have become, in the eyes of the audience, a monster. She redeems herself only by being prepared to bear considerable risks to save the boy.

At the end of the movie, in cinemas in the affluent nations of the world, people who would have been quick to condemn Dora if she had not rescued the boy go home to places far more comfortable than her apartment. In fact, the average family in the United States spends almost one-third of its income on things that are no more necessary to them than Dora's new TV was to her. Going out to nice restaurants, buying new clothes because the old ones are no longer stylish, vacationing at beach resorts—so much of our income is spent on things not essential to the preservation of our lives and health. Donated to one of a number of charitable agencies, that money could mean the difference between life and death for children in need.

All of which raises a question: In the end, what is the ethical distinction between a Brazilian who sells a homeless child to organ peddlers and an American who already has a TV and upgrades to a better one—knowing that the money could be donated to an organization that would use it to save the lives of kids in need?

Of course, there are several differences between the two situations that could support different moral judgments about them. For one thing, to be able to consign a child to death when he is standing right in front of you takes a chilling kind of heartlessness; it is much easier to ignore an appeal for money to help children you will never meet. Yet for a utilitarian philosopher like myself—that is, one who judges whether acts are right or wrong by their consequences—if the upshot of the American's failure to donate the money is that one more kid dies on the streets of a Brazilian city, then it is, in some sense, just as bad as selling the kid to the organ peddlers. But one doesn't need to embrace my utilitarian ethic to see that, at the very least, there is a troubling incongruity in being so quick to condemn Dora for taking the child to the organ peddlers while, at the same time, not regarding the American consumer's behavior as raising a serious moral issue.

In his 1996 book, *Living High and Letting Die,* the New York University philosopher Peter Unger presented an ingenious series of imaginary examples designed to probe our intuitions about whether it is wrong to live well without giving substantial amounts of money to help people who are hungry, malnourished, or dying from easily treatable illnesses like diarrhea. Here's my paraphrase of one of these examples:

Bob is close to retirement. He has invested most of his savings in a very rare and valuable old car, a Bugatti, which he has not been able to insure. The Bugatti is his pride and joy. In addition to the pleasure he gets from driving and caring for his car, Bob knows that its rising market value means that he will always be able to sell it and live comfortably after retirement. One day when Bob is out for a drive, he parks the Bugatti near the end of a railway siding and goes for a walk up the track. As he does so, he sees that a runaway train, with no one aboard, is running down the railway track. Looking farther down the track, he sees the small figure of a child very likely to be killed by the runaway train. He can't stop the train and the child is too far away to warn of the danger, but he can throw a switch that will divert the train down the siding where his Bugatti is parked. Then nobody will be killed—but the train will destroy his Bugatti. Thinking of his joy in owning the car and the financial security it represents, Bob decides not to throw the switch. The child is killed. For many years to come, Bob enjoys owning his Bugatti and the financial security it represents.

Bob's conduct, most of us will immediately respond, was gravely wrong. Unger agrees. But then he reminds us that we, too, have opportunities to save the lives of children. We can give to organizations like UNICEF or Oxfam America. How much would we have to give one of these organizations to have a high probability of saving the life of a child threatened by easily preventable diseases? (I do not believe that children are more worth saving than adults, but since no one can argue that children have brought their poverty on themselves, focusing on them simplifies the issues.) Unger called up some experts and used the information they provided to offer some plausible estimates that include the cost of raising money, administrative expenses, and the cost of delivering aid where it is most needed. By his calculation, $200 in donations would help transform a sickly 2-year-old into a healthy 6-year-old—offering safe passage through childhood's most dangerous years. To show how practical philosophical argument can be, Unger even tells his readers that they can easily donate funds by using their credit card and calling one of these toll-free numbers: (800) 367-5437 for UNICEF; (800) 693-2687 for Oxfam America.

Now you, too, have the information you need to save a child's life. How should you judge yourself if you don't do it? Think again about Bob and his Bugatti. Unlike Dora, Bob did not have to look into the eyes of the child he was sacrificing for his own material comfort. The child was a complete stranger to him and too far away to relate to in an intimate, personal way. Unlike Dora, too, he did not mislead the child or initiate the chain of events imperiling him. In all these respects, Bob's situation resembles that of people able but unwilling to donate to overseas aid and differs from Dora's situation.

If you still think that it was very wrong of Bob not to throw the switch that would have diverted the train and saved the child's life, then it is hard to see how you could deny that it is also very wrong not to send money to one of the organizations listed above. Unless, that is, there is some morally important difference between the two situations that I have overlooked.

Is it the practical uncertainties about whether aid will really reach the people who need it? Nobody who knows the world of overseas aid can doubt that such uncertainties exist. But Unger's figure of $200 to save a child's life was reached after he had made conservative assumptions about the proportion of the money donated that will actually reach its target.

One genuine difference between Bob and those who can afford to donate to overseas aid organizations but don't is that only Bob can save the child on the tracks, whereas there are hundreds of millions of people who can give $200 to overseas aid organizations. The problem is that most of them aren't doing it. Does this mean that it is all right for you not to do it?

Suppose that there were more owners of priceless vintage cars—Carol, Dave, Emma, Fred, and so on, down to Ziggy—all in exactly the same situation as Bob, with their own siding and their own switch, all sacrificing the child in order to preserve their own cherished car. Would that make it all right for Bob to do the same? To answer this question affirmatively is to endorse follow-the-crowd ethics—the kind of ethics that led many Germans to look away when the Nazi atrocities were being committed. We do not excuse them because others were behaving no better.

We seem to lack a sound basis for drawing a clear moral line between Bob's situation and that of any reader of this article with $200 to spare who does not donate it to an overseas aid agency. These readers seem to be acting at least as badly as Bob was acting when he chose to let the runaway train hurtle toward the unsuspecting child. In the light of this conclusion, I trust that many readers will reach for the phone and donate that $200. Perhaps you should do it before reading further.

Now that you have distinguished yourself morally from people who put their vintage cars ahead of a child's life, how about treating yourself and your partner to dinner at your favorite restaurant? But wait. The money you will spend at the restaurant could also help save the lives of children overseas! True, you weren't planning to blow $200 tonight, but if you were to give up dining out just for one month, you would easily save that amount. And what is one month's dining out, compared with a child's life? There's the rub. Since there are a lot of desperately needy children in the world, there will always be another child whose life you could save for another $200. Are you therefore obliged to keep giving until you have nothing left? At what point can you stop?

Hypothetical examples can easily become farcical. Consider Bob. How far past losing the Bugatti should he go? Imagine that Bob had got his foot stuck in the track of the siding, and if he diverted the train, then before it rammed the car it would also amputate his big toe. Should he still throw the switch? What if it would amputate his foot? His entire leg?

As absurd as the Bugatti scenario gets when pushed to extremes, the point it raises is a serious one: only when the sacrifices become very significant indeed would most people be prepared to say that Bob does nothing wrong when he decides not to throw the switch. Of course, most people could be wrong; we can't decide moral issues by taking opinion polls. But consider for yourself the level of sacrifice that you would demand of Bob, and then think about how much money you would have to give away in order to make a sacrifice that is roughly equal to that. It's almost certainly much, much more than $200. For most middle-class Americans, it could easily be more like $200,000.

Isn't it counterproductive to ask people to do so much? Don't we run the risk that many will shrug their shoulders and say that morality, so conceived, is fine for saints but not for them? I accept that we are unlikely to see, in the near or even medium-term future, a world in which it is normal for wealthy Americans to give the bulk of their wealth to strangers. When it comes to praising or blaming people for what they do, we tend to use a standard that is relative to some conception of normal behavior. Comfortably off Americans who give, say, 10 percent of their income to overseas aid organizations are so far ahead of most of their equally comfortable fellow citizens that I wouldn't go out of my way to chastise them for not doing more. Nevertheless, they should be doing much more, and they are in no position to criticize Bob for failing to make the much greater sacrifice of his Bugatti.

At this point various objections may crop up. Someone may say: "If every citizen living in the affluent nations contributed his or her share, I wouldn't have to make such a drastic sacrifice, because long before such levels were reached, the resources would have been there to save the lives of all those children dying from lack of food or medical care. So why should I give more than my fair share?" Another, related objection is that the government ought to increase its overseas aid allocations, since that would spread the burden more equitably across all taxpayers.

Yet the question of how much we ought to give is a matter to be decided in the real world—and that, sadly, is a world in which we know that most people do not, and in the immediate future will not, give substantial amounts to overseas aid agencies. We know, too, that at least in the next year, the United States government is not going to meet even the very modest target, recommended by the United Nations, of 0.7 percent of gross national product; at the moment it lags far below that, at 0.09 percent, not even half of Japan's 0.22 percent or a tenth of Denmark's 0.97 percent. Thus, we know that the money we can give beyond that theoretical "fair share" is still going to save lives that would otherwise be lost. While the idea that no one need do more than his or her fair share is a powerful one, should it prevail if we know that others are not doing their fair share and that children will die preventable deaths unless we do more than our fair share? That would be taking fairness too far.

Thus, this ground for limiting how much we ought to give also fails. In the world as it is now, I can see no escape from the conclusion that each one of us with wealth surplus to his or her essential needs should be giving most of it to help people suffering from poverty so dire as to be life-threatening. That's right: I'm saying that you shouldn't buy that new car, take that cruise, redecorate the house, or get that pricey new suit. After all, a $1,000 suit could save five children's lives.

So how does my philosophy break down in dollars and cents? An American household with an income of $50,000 spends around $30,000 annually on necessities, according to the Conference Board, a nonprofit economic research organization. Therefore, for a household bringing in $50,000 a year, donations to help the world's poor should be as close as possible to $20,000. The $30,000 required for necessities holds for higher incomes as well. So a household making $100,000 could write a yearly check for $70,000. Again, the formula is simple: whatever money you're spending on luxuries, not necessities, should be given away.

Now, evolutionary psychologists tell us that human nature just isn't sufficiently altruistic to make it plausible that many people will sacrifice so much for strangers. On the facts of human nature, they might be right, but they would be wrong to draw a moral conclusion from those facts. If it is the case that we ought to do things that, predictably, most of us won't do, then let's face that fact head-on. Then, if we value the life of a child more than going to fancy restaurants, the next time we dine out we will know that we could have done something better with our money. If that makes living a morally decent life extremely arduous, well, then that is the way things are. If we don't do it, then we should at least know that we are failing to live a morally decent life—not because it is good to wallow in guilt but because knowing where we should be going is the first step toward heading in that direction.

When Bob first grasped the dilemma that faced him as he stood by that railway switch, he must have thought how extraordinarily unlucky he was to be placed in a situation in which he must choose between the life of an innocent child and the sacrifice of most of his savings. But he was not unlucky at all. We are all in that situation.

CHAPTER 19

The Ethics of War and Peace

Douglas P. Lackey

Is it ever right to wage war? According to Saint Matthew, Jesus taught his disciples that it is never right:

> You have heard that it was said, "An eye for an eye and a tooth for a tooth." But I say to you, Do not resist the one who is evil. But if anyone slaps you on the right cheek, turn to him the other also. And if any one would sue you and take your tunic, let him have your cloak as well. And if anyone forces you to go one mile, go with him two miles. . . .
>
> You have heard that it was said, "You shall love your neighbor and hate your enemy." But I say to you, Love your enemies and pray for those who persecute you, so that you may be sons of your Father who is in heaven.

Since this teaching is so clear, we might expect Christians to be pacifists; and since Christianity is the dominant religion of our culture, we might expect pacifism to be widespread. Surprisingly, however, there are very few pacifists in our culture, and very few Christians oppose war as a matter of principle.

This was not always so. The early Christians, living when the New Testament was being written and shortly afterward, thought that Jesus's teaching was perfectly unambiguous: He did not permit meeting violence with violence. This was Saint Paul's understanding, as he emphasizes in the 12th chapter of Romans. And Tertullian, who lived around 200 A.D., wrote: "Can it be lawful to handle the sword, when the Lord himself has declared that he who uses the sword shall perish by it?"

But as Christianity grew larger and more influential, it had to accommodate the state. Christianity could not become a state religion

---

Excerpted from Douglas P. Lackey, *The Ethics of War and Peace,* pp. 28–37, 39–40, 43–44, 58–61, © 1989. Reprinted by permission of Prentice-Hall, Inc., Upper Saddle River, NJ.

if it continued to condemn war—waging war was, after all, something that all states did. So the church's doctrine changed. Church thinkers adopted the Greek notion that some wars are just and some are not. Theologians from Saint Augustine on have therefore concentrated on defining the conditions under which war is just. Thomas Aquinas, for example, said that a war is just when three conditions are met: a legitimate authority declares the war; the war is waged for a "just cause"; and the war is fought using "just means."

In the modern era, the Doctrine of the Just War has provided both religious and secular thinkers with a framework for thinking about the ethics of warfare. In the following selection, Douglas P. Lackey, a professor of philosophy at Baruch College of the City University of New York, outlines the essential points of the doctrine.

When to Fight

1. Introduction. Rightly or wrongly, pacifism has always been a minority view. Most people believe that *some* wars are morally justifiable; the majority of Americans believe that World War II was a moral war. But though most people have clear-cut intuitions about the moral acceptability of World War II, the Vietnam War, and so forth, few people have a theory that justifies and organizes their intuitive judgments. If morally concerned nonpacifists are to defeat the pacifists to their moral left and the cynics to their moral right, they must develop a theory that will distinguish justifiable wars from unjustifiable wars, using a set of consistent and consistently applied rules.

The work of specifying these rules, which dates at least from Aristotle's *Politics*, traditionally goes under the heading of "just war theory." The name is slightly misleading, since justice is only one of several primary moral concepts, all of which must be consulted in a complete moral evaluation of war. A just war—a morally good war—is not merely a war dictated by principles of justice. A just war is a morally justifiable war after justice, human rights, the common good, and all other relevant moral concepts have been consulted and weighed against the facts and against each other. . . .

2. Competent Authority. From the time of Augustine, theorists have maintained that a just war can be prosecuted only by a "competent authority." Augustine . . . considered the use of force by private persons to be immoral; consequently the only permissible uses of force were those sanctioned by public authorities. Medieval authors, with a watchful eye for peasant revolts, followed Augustine in confining the just use of force to princes, whose authority and patronage were divinely sanctioned. Given these scholastic roots, considerations of competent authority might appear archaic, but it is still helpful for purposes of moral judgment to distinguish wars from spontaneous uprisings, and soldiers and officers from pirates and brigands. Just war must, first of all, be war.

To begin, most scholars agree that war is a controlled use of force, undertaken by persons organized in a functioning chain of command. An isolated assassin cannot wage war; New York City's Mad Bomber in the 1950s only metaphorically waged war against Con Edison. In some sense, then, war is the contrary of violence. Second, the use of force in war must be directed to an identifiable political result, a requirement forever associated with the Prussian theorist Karl von Clauswitz. An "identifiable political result" is some change in a government's policy, some alteration in a form of government, or some extension or limitation of the scope of its authority. Since the extermination of a people is not an identifiable political result, most acts of genocide are not acts of war: the Turks did not wage war against the Armenians, nor did Hitler wage war on the Jews. (The American frontier cliché, "the only good Indian is a dead Indian," expresses the hopes of murderers, not soldiers.) And since the religious conversion of people is, in most cases, not a political result, many holy wars, by this definition, have not been wars. . . .

3. Right Intention. One can imagine cases in which a use of military force might satisfy all the external standards of just war while those who order this use of force have no concern for justice. Unpopular political leaders, for example, might choose to make war in order to stifle domestic dissent and win the next election. The traditional theory of just war insists that a just war be a war for the right, fought for the sake of the right.

In the modern climate of political realism, many authors are inclined to treat the standard of right intention as a quaint relic of a more idealistic age, either on the grounds that moral motives produce disastrous results in international politics or on the grounds that motives are subjective and unobservable. ("I will not speculate on the motives of the North Vietnamese," Henry Kissinger once remarked, "I have too much difficulty understanding our own.") But it is unfair to dismiss idealistic motives on the grounds that they produce disaster in international politics, since realistic motives have produced their own fair share of disasters. It is a mistake to dismiss motives as unobservable, when they are so often clearly exhibited in behavior. . . .

4. Just Cause. The most important of the *jus ad bellum* rules is the rule that the moral use of military force requires a just cause. From the earliest writings, just war theorists rejected love of war and love of conquest as morally acceptable causes for war: "We [should] wage war," Aristotle wrote, "for the sake of peace" (*Politics,* 1333A). Likewise, the seizure of plunder was always rejected as an acceptable cause for war. Beyond these elementary restrictions, however, a wide variety of "just causes" were recognized. The history of the subject is the history of how this repertoire of just causes was progressively cut down to the modern standard, which accepts only the single cause of self-defense.

As early as Cicero in the first century B.C., analysts of just war recognized that the only proper occasion for the use of force was a "wrong received." It follows from this that the condition or characteristics of potential enemies, apart from their actions, cannot supply a just cause for war. Aristotle's suggestion that a war is justified to enslave those who naturally deserve to be slaves, John Stuart Mill's claim that military intervention is justified in order to bestow the benefits of Western civilization on less advanced peoples, and the historically common view that forcible conversion to some true faith is justified as obedience to divine command are all invalidated by the absence of a "wrong received."

Obviously, the concept of a "wrong received" stands in need of considerable analysis. In the eighteenth century, the notion of wrong included the notion of insult, and sovereigns considered it legitimate to initiate war in response to verbal disrespect, desecrations of national symbols, and so forth. The nineteenth century, which saw the abolition of private duels, likewise saw national honor reduced to a secondary role in the moral justification of war. For most nineteenth-century theorists, the primary wrongs were not insults, but acts or policies of a government resulting in violations of the rights of the nation waging just war.

By twentieth-century standards, this definition of international wrongs providing conditions of just war was both too restrictive and too loose. It was too restrictive in that it failed to recognize any rights of *peoples,* as opposed to *states:* rights to cultural integrity, national self-determination, and so forth. It was too loose in that it sanctioned the use of military force in response to wrongs the commission of which may not have involved military force, thus condoning, on occasion, the first use of arms.

These two excesses were abolished in twentieth-century international law. The right to national self-determination was a prevailing theme at the Versailles conference in 1919 and was repeatedly invoked in the period of decolonization following World War II. Prohibition of first use of force was attempted in drafting of the U.N. Charter in 1945:

> Article 2(4): All Members shall refrain in their international relations from the threat or use of force against the territorial integrity or political independence of any state or in any other manner inconsistent with the Purposes of the United Nations.

> Article 51: Nothing in the present Charter shall impair the inherent right of individual or collective self-defense if an armed attack occurs against a member of the United Nations, until the Security Council has taken the measures necessary to maintain international peace and security.

Strictly speaking, Article 51 does not prohibit first use of military force: to say that explicitly, the phrase "if an armed attack occurs" would have to be replaced by "if and only if an armed attack occurs." Nevertheless, Article 51, coupled with Article 2(4), rules out anticipatory self-defense. Legitimate self-defense must be self-defense against an actual attack. . . .

5. Anticipation and Just Cause. One of the most radical features of the United Nations analysis of just cause is its rejection of anticipatory self-defense. The decision of those who framed the Charter was informed by history: the argument of anticipatory self-defense had been repeatedly and cynically invoked by political leaders set on military adventures, and the framers were determined to prevent a repetition of August 1914, when nations declared war in response to mobilizations, that is, to anticipated attacks rather than actual attacks. The U.N. view stands on good logical ground: if the use of force by nation A is justified on the grounds that its rights have been violated by nation B, then nation B must have already done something that has violated A's rights. To argue that force is necessary in order to *prevent* a future rights violation by nation B is not to make an argument based on rights at all: it is a call to use force in order to make a better world—a very different sort of moral argument than the argument that a right has been violated, and one rejected by the mainstream tradition that defines just war as a response to a "wrong received."

Nevertheless, many scholars are uncomfortable with an absolute ban on anticipatory self-defense. It might be wise, as a point of international law, to reject anticipatory self-defense in order to deprive nations of a convenient legal pretext for war, but from the point of view of moral principles, it is implausible that *every* case of anticipatory self-defense should be morally wicked. After all, people accept the morality of ordinary self-defense on the grounds that cases arise in which survival requires force directed against the attacker, and the use of force is morally proper in such cases. But exactly the same argument, "the use of force when necessary for survival," could be made in some cases of anticipatory self-defense. . . .

6. Intervention and Just Cause. At first sight it would appear that the U.N. Charter rules out the use of force by all nations except the victims of aggression. But there is an escape clause in Article 51, which grants nations the right of *collective* self-defense. In cases of legitimate collective self-defense, a nation can permissibly use force against an aggressor without itself being the victim of aggression.

So far as international law and custom are concerned, most scholars are agreed that legitimate use of force by A on behalf of B against aggressor C requires some prior mutual defense agreement between A and B. The legal logic of this interpretation of collective self-defense is straightforward: the main intent of the U.N. Charter is to prevent nations from having recourse to force, and to achieve this end it would not be a good idea to let any nation rush to the aid of any other nation that seems to be the victim of aggression. But international law here may be too strict for our moral sensibilities. We do not, at the personal level, require that Good Samaritans have prior contracts with those they seek to aid, even if the Good Samaritan, unlike his biblical predecessor, must use force to rescue the victim of attack. By analogy it seems unreasonable to require prior collective defense agreements between international Good Samaritans and nations that are the victims of aggression. . . .

7. The Rule of Proportionality. It is a superficially paradoxical feature of just war theory that a just cause need not make for a just war. If the just cause can be achieved by some means other than war, then war for that just cause is not morally justified. If the just cause *might* be achieved by other means that have not been attempted, then war for that just cause is not just war. If the cause is just but cannot be achieved by war, then war for that cause is not just war. These rules, sometimes called the rule of necessity, the rule of last resort, or the "chance of victory" requirement, are part of that section of just war theory which acknowledges that some just causes are not sufficiently weighty, on the moral scales, to justify the evils that war for those just causes might produce. The rule of proportionality states that a war cannot be just unless the evil that can reasonably be expected to ensue from the war is less than the evil that can reasonably be expected to ensue if the war is not fought. . . .

8. The Rule of Just Peace. The preceding sections considered all the traditional rules of *jus ad bellum*. Since the rules are addressed to decision makers contemplating war, they take into consideration only such facts as are available to decision makers before war begins. There is room for one further rule, a rule that takes into consideration facts available to moral judges after the war ends. For war to be just, the winning side must not only have obtained justice for itself; it must not have achieved it at the price of violating the rights of others. A just war must lead to a just peace.

The rule of just outcome provides a solution to an ancient controversy concerning just cause. In the modern analysis, for nation A to have just cause, its rights must have been violated by nation B. Pursuit of this just cause permits nation A to use force to restore its rights. But do the rules of morality restrict A to just the restoration of its rights? In civil law, if party B has wrongfully injured party A, A is often entitled not just to compensation for the loss sustained through the injury but also to damages. By analogy, a nation acting in self-defense is entitled not merely to a restoration of the status quo ante but also to further rewards. In considering the scope of these rewards, authors have looked charitably on such rewards as might provide nation A with improved security in the future and teach the lesson that international crime does not pay.

The analogy, however, between civil law and international affairs is weak. The party that pays damages in civil law deserves to be forced to pay, but changes in international arrangements resulting from successful wars fought in self-defense may involve thousands of persons who were not parties to the conflict. It is in the interest of these victims of international upheaval that the rule of just outcome be applied. Such acts as go beyond the restoration of the status quo ante, acts that provide the victor with improved security or assess damages against the loser, must not violate the rights of the citizens in the losing nation or the rights of third parties. . . .

How to Fight

1. Introduction. People who believe that there are moral limits defining *when* wars should be fought naturally believe that there are moral limits defining *how* they should be fought. The idea that there are right and wrong ways to conduct war is an ancient one. In the Hebrew Bible, God states that though it may be necessary to kill one's enemy, it is never permissible to cut down his fruit trees (Deut. 20:19). In the sixth century B.C. the Hindu Laws of Manu specified, "When the King fights with his foes in battle, let him not strike with weapons concealed in wood, nor with barbed, poisoned, or flaming arrows."

Over the centuries, a vast array of rules and customs constituting *jus in bello* have been elaborated. There are rules that specify proper behavior toward neutral countries, toward the citizens of neutral countries, and toward neutral ships. There are rules governing what can and cannot be done to enemy civilians, to enemy soldiers on the battlefield, and to enemy soldiers when they are wounded and when they have surrendered. There are rules concerning proper and improper weapons of war, and proper and improper tactics on the battlefield. . . .

2. Necessity, Proportionality, and Discrimination. For the student approaching the laws of war for the first time, the profusion of covenants, treaties, customs, and precedents can be bewildering. But fortunately there are a few leading ideas that have governed the development of the laws of war. The first is that the destruction of life and property, even enemy life and property, is inherently bad. It follows that military forces should cause no more destruction than is strictly necessary to achieve their objectives. (Notice that the principle does not say that whatever is necessary is permissible, but that everything permissible must be necessary.) This is the principle of necessity: that *wanton* destruction is forbidden. More precisely, the principle of necessity specifies that a military operation is forbidden if there is some alternative operation that causes less destruction but has the same probability of producing a successful military result.

The second leading idea is that the amount of destruction permitted in pursuit of a military objective must be proportionate to the importance of the objective. This is the *military* principle of

proportionality (which must be distinguished from the *political* principle of proportionality in the *jus ad bellum*). It follows from the military
principle of proportionality that certain objectives should be ruled
out of consideration on the grounds that too much destruction would
be caused in obtaining them.

The third leading idea, the principle of noncombatant immunity, is that civilian life and property should not be subjected to
military force: military force must be directed only at military objectives. Obviously, the principle of noncombatant immunity is useful only if there is a consensus about what counts as "civilian" and
what counts as "military." In the older Hague Conventions, a list of
explicit nonmilitary targets is developed: "buildings dedicated to
religion, art, science, or charitable purposes, historic monuments,
hospitals . . . undefended towns, buildings, or dwellings." Anything
that is not explicitly mentioned qualifies as a military target. But this
list is overly restrictive, and the consensus of modern thought takes
"military" targets to include servicemen, weapons, and supplies; the
ships and vehicles that transport them; and the factories and workers that produce them. Anything that is not "military" is "civilian."
Since, on either definition, the principle of noncombatant immunity
distinguishes acceptable military objectives from unacceptable civilian objectives, it is often referred to as the principle of discrimination.
(In the morality of war, discrimination is good, not evil.)

There is an objective and subjective version of the principle of
noncombatant immunity. The objective version holds that if civilians
are killed as a result of military operations, the principle is violated.
The subjective version holds that if civilians are *intentionally* killed as
a result of military operations, the principle is violated. The interpretation of "intentional" in the subjective version is disputed, but the
general idea is that the killing of civilians is intentional if, and only if,
they are the chosen *targets* of military force. It follows, on the subjective version, that if civilians are killed in the course of a military operation directed at a military target, the principle of discrimination has
not been violated. Obviously, the objective version of the principle of
discrimination is far more restrictive than the subjective. . . .

The principles of necessity, proportionality, and discrimination
apply with equal force to all sides in war. Violation of the rules cannot be justified or excused on the grounds that one is fighting on the
side of justice. Those who developed the laws of war learned through
experience that just causes must have moral limits.

CHAPTER 20

Fifty Years after Hiroshima

John Rawls

In the spring of 1945, the Allies finally captured land so close to Japan that they could start a bombing campaign against the Japanese home islands. Many of the bombs used were incendiary, designed to spread fires which the Japanese cities were not constructed to withstand. Hundreds of thousands of civilians perished in those infernos.

On August 6 and August 9 of 1945, the United States dropped atomic bombs on Hiroshima and Nagasaki, killing tens of thousands of people instantly and leaving many more to die horrible deaths. Hiroshima and Nagasaki were chosen mostly for a pragmatic reason: few other Japanese cities were still standing.

John Rawls was an infantryman in the Pacific during World War II, and fifty years after the bombings, he wrote this essay about the conduct of war. According to Rawls, the Americans' actions violated the rights of Japanese civilians. President Truman, who ordered the atomic bombings, acted like a politician but not like a statesman.

John Rawls (1921–2002) taught for many years at Harvard University. He will long be remembered as the author of *A Theory of Justice* (1971), the most influential work in political philosophy of the twentieth century.

The fiftieth year since the bombing of Hiroshima is a time to reflect about what one should think of it. Is it really a great wrong, as many now think, and many also thought then, or is it perhaps justified after

From John Rawls, *Collected Papers,* edited by Samuel Freeman (Cambridge, MA: Harvard University Press, 1999), pp. 565–572, originally published in *Dissent* (Summer 1995), pp. 323–327. Reprinted by permission of the Estate of John Rawls.

all? I believe that both the fire-bombing of Japanese cities beginning in the spring of 1945 and the later atomic bombing of Hiroshima on August 6 were very great wrongs, and rightly seen as such. In order to support this opinion, I set out what I think to be the principles governing the conduct of war—*jus in bello*—of democratic peoples. These peoples have different ends of war than nondemocratic, especially totalitarian, states, such as Germany and Japan, which sought the domination and exploitation of subjected peoples, and in Germany's case, their enslavement if not extermination.

Although I cannot properly justify them here, I begin by setting out six principles and assumptions in support of these judgments. I hope they seem not unreasonable; and certainly they are familiar, as they are closely related to much traditional thought on this subject.

1. The aim of a just war waged by a decent democratic society is a just and lasting peace between peoples, especially with its present enemy.

2. A decent democratic society is fighting against a state that is not democratic. This follows from the fact that democratic peoples do not wage war against each other; and since we are concerned with the rules of war as they apply to such peoples, we assume the society fought against is nondemocratic and that its expansionist aims threatened the security and free institutions of democratic regimes and caused the war.

3. In the conduct of war, a democratic society must carefully distinguish three groups: the state's leaders and officials, its soldiers, and its civilian population. The reason for these distinctions rests on the principle of responsibility: since the state fought against is not democratic, the civilian members of the society cannot be those who organized and brought on the war. This was done by its leaders and officials assisted by other elites who control and staff the state apparatus. They are responsible, they willed the war, and for doing that, they are criminals. But civilians, often kept in ignorance and swayed by state propaganda, are not. And this is so even if some civilians knew better and were enthusiastic for the war. In a nation's conduct of war many such marginal cases may exist, but they are irrelevant. As for soldiers, they, just as civilians, and leaving aside the upper ranks of an officer class, are not responsible for the war, but are conscripted or in other ways forced into it, their patriotism often cruelly and cynically exploited. The grounds on which they may be attacked directly are not that they are responsible for the war but that a democratic people cannot defend itself in any other way, and defend itself it must do. About this there is no choice.

4. A decent democratic society must respect the human rights of the members of the other side, both civilians and soldiers, for two reasons. One is because they simply have these rights by the law of peoples. The other reason is to teach enemy soldiers and civilians the content of those rights by the example of how they hold in their own case. In this way their significance is best brought home to them. They are assigned a certain status, the status of the members of some human society who possess rights as human persons. In the case of human rights in war the aspect of status as applied to civilians is given a strict interpretation. This means, as I understand it here, that they can never be attacked directly except in times of extreme crisis, the nature of which I discuss below.

5. Continuing with the thought of teaching the content of human rights, the next principle is that just peoples by their actions and proclamations are to foreshadow during war the kind of peace they aim for and the kind of relations they seek between nations. By doing so, they show in an open and public way the nature of their aims and the kind of people they are. These last duties fall largely on the leaders and officials of the governments of democratic peoples, since they are in the best position to speak for the whole people and to act as the principle applies. Although all the preceding principles also specify duties of statesmanship, this is especially true of 4 and 5. The way a war is fought and the actions ending it endure in the historical memory of peoples and may set the stage for future war. This duty of statesmanship must always be held in view.

6. Finally, we note the place of practical means-end reasoning in judging the appropriateness of an action or policy for achieving the aim of war or for not causing more harm than good. This mode of thought—whether carried on by (classical) utilitarian reasoning, or by cost-benefit analysis, or by weighing national interests, or in other ways—must always be framed within and strictly limited by the preceding principles. The norms of the conduct of war set up certain lines that bound just action. War plans and strategies, and the conduct of battles, must lie within their limits. (The only exception, I repeat, is in times of extreme crisis.)

In connection with the fourth and fifth principles of the conduct of war, I have said that they are binding especially on the leaders of nations. They are in the most effective position to represent their people's aims and obligations, and sometimes they become statesmen. But who is a statesman? There is no office of statesman, as there is of president, or chancellor, or prime minister. The statesman is an ideal, like the ideal of the truthful or virtuous individual. Statesmen are presidents or prime ministers who become statesmen through their exemplary performance and leadership in their office in difficult and trying times and manifest strength, wisdom, and courage. They guide their people through turbulent and dangerous periods for which they are esteemed always, as one of their great statesmen.

The ideal of the statesman is suggested by the saying: the politician looks to the next election, the statesman to the next generation. It is the task of the student of philosophy to look to the permanent conditions and the real interests of a just and good democratic society. It is the task of the statesman, however, to discern these conditions and interests in practice; the statesman sees deeper and further than most others and grasps what needs to be done. The statesman must get it right, or nearly so, and hold fast to it. Washington and Lincoln were statesmen. Bismarck was not. He did not see Germany's real interests far enough into the future, and his judgment and motives were often distorted by his class interests and his wanting himself alone to be chancellor of Germany. Statesmen need not be selfless and may have their own interests when they hold office, yet they must be selfless in their judgments and assessments of society's interests and not be swayed, especially in war and crisis, by passions of revenge and retaliation against the enemy.

Above all, they are to hold fast to the aim of gaining a just peace, and avoid the things that make achieving such a peace more difficult. Here the proclamations of a nation should make clear (the statesman must see to this) that the enemy people are to be granted an autonomous regime of their own and a decent and full life once peace is securely reestablished. Whatever they may be told by their leaders, whatever reprisals they may reasonably fear, they are not to be held as slaves or serfs after surrender, or denied in due course their full liberties; and they may well achieve freedoms they did not enjoy before, as the Germans and the Japanese eventually did. The statesman knows, if others do not, that all descriptions of the enemy people (not their rulers) inconsistent with this are impulsive and false.

Turning now to Hiroshima and the fire-bombing of Tokyo, we find that neither falls under the exemption of extreme crisis. One aspect of this is that since (let's suppose) there are no absolute rights—rights that must be respected in all circumstances—there are occasions when civilians can be attacked directly by aerial bombing. Were there times during the war when Britain could properly have bombed Hamburg and Berlin? Yes, when Britain was alone and desperately facing Germany's superior might; moreover, this period would extend until Russia had clearly beat off the first German assault in the summer and fall of 1941, and would be able to fight Germany until the end. Here the cutoff point might be placed differently, say the summer of 1942, and certainly by Stalingrad. I shall not dwell on this, as the crucial matter is that under no conditions could Germany be allowed to win the war, and this for two basic reasons: first, the nature and history of constitutional democracy and its place in European culture; and second, the peculiar evil of Nazism and the enormous and uncalculable moral and political evil it represented for civilized society.

The peculiar evil of Nazism needs to be understood, since in some circumstances a democratic people might better accept defeat if the terms of peace offered by the adversary were reasonable and moderate, did not subject them to humiliation, and looked forward to a workable and decent political relationship. Yet characteristic of Hitler was that he accepted no possibility at all of a political relationship with his enemies. They were always to be cowed by terror and brutality, and ruled by force. From the beginning the campaign against Russia, for example, was a war of destruction against Slavic peoples, with the original inhabitants remaining, if at all, only as serfs. When Goebbels and others protested that the war could not be won that way, Hitler refused to listen.

Yet it is clear that while the extreme crisis exemption held for Britain in the early stages of the war, it never held at any time for the United States in its war with Japan. The principles of the conduct of war were always applicable to it. Indeed, in the case of Hiroshima many involved in higher reaches of the government recognized the questionable character of the bombing and that limits were being crossed. Yet during the discussions among allied leaders in June and July 1945, the weight of the practical means-end reasoning carried the day. Under the continuing pressure of war, such moral doubts as there were failed to gain an express and articulated view. As the war progressed, the heavy fire-bombing of civilians in the capitals of Berlin and Tokyo and elsewhere was increasingly accepted on the allied side. Although after the outbreak of war Roosevelt had urged both sides not to commit the inhuman barbarism of bombing civilians, by 1945 allied leaders came to assume that Roosevelt would have used the bomb on Hiroshima. The bombing grew out of what had happened before.

The practical means-end reasons to justify using the atomic bomb on Hiroshima were the following:

The bomb was dropped to hasten the end of the war. It is clear that Truman and most other allied leaders thought it would do that. Another reason was that it would save lives where the lives counted are the lives of American soldiers. The lives of Japanese, military or civilian, presumably counted for less. Here the calculations of least time and most lives saved were mutually supporting. Moreover, dropping the bomb would give the Emperor and the Japanese leaders a way to save face, an important matter given Japanese samurai culture. Indeed, at the end a few top Japanese leaders wanted to make a last sacrificial stand but were overruled by others supported by the Emperor, who ordered surrender on August 12, having received word from Washington that the Emperor could stay provided it was understood that he had to comply with the orders of the American military commander. The last reason I mention is that the bomb was dropped to impress the Russians with American power and make them more agreeable with our demands. This reason is highly disputed but is urged by some critics and scholars as important.

The failure of these reasons to reflect the limits on the conduct of war is evident, so I focus on a different matter: the failure of statesmanship on the part of allied leaders and why it might have occurred. Truman once described the Japanese as beasts and to be treated as such; yet how foolish it sounds now to call the Germans or the Japanese barbarians and beasts! Of the Nazis and Tojo militarists, yes, but they are not the German and the Japanese people. Churchill later granted that he carried the bombing too far, led by passion and the intensity of the conflict. A duty of statesmanship is not to allow such feelings, natural and inevitable as they may be, to alter the course a democratic people should best follow in striving for peace. The statesman understands that relations with the present enemy have special importance: for as I have said, war must be openly and publicly conducted in ways that make a lasting and amicable peace possible with a defeated enemy, and prepare its people for how they may expect to be treated. Their present fears of being subjected to acts of revenge and retaliation must be put to rest; present enemies must be seen as associates in a shared and just future peace.

These remarks make it clear that, in my judgment, both Hiroshima and the fire-bombing of Japanese cities were great evils that the duties of statesmanship require political leaders to avoid in the absence of the crisis exemption. I also believe this could have been done at little cost in further casualties. An invasion was unnecessary at that date, as the war was effectively over. However, whether that is true or not makes no difference. Without the crisis exemption, those bombings are great evils. Yet it is clear that an articulate expression of the principles of just war introduced at that time would not have altered the outcome. It was simply too late. A president or prime minister must have carefully considered these questions, preferably long before, or at least when they had the time and leisure to think things out. Reflections on just war cannot be heard in the daily round of the pressure of events near the end of the hostilities; too many are anxious and impatient, and simply worn out.

Similarly, the justification of constitutional democracy and the basis of the rights and duties it must respect should be part of the public political culture and discussed in the many associations of civic society as part of one's education. It is not clearly heard in day-to-day ordinary politics, but must be presupposed as the background, not the daily subject of politics, except in special circumstances. In the same way, there was not sufficient prior grasp of the fundamental importance of the principles of just war for the expression of them to have blocked the appeal of practical means-end reasoning in terms of a calculus of lives, or of the least time to end the war, or of some other balancing of costs and benefits. This practical reasoning justifies too much, too easily, and provides a way for a dominant power to quiet any moral worries that may arise. If the principles of war are put forward at that time, they easily become so many more considerations to be balanced in the scales.

Another failure of statesmanship was not to try to enter into negotiations with the Japanese before any drastic steps such as the fire-bombing of cities or the bombing of Hiroshima were taken. A conscientious attempt to do so was morally necessary. As a democratic people, we owed that to the Japanese people—whether to their government is another matter. There had been discussions in Japan for some time about finding a way to end the war, and on June 26 the government had been instructed by the Emperor to do so. It must surely have realized that with the navy destroyed and the outer islands taken, the war was lost. True, the Japanese were deluded by the hope that the Russians might prove to be their allies, but negotiations are precisely to disabuse the other side of delusions of that kind. A statesman is not free to consider that such negotiations may lessen the desired shock value of subsequent attacks.

Truman was in many ways a good, at times a very good president. But the way he ended the war showed he failed as a statesman. For him it was an opportunity missed, and a loss to the country and its armed forces as well. It is sometimes said that questioning the bombing of Hiroshima is an insult to the American troops who fought the war. This is hard to understand. We should be able to look back and consider our faults after fifty years. We expect the Germans and the Japanese to do that. . . . Why shouldn't we? It can't be that we think we waged the war without moral error!

None of this alters Germany's and Japan's responsibility for the war nor their behavior in conducting it. Emphatically to be repudiated are two nihilist doctrines. One is expressed by Sherman's remark, "War is hell," so anything goes to get it over with as soon as one can. The other says that we are all guilty so we stand on a level and no one can blame anyone else. These are both superficial and deny all reasonable distinctions; they are invoked falsely to try to excuse our misconduct or to plead that we cannot be condemned.

The moral emptiness of these nihilisms is manifest in the fact that just and decent civilized societies—their institutions and laws, their civil life and background culture and mores—all depend absolutely on making significant moral and political distinctions in all situations. Certainly war is a kind of hell, but why should that mean that all moral distinctions cease to hold? And granted also that sometimes all or nearly all may be to some degree guilty, that does not mean that all are equally so. There is never a time when we are free from all moral and political principles and restraints. These nihilisms are pretenses to be free of those principles and restraints that always apply to us fully.

CHAPTER 21

What Is Wrong with Terrorism?

Thomas Nagel

After the terrorist attacks of September 11, 2001, Thomas Nagel wrote this short piece about why terrorism is immoral. Professor Nagel (1937–) is jointly appointed in Philosophy and Law at New York University. He has written 10 books and over 100 articles.

People all over the world react with visceral horror to attacks on civilians by Al-Qaeda, by Palestinian suicide bombers, by Basque or Chechen separatists, or by IRA militants. As there now seems to be a pause in the spate of suicide bombings and other terrorist acts—if only momentary—perhaps now is a moment to grapple with a fundamental question: What makes *terrorist* killings any more worthy of condemnation than other forms of murder?

The special opprobrium associated with the word "terrorism" must be understood as a condemnation of means, not ends. Of course, those who condemn terrorist attacks on civilians often also reject the ends that the attackers are trying to achieve. They think that a separate Basque state, or the withdrawal of U.S. forces from the Middle East, for example, are not aims that anyone should be pursuing, let alone by violent means.

But the condemnation does not depend on rejecting the aims of the terrorists. The reaction to the attacks of September 11, 2001 on New York and Washington and their like underscores that such

From www.project-syndicate.org, November 2002. Reprinted by permission of Project Syndicate.

means are outrageous whatever the end; they should not be used to achieve even a good end—indeed, even if there is no other way to achieve it. The normal balancing of costs against benefits is not allowable here.

This claim is not as simple as it appears because it does not depend on a general moral principle forbidding all killing of non-combatants. Similarly, those who condemn terrorism as beyond the pale are usually not pacifists. They believe not only that it is all right to kill soldiers and bomb munitions depots in times of war, but that inflicting "collateral damage" on non-combatants is sometimes unavoidable—and morally permissible.

But if that is permissible, why is it wrong to aim *directly* at non-combatants if killing them will have a good chance of inducing the enemy to cease hostilities, withdraw from occupied territory, or grant independence? Dying is bad, however one is killed. So why should a civilian death be acceptable if it occurs as a side-effect of combat that serves a worthy end, whereas a civilian death that is inflicted deliberately as a means to the *same* end is a terrorist outrage?

The distinction is not universally accepted—certainly not by the major belligerents in World War II. Hiroshima is the most famous example of terror bombing, but the Germans, the Japanese, and the British as well as the Americans deliberately slaughtered civilian non-combatants in large numbers. Today, however, terrorism inspires widespread revulsion, which in turn helps to justify military action against it. So it is essential that the reason for that revulsion become better understood.

The core moral idea is a prohibition against *aiming* at the death of a harmless person. Everyone is presumed to be inviolable in this way until he himself becomes a danger to others; so we are permitted to kill in self-defense, and to attack enemy combatants in war. But this is an exception to a general and strict requirement of respect for human life. So long as we are not doing any harm, no one may kill us just because it would be useful to do so. This minimal basic respect is owed to *every* individual, and it may not be violated even to achieve valuable long-term goals.

However, there are some activities, including legitimate self-defense or warfare, that create an unavoidable risk of harm to innocent parties. This is true not only of violent military or police actions but also of peaceful projects like major construction in densely populated cities. In those cases, if the aim is important enough, the activity is not morally prohibited provided due care is taken to minimize the risk of harm to innocent parties, consistent with the achievement of the aim.

The moral point is that we are obliged to do our best to avoid or minimize civilian casualties in warfare, even if we know that we cannot avoid them completely. Those deaths do not violate the strictest protection of human life—that we may not *aim* to kill a harmless person. On the contrary, our aim is if possible to avoid such collateral deaths.

Of course, the victim ends up dead whether killed deliberately by a terrorist or regrettably as the side effect of an attack on a legitimate military target. But in our sense of what we are owed morally by our fellow human beings, there is a huge difference between these two acts, and the attitudes they express toward human life.

So long as it remains an effective means for weak parties to exert pressure on their more powerful enemies, terrorism cannot be expected to disappear. But we should hope nonetheless that the recognition of its special form of contempt for humanity will spread, rather than being lost as a result of its recent successes.

CHAPTER 22

The War on Terrorism and the End of Human Rights

David Luban

Terrorism is as old as human conflict. It is the poor man's war: if you are much weaker than your enemy, then you know you cannot march into his cities or land on his beaches without being annihilated. So, you try to achieve your goals or seek your revenge through stealth and surprise, which usually means attacking unarmed civilians. The weaker side has always, everywhere, used terrorist tactics.

Terrorism, understood in this way, will never disappear completely. There will always be violent factions who know they cannot win a fair fight. So, when President George W. Bush declared war on terrorism following the attacks of September 11, he was embarking on a war that can never be finally won. In this selection, David Luban explains how Bush's war on terrorism combined elements of what he calls the "war model" with elements of what he calls the "law model." This combination increased American power while decreasing the rights of both the enemy and the innocent bystander. It remains to be seen how Bush's successors, beginning with Barack Obama, will continue this struggle against America's enemies.

David Luban (1949–) is a professor at the Georgetown University Law Center in Washington, DC.

In the immediate aftermath of September 11, President Bush stated that the perpetrators of the deed would be brought to justice. Soon

From *War after September 11,* edited by Verna V. Gehring (Rowman & Littlefield, 2003), pp. 51–62. Reprinted by permission.

afterwards, the President announced that the United States would engage in a war on terrorism. The first of these statements adopts the familiar language of criminal law and criminal justice. It treats the September 11 attacks as horrific crimes—mass murders—and the government's mission as apprehending and punishing the surviving planners and conspirators for their roles in the crimes. The War on Terrorism is a different proposition, however, and a different model of governmental action—not law but war. Most obviously, it dramatically broadens the scope of action, because now terrorists who knew nothing about September 11 have been earmarked as enemies. But that is only the beginning.

The Hybrid War-Law Approach

The model of war offers much freer rein than that of law, and therein lies its appeal in the wake of 9/11. First, in war but not in law it is permissible to use lethal force on enemy troops regardless of their degree of personal involvement with the adversary. The conscripted cook is as legitimate a target as the enemy general. Second, in war but not in law "collateral damage," that is, foreseen but unintended killing of non-combatants, is permissible. (Police cannot blow up an apartment building full of people because a murderer is inside, but an air force can bomb the building if it contains a military target.) Third, the requirements of evidence and proof are drastically weaker in war than in criminal justice. Soldiers do not need proof beyond a reasonable doubt, or even proof by a preponderance of evidence, that someone is an enemy soldier before firing on him or capturing and imprisoning him. They don't need proof at all, merely plausible intelligence. Thus, the U.S. military remains regretful but unapologetic about its January 2002 attack on the Afghani town of Uruzgan, in which twenty-one innocent civilians were killed, based on faulty intelligence that they were al Qaeda fighters. Fourth, in war one can attack an enemy without concern over whether he has done anything. Legitimate targets are those who in the course of combat *might* harm us, not those who *have* harmed us. No doubt there are other significant differences as well. But the basic point should be clear: given Washington's mandate to eliminate the danger of future 9/11s, so far as humanly possible, the model of war offers important advantages over the model of law.

There are disadvantages as well. Most obviously, in war but not in law, fighting back is a *legitimate* response of the enemy. Second, when nations fight a war, other nations may opt for neutrality. Third, because fighting back is legitimate, in war the enemy soldier deserves special regard once he is rendered harmless through injury or surrender. It is impermissible to punish him for his role in fighting the war. Nor can he be harshly interrogated after he is captured. The Third Geneva Convention provides: "Prisoners of war who refuse to answer [questions] may not be threatened, insulted, or exposed to unpleasant or disadvantageous treatment of any kind." And, when the war concludes, the enemy soldier must be repatriated.

Here, however, Washington has different ideas, designed to eliminate these tactical disadvantages in the traditional war model. Washington regards international terrorism not only as a military adversary, but also as a criminal activity and criminal conspiracy. In the law model, criminals don't get to shoot back, and their acts of violence subject them to legitimate punishment. That is what we see in Washington's prosecution of the War on Terrorism. Captured terrorists may be tried before military or civilian tribunals, and shooting back at Americans, including American troops, is a federal crime. . . . Furthermore, the U.S. may rightly demand that other countries not be neutral about murder and terrorism. Unlike the war model, a nation may insist that those who are not with us in fighting murder and terror are against us, because by not joining our operations they are providing a safe haven for terrorists or their bank accounts. By selectively combining elements of the war model and elements of the law model, Washington is able to maximize its own ability to mobilize lethal force against terrorists while eliminating most traditional rights of a military adversary, as well as the rights of innocent bystanders caught in the crossfire.

A Limbo of Rightlessness

The legal status of al Qaeda suspects imprisoned at the Guantanamo Bay Naval Base in Cuba is emblematic of this hybrid war-law approach to the threat of terrorism. In line with the war model, they lack the usual rights of criminal suspects—the presumption of innocence, the right to a hearing to determine guilt, the opportunity to prove that the authorities have grabbed the wrong man. But, in line with the law model, they are considered *unlawful* combatants. Because they are not uniformed forces, they lack the rights of prisoners of war and are liable to criminal punishment. Initially, the American government declared that the Guantanamo Bay prisoners have no rights under the Geneva Conventions. In the face of international protests, Washington quickly backpedaled and announced that the Guantanamo Bay prisoners would indeed be treated as decently as POWs—but it also made clear that the prisoners have no right to such treatment. Neither criminal suspects nor POWs, neither fish nor fowl, they inhabit a limbo of rightlessness. . . .

More recently, two American citizens alleged to be al Qaeda operatives (Jose Padilla, a.k.a. Abdullah al Muhajir, and Yasser Esam Hamdi) have been held in American military prisons, with no crimes charged, no opportunity to consult counsel, and no hearing. The President described Padilla as "a bad man" who aimed to build a nuclear "dirty" bomb and use it against America; and the Justice Department has classified both men as "enemy combatants" who may be held indefinitely. Yet, as military law expert Gary Solis points out, "Until now, as used by the attorney general, the term 'enemy combatant' appeared nowhere in U.S. criminal law, international law or in the law of war." The phrase comes from the 1942 Supreme Court case *Ex parte Quirin,* but all the Court says there is that "an enemy combatant who without uniform comes secretly through the lines for the purpose of waging war by destruction of life or property" would "not . . . be entitled to the status of prisoner of war, but . . . [they would] be offenders against the law of war subject to trial and punishment by military tribunals." For the Court, in other words, the status of a person as a nonuniformed enemy combatant makes him a criminal rather than a warrior, and determines *where* he is tried (in a military, rather than a civilian, tribunal) but not *whether* he is tried. Far from authorizing open-ended confinement, *Ex parte Quirin* presupposes that criminals are entitled to hearings: without a hearing how can suspects prove that the government made a mistake? *Quirin* embeds the concept of "enemy combatant" firmly in the law model. In the war model, by contrast, POWs may be detained without a hearing until hostilities are over. But POWs were captured in uniform, and only their undoubted identity as enemy soldiers justifies such open-ended custody. Apparently, Hamdi and Padilla will get the worst of both models— open-ended custody with no trial, like POWs, but no certainty beyond the US government's say-so that they really are "bad men." This is the hybrid war-law model. It combines the *Quirin* category of "enemy combatant without uniform," used in the law model to justify a military trial, with the war model's practice of indefinite confinement with no trial at all.

The Case for the Hybrid Approach

Is there any justification for the hybrid war-law model, which so drastically diminishes the rights of the enemy? An argument can be offered along the following lines. In ordinary cases of war among states, enemy soldiers may well be morally and politically innocent. Many of them are conscripts, and those who aren't do not necessarily endorse the state policies they are fighting to defend. But enemy soldiers in the War on Terrorism are, by definition, those who have embarked on a path of terrorism. They are neither morally nor politically innocent. Their sworn aim—"Death to America!"—is to create more 9/11s. In this respect, they are much more akin to criminal conspirators than to conscript soldiers. Terrorists will fight as soldiers when they must, and metamorphose into mass murderers when they can.

Furthermore, suicide terrorists pose a special, unique danger. Ordinary criminals do not target innocent bystanders. They may be willing to kill them if necessary, but bystanders enjoy at least some measure of security because they are not primary targets. Not so with terrorists, who aim to kill as many innocent people as possible. Likewise, innocent bystanders are protected from ordinary criminals by whatever deterrent force the threat of punishment and the risk of getting killed in the act of committing a crime offer. For a suicide bomber, neither of these threats is a deterrent at all—after all, for the suicide bomber one of the hallmarks of a *successful* operation is that he winds up dead at day's end. Given the unique and heightened danger that suicide terrorists pose, a stronger response that grants potential terrorists fewer rights may be justified. Add to this the danger that terrorists may come to possess weapons of mass destruction, including nuclear devices in suitcases. Under circumstances of such dire menace, it is appropriate to treat terrorists as though they embody the most dangerous aspects of both warriors and criminals. That is the basis of the hybrid war-law model.

The Case against Expediency

The argument against the hybrid war-law model is equally clear. The U.S. has simply chosen the bits of the law model and the bits of the war model that are most convenient for American interests, and ignored the rest. The model abolishes the rights of potential enemies (and their innocent shields) by fiat—not for reasons of moral or legal principle, but solely because the U.S. does not want them to have rights.

The more rights they have, the more risk they pose. But Americans' urgent desire to minimize our risks doesn't make other people's rights disappear. Calling our policy a War on Terrorism obscures this point.

The theoretical basis of the objection is that the law model and the war model each comes as a package, with a kind of intellectual integrity. The law model grows out of relationships within states, while the war model arises from relationships between states. The law model imputes a ground-level community of values to those subject to the law. . . . Only because law imputes shared basic values to the community can a state condemn the conduct of criminals and inflict punishment on them. Criminals deserve condemnation and punishment because their conduct violates norms that we are entitled to count on their sharing. But . . . the government cannot simply grab them and confine them without making sure they have broken the law, nor can it condemn them without due process for ensuring that it has the right person, nor can it knowingly place bystanders in mortal peril in the course of fighting crime. They are our fellows, and the community should protect them just as it protects us. The same imputed community of values that justifies condemnation and punishment creates rights to due care and due process.

War is different. War is the ultimate acknowledgment that human beings do not live in a single community with shared norms. If their norms conflict enough, communities pose a physical danger to each other, and nothing can safeguard a community against its enemies except force of arms. That makes enemy soldiers legitimate targets; but it makes our soldiers legitimate targets as well, and, once the enemy no longer poses a danger, he should be immune from punishment, because if he has fought cleanly he has violated no norms that we are entitled to presume he honors. . . .

Because the law model and war model come as conceptual packages, it is unprincipled to wrench them apart and recombine them simply because it is in America's interest to do so. To declare that Americans can fight enemies with the latitude of warriors, but if the enemies fight back they are not warriors but criminals, amounts to a kind of heads-I-win-tails-you-lose international morality in which whatever it takes to reduce American risk, no matter what the cost to others, turns out to be justified. This, in brief, is the criticism of the hybrid war-law model.

To be sure, the law model could be made to incorporate the war model merely by rewriting a handful of statutes. Congress could enact laws permitting imprisonment or execution of persons who pose a significant threat of terrorism whether or not they have already done anything wrong. The standard of evidence could be set low and the requirement of a hearing eliminated. Finally, Congress could authorize the use of lethal force against terrorists regardless of the danger to innocent bystanders, and it could immunize officials from lawsuits or prosecution by victims of collateral damage. Such statutes would violate the Constitution, but the Constitution could be amended to incorporate antiterrorist exceptions to the Fourth, Fifth, and Sixth Amendments. In the end, we would have a system of law that includes all the essential features of the war model.

It would, however, be a system that imprisons people for their intentions rather than their actions, and that offers the innocent few protections against mistaken detention or inadvertent death through collateral damage. Gone are the principles that people should never be punished for their thoughts, only for their deeds, and that innocent people must be protected rather than injured by their own government. . . . The hypothetical legislation incorporates war into law only by making law as partisan and ruthless as war. It no longer resembles law as Americans generally understand it.

The Threat to International Human Rights

In the War on Terrorism, what becomes of international human rights? It seems beyond dispute that the war model poses a threat to international human rights, because honoring human rights is neither practically possible nor theoretically required during war. Combatants are legitimate targets; noncombatants maimed by accident or mistake are regarded as collateral damage rather than victims of atrocities; cases of mistaken identity get killed or confined without a hearing because combat conditions preclude due process. To be sure, the laws of war specify minimum human rights, but these are far less robust than rights in peacetime—and the hybrid war-law model reduces this schedule of rights even further by classifying the enemy as unlawful combatants. . . .

It is natural to suggest that this suspension of human rights is an exceptional emergency measure to deal with an unprecedented threat. This raises the question of how long human rights will remain suspended. When will the war be over?

Here, the chief problem is that the War on Terrorism is not like any other kind of war. The enemy, Terrorism, is not a territorial state or nation or government. There is no opposite number to negotiate with. There is no one on the other side to call a truce or declare a ceasefire, no one among the enemy authorized to surrender. In traditional wars among states, the war aim is to impose one state's political will on another's. The *aim* of the war is not to kill the enemy—killing the enemy is the *means* used to achieve the real end, which is to force capitulation. In the War on Terrorism, no capitulation is possible. That means that the real aim of the war is, quite simply, to kill or capture all of the terrorists—to keep on killing and killing, capturing and capturing, until they are all gone.

Of course, no one expects that terrorism will ever disappear completely. Everyone understands that new anti-American extremists, new terrorists, will always arise and always be available for recruitment and deployment. Everyone understands that even if al Qaeda is destroyed or decapitated, other groups, with other leaders, will arise in its place. It follows, then, that the War on Terrorism will be a war that can only be abandoned, never concluded. The War has no natural resting point, no moment of victory or finality. It requires a mission of killing and capturing, in territories all over the globe, that will go on in perpetuity. It follows as well that the suspension of human rights implicit in the hybrid war-law model is not temporary but permanent.

. . . The War on Terrorism has become a model of politics, a worldview with its own distinctive premises and consequences. As I have argued, it includes a new model of state action, the hybrid war-law model, which depresses human rights from their peacetime standard to the war-time standard, and indeed even further. So long as it continues, the War on Terrorism means the end of human rights, at least for those near enough to be touched by the fire of battle.

CHAPTER 23

*L*iberalism, Torture, and the Ticking Bomb

David Luban

After September 11, 2001, many Americans were afraid that Al-Qaeda terrorists would strike again. Ordinary citizens were apprehensive about riding on airplanes; rumors spread that terrorists might use a "dirty bomb" to destroy an American city; and Muslim-Americans dressed patriotically to avoid angry confrontations with strangers. Meanwhile, President George W. Bush's popularity soared—Americans wanted to believe in their leader.

In this climate of patriotism and fear, the Bush administration began using torture in its "War on Terror." The torturing was done in secret, because torture violates both international law and official American policy. Word began to leak out, however, and some people opposed this new development. But others defended the president: If a terrorist has planted a bomb in midtown Manhattan and won't tell you where it is, surely you would be willing to torture this information out of him?

In this selection, David Luban describes how unrealistic this "ticking bomb" scenario is, and how dangerous a policy of torture is in practice. Luban makes a strong case without even mentioning a number of military and geopolitical reasons not to torture: (1) If you torture the enemy, the enemy will be more likely to torture you; (2) the enemy will be less likely to surrender if they fear being tortured, so the battle will rage on; (3) the enemy may cite your harsh tactics in recruiting volunteers; (4) in a military occupation, torturing the enemy will turn the local population against you, thus resulting in more enemies

---

From the *Virginia Law Review*, vol. 91, no. 6 (October 2005), pp. 1425–1461. Reprinted by permission.

and fewer informants; (5) a country that violates human rights will find other countries less cooperative, both economically and militarily; (6) a country that breaks international law cannot object when other countries do the same; (7) someone being severely interrogated will answer a question, regardless of whether he knows the answer—he might make a guess; he might say what he thinks the interrogator wants to hear; or, he might have been trained to tell a particular lie; (8) a country that tortures will find it difficult to prosecute terrorists for crimes, because the defendants can always say that the evidence was obtained illegally, through torture; and (9) to obtain useful information, bribes often work better than torture—but once you start torturing, it's hard to develop a cooperative relationship with the enemy.

David Luban (1949–) is a professor at the Georgetown University Law Center in Washington, DC.

Torture used to be incompatible with American values. Our Bill of Rights forbids cruel and unusual punishment, and that has come to include all forms of corporal punishment except prison and death by methods purported to be painless. Americans and our government have historically condemned states that torture; we have granted asylum or refuge to those who fear it. The Senate ratified the Convention Against Torture, Congress enacted antitorture legislation, and judicial opinions spoke of "the dastardly and totally inhuman act of torture."

Then came September 11. Less than one week later, a feature story reported that a quiz in a university ethics class "gave four choices for the proper U.S. response to the terrorist attacks: A.) execute the perpetrators on sight; B.) bring them back for trial in the United States; C.) subject the perpetrators to an international tribunal; or D.) torture and interrogate those involved." Most students chose A and D—execute them on sight and torture them. Six weeks after September 11, the press reported that frustrated FBI interrogators were considering harsh interrogation tactics; a few weeks after that, the *New York Times* reported that torture had become a topic of conversation "in bars, on commuter trains, and at dinner tables." By mid-November 2001, the *Christian Science Monitor* found that thirty-two percent of surveyed Americans favored torturing terror suspects. Alan Dershowitz reported in 2002 that "[d]uring numerous public appearances since September 11, 2001, I have asked audiences for a show of hands as to how many would support the use of nonlethal torture in a ticking-bomb case. Virtually every hand is raised." American abhorrence to torture now appears to have extraordinarily shallow roots.

To an important extent, one's stance on torture runs independent of progressive or conservative ideology. Alan Dershowitz suggests that torture should be regulated by a judicial warrant requirement. Liberal Senator Charles Schumer has publicly rejected the idea "that torture should never, ever be used." He argues that most U.S. senators would back torture to find out where a ticking time bomb is planted. By contrast, William Safire, a self-described "conservative . . . and card-carrying hard-liner," expresses revulsion at "phony-tough" pro-torture arguments, and forthrightly labels torture "barbarism." Examples like these illustrate how vital it is to avoid a simple left-right reductionism. For the most part, American conservatives belong no less than progressives to liberal culture, broadly understood. Henceforth, when I speak of "liberalism," I mean it in the broad sense used by political philosophers from John Stuart Mill on, a sense that includes conservatives as well as progressives, so long as they believe in limited government and the importance of human dignity and individual rights. . . .

I. The Five Aims of Torture

What makes torture, the deliberate infliction of suffering and pain, especially abhorrent to liberals? This may seem like a bizarre question, because the answer seems self-evident: making people suffer is a horrible thing. Pain hurts and bad pain hurts badly. But let me pose the question in different terms. Realistically, the abuses of detainees at Abu Ghraib, Baghram, and Guantanamo pale by comparison with the death, maiming, and suffering in collateral damage during the Afghan and Iraq wars. Bombs crush limbs and burn people's faces off; nothing even remotely as horrifying has been reported in American prisoner abuse cases. Yet as much as we may regret or in some cases decry the wartime suffering of innocents, we do not seem to regard it with the special abhorrence that we do torture. This seems hypocritical and irrational, almost fetishistic, and it raises the question of what makes torture more illiberal than bombing and killing. The answer lies in the relationship between torturer and victim. The self-conscious aim of torture is to turn its victim into someone who is isolated, overwhelmed, terrorized, and humiliated. Torture aims to strip away from its victim all the qualities of human dignity that liberalism prizes. The torturer inflicts pain one-on-one, deliberately, up close and personal, in order to break the spirit of the victim—in other words, to tyrannize and dominate the victim. The relationship between them becomes a perverse parody of friendship and intimacy: intimacy transformed into its inverse image, where the torturer focuses on the victim's body with the intensity of a lover, except that every bit of that focus is bent to causing pain and tyrannizing the victim's spirit.

I am arguing that torture is a microcosm, raised to the highest level of intensity, of the tyrannical political relationships that liberalism hates the most. I have said that torture isolates and privatizes. Pain forcibly severs our concentration on anything outside of us; it collapses our horizon to our own body and the damage we feel in it. Even much milder sensations of prolonged discomfort can distract us so much that it becomes impossible to pay attention to anything else, as anyone knows who has had to go to the bathroom in a situation where it cannot be done. . . . The world of the man or woman in great pain is a world without relationships or engagements, a world without an exterior. It is a world reduced to a point, a world that makes no sense and in which the human soul finds no home and no repose.

And torture terrorizes. The body in pain winces; it trembles. The muscles themselves register fear. This is rooted in pain's biological function of impelling us in the most urgent way possible to escape from the source of pain—for that impulse is indistinguishable from panic. U.S. interrogators have reportedly used the technique of "waterboarding" to break the will of detainees. Waterboarding involves immersing the victim's face in water or wrapping it in a wet towel to induce drowning sensations. As anyone who has ever come close to drowning or suffocating knows, the oxygen-starved brain sends panic signals that overwhelm everything else. . . .

And torture humiliates. It makes the victim scream and beg; the terror makes him lose control of his bowels and bladder. The essence of cruelty is inflicting pain for the purpose of lording it over someone—we sometimes say "breaking" them—and the mechanism of cruelty is making the victim the audience of your own mastery. Cruelty always aims at humiliation. . . .

The predominant setting for torture has always been military victory. The victor captures the enemy and tortures him. . . .

Underneath whatever religious significance that attaches to torturing the vanquished, the victor tortures captives for the simplest of motives: to relive the victory, to demonstrate the absoluteness of his mastery, to rub the loser's face in it, and to humiliate the loser by making him scream and beg. For the victorious warrior, it's fun; it's entertainment. . . .

Already we can see why liberals abhor torture. Liberalism incorporates a vision of engaged, active human beings possessing an inherent dignity regardless of their social station. The victim of torture is in every respect the opposite of this vision. The torture victim is isolated and reduced instead of engaged and enlarged, terrified instead of active, humiliated instead of dignified. And, in the paradigm case of torture, the victor's torment of defeated captives, liberals perceive the living embodiment of their worst nightmare: tyrannical rulers who take their pleasure from the degradation of those unfortunate enough to be subject to their will.

There are at least four other historically significant reasons for torture besides victor's cruelty. . . .

First, there is torture for the purpose of terrorizing people into submission. Dictators from Hitler to Pinochet to Saddam Hussein tortured their political prisoners so that their enemies, knowing that they might face a fate far worse than death, would be afraid to oppose them. . . .

Second, until the last two centuries, torture was used as a form of criminal punishment. . . .

Curiously, when Beccaria writes explicitly about the subject of torture, he does not mention torture as punishment. Rather, he polemicizes against judicial torture in order to extract confessions from criminal suspects. This is the third historically significant use of torture, distinct from punishment, even though judges administer both. . . .

These, then, are the four illiberal motives for torture: victor's pleasure, terror, punishment, and extracting confessions. That leaves only one rationale for torture that might conceivably be acceptable to a liberal: torture as a technique of intelligence gathering from captives who will not talk. This may seem indistinguishable from torture to extract confessions, because both practices couple torture with interrogation. The crucial difference lies in the fact that the confession is backward-looking, in that it aims to document and ratify the past for purposes of retribution, while intelligence gathering is forward-looking because it aims to gain information to forestall future evils like terrorist attacks.

It is striking, and in obvious ways reassuring, that this is the only rationale for torture that liberal political culture admits could even possibly be legitimate. To speak in a somewhat perverse and paradoxical way, liberalism's insistence on limited governments that exercise their power only for . . . pragmatic purposes creates the possibility of seeing torture as a civilized . . . practice, provided that its sole purpose is preventing future harms. . . . But more importantly, the liberal rationale for torture as intelligence gathering in gravely dangerous situations transforms and rationalizes the motivation for torture. Now, for the first time, it becomes possible to think of torture as a last resort of men and women who are profoundly reluctant to torture. And in that way, liberals can for the first time think of torture dissociated from cruelty—torture authorized and administered by decent human beings who abhor what circumstances force them to do. Torture to gather intelligence and save lives seems almost heroic. For the first time, we can think of kindly torturers rather than tyrants. . . .

Let me summarize this part of my argument. Liberals, I have said, rank cruelty first among vices—not because liberals are more compassionate than anyone else, but because of the close connection between cruelty and tyranny. Torture is the living manifestation of cruelty, and the peculiar horror of torture within liberalism arises from the fact that torture is tyranny in microcosm, at its highest level of intensity. . . . It should hardly surprise us that liberals wish to ban torture absolutely—a wish that became legislative reality in the Torture Convention's insistence that nothing can justify torture.

But what about torture as intelligence gathering, torture to forestall greater evils? I suspect that throughout history this has been the least common motivation for torture, and thus the one most readily overlooked. And yet it alone bears no essential connection with tyranny. This is not to say that the torture victim experiences it as any less terrifying, humiliating, or tyrannical. . . . But the torturer's goal of forestalling greater evils is one that liberals share. It seems like a rational motivation, far removed from cruelty and power-lust. In fact, the liberal may for the first time find it possible to view torture from the torturer's point of view rather than the victim's.

Thus, even though absolute prohibition remains liberalism's primary teaching about torture, and the basic liberal stance is empathy for the torture victim, a more permissive stance remains an unspoken possibility. . . . As long as the intelligence needs of a liberal society are slight, this possibility within liberalism remains dormant. . . . But when a catastrophe like 9/11 happens, liberals may cautiously conclude that, in the words of a well-known *Newsweek* article, it is "Time to Think About Torture."

But the pressure of liberalism will compel them to think about it in a highly stylized and artificial way, what I will call the "liberal ideology of torture." The liberal ideology insists that the sole purpose of torture must be intelligence gathering to prevent a catastrophe; that torture is necessary to prevent the catastrophe; that torturing is the exception, not the rule, so that it has nothing to do with state tyranny; that those who inflict the torture are motivated solely by the looming catastrophe, with no tincture of cruelty; that torture in such circumstances is, in fact, little more than self-defense; and that, because of the associations of torture with the horrors of yesteryear, perhaps one should not even call harsh interrogation "torture."

And the liberal ideology will crystallize all of these ideas in a single, mesmerizing example: the ticking time bomb.

II. The Ticking Bomb

Suppose the bomb is planted somewhere in the crowded heart of an American city, and you have custody of the man who planted it. He won't talk. Surely, the hypothetical suggests, we shouldn't be too squeamish to torture the information out of him and save hundreds of lives. Consequences count, and abstract moral prohibitions must yield to the calculus of consequences.

Everyone argues the pros and cons of torture through the ticking time bomb. Senator Schumer and Professor Dershowitz, the Israeli Supreme Court and indeed every journalist devoting a think-piece to the unpleasant question of torture, begins with the ticking time bomb and ends there as well. . . . I mean to disarm the ticking time bomb and argue that it is the wrong thing to think about. If so, then the liberal ideology of torture begins to unravel.

But before beginning these arguments, I want to pause and ask why this jejune example has become the alpha and omega of our thinking about torture. I believe the answer is this: The ticking time bomb is proffered against liberals who believe in an absolute prohibition against torture. The idea is to force the liberal prohibitionist to admit that yes, even he or even she would agree to torture in at least this one situation. Once the prohibitionist admits that, then she has conceded that her opposition to torture is not based on principle. Now that the prohibitionist has admitted that her moral principles can be breached, all that is left is haggling about the price. No longer can the prohibitionist claim the moral high ground; no longer can she put the burden of proof on her opponent. She is down in the mud with them, and the only question left is how much further down she will go. Dialectically, getting the prohibitionist to address the ticking time bomb is like getting the vegetarian to eat just one little oyster because it has no nervous system. Once she does that—*gotcha!*

The ticking time-bomb scenario serves a second rhetorical goal, one that is equally important to the proponent of torture. It makes us see the torturer in a different light. . . . Now, he is not a cruel man or a sadistic man or a coarse, insensitive brutish man. The torturer is instead a conscientious public servant, heroic the way that New York firefighters were heroic, willing to do desperate things only because the plight is so desperate and so many innocent lives are weighing on the public servant's conscience. . . .

Wittgenstein once wrote that confusion arises when we become bewitched by a picture. He meant that it's easy to get seduced by simplistic examples that look compelling but actually misrepresent the world in which we live. If the subject is the morality of torture, philosophical confusions can have life-or-death consequences. I believe the ticking time bomb is the picture that bewitches us.

I don't mean that the time-bomb scenario is completely unreal. To take a real-life counterpart: in 1995, an al Qaeda plot to bomb eleven U.S. airliners and assassinate the Pope was thwarted by information tortured out of a Pakistani bomb-maker by the Philippine police. According to journalists Marites Dañguilan Vitug and Glenda M. Gloria, the police had received word of possible threats against the Pope. They went to work. "For weeks, agents hit him with a chair and a long piece of wood, forced water into his mouth, and crushed lighted cigarettes into his private parts. . . . His ribs were almost totally broken, and his captors were surprised that he survived. . . ." Grisly, to be sure—but if they hadn't done it, thousands of innocent travelers might have died horrible deaths.

But look at the example one more time. The Philippine agents were surprised he survived—in other words, they came close to torturing him to death *before* he talked. And they tortured him *for weeks,* during which time they didn't know about any specific al Qaeda plot. What if he too didn't know? Or what if there had been no al Qaeda plot? Then they would have tortured him for weeks, possibly tortured him to death, for nothing. For all they knew at the time, that is exactly what they were doing. You cannot use the argument that preventing the al Qaeda attack justified the decision to torture, because *at the moment the decision was made* no one knew about the al Qaeda attack.

The ticking-bomb scenario cheats its way around these difficulties by stipulating that the bomb is there, ticking away, and that officials know it and know they have the man who planted it. Those conditions will seldom be met. Let us try some more realistic hypotheticals and the questions they raise:

1. The authorities know there may be a bomb plot in the offing, and they have captured a man who may know something about it, but may not. Torture him? How much? For weeks? For months? The chances are considerable that you are torturing a man with nothing to tell you. If he doesn't talk, does that mean it's time to stop, or time to ramp up the level of torture? How likely does it have to be that he knows something important? Fifty-fifty? Thirty-seventy? Will one out of a hundred suffice to land him on the waterboard?

2. Do you really want to make the torture decision by running the numbers? A one-percent chance of saving a thousand lives yields ten statistical lives. Does that mean that you can torture up to nine people on a one-percent chance of finding crucial information?

3. The authorities think that one out of a group of fifty captives in Guantanamo might know where Osama bin Laden is hiding, but they do not know which captive. Torture them all? That is: Do you torture forty-nine captives with nothing to tell you on the uncertain chance of capturing bin Laden?

4. For that matter, would capturing Osama bin Laden demonstrably save a single human life? . . . Or does it not matter whether torture is intended to save human lives from a specific threat, as long as it furthers some goal in the War on Terror? This last question is especially important once we realize that the interrogation of al Qaeda suspects will almost never be employed to find out where the ticking bomb is hidden. Instead, interrogation is a more general fishing expedition for any intelligence that might be used to help "unwind" the terrorist organization. Now one might reply that al Qaeda is itself the ticking time bomb, so that unwinding the organization meets the formal conditions of the ticking-bomb hypothetical. This is equivalent to asserting that any intelligence that promotes victory in the War on Terror justifies torture. . . . But at this point, we verge on declaring all military threats and adversaries that menace American civilians to be ticking bombs whose defeat justifies torture. The limitation of torture to emergency exceptions, implicit in the ticking-bomb story, now threatens to unravel, making torture a legitimate instrument of military policy. And then the question becomes inevitable: Why not torture in pursuit of any worthwhile goal?

5. Indeed, if you are willing to torture forty-nine innocent people to get information from the one who has it, why stop there? If suspects will not break under torture, why not torture their loved ones in front of them? They are no more innocent than the forty-nine you have already shown you are prepared to torture. In fact, if only the numbers matter, torturing loved ones is almost a no-brainer if you think it will work. Of course, you won't know until you try whether torturing his child will break the suspect. But that just changes the odds; it does not alter the argument.

The point of the examples is that in a world of uncertainty and imperfect knowledge, the ticking-bomb scenario should not form the point of reference. The ticking bomb is the picture that bewitches us. The real debate is not between one guilty man's pain and hundreds of innocent lives. It is the debate between the certainty of anguish and the mere possibility of learning something vital and saving lives. And, above all, it is the question about whether a responsible citizen must unblinkingly think the unthinkable and accept that the morality of torture should be decided purely by totaling up costs and benefits. Once you accept that only the numbers count, then anything, no matter how gruesome, becomes possible. . . .

III. Torture as a Practice

There is a second, insidious, error built into the ticking-bomb hypothetical. It assumes a single, ad hoc decision about whether to torture, by officials who ordinarily would do no such thing except in a desperate emergency. But in the real world of interrogations, decisions are not made one-off. The real world is a world of policies, guidelines, and directives. It is a world of *practices*, not of ad hoc emergency measures. Therefore, any responsible discussion of torture must address the practice of torture, not the ticking-bomb hypothetical. I am not saying anything original here; other writers have made exactly this point. But somehow, we always manage to forget this and circle back to the ticking time bomb. . . .

Treating torture as a practice rather than as a desperate improvisation in an emergency means changing the subject from the ticking bomb to other issues like these: Should we create a professional cadre of trained torturers? That means a group of interrogators who know the techniques, who learn to overcome their instinctive revulsion against causing physical pain, and who acquire the legendary surgeon's arrogance about their own infallibility. . . . Should universities create an undergraduate course in torture? Or should the subject be offered only in police and military academies? Do we want federal grants for research to devise new and better techniques? Patents issued on high-tech torture devices? Companies competing to manufacture them? Trade conventions in Las Vegas? Should there be a medical sub-specialty of torture doctors, who ensure that captives do not die before they talk? The questions amount to this: Do we really want to create a torture culture and the kind of people who inhabit it? The ticking time bomb distracts us from the real issue, which is not about emergencies, but about the normalization of torture.

Perhaps the solution is to keep the practice of torture secret in order to avoid the moral corruption that comes from creating a public culture of torture. But this so-called "solution" does not reject the normalization of torture. It accepts it, but layers on top of it the normalization of state secrecy. The result would be a shadow culture of torturers and those who train and support them, operating outside the public eye and accountable only to other insiders of the torture culture.

Just as importantly: Who guarantees that case-hardened torturers, inured to levels of violence and pain that would make ordinary people vomit at the sight, will know where to draw the line on when torture should be used? They rarely have in the past. They didn't in Algeria. They didn't in Israel, where in 1999, the Israeli Supreme Court backpedaled from an earlier consent to torture lite because the interrogators were running amok and torturing two-thirds of their Palestinian captives. In the Argentinian Dirty War, the tortures began because terrorist cells had a policy of fleeing when one of their members had disappeared for forty-eight hours, leaving authorities two days to wring the information out of the captive. Mark Osiel, who has studied the Argentinean military in the Dirty War, reports that many of the torturers initially had qualms about what they were doing, until their priests reassured them that they were fighting God's fight.

By the end of the Dirty War, the qualms were gone, and, as John Simpson and Jana Bennett report, hardened young officers were placing bets on who could kidnap the prettiest girl to rape and torture. Escalation is the rule, not the aberration.

There are two fundamental reasons for this: one rooted in the nature of bureaucracy and the other in social psychology. The liberal ideology of torture presupposes a torturer impelled by the desire to stop a looming catastrophe, not by cruelty. Implicitly, this image presumes that the interrogator and the decisionmaker are the same person. But the defining fact about real organizations is the division of labor. The person who decides whether this prisoner presents a genuine ticking-bomb case is not the interrogator. The decision about what counts as a ticking-bomb case—one where torture is the lesser evil—depends on complex value judgments, and these are made further up the chain of command. The interrogator simply executes decisions made elsewhere.

Interrogators do not inhabit a world of loving kindness, or of equal concern and respect for all human beings. Interrogating resistant prisoners non-violently and non-abusively still requires a relationship that in any other context would be morally abhorrent. It requires tricking information out of the subject, and the interrogator does this by setting up elaborate scenarios to disorient the subject and propel him into an alternative reality. The subject must be deceived into thinking that his high-value intelligence has already been revealed by someone else, so that it is no longer of any value. He must be fooled into thinking that his friends have betrayed him or that the interrogator is his friend. The interrogator disrupts his sense of time and place, disorients him with sessions that never take place at predictable times or intervals, and manipulates his emotions. The very names of interrogation techniques show this: "Emotional Love," "Emotional Hate," "Fear Up Harsh," "Fear Up Mild," "Reduced Fear," "Pride and Ego Up," "Pride and Ego Down," "Futility." The interrogator may set up a scenario to make the subject think he is in the clutches of a much-feared secret police organization from a different country ("False Flag"). Every bit of the subject's environment is fair game for manipulation and deception, as the interrogator aims to create the total lie that gets the subject talking.

. . . The liberal fiction that interrogation can be done by people who are neither cruel nor tyrannical runs aground on the fact that regardless of the interrogator's character off the job, on the job, every fiber of his concentration is devoted to dominating the mind of the subject.

Only one thing prevents this from turning into abuse and torture, and that is a clear set of bright-line rules, drummed into the interrogator with the intensity of a religious indoctrination, complete with warnings of fire and brimstone. . . .

But what happens when the line is breached? When, as in Afghanistan, the interrogator gets mixed messages about whether Geneva applies, or hears rumors of ghost detainees, of high-value captives held for years of interrogation in the top-secret facility known as "Hotel California," located in some nation somewhere? Or when the interrogator observes around him the move from deception to abuse, from abuse to torture lite, from torture lite to beatings and waterboarding? Without clear lines, the tyranny innate in the interrogator's job has nothing to hold it in check. Perhaps someone, somewhere in the chain of command, is wringing hands over whether this interrogation qualifies as a ticking-bomb case; but the interrogator knows only that the rules of the road have changed and the posted speed limits no longer apply. The liberal fiction of the conscientious interrogator overlooks a division of moral labor in which the person with the fastidious conscience and the person doing the interrogation are not the same.

The fiction must presume, therefore, that the interrogator operates only under the strictest supervision, in a chain of command where his every move gets vetted and controlled by the superiors who are actually doing the deliberating. The trouble is that this assumption flies in the face of everything that we know about how organizations work. The basic rule in every bureaucratic organization is that operational details and the guilty knowledge that goes with them get pushed down the chain of command as far as possible. . . .

We saw this phenomenon at Abu Ghraib, where military intelligence officers gave military police vague orders like: "'Loosen this guy up for us;' 'Make sure he has a bad night.' 'Make sure he gets the treatment.'" Suppose that the eighteen-year-old guard interprets "[m]ake sure he has a bad night" to mean, simply, "keep him awake all night." How do you do that without physical abuse? Furthermore, personnel at Abu Ghraib witnessed far harsher treatment of prisoners by "other governmental agencies" (OGA), a euphemism for the Central Intelligence Agency. They saw OGA spirit away the dead body of an interrogation subject, and allegedly witnessed a contract employee rape a youthful prisoner. When that is what you see, abuses like those in the Abu Ghraib photos will not look outrageous. Outrageous compared with what?

This brings me to the point of social psychology. Simply stated, it is this: we judge right and wrong against the baseline of whatever we have come to consider "normal" behavior, and if the norm shifts in the direction of violence, we will come to tolerate and accept violence as a normal response. . . . I will illustrate the point with the most salient example. This is the famous Stanford Prison Experiment. Male volunteers were divided randomly into two groups who would simulate the guards and inmates in a mock prison. Within a matter of days, the inmates began acting like actual prison inmates—depressed, enraged, and anxious. And the guards began to abuse the inmates to such an alarming degree that the researchers had to halt the two-week experiment after just seven days. . . . It took only five days before a guard, who prior to the experiment described himself as a pacifist, was forcing greasy sausages down the throat of a prisoner who refused to eat; and in less than a week, the guards were placing bags over prisoners' heads, making them strip, and sexually humiliating them in ways reminiscent of Abu Ghraib.

My conclusion is very simple. Abu Ghraib is the fully predictable image of what a torture culture looks like. Abu Ghraib is not a few bad apples—it is the apple tree. And you cannot reasonably expect that interrogators in a torture culture will be the fastidious and well-meaning torturers that the liberal ideology fantasizes. . . .

For all these reasons, the ticking-bomb scenario is an intellectual fraud. In its place, we must address the real questions about torture—questions about uncertainty, questions about the morality of consequences, and questions about what it does to a culture and the torturers themselves to introduce the practice. Once we do so, I suspect that few Americans will be willing to accept that everything is possible. . . .

CHAPTER 24

A Defense of the Death Penalty

Louis P. Pojman

Louis P. Pojman (1935–2005) was Professor Emeritus at the United States Military Academy. He argues that the death penalty is justified for two reasons: it gives killers what they deserve, and it effectively deters potential killers. However, he does not believe that the death penalty should be used *only* on those who murder.

Who so sheddeth man's blood, by man shall his blood be shed.
(Genesis 9:6)

There is an ancient tradition, going back to biblical times, but endorsed by the mainstream of philosophers, from Plato to Thomas Aquinas, from Thomas Hobbes to Immanuel Kant, Thomas Jefferson, John Stuart Mill, and C. S. Lewis, that a fitting punishment for murder is the execution of the murderer. One prong of this tradition, the *backward-looking* or deontological position, epitomized in Aquinas and Kant, holds that because human beings, as rational agents, have dignity, one who with malice aforethought kills a human being forfeits his right to life and deserves to die. The other, the *forward-looking* or consequentialist, tradition, exemplified by Jeremy Bentham, Mill, and Ernest van den Haag, holds that punishment ought to serve as a deterrent, and that capital punishment is an adequate deterrent to prospective murderers. . . . I will argue that both traditional defenses are sound and together they make a strong case for retaining the death penalty. That is, I hold a combined theory of punishment. A backward-looking

Excerpted from Louis P. Pojman, "Why the Death Penalty Is Morally Permissible," in *Debating the Death Penalty*, edited by Hugo Adam Bedau and Paul G. Cassell (Oxford University Press, 2004), pp. 51–75. Reprinted by permission of Oxford University Press.

judgment that the criminal has committed a heinous crime plus a forward-looking judgment that a harsh punishment will deter would-be murderers is sufficient to justify the death penalty. I turn first to the retributivist theory in favor of capital punishment.

Retribution

> . . . I remember the grocer's wife. She was a plump, happy woman who enjoyed the long workday she shared with her husband in their ma-and-pa store. One evening, two young men came in and showed guns, and the grocer gave them everything in the cash register.
>
> For no reason, almost as an afterthought, one of the men shot the grocer in the face. The woman stood only a few feet from her husband when he was turned into a dead, bloody mess.
>
> She was about 50 when it happened. In a few years her mind was almost gone, and she looked 80. They might as well have killed her too. . . .

Human beings have dignity as self-conscious rational agents who are able to act morally. One could maintain that it is precisely their moral goodness or innocence that bestows dignity and a right to life on them. Intentionally taking the life of an innocent human being is so evil that absent mitigating circumstances, the perpetrator forfeits his own right to life. He or she deserves to die.

The retributivist holds three propositions: (1) that all the guilty deserve to be punished; (2) that only the guilty deserve to be punished; and (3) that the guilty deserve to be punished in proportion to the severity of their crime. . . .

Criminals like Steven Judy, Jeffrey Dahmer, Timothy McVeigh, Ted Bundy (who is reported to have raped and murdered over 100 women), John Mohammed and John Lee Malvo, who murdered 12 people in the killing spree of 2002, and the two men who gunned down the grocer have committed capital offenses and deserve nothing less than capital punishment. No doubt malicious acts like the ones committed by these criminals deserve worse punishment than death, and I would be open to suggestions of torture (why not?), but at a minimum, the death penalty seems warranted.

People often confuse *retribution* with *revenge.* . . . While moral people will feel outrage at acts of heinous crimes, the moral justification of punishment is not *vengeance,* but *desert.* Vengeance signifies inflicting harm on the offender out of anger because of what he has done. Retribution is the rationally supported theory that the criminal deserves a punishment fitting the gravity of his crime. . . .

Our natural instinct is for *vengeance,* but civilization demands that we restrain our anger and go through a legal process, letting the outcome determine whether and to what degree to punish the accused. Civilization demands that we not take the law into our own hands, but it should also satisfy our deepest instincts when they are consonant with reason. Our instincts tell us that some crimes, like McVeigh's, Judy's, and Bundy's, should be severely punished, but we refrain from personally carrying out those punishments, committing ourselves to the legal processes. The death penalty is supported by our gut animal instincts as well as our sense of justice as desert.

The death penalty reminds us that there are consequences to our actions, that we are responsible for what we do, so that dire consequences for immoral actions are eminently appropriate. The death penalty is such a fitting response to evil.

Deterrence

The second tradition justifying the death penalty is the utilitarian theory of deterrence. This holds that by executing convicted murderers we will deter would-be murderers from killing innocent people. The evidence for deterrence is controversial. . . . However, one often hears abolitionists claiming the evidence shows that the death penalty fails to deter homicide. This is too strong a claim. The sociological evidence doesn't show either that the death penalty deters or that it fails to deter. The evidence is simply inconclusive. But a common-sense case can be made for deterrence.

Imagine that every time someone intentionally killed an innocent person he was immediately struck down by lightning. When mugger Mike slashed his knife into the neck of the elderly pensioner, lightning struck, killing Mike. His fellow muggers witnessed the sequence of events. When burglar Bob pulled his pistol out and shot the bank teller through her breast, a bolt leveled Bob, his compatriots beholding the spectacle. Soon men with their guns lying next to them were found all across the world in proximity to the corpses of their presumed victims. Do you think that the evidence of cosmic retribution would go unheeded?

We can imagine the murder rate in the United States and everywhere else plummeting. The close correlation between murder and cosmic retribution would serve as a deterrent to would-be murderers. If this thought experiment is sound, we have a prima facie argument for the deterrent effect of capital punishment. In its ideal, prompt performance, the death penalty would likely deter. . . . The question then becomes how do we institute the death penalty so as to have the maximal deterrent effect without violating the rights of the accused.

We would have to bring the accused to trial more quickly and limit the appeals process of those found guilty "beyond reasonable doubt." Having DNA evidence should make this more feasible than hitherto. Furthermore, public executions of the convicted murderer would serve as a reminder that crime does not pay. Public executions of criminals seem an efficient way to communicate the message that if you shed innocent blood, you will pay a high price. . . .

Common sense informs us that most people would prefer to remain out of jail, that the threat of public humiliation is enough to deter some people, that a sentence of 20 years will deter most people more than a sentence of two years, that a life sentence will deter most would-be criminals more than a sentence of 20 years. I think that we have commonsense evidence that the death penalty is a better deterrent than prison sentences. For one thing, as Richard Herrnstein and James Q. Wilson have argued in *Crime and Human Nature,* a great deal of crime is committed on a cost-benefit schema, wherein the criminal engages in some form of risk assessment as to his or her chances of getting caught and punished in some manner. If he or she estimates the punishment mild, the crime becomes inversely attractive, and vice versa. The fact that those who are condemned to death do everything in their power to get their sentences postponed or reduced to long-term prison sentences, in the way *lifers* do not, shows that they fear death more than life in prison. . . .

Former Prosecuting Attorney for the State of Florida, Richard Gernstein, has set forth the commonsense case for deterrence. First of all, he claims, the death penalty certainly deters the murderer from any further murders, including those he or she might commit within the prison where he is confined. Second, statistics cannot tell us how many potential criminals have refrained from taking another's life through fear of the death penalty. He quotes Judge Hyman Barshay of New York: "The death penalty is a warning, just like a lighthouse throwing its beams out to sea. We hear about shipwrecks, but we do not hear about the ships the lighthouse guides safely on their way. We do not have proof of the number of ships it saves, but we do not tear the lighthouse down."

Some of the commonsense evidence is anecdotal. . . . Growing up in the infamous Cicero, Illinois, home of Al Capone and the Mafia, I had friends who went into crime, mainly burglary and larceny. It was common knowledge that one stopped short of killing in the act of robbery. A prison sentence could be dealt with—especially with a good lawyer—but being convicted of murder, which at that time included a reasonable chance of being electrocuted, was an altogether different matter. No doubt exists in my mind that the threat of the electric chair saved the lives of some of those who were robbed in my town. . . .

It seems likely that the death penalty does not deter as much as it could due to its inconsistent and rare use. For example, . . . in 1994, there were 23,305 cases of murder and nonnegligent manslaughter and only 31 executions—for a ratio of better than 750 to 1. The average length of stay for a prisoner executed in 1994 was 10 years and two months. If potential murderers perceived the death penalty as a highly probable outcome of murder, would they not be more reluctant to kill? . . .

The late Ernest van den Haag has set forth what he called the Best Bet Argument. He argued that even though we don't know for certain whether the death penalty deters or prevents other murders, we should bet that it does. Indeed, due to our ignorance, any social policy we take is a gamble. Not to choose capital punishment for first-degree murder is as much a bet that capital punishment doesn't deter as choosing the policy is a bet that it does. There is a significant difference in the betting, however, in that to bet against capital punishment is to bet against the innocent and for the murderer, while to bet for it is to bet against the murderer and for the innocent. . . .

Suppose that we choose a policy of capital punishment for capital crimes. In this case we are betting that the death of some murderers will be more than compensated for by the lives of some innocents not being murdered (either by these murderers or others who would have murdered). If we're right, we have saved the lives of the innocent. If we're wrong, unfortunately, we've sacrificed the lives of some murderers. But say we choose not to have a social policy of capital punishment. If capital punishment doesn't work as a deterrent, we've come out ahead, but if it does work, then we've missed an opportunity to save innocent lives. If we value the saving of innocent lives more highly than the loss of the guilty, then to bet on a policy of capital punishment turns out to be rational. Since the innocent have a greater right to life than the guilty, it is our moral duty to adopt a policy that has a chance of protecting them from potential murderers. . . .

If the Best Bet Argument is sound, or if the death penalty does deter would-be murderers, as common sense suggests, then we should support some uses of the death penalty. It should be used for those who commit first-degree murder, for whom no mitigating factors are present, and especially for those who murder police officers, prison guards, and political leaders. Many states rightly favor it for those who murder while committing another crime, such as burglary or rape. It should be used in cases of treason and terrorist bombings. It should also be considered for the perpetrators of egregious white collar crimes such as bank managers embezzling the savings of the public. . . .

Let me consider two objections often made to the implementation of the death penalty: that it sometimes leads to the death of innocents and that it discriminates against blacks.

Objection 1: Miscarriages of justice occur. Capital punishment is to be rejected because of human fallibility in convicting innocent parties and sentencing them to death. In a survey done in 1985, Hugo Adam Bedau and Michael Radelet found that of the 7,000 persons executed in the United States between 1900 and 1985, 25 were innocent of capital crimes. While some compensation is available to those unjustly imprisoned, the death sentence is irrevocable. We can't compensate the dead. As John Maxton, a member of the British Parliament puts it, "If we allow one innocent person to be executed, morally we are committing the same, or, in some ways, a worse crime than the person who committed the murder."

Response: Mr. Maxton is incorrect in saying that mistaken judicial execution is morally the same as or worse than murder, for a deliberate intention to kill the innocent occurs in a murder, whereas no such intention occurs in wrongful capital punishment.

Sometimes the objection is framed this way: It is better to let ten criminals go free than to execute one innocent person. If this dictum is a call for safeguards, then it is well taken; but somewhere there seems to be a limit on the tolerance of society toward capital offenses. Would these abolitionists argue that it is better that 50 or 100 or 1,000 murderers go free than that one innocent person be executed? Society has a right to protect itself from capital offenses even if this means taking a finite chance of executing an innocent person. If the basic activity or process is justified, then it is regrettable, but morally acceptable, that some mistakes are made. Fire trucks occasionally kill innocent pedestrians while racing to fires, but we accept these losses as justified by the greater good of the activity of using fire trucks. We judge the use of automobiles to be acceptable even though such use causes an average of 50,000 traffic fatalities each year. We accept the morality of a defensive war even though it will result in our troops accidentally or mistakenly killing innocent people. . . .

The abolitionist is incorrect in arguing that death is different from long-term prison sentences because it is irrevocable. Imprisonment also takes good things away from us that may never be returned. We cannot restore to the inmate the freedom or opportunities he or she lost. Suppose an innocent 25-year-old man is given a life sentence for murder. Thirty years later the error is discovered and he is set free. Suppose he values three years of freedom to every one year of life. That is, he would rather live 10 years as a free man than 30 as a prisoner. Given this man's values, the criminal justice system has taken the equivalent of 10 years of life from him. If he lives until he is 65, he has, as far as his estimation is concerned, lost 10 years, so that he may be said to have lived only 55 years.

The numbers in this example are arbitrary, but the basic point is sound. Most of us would prefer a shorter life of higher quality to a longer one of low quality. Death prevents all subsequent quality, but imprisonment also irrevocably harms one by diminishing the quality of life of the prisoner.

Objection 2: The second objection made against the death penalty is that it is unjust because it discriminates against the poor and minorities, particularly African Americans, over rich people and whites. . . .

Response: First of all, it is not true that a law that is applied in a discriminatory manner is unjust. . . . The discriminatory application, not the law itself, is unjust. . . . For example, a friend once got two speeding tickets during a 100-mile trip (having borrowed my car). He complained to the police officer who gave him his second ticket that many drivers were driving faster than he was at the time. They had escaped detection, he argued, so it wasn't fair for him to get two tickets on one trip. The officer acknowledged the imperfections of the system but, justifiably, had no qualms about giving him the second ticket. . . . Discriminatory practices should be reformed, and in many cases they can be. But imperfect practices in themselves do not entail that the laws engendering these practices themselves are unjust. . . .

. . . If we concluded that we should abolish a rule or practice, unless we treated everyone exactly by the same rules all the time, we would have to abolish, for example, traffic laws and laws against imprisonment for rape, theft, and even murder. Carried to its logical limits, we would also have to refrain from saving drowning victims if a number of people were drowning but we could only save a few of them. Imperfect justice is the best that we humans can attain. We should reform our practices as much as possible to eradicate unjust discrimination wherever we can, but if we are not allowed to have a law without perfect application, we will be forced to have no laws at all.

Nathanson . . . argues that the case of death is different. "Because of its finality and extreme severity of the death penalty, we need to be more scrupulous in applying it as punishment than is necessary with any other punishment." The retentionist agrees that the death penalty is a severe punishment and that we need to be scrupulous in applying it. The difference between the abolitionist and the reten- tionist seems to lie in whether we are wise and committed enough as a nation to reform our institutions so that they approximate fairness. Apparently, Nathanson is pessimistic here, whereas I have faith in our ability to learn from our mistakes and reform our systems. If we can't reform our legal system, what hope is there for us?

More specifically, the charge that a higher percentage of blacks than whites are executed was once true but is no longer so. Many states have made significant changes in sentencing procedures, with the result that currently whites convicted of first-degree murder are sentenced to death at a higher rate than blacks. . . .

Abolitionists often make the complaint that only the poor get death sentences for murder. If their trials are fair, then they deserve the death penalty, but rich murderers may be equally deserving. At the moment only first-degree murder and treason are crimes deemed worthy of the death penalty. Perhaps our notion of treason should be expanded to include those who betray the trust of the public: cor- poration executives who have the trust of ordinary people, but who, through selfish and dishonest practices, ruin their lives. As noted above, my proposal is to consider broadening, not narrowing, the scope of capital punishment, to include business personnel who unfairly harm the public. The executives in the recent corporation scandals who bailed out of sinking corporations with golden, million- dollar lifeboats while the pension plans of thousands of employees went to the bottom of the economic ocean, may deserve severe pun- ishment, and if convicted, they should receive what they deserve. My guess is that the threat of the death sentence would have a deterrent effect here. Whether it is feasible to apply the death penalty for hor- rendous white-collar crimes is debatable. But there is something to be said in its favor. It would remove the impression that only the poor get executed. . . .

CHAPTER 25

Why the United States Will Join the Rest of the World in Abandoning Capital Punishment

Stephen B. Bright

As a nation that executes prisoners, the United States is in poor company. Most countries with the death penalty are terrible violators of human rights. In 2007, the top executors in the world were China, Iran, Saudi Arabia, Pakistan, and the USA.

However, even where the death penalty is used—in about 33% of the world's countries—it is not used very much. In 2008, the United States executed only 37 prisoners. Most death-row inmates in America will never be executed; they will die of natural causes.

Stephen B. Bright (1948–) believes that the United States should and will get out of the execution business. Mr. Bright is president and senior counsel at the Southern Center for Human Rights in Atlanta, Georgia.

The United States will inevitably join other industrialized nations in abandoning the death penalty, just as it has abandoned whipping, the stocks, branding, cutting off appendages, maiming, and other

From *Debating the Death Penalty*, edited by Hugo Adam Bedau and Paul G. Cassell (Oxford University Press, 2004), pp. 152–182. Reprinted by permission of Oxford University Press.

primitive forms of punishment. It remains to be seen how long it will be until the use of the death penalty becomes so infrequent as to be pointless, and it is eventually abandoned. In the meantime, capital punishment is arbitrarily and unfairly imposed, undermines the standing and moral authority of the United States in the community of nations, and diminishes the credibility and legitimacy of the courts within the United States.

Although death may intuitively seem to be an appropriate punishment for a person who kills another person and polls show strong support for the death penalty, most Americans know little about realities of capital punishment, past and present. The death penalty is a direct descendant of the darkest aspects of American history—slavery, lynching, racial oppression, and perfunctory capital trials known as "legal lynchings"—and racial discrimination remains a prominent feature of capital punishment. The death penalty is not imposed to avenge every killing and—as some contend—to bring "closure" to the family of every victim, but is inflicted in less than 1 percent of all murder cases. Of more than 20,000 murders in the United States annually, an average of fewer than 300 people are sentenced to death, and only 55 are executed each year. Only 19 states actually carried out executions between 1976, when the U.S. Supreme Court authorized the resumption of capital punishment after declaring it unconstitutional in 1972, and the end of 2002. Eighty-six percent of those executions were in the South. Just two states—Texas and Virginia—carried out 45 percent of them.

Any assessment of the death penalty must not be based on abstract theories about how it should work in practice or the experiences of states like Oregon, which seldom impose the death penalty and carry it out even less. To understand the realities of the death penalty, one must look to the states that sentence people to death by the hundreds and have carried out scores of executions. In those states, innocent people have been sentenced to die based on such things as mistaken eyewitness identifications, false confessions, the testimony of partisan experts who render opinions that are not supported by science, failure of police and prosecutors to turn over evidence of innocence, and testimony of prisoners who get their own charges dismissed by testifying that the accused admitted the crime to them. Even the guilty are sentenced to death as opposed to life imprisonment without the possibility of parole not because they committed the worst crimes but because of where they happen to be prosecuted, the incompetence of their court-appointed lawyers, their race, or the race of their victim. . . .

Further experimentation with lethal punishment after centuries of failure has no place in a conservative society that is wary of too much government power and skeptical of the government's ability to do things well. Further experimentation might be justified if it served some purpose. But capital punishment is not needed to protect society or to punish offenders, as shown by over 100 countries around the world that do not have the death penalty and states such as Michigan and Wisconsin, neither of which have had the death penalty since the mid-1800s. It can be argued that capital punishment was necessary when America was a frontier society and had no prisons. But today the United States has not only maximum security prisons, but "super maximum" prisons where serial killers, mass murderers, and sadistic murderers can be severely punished and completely isolated from guards and other inmates.

Nor is crime deterred by the executions in fewer than half the states of an arbitrarily selected 1 percent of those who commit murders, many of whom are mentally ill or have limited intellectual functioning. The South, which has carried out 85 percent of the nation's executions since 1976, has the highest murder rate of any region of the country. The Northeast, which has the fewest executions by far—only 3 executions between 1976 and the end of 2002—has the lowest murder rate.

The United States does not need to keep this relic of the past to show its abhorrence of murder. As previously noted, 99 percent of the murders in the United States are not punished by death. Even at war crimes trials in The Hague, genocide and other crimes against humanity are not punished with the death penalty. The societies that do not have capital punishment surely abhor murder as much as any other, but they do not find it necessary to engage in killing in order to punish, protect, or show their abhorrence with killing.

Finally, capital punishment has no place in a decent society that places some practices, such as torture, off limits—not because some individuals have not done things so bad that they arguably deserved to be tortured, but because a civilized society simply does not engage in such acts. It can be argued that rapists deserve to be raped, that mutilators deserve to be mutilated. Most societies, however, refrain from responding in this way because the punishment is not only degrading to those on whom it is imposed, but it is also degrading to the society that engages in the same behavior as the criminals. When death sentences are carried out, small groups of people gather in execution chambers and watch as a human being is tied down and put down. Some make no effort to suppress their glee when the sentence is carried out and celebrations occur inside and outside the prison. These celebrations of death reflect the dark side of the human spirit—an arrogant, vengeful, unforgiving, uncaring side that either does not admit the possibility of innocence or redemption or is willing to kill people despite those possibilities.

A Human Rights Violation That Undermines the Standing and Moral Authority of the United States

If people were asked 50 years ago which one of the following three countries—Russia, South Africa, or the United States—would be most likely to have the death penalty at the turn of the century, few people would have answered the United States. And yet, the United States was one of four countries that accounted for 90 percent of all the executions in the world in 2001 (the others were China, Iran, and Saudi Arabia), while Russia and South Africa are among the nations that no longer practice capital punishment. Since 1985, over 40 countries have abandoned capital punishment whereas only four countries that did not have it have adopted it. One of those, Nepal, has since abolished it. Turkey abolished the death penalty in 2001 in its efforts to join the European Union, leaving the United States the only NATO country that still has the death penalty. . . .

The retention of capital punishment in the United States draws harsh criticism from throughout the world. . . . Capital punishment also affects the United States's relations with other countries in other ways. Canada and Mexico have repeatedly protested when their nationals are executed by the United States, as have other countries. Canada, Mexico, and most European countries will not extradite suspects to the United States if they are subject to capital punishment and will not assist in the prosecution of people facing the death penalty. Just as the United States could not assert moral leadership in the world as long as it allowed segregation, it will not be a leader on human rights as long as it allows capital punishment.

Arbitrary and Unfair Infliction

Regardless of the practices of the rest of the world or the morality of capital punishment, the process leading to a death sentence is so unfair and influenced by so many improper factors and the infliction of death sentences is so inconsistent that this punishment should be abandoned.

The exoneration of many people who spent years of their lives in prisons for crimes they did not commit—many of them on death rows—has dramatically brought to light defects in the criminal justice system that have surprised and appalled people who do not observe the system every day and assumed that it was working properly. The average person has little or no contact with the criminal courts, which deal primarily with crimes committed against and by poor people and members of racial minorities. It is a system that is overworked and underfunded, and particularly underfunded when it comes to protecting the rights of those accused.

Law enforcement officers, usually overworked and often under tremendous public pressure to solve terrible crimes, make mistakes, fail to pursue all lines of investigation, and, on occasion, overreach or take shortcuts in pursuing arrests. Prosecutors exercise vast and unchecked discretion in deciding which cases are to be prosecuted as capital cases. The race of the victim and the defendant, political considerations, and other extraneous factors influence whether prosecutors seek the death penalty and whether juries or judges impose it.

A person facing the death penalty usually cannot afford to hire an attorney and is at the mercy of the system to provide a court-appointed lawyer. While many receive adequate representation (and often are not sentenced to death as a result), many others are assigned lawyers who lack the knowledge, skill, resources—and sometimes even the inclination—to handle a serious criminal case. People who would not be sentenced to death if properly represented are sentenced to death because of incompetent court-appointed lawyers. In many communities, racial minorities are still excluded from participation as jurors, judges, prosecutors, and lawyers in the system. In too many cases, defendants are convicted on flimsy evidence, such as eyewitness identifications, which are notoriously unreliable but are seen as very credible by juries; the testimony of convicts who, in exchange for lenient treatment in their own cases, testify that the accused admitted to them that he or she committed the crime; and confessions obtained from people of limited intellect through lengthy and overbearing interrogations.

. . . These are not minor, isolated incidents; they are long-standing, pervasive, systemic deficiencies in the criminal justice system that are not being corrected and, in some places, are even becoming worse. . . . Law enforcement agencies have been unwilling to videotape interrogations and use identification procedures that are more reliable than those presently employed. People who support capital punishment as a concept are unwilling to spend millions of tax dollars to provide competent legal representation for those accused of crimes. And courts have yet to find ways to overcome centuries of racial discrimination that often influence, consciously or subconsciously, the decisions of prosecutors, judges, and juries.

A Warning That Something Is Terribly Wrong: Innocent People Condemned to Death. Over 100 people condemned to death in the last 30 years have been exonerated and released after new evidence established their innocence or cast such doubt on their guilt that they could not be convicted. The 100th of those people, Ray Krone, was convicted and sentenced to death in Arizona based on the testimony of an expert witness that his teeth matched bite marks on the victim. During the ten years that Krone spent on death row, scientists developed the ability to compare biological evidence recovered at crime scenes with the DNA of suspects. DNA testing established that Krone was innocent. On Krone's release, the prosecutor said, "[Krone] deserves an apology from us, that's for sure. A mistake was made here. . . . What do you say to him? An injustice was done and we will try to do better. And we're sorry." Although unfortunate to be wrongfully convicted, Krone was very fortunate that there was DNA evidence in his case. In most cases, there is no biological evidence for DNA testing.

Other defendants had their death sentences commuted to life imprisonment without the possibility of parole because of questions about their innocence. For example, in 1994, the governor of Virginia commuted the death sentence of a mentally retarded man, Earl Washington, to life imprisonment without parole because of questions regarding his guilt. Washington, an easily persuaded, somewhat childlike special-education dropout, had been convicted of murder and rape based on a confession he gave to police, even though it was full of inconsistencies. For example, at one point in the confession Washington said that the victim was white and at another that the victim was black. Six years later, DNA evidence—not available at the time of Washington's trial or the commutation—established that Washington was innocent and he was released.

Although DNA testing has been available only in cases where there was biological evidence and the evidence has been preserved, it has established the innocence of many people who were not sentenced to death. A Michigan judge in 1984 lamented the fact that the state did not have the death penalty, saying that life imprisonment was inadequate for Eddie Joe Lloyd for the rape and murder of a 16-year-old girl. Police had obtained a confession from Lloyd while he was in a mental hospital. Seventeen years later, DNA evidence established that Lloyd did not commit the crime. On his release, Lloyd commented, "If Michigan had the death penalty, I would have been through, the angels would have sung a long time ago."

Sometimes evidence of innocence has surfaced only at the last minute. Anthony Porter, sentenced to death in Illinois, went through all the appeals and review that are available for one so sentenced. Every court upheld his conviction and sentence. As Illinois prepared to put him to death, a question arose as to whether Porter, who was brain damaged and mentally retarded, understood what was happening to him. A person who lacks the mental ability to understand that he is being put to death in punishment for a crime cannot be executed unless he is treated and becomes capable of understanding why he is being executed. Just two days before Porter was to be executed, a court stayed his execution in order to examine his mental condition. After the stay was granted, a journalism class at Northwestern University and a private investigator examined the case and proved that Anthony Porter was innocent. They obtained a confession from the person who committed the crime. Anthony Porter was released, becoming the third person released from Illinois's death row after being proven innocent by a journalism class at Northwestern.

Some people have been executed despite questions of their innocence. Gary Graham was sentenced to death in Texas based on the identification of a witness who said she saw a murder from 40 feet away. Studies have demonstrated that such identifications are often unreliable. But Graham had the misfortune to be assigned a notoriously incompetent lawyer, Ron Mock, who had so many clients sentenced to death that some refer to the "Mock Wing" of death row. Mock failed to seriously contest the state's case, conduct an independent investigation, and present witnesses at the scene who would have testified that Graham was not the person who committed the crime and that the perpetrator was much shorter than Graham. Although it was apparent that Graham did not receive a fair trial and adequate legal representation, he was executed by Texas in 2000. Whether Graham was innocent or guilty will never be resolved because in his case, like most others, there was no DNA evidence that would conclusively establish guilt or innocence.

Some proponents of capital punishment argue that the exoneration of Porter and others shows that the system works and that no innocent people have been executed. However, someone spending years on death row for a crime he did not commit is not an example of the system working. When journalism students prove that police, prosecutors, judges, defense lawyers, and the entire legal system failed to discover the perpetrator of a crime and instead condemned the wrong person to die, the system is not working. Porter and others were spared, as Chief Justice Moses Harrison of the Illinois Supreme Court observed, "only because of luck and the dedication of the attorneys, reporters, family members and volunteers who labored to win their release. They survived despite the criminal justice system, not because of it. . . .

. . . Courts will always be fallible and reversible, while death will always be final and irreversible.

The Two Most Important Decisions—Made by Prosecutors. The two most important decisions in every death penalty case are made not by juries or judges, but by prosecutors. No state or federal law ever requires prosecutors to seek the death penalty or take a capital case to trial. A prosecutor has complete discretion in deciding whether to seek the death penalty and, even if death is sought, whether to offer a sentence less than death in exchange for the defendant's guilty plea. The overwhelming majority of all criminal cases, including capital cases, are resolved not by trials but by plea bargains. Whether death is sought or imposed is based on the discretion and proclivities of the thousands of people who occupy the offices of prosecutor in judicial districts throughout the nation. . . . Some prosecutors seek the death penalty at every opportunity, and others never seek it; some seldom seek it; some frequently seek it. There is no requirement that individual prosecutors—who, in most states, are elected by districts—be consistent in their practices in seeking the death penalty.

As a result of this discretion, there are great geographical disparities in where death is imposed within states. Prosecutors in Houston and Philadelphia have sought the death penalty in virtually every case in which it can be imposed. As a result of aggressive prosecutors and inept court-appointed lawyers, Houston and Philadelphia have each condemned over 100 people to death—more than most states. Harris County, which includes Houston, has had more executions in the last 30 years than any *state* except Texas and Virginia. . . .

Whether death is sought may depend on the side of the county line where the crime was committed. A murder was committed in a parking lot that contained the boundary between Lexington

County, South Carolina, which at the time had sentenced 12 people to death, and Richland County, which had sent only one person to death row. The crime was determined to have occurred a few feet on the Lexington County side of the line. The defendant was tried in Lexington County and sentenced to death. Had the crime occurred a few feet in the other direction, the death penalty almost certainly would not have been imposed. . . .

Thus, whether the death sentence is imposed may depend more on the personal predilections and politics of local prosecutors than the heinousness of the crime or the incorrigibility of the defendant.

The Role of Racial Bias. The complete discretion given to prosecutors in deciding whether to seek the death penalty and whether to drop the death penalty in exchange for guilty pleas also contributes to racial disparities in the infliction of the death penalty. In the 38 states that have the death penalty, 97.5 percent of the chief prosecutors are white. In 18 of the states, all of the chief prosecutors are white. Even the most conscientious prosecutors who have had little experience with people of other races may be influenced in their decisions by racial stereotypes and attitudes they have developed over their lives.

But the rest of the criminal justice system is almost as unrepresentative of Americans' racial diversity as prosecutors' offices. In the South, where the death penalty is most often imposed and carried out, over half the victims of crime are people of color, well over 60 percent of the prison population is made up of people of color, and half of those sentenced to death are members of racial minorities. Yet people of color are seldom involved as judges, jurors, prosecutors, and lawyers in the courts. . . .

Although African Americans constitute only 12 percent of the national population, they are victims of half the murders that are committed in the United States. Yet 80 percent of those on death row were convicted of crimes against white people. The discrepancy is even greater in the Death Belt states of the South. In Georgia and Alabama, for example, African Americans are the victims of 65 percent of the homicides, yet 80 percent of those on death rows are there for crimes against white persons. . . .

Study after study has confirmed what lawyers practicing in the criminal courts observe every day: People of color are treated more harshly than white people. A person of color is more likely than a white person to be stopped by the police, to be abused by the police during that stop, to be arrested, to be denied bail when taken to court, to be charged with a serious crime as opposed to a less serious one that could be charged, to be convicted, and to receive a harsher sentence. But a person of color is much *less* likely to be a participant in the criminal justice system as a judge, juror, prosecutor, or lawyer.

It would be quite remarkable if race affected every aspect of the criminal justice system except with regard to the death penalty—the area in which decision makers have the broadest discretion and base their decisions on evidence with tremendous emotional impact. The sad reality is that race continues to influence who is sentenced to death as it has throughout American history.

The Death Sentence for Being Assigned the Worst Lawyer. Capital cases—complex cases with the highest stakes of any in the legal system—should be handled by the most capable lawyers, with the resources to conduct thorough investigations and consult with various experts on everything from the prosecution's scientific evidence to psychologists and psychiatrists to investigate the defendant's mental health. The right to counsel is the most fundamental constitutional right of a person charged with a crime. A person accused of a crime depends on a lawyer to investigate the prosecution's case; to present any facts that may be helpful to the accused and necessary for a fair and reliable determination of guilt or innocence and, if guilty, a proper sentence; and to protect every other right of the accused. However, U.S. Supreme Court Justice Ruth Bader Ginsburg observed in 2001 that she had "yet to see a death case among the dozens coming to the Supreme Court . . . in which the defendant was well represented at trial. People who are well-represented at trial do not get the death penalty."

Those receiving the death penalty are not well represented because many states do not provide the structure, resources, independence, and accountability that is required to insure competent representation in an area of such specialization. . . .

In states with no public defender offices, lawyers in private practice are assigned to defend capital cases and paid well below market rates. Lawyers, like many people, are attracted to work that pays well. Few lawyers are willing to take the most difficult and emotionally demanding cases with the highest stakes for wages that are among the lowest in the legal profession. A paralegal who works on a federal bankruptcy case is compensated at a higher hourly rate than a lawyer who defends a capital case in Alabama, Georgia, Mississippi, Virginia, and many other states that send many people to death rows. . . .

In several states where journalists have investigated—Illinois, Kentucky, Tennessee, and Texas—they have found that a fourth to a third of those sentenced to death were represented at their trials by lawyers who were later disbarred, suspended, or convicted of crimes. . . .

Many courts continue to operate on the fiction that anyone licensed to practice law—even someone whose practice is mostly real estate or divorce law—is competent to handle capital cases. This is like saying that every doctor is competent to do brain surgery. . . .

Justice Hugo Black wrote for the U.S. Supreme Court in 1956 that "[t]here can be no equal justice where the kind of trial a [person] gets depends on the amount of money he [or she] has." But today, no one seriously doubts that the kind of trial, and the kind of justice, a person receives depends very much on the amount of money he or she has. The quality of legal representation tolerated by some courts shocks the conscience of a person of average sensibilities. But poor representation resulting from lack of funding and structure has been accepted as the best that can be done with the limited resources available. The commitment of many states to providing lawyers for those who cannot afford them was aptly described by a Chief Justice of the Georgia Supreme Court: "[W]e set our sights on the embarrassing target of mediocrity. I guess that means about halfway. And that raises a question. Are we willing to put up with halfway justice? To my way of thinking, one-half justice must mean one-half injustice, and one-half injustice is no justice at all."

The proponents of capital punishment are always quick to say that people facing the death penalty *should* receive better legal representation. But they do not explain how this is going to be accomplished— whether by a sudden burst of altruism on the part of members of the legal profession, who are going to suddenly start taking capital cases for a fraction of what they can make doing other work; a massive infusion of funding from state legislatures that are searching for revenue for education, transportation, and other areas that have a constituency; or some other miracle. The right to competent representation is celebrated in the abstract, but most states—and most supporters of capital punishment—are unwilling to pay for it. As a result the death penalty will continue to be imposed not upon those who commit the worst crimes, but upon those who have the misfortune to be assigned the worst lawyers. . . .

Conclusion

. . . We should have the humility to admit that the legal system is not infallible and that mistakes are made. We should have the honesty to admit that our society is unwilling to pay the price of providing every poor person with competent legal representation, even in capital cases. We should have the courage to acknowledge the role that race plays in the criminal justice system and make a commitment to do something about it instead of pretending that racial prejudice no longer exists. And we should have the compassion and decency to recognize the dignity of every person, even those who have offended us most grievously. The Constitutional Court of South Africa addressed many of these issues in deciding whether the death penalty violated that country's constitution. Despite a staggering crime rate and a long history of racial violence and oppression, the Court unanimously concluded that in a society in transition from hatred to understanding, from vengeance to reconciliation, there was no place for the death penalty. The American people will ultimately reach the same conclusion, deciding that, like slavery and segregation, the death penalty is a relic of another era, and that this society of such vast wealth is capable of more constructive approaches to crime. And the United States will join the rest of the civilized world in abandoning capital punishment.

CHAPTER 26

*A*merica's Unjust Drug War

Michael Huemer

Over 2.3 million Americans are imprisoned; 5 million more are on probation or parole. The United States has the highest rate of incarceration of any country in the world. With only one-twentieth of the world's population, America has one-fourth of the world's prison population.

There were not always so many people behind bars. Since the early 1970s, the federal government has waged a "war on drugs," and the ballooning prison population is a result. More than half of the inmates in federal prisons were convicted of drug possession or trafficking. In the larger system of state prisons, around 20% of the inmates are drug offenders. Each year the government spends billions of dollars on the war on drugs.

Michael Huemer, who teaches philosophy at the University of Colorado at Boulder, thinks we should call off this war. Drug use, he says, is less harmful than smoking or obesity, but no one wants to outlaw french fries or cigarettes. Huemer thinks drug laws are seriously unjust because they violate one's right to control one's own body.

Should the recreational use of drugs such as marijuana, cocaine, heroin, and LSD, be prohibited by law? *Prohibitionists* answer yes. They usually argue that drug use is extremely harmful both to drug users and to society in general, and possibly even immoral, and they believe that these facts provide sufficient reasons for prohibition. *Legalizers* answer no. They usually give one or more of three arguments: First, some

---

From Bill Masters, *The New Prohibition*, Accurate Press, 2004. Reprinted by permission of the author and Accurate Press. Updated by the author in January 2009.

argue that drug use is not as harmful as prohibitionists believe, and even that it is sometimes beneficial. Second, some argue that drug prohibition "does not work," in other words, it is not very successful in preventing drug use and/or has a number of very bad consequences. Lastly, some argue that drug prohibition is unjust or violates rights.

I won't attempt to discuss all these arguments here. Instead, I will focus on what seem to me the three most prominent arguments in the drug legalization debate: first, the argument that drugs should be outlawed because of the harm they cause to drug users; second, the argument that they should be outlawed because they harm people other than the user; and third, the argument that drugs should be legalized because drug prohibition violates rights. I shall focus on the moral/philosophical issues that these arguments raise, rather than medical or sociological issues. I shall show that the two arguments for prohibition fail, while the third argument, for legalization, succeeds.

I. Drugs and Harm to Users

The first major argument for prohibition holds that drugs should be prohibited because drug use is extremely harmful to the users themselves, and prohibition decreases the rate of drug abuse. This argument assumes that the proper function of government includes preventing people from harming themselves. Thus, the argument is something like this:

1. Drug use is very harmful to users.
2. The government should prohibit people from doing things that harm themselves.
3. Therefore, the government should prohibit drug use.

Obviously, the second premise is essential to the argument; if I believed that drug use was very harmful, but I did *not* think that the government should prohibit people from harming themselves, then I would not take this as a reason for prohibiting drug use. But premise (2), if taken without qualification, is extremely implausible. Consider some examples of things people do that are harmful (or entail a risk of harm) to themselves: smoking tobacco, drinking alcohol, eating too much, riding motorcycles, having unprotected or promiscuous sex, maintaining relationships with inconsiderate or abusive boyfriends and girlfriends, maxing out their credit cards, working in dead-end jobs, dropping out of college, moving to New Jersey, and being rude to their bosses. Should the government prohibit all of these things?[1]

Most of us would agree that the government should not prohibit *any* of these things, let alone all of them. And this is not merely for logistical or practical reasons; rather, we think that controlling those activities is not the business of government.

Perhaps the prohibitionist will argue, not that the government should prohibit *all* activities that are harmful to oneself, but that it should prohibit activities that harm oneself in a certain way, or to a certain degree, or that also have some other characteristic. It would then be up to the prohibitionist to explain how the self-inflicted harm of drug use differs from the self-inflicted harms of the other activities mentioned above. Let us consider three possibilities.

(1) One suggestion would be that drug use also harms people other than the user; we will discuss this harm to others in section II below. If, as I will contend, neither the harm to drug users nor the harm to others justifies prohibition, then there will be little plausibility in the suggestion that the combination of harms justifies prohibition. Of course, one could hold that a certain threshold level of total harm must be reached before prohibition of an activity is justified, and that the combination of the harm of drugs to users and their harm to others passes that threshold even though neither kind of harm does so by itself. But if, as I will contend, the "harm to users" and "harm to others" arguments both fail because it is not the government's business to apply criminal sanctions to prevent the kinds of harms in question, *then* the combination of the two harms will not make a convincing case for prohibition.

(2) A second suggestion is that drug use is generally *more* harmful than the other activities listed above. But there seems to be no reason to believe this. As one (admittedly limited) measure of harmfulness, consider the mortality statistics. In the year 2000, illicit drug use directly or indirectly caused an estimated 17,000 deaths in the United States.[2] By contrast, tobacco caused an estimated 435,000 deaths.[3] Of course, more people use tobacco than use illegal drugs,[4] so let us divide by the number of users: tobacco kills 4.5 people per 1000 at-risk persons per year; illegal drugs kill 0.66 people per 1000 at-risk persons per year.[5] Yet almost no one favors outlawing tobacco and putting smokers in prison. On a similar note, obesity caused an estimated 112,000 deaths in the same year (due to increased incidence of heart disease, strokes, and so on), or 1.8 per 1000 at-risk persons.[6] Health professionals have warned about the pandemic of obesity, but no one has yet called for imprisoning obese people.

There are less tangible harms of drug use—harms to one's general quality of life. These are difficult to quantify. But compare the magnitude of the harm to one's quality of life that one can bring about by, say, dropping out of high school, working in a dead-end job for several years, or marrying a jerk—these things can cause extreme and lasting detriment to one's well-being. And yet no one proposes jailing those who drop out, work in bad jobs, or make poor marriage decisions. The idea of doing so would seem ridiculous, clearly beyond the state's prerogatives.

(3) Another suggestion is that drug use harms users *in a different way* than the other listed activities. What sorts of harms do drugs cause? First, illicit drugs may worsen users' health and, in some cases, entail a risk of death. But many other activities—including the consumption of alcohol, tobacco, and fatty foods; sex; and (on a broad construal of "health") automobiles—entail health risks, and yet almost no one believes those activities should be criminalized.

Second, drugs may damage users' relationships with others—particularly family, friends, and lovers—and prevent one from developing more satisfying personal relationships.[7] Being rude to others can also have this effect, yet no one believes you should be put in jail for being rude. Moreover, it is very implausible to suppose that people should be subject to criminal sanctions for ruining their personal relationships. I have no general theory of what sort of things people should be punished for, but consider the following example: suppose that I decide to break up with my girlfriend, stop calling my family, and push away all my friends. I do this for no good reason—I just feel like it. This would damage my personal relationships as much as anything could. Should the police now arrest me and put me in jail? If not, then why should they arrest me for doing something that only has a *chance* of indirectly bringing about a similar result? The following seems like a reasonable political principle: If it would be wrong (because not part of the government's legitimate functions) to punish people for *directly bringing about* some result, then it would also be wrong to punish people for doing some other action on the grounds that the action has a *chance* of bringing about that result indirectly. If the state may not prohibit me from *directly cutting off* my relationships with others, then the fact that my drug use *might have the result* of damaging those relationships does not provide a good reason to prohibit me from using drugs.

Third, drugs may harm users' financial lives, costing them money, causing them to lose their jobs or not find jobs, and preventing them from getting promotions. The same principle applies here: if it would be an abuse of government power to prohibit me from directly bringing about those sorts of negative financial consequences, then surely the fact that drug use might indirectly bring them about is not a good reason to prohibit drug use. Suppose that I decide to quit my job and throw all my money out the window, for no reason. Should the police arrest me and put me in prison?

Fourth and finally, drugs may damage users' moral character, as James Q. Wilson believes:

> [I]f we believe—as I do—that dependency on certain mind-altering drugs *is* a moral issue and that their illegality rests in part on their immorality, then legalizing them undercuts, if it does not eliminate altogether, the moral message. That message is at the root of the distinction between nicotine and cocaine. Both are highly addictive; both have harmful physical effects. But we treat the two drugs differently not simply because nicotine is so widely used as to be beyond the reach of effective prohibition, but because its use does not destroy the user's essential humanity. Tobacco shortens one's life, cocaine debases it. Nicotine alters one's habits, cocaine alters one's soul. The heavy use of crack, unlike the heavy use of tobacco, corrodes those natural sentiments of sympathy and duty that constitute our human nature and make possible our social life.[8]

In this passage, Wilson claims that the use of cocaine (a) is immoral, (b) destroys one's humanity, (c) alters one's soul, and (d) corrodes one's sense of sympathy and duty. One problem with Wilson's argument is the lack of evidence supporting claims (a)–(d). Before we put people in prison for corrupting their souls, we should require some objective evidence that their souls are in fact being corrupted. Before we put people in prison for being immoral, we should require some argument showing that their actions are in fact immoral. Perhaps Wilson's charges of immorality and corruption all come down to the charge that drug users lose their sense of sympathy and duty—that is, claims (a)–(c) all rest upon claim (d). It is plausible that *heavy* drug users experience a decreased sense of sympathy with others and a decreased sense of duty and responsibility. Does this provide a good reason to prohibit drug use?

Again, it seems that one should not prohibit an activity on the grounds that it may indirectly cause some result, unless it would be appropriate to prohibit the direct bringing about of that result. Would it be appropriate, and within the legitimate functions of the state, to punish people for being unsympathetic and undutiful, or for behaving in an unsympathetic and undutiful way? Suppose that Howard—though not a drug user—doesn't sympathize with others. When people try to tell Howard their problems, he just tells them to quit whining. Friends and coworkers who ask Howard for favors are rudely rebuffed. Furthermore—though he does not harm others in ways that would be against our current laws—Howard has a poor sense of duty. He doesn't bother to show up for work on time, nor does he take any pride in his work; he doesn't donate to charity; he doesn't try to improve his community. All around, Howard is an ignoble and unpleasant individual. Should he be put in jail?

If not, then why should someone be put in jail merely for doing something that would have a *chance* of causing them to become like Howard? If it would be an abuse of governmental power to punish people for being jerks, then the fact that drug use may cause one to become a jerk is not a good reason to prohibit drug use.

II. Drugs and Harm to Others

Some argue that drug use must be outlawed because drug use harms the user's family, friends, and coworkers, and/or society in general. A report produced by the Office of National Drug Control Policy states:

> Democracies can flourish only when their citizens value their freedom and embrace personal responsibility. Drug use erodes the individual's capacity to pursue both ideals. It diminishes the individual's capacity to operate effectively in many of life's spheres—as a student, a parent, a spouse, an employee—even as a coworker or fellow motorist. And, while some claim it represents an expression of individual autonomy, drug use is in fact inimical to personal freedom, producing a reduced capacity to participate in the life of the community and the promise of America.[9]

At least one of these alleged harms—dangerous driving—*is* clearly the business of the state. For this reason, I entirely agree that people should be prohibited from driving while under the influence of drugs. But what about the rest of the alleged harms?

Return to our hypothetical citizen Howard. Imagine that Howard—again, for reasons having nothing to do with drugs—does not value freedom, nor does he embrace personal responsibility. It is unclear exactly what this means, but, for good measure, let us suppose that Howard embraces a totalitarian political ideology and denies the existence of free will. He constantly blames other people for his problems and tries to avoid making decisions. Howard is a college student with a part-time job. However, he is a terrible student and worker. He hardly ever studies and frequently misses assignments, as a result of which he gets poor grades. As mentioned earlier, Howard comes to work late and takes no pride in his work. Though he does nothing against our current laws, he is an inattentive and inconsiderate spouse and parent. Nor does he make any effort to participate in the life of his community, or the promise of America. He would rather lie around the house, watching television and cursing the rest of the world for his problems. In short, Howard does all the bad things to his family, friends, coworkers, and society that the ONDCP says *may* result from drug use. And most of this is voluntary.

Should Congress pass laws against what Howard is doing? Should the police then arrest him, and the district attorney prosecute him, for being a loser?

Once again, it seems absurd to suppose that we would arrest and jail someone for behaving in these ways, undesirable as they may be. Since drug use only has a *chance* of causing one to behave in each of these ways, it is even more absurd to suppose that we should arrest and jail people for drug use on the grounds that drug use has these potential effects.

III. The Injustice of Drug Prohibition

Philosopher Douglas Husak has characterized drug prohibition as the greatest injustice perpetrated in the United States since slavery.[10] This is no hyperbole. If the drug laws are unjust, then America has over half a million people unjustly imprisoned.[11]

Why think the drug laws are *unjust*? Husak's argument invokes a principle with which few could disagree: it is unjust for the state to punish people without having a good reason for doing so.[12] We have seen the failure of the most common proposed rationales for drug prohibition. If nothing better is forthcoming, then we must conclude that prohibitionists have no rational justification for punishing drug users. We have deprived hundreds of thousands of people of basic liberties and subjected them to severe hardship conditions, for no good reason.

This is bad enough. But I want to say something stronger: it is not merely that we are punishing people for no good reason. We are punishing people for exercising their natural rights. Individuals have a right to use drugs. This right is neither absolute nor exceptionless; suppose, for example, that there existed a drug which, once ingested, caused a significant proportion of users, without any further free choices on their part, to attack other people without provocation. I would think that stopping the use of this drug would be the business of the government. But no existing drug satisfies this description. Indeed, though I cannot take time to delve into the matter here, I think it is clear that the drug *laws* cause far more crime than drugs themselves do.

The idea of a right to use drugs derives from the idea that individuals own their own bodies. That is, a person has the right to exercise control over his own body—including the right to decide how it should be used, and to exclude others from using it—in a manner similar to the way one may exercise control over one's (other) property. This statement is somewhat vague; nevertheless, we can see the general idea embodied in commonsense morality. Indeed, it seems that if there is *anything* one would have rights to, it would be one's own body. This explains why we think others may not physically attack you or kidnap you. It explains why we do not accept the use of unwilling human subjects for medical experiments, even if the experiments are beneficial to society—the rest of society may not decide to use your body for its own purposes without your permission. It explains why some believe that women have a right to an abortion—and why some others do not. The former believe that a woman has the right to do what she wants with her own body; the latter believe that the fetus is a distinct person, and a woman does not have the right to harm *its* body. Virtually no one disputes that, *if* a fetus is merely a part of the woman's body, *then* a woman has a right to choose whether to have an abortion; just as virtually no one disputes that, *if* a fetus is a distinct person, then a woman lacks the right to destroy it. Almost no one disputes that persons have rights over their own bodies but not over others' bodies.

The right to control one's body cannot be interpreted as implying a right to use one's body in *every* conceivable way, any more than we have the right to use our property in every conceivable way. Most importantly, we may not use our bodies to harm others in certain ways, just as we may not use our property to harm others. But drug use seems to be a paradigm case of a legitimate exercise of the right to control one's own body. Drug consumption takes place in and immediately around the user's own body; the salient effects occur *inside* the user's body. If we consider drug use merely as altering the user's own body and mind, it is hard to see how anyone who believes in rights at all could deny that it is protected by a right, for: (a) it is hard to see how anyone who believes in rights could deny that individuals have rights over their own bodies and minds, and (b) it is hard to see how anyone who believes in such rights could deny that drug use, considered merely as altering the user's body and mind, is an example of the exercise of one's rights over one's own body and mind.

Consider two ways a prohibitionist might object to this argument. First, a prohibitionist might argue that drug use does not *merely* alter the user's own body and mind, but also harms the user's family, friends, co-workers, and society. I responded to this sort of argument in section II. Not just *any* way in which an action might be said to "harm" other people makes the action worthy of criminal sanctions. Here we need not try to state a general criterion for what sorts of harms make an action worthy of criminalization; it is enough to note that there are some kinds of "harms" that virtually no one would take to warrant criminal sanctions, and that these include the "harms" I cause to others by being a poor student, an incompetent worker, or an apathetic citizen.[13] That said, I agree with the prohibitionists at least this far: no one should be permitted to drive or operate heavy machinery while under the influence of drugs that impair their ability to do those things; nor should pregnant mothers be permitted to ingest drugs, if it can be proven that those drugs cause substantial risks to their babies (I leave open the question of what the threshold level of risk should be, as well as the empirical questions concerning the actual level of risk created by illegal drugs). But, in the great majority of cases, drug use does not harm anyone in any *relevant* ways—that is, ways that we normally take to merit criminal penalties—and should not be outlawed.

Second, a prohibitionist might argue that drug use fails to qualify as an exercise of the user's rights over his own body, because the individual is not truly acting freely in deciding to use drugs. Perhaps individuals only use drugs because they have fallen prey to some sort of psychological compulsion, because drugs exercise a siren-like allure that distorts users' perceptions, because users don't realize how bad drugs are, or something of that sort. The exact form of this objection doesn't matter; in any case, the prohibitionist faces a dilemma. If users do not freely choose to use drugs, then it is unjust to *punish* them for using drugs. For if users do not choose freely, then they are not morally responsible for their decision, and it is unjust to punish a person for something he is not responsible for. But if users *do* choose freely in deciding to use drugs, then this choice is an exercise of their rights over their own bodies.

I have tried to think of the best arguments prohibitionists could give, but in fact prohibitionists have remained puzzlingly silent on this issue. When a country goes to war, it tends to focus on how to win, sparing little thought for the rights of the victims in the enemy country. Similarly, one effect of America's declaring "war" on drug users seems to have been that prohibitionists have given almost no thought to the rights of drug users. Most either ignore the issue or mention it briefly only to dismiss it without argument.[14] In an effort to discredit legalizers, the Office of National Drug Control Policy produced the following caricature—

> The easy cynicism that has grown up around the drug issue is no accident. Sowing it has been the deliberate aim of a decades-long campaign by proponents of legalization, critics whose mantra is "nothing works," and whose central insight appears to be that they can avoid having to propose the unmentionable—a world where drugs are ubiquitous and where use and addiction would skyrocket—if they can hide behind the bland management critique that drug control efforts are "unworkable."[15]

—apparently denying the existence of the central issues I have discussed in this essay. It seems reasonable to assume that an account of the state's right to forcibly interfere with individuals' decisions regarding their own bodies is not forthcoming from these prohibitionists.

IV. Conclusion

Undoubtedly, the drug war has been disastrous in many ways that others can more ably describe—in terms of its effects on crime, on police corruption, and on other civil liberties, to name a few. But more than that, the drug war is morally outrageous in its very conception. If we are to call ours a free society, we cannot deploy force to deprive people of their liberty and property for whimsical reasons. The exercise of such coercion requires a powerful and clearly stated rationale. Most of the reasons that have been proposed in the case of drug prohibition would be considered feeble if advanced in other contexts. Few would take seriously the suggestion that people should be imprisoned for harming their own health, being poor students, or failing to share in the American dream. It is still less credible that we should imprison people for an activity that only *may* lead to those consequences. Yet these and other, similarly weak arguments form the core of prohibition's defense.

Prohibitionists are likewise unable to answer the argument that individuals have a right to use drugs. Any such answer would have to deny either that persons have rights of control over their own bodies, or that consuming drugs constituted an exercise of those rights. We have seen that the sort of harms drug use allegedly causes to society do not make a case against its being an exercise of the user's rights over his own body. And the claim that drug users can't control their behavior or don't know what they are doing renders it even more mysterious why one would believe drug users deserve to be punished for what they are doing.

I will close by responding to a query posed by prohibition-advocate James Inciardi:

> The government of the United States is not going to legalize drugs anytime soon, if ever, and certainly not in this [the 20th] century. So why spend so much time, expense, and intellectual and emotional effort on a quixotic undertaking? . . . [W]e should know by now that neither politicians nor the polity respond positively to abrupt and drastic strategy alterations.[16]

The United States presently has 553,000 people unjustly imprisoned. Inciardi may—tragically—be correct that our government has no intention of stopping its flagrant violations of the rights of its people any time soon. Nevertheless, it remains the duty of citizens and of political and social theorists to identify the injustice, and not to tacitly assent to it. Imagine a slavery advocate, decades before the Civil War, arguing that abolitionists were wasting their breath and should move on to more productive activities, such as arguing for incremental changes in the way slaves are treated, since the southern states had no intention of ending slavery any time soon. The institution of slavery is a black mark on our nation's history, but our history would be even more shameful if no one at the time had spoken against the injustice.

Is this comparison overdrawn? I don't think so. The harm of being unjustly imprisoned is qualitatively comparable (though it usually ends sooner) to the harm of being enslaved. The increasingly popular scapegoating and stereotyping of drug users and sellers on the part of our nation's leaders is comparable to the racial prejudices of previous generations. Yet very few seem willing to speak on behalf of drug users. Perhaps the unwillingness of those in public life to defend drug users' rights stems from the negative image we have of drug users and the fear of being associated with them. Yet these attitudes remain baffling. I have used illegal drugs myself. I know many decent and successful individuals, both in and out of my profession, who have used illegal drugs. Two United States Presidents, one Vice-President, a Speaker of the House, and a Supreme Court Justice have all admitted to having used illegal drugs.[17] Nearly half of all Americans over the age of 11 have used illegal drugs.[18] But now leave aside the absurdity of recommending criminal sanctions for all these people. My point is this: if we are convinced of the injustice of drug prohibition, then—even if our protests should fall on deaf ears—we cannot remain silent in the face of such a large-scale injustice in our own country. And, fortunately, radical social reforms *have* occurred, more than once in our history, in response to moral arguments.

Notes

1. Douglas Husak (*Legalize This! The Case for Decriminalizing Drugs*, London: Verso, 2002, pages 7, 101–3) makes this sort of argument. I have added my own examples of harmful activities to his list.

2. Ali Mokdad, James Marks, Donna Stroup, and Julie Gerberding, "Actual Causes of Death in the United States, 2000," *Journal of the American Medical Association* 291, no. 10, 2004: 1238–45, page 1242. The statistic includes estimated contributions of drug use to such causes of death as suicide, homicide, motor vehicle accidents, and HIV infection.

3. Mokdad et al., page 1239; the statistic includes estimated effects of secondhand smoke. The Centers for Disease Control and Prevention provides an estimate of 440,000 ("Annual Smoking-Attributable Mortality, Years of Potential Life Lost, and Economic Costs—United States, 1995–1999," *Morbidity and Mortality Weekly Report* 51, 2002: 300–303, http://www.cdc.gov/mmwr/PDF/wk/mm5114.pdf, page 300).

4. James Inciardi ("Against Legalization of Drugs" in Arnold Trebach and James Inciardi, *Legalize It? Debating American Drug Policy*, Washington, DC: American University Press, 1993, pages 161, 165) makes this point, accusing drug legalizers of "sophism." He does not go on to calculate the number of deaths per user, however.

5. I include both current and former smokers among "at risk persons." The calculation for tobacco is based on Mokdad et al.'s report (page 1239) that 22.2% of the adult population were smokers and 24.4% were former smokers in 2000, and the U.S. Census Bureau's estimate of an adult population of 209 million in the year 2000 ("Table 2: Annual Estimates of the Population by Sex and Selected Age Groups for the United States: April 1, 2000 to July 1, 2007 [NC-EST2007-02]," release date May 1, 2008, http://www.census.gov/popest/national/asrh/NC-EST2007/NC-EST2007-02.xls). The calculation for illicit drugs is based on the report of the Office of National

Drug Control Policy (hereafter, ONDCP) that, in the year 2000, 11% of persons aged 12 and older had used illegal drugs in the previous year ("Drug Use Trends," October 2002, http://www.whitehousedrugpolicy.gov/publications/factsht/druguse/), and the U.S. Census Bureau's report of a population of about 233 million Americans aged 12 and over in 2000 ("Table 1: Annual Estimates of the Population by Sex and Five-Year Age Groups for the United States: April 1, 2000 to July 1, 2007 [NC-EST2007-01]," release date May 1, 2008, http://www.census.gov/popest/national/asrh/NC-EST2007/NC-EST2007-02.xls). Interpolation was applied to the Census Bureau's "10 to 14" age category to estimate the number of persons aged 12 to 14. In the case of drugs, if "at risk persons" are considered to include only those who admit to having used illegal drugs in the past month, then the death rate is 1.2 per 1000 at-risk persons.

6. Based on 112,000 premature deaths caused by obesity in 2000 (Katherine Flegal, Barry Graubard, David Williamson, and Mitchell Gail, "Excess Deaths Associated with Underweight, Overweight, and Obesity," *Journal of the American Medical Association* 293, no. 15, 2005: 1861–7), a 30.5% obesity rate among U.S. adults in 2000 (Allison Hedley, Cynthia Ogden, Clifford Johnson, Margaret Carroll, Lester Curtin, and Katherine Flegal, "Prevalence of Overweight and Obesity Among U.S. Children, Adolescents, and Adults, 1999–2002," *Journal of the American Medical Association* 291, no. 23, 2004: 2847–50) and a U.S. adult population of 209 million in 2000 (U.S. Census Bureau, "Table 2," *op. cit.*).

7. Inciardi, pages 167, 172.

8. James Q. Wilson, "Against the Legalization of Drugs," *Commentary* 89, 1990: 21–8, page 26.

9. ONDCP, *National Drug Control Strategy 2002*, Washington, DC: Government Printing Office, http://www.whitehousedrugpolicy.gov/publications/policy/03ndcs/, pages 1–2.

10. Husak, *Legalize This!*, page 2.

11. In 2006, there were approximately 553,000 people in American prisons and jails whose most serious offense was a drug offense. This included 93,751 federal inmates (U.S. Department of Justice, "Prisoners in 2006," December 2007, http://www.ojp.usdoj.gov/bjs/pub/pdf/p06.pdf, page 9). State prisons held another 269,596 drug inmates, based on the 2006 state prison population of 1,377,815 ("Prisoners in 2006," page 2) and the 2004 rate of 19.57% of state prisoners held on drug charges ("Prisoners in 2006," page 24). Local jails held another 189,204 drug inmates, based on the 2006 local jail population of 766,010 ("Prisoners in 2006," page 3) and the 2002 rate of 24.7% of local inmates held on drug charges (U.S. Department of Justice, "Profile of Jail Inmates 2002," published July 2004, revised October 12, 2004, http://www.ojp.usdoj.gov/bjs/pub/pdf/pji02.pdf, page 1). In all cases, I have used the latest statistics available as of this writing.

12. Husak, *Legalize This!*, page 15. See his chapter 2 for an extended discussion of various proposed rationales for drug prohibition, including many issues that I lack space to discuss here.

13. Husak (*Drugs and Rights*, Cambridge University Press, 1992, pages 166–8) similarly argues that no one has a *right* that I be a good neighbor, proficient student, and so on, and that only harms that violate rights can justify criminal sanctions.

14. See Inciardi for an instance of ignoring and Daniel Lungren ("Legalization Would Be a Mistake" in Timothy Lynch, ed., *After Prohibition*, Washington, DC: Cato Institute, 2000, page 180) for an instance of unargued dismissal. Wilson (page 24) addresses the issue, if at all, only by arguing that drug use makes users worse parents, spouses, employers, and co-workers. This fails to refute the contention that individuals have a right to use drugs.

15. ONDCP, *National Drug Control Strategy 2002*, page 3.

16. Inciardi, page 205.

17. Bill Clinton, Al Gore, Newt Gingrich and Clarence Thomas (reported by David Phinney, "Dodging the Drug Question," ABC News, August 19, 1999, http://abcnews.go.com/sections/politics/DailyNews/prez_questions990819.html). George W. Bush has refused to state whether he has ever used illegal drugs. Barack Obama has acknowledged using cocaine and marijuana (*Dreams from My Father*, New York: Random House, 2004, page 93).

18. In 2006, 45% of Americans aged 12 and over reported having used at least one illegal drug (U.S. Department of Health and Human Services, "National Survey on Drug Use and Health," 2006, Table 1.1B, http://www.oas.samhsa.gov/NSDUH/2k6NSDUH/tabs/Sect1peTabs1to46.htm).

CHAPTER 27

*I*s Homosexuality Unnatural?

Burton M. Leiser

Western attitudes toward homosexuality have been shaped largely by Christianity; and within the Christian tradition, homosexuality has been condemned time and again. Saint Paul declared that "idolaters, thieves, homosexuals, drunkards, and robbers" cannot inherit the Kingdom of God. But why not? What is so bad about them? Subsequent theologians said that homosexuality is *unnatural,* and this became the key term in the debate. Saint Thomas Aquinas held that morality is a matter of acting in accordance with "the laws of nature," and he cited "unisexual lust" as a particularly noxious "sin against nature."

Today, gay marriage is legal in only six countries: The Netherlands, Belgium, Canada, Norway, South Africa, and Spain. In the United States, homosexuals can marry only in Massachusetts and Connecticut, while several other states allow same-sex civil unions or domestic partnerships. When people debate the legitimacy of gay marriage, their opinions are often shaped by whether they think that homosexuality, in general, is unnatural and therefore wrong.

Burton M. Leiser is Professor Emeritus at Pace University in New York. In the following selection, he discusses the claim that gay sex is "unnatural." As he points out, this term can have several different meanings, and it is important to distinguish them in order to assess the traditional argument against homosexuality.

From Burton M. Leiser, *Liberty, Justice, and Morals: Contemporary Value Conflicts,* 3rd ed., pp. 51–57, © 1986. Reprinted by permission of Prentice-Hall, Inc., Upper Saddle River, NJ.

Theologians and other moralists have said homosexual acts violate the "natural law," and that they are therefore immoral and ought to be prohibited by the state.

The word *nature* has a built-in ambiguity that can lead to serious misunderstandings. When something is said to be "natural" or in conformity with "natural law" or the "law of nature," this may mean either (1) that it is in conformity with the descriptive laws of nature, or (2) that it is not artificial, that man has not imposed his will or his devices upon events or conditions as they exist or would have existed without such interference.

1. *The descriptive laws of nature.* The laws of nature, as these are understood by the scientist, differ from the laws of man. The former are purely descriptive, where the latter are prescriptive. When a scientist says that water boils at 212° Fahrenheit or that the volume of a gas varies directly with the heat that is applied to it and inversely with the pressure, he means merely that as a matter of recorded and observable fact, pure water under standard conditions always boils at precisely 212° Fahrenheit and that as a matter of observed fact, the volume of a gas rises as it is heated and falls as pressure is applied to it. These "laws" merely *describe* the manner in which physical substances *actually behave.* They differ from municipal and federal laws in that they *do not prescribe behavior.* Unlike man-made laws, natural laws are not passed by any legislator or group of legislators; they are not proclaimed or announced; they impose no obligation upon anyone or anything; their violation entails no penalty, and there is no reward for following them or abiding by them. When a scientist says that the air in a tire obeys the laws of nature that govern gases, he does *not* mean that the air, having been informed that it *ought* to behave in a certain way, behaves appropriately under the right conditions. He means, rather, that as a matter of fact, the air in a tire *will* behave like all other gases. In saying that Boyle's law governs the behavior of gases, he means merely that gases do, as a matter of fact, behave in accordance with Boyle's law, and that Boyle's law enables one to predict accurately what will happen to a given quantity of a gas as its pressure is raised; he does *not* mean to suggest that some heavenly voice has proclaimed that all gases should henceforth behave in accordance with the terms of Boyle's law and that a ghostly policeman patrols the world, ready to mete out punishments to any gases that violate the heavenly decree. In fact, according to the scientist, it does not make sense to speak of a natural law being violated. For if there were a true exception to a so-called law of nature, the exception would require a change in the description of those phenomena, and the law would have been shown to be no law at all. The laws of nature are revised as scientists discover new phenomena that require new refinements in their descriptions of the way things actually happen. In this respect they differ fundamentally from human laws, which are revised periodically by legislators who are not so interested in *describing* human behavior as they are in *prescribing* what human behavior *should* be.

2. *The artificial as a form of the unnatural.* On occasion when we say that something is not natural, we mean that it is a product of human artifice. A typewriter is not a natural object, in this sense, for the substances of which it is composed have been removed from their natural state—the state in which they existed before men came along—and have been transformed by a series of chemical and physical and mechanical processes into other substances. They have been rearranged into a whole that is quite different from anything found in nature. In short, a typewriter is an artificial object. In this sense, clothing is not natural, for it has been transformed considerably from the state in which it was found in nature; and wearing clothing is also not natural, in this sense, for in one's natural state, before the application of anything artificial, before any human interference with things as they are, one is quite naked. Human laws, being artificial conventions designed to exercise a degree of control over the natural inclinations and propensities of men, may in this sense be considered to be unnatural.

When theologians and moralists speak of homosexuality, contraception, abortion, and other forms of human behavior as being unnatural and say that for that reason such behavior must be considered to be wrong, in what sense are they using the word *unnatural*? Are they saying that homosexual behavior and the use of contraceptives are contrary to the scientific laws of nature, are they saying that they are artificial forms of behavior, or are they using the terms *natural* and *unnatural* in some third sense?

They cannot mean that homosexual behavior (to stick to the subject presently under discussion) violates the laws of nature in the first sense, for, as has been pointed out, in *that* sense it is impossible to violate the laws of nature. Those laws, being merely descriptive of what actually does happen, would have to *include* homosexual behavior if such behavior does actually take place. Even if the defenders of the theological view that homosexuality is unnatural were to appeal to a statistical analysis by pointing out that such behavior is not normal from a statistical point of view, and therefore not what the laws of nature require, it would be open to their critics to reply that any descriptive law of nature must account for and incorporate all statistical deviations, and that the laws of nature, in this sense, do not *require* anything. These critics might also note that the best statistics available reveal that about half of all American males engage in homosexual activity at some time in their lives, and that a very large percentage of American males have exclusively homosexual relations for a fairly extensive period of time; from which it would follow that such behavior is natural, for them, at any rate, in this sense of the word *natural.*

If those who say that homosexual behavior is unnatural are using the term *unnatural* in the second sense as artificial, it is difficult to understand their objection. That which is artificial is often far better than what is natural. Artificial homes seem, at any rate, to be more suited to human habitation and more conducive to longer life and better health than are caves and other natural shelters. There are distinct advantages to the use of such unnatural (artificial) amenities as clothes, furniture, and books. Although we may dream of an idyllic return to nature in our more wistful moments, we would soon discover, as Thoreau did in his attempt to escape from the artificiality of civilization, that needles and thread, knives and matches, ploughs and nails, and countless other products of human artifice are essential to human life. We would discover, as Plato pointed out in the *Republic,* that no man can be truly self-sufficient. Some of the by-products of industry are less than desirable, but neither industry nor the products of industry are intrinsically evil, even though both are unnatural in this sense of the word.

Interference with nature is not evil in itself. Nature, as some writers have put it, must be tamed. In some respects man must look upon it as an enemy to be conquered. If nature were left to its own devices, without the intervention of human artifice, men would be consumed by disease, they would be plagued by insects, they would be chained to the places where they were born with no means of swift communication or transport, and they would suffer the discomforts and the torments of wind and weather and flood and fire with no practical means of combating any of them. Interfering with nature, doing battle with nature, using human will and reason and skill to thwart what might otherwise follow from the conditions that prevail in the world is a peculiarly human enterprise, one that can hardly be condemned merely because it does what is not natural.

Homosexual behavior can hardly be considered to be unnatural in this sense. There is nothing artificial about such behavior. On the contrary, it is quite natural, in this sense, to those who engage in it.

And even if it were not, even if it were quite artificial, this is not in itself a ground for condemning it.

It would seem, then, that those who condemn homosexuality as an unnatural form of behavior must mean something else by the word *unnatural,* something not covered by either of the preceding definitions. A third possibility is this:

3. *Anything uncommon or abnormal is unnatural.* If this is what is meant by those who condemn homosexuality on the ground that it is unnatural, it is quite obvious that their condemnation cannot be accepted without further argument. The fact that a given form of behavior is uncommon provides no justification for condemning it. Playing viola in a string quartet may be an uncommon form of human behavior. Yet there is no reason to suppose that such uncommon behavior is, by virtue of its uncommonness, deserving of condemnation or ethically or morally wrong. On the contrary, many forms of behavior are praised precisely because they are so uncommon. Great artists, poets, musicians, and scientists are uncommon in this sense; but clearly the world is better off for having them, and it would be absurd to condemn them or their activities for their failure to be common and normal. If homosexual behavior is wrong, then, it must be for some reason other than its unnaturalness in this sense of the word.

4. *Any use of an organ or an instrument that is contrary to its principal purpose or function is unnatural.* Every organ and every instrument—perhaps even every creature—has a function to perform, one for which it is particularly designed. Any use of those instruments and organs that is consonant with their purposes is natural and proper, but any use that is inconsistent with their principal functions is unnatural and improper, and to that extent, evil or harmful. Human teeth, for example, are admirably designed for their principal functions—biting and chewing the kinds of food suitable for human consumption. But they are not particularly well suited for prying the caps from beer bottles. If they are used for that purpose, which is not natural to them, they are likely to crack or break under the strain. The abuse of one's teeth leads to their destruction and to a consequent deterioration in one's overall health. If they are used only for their proper function, however, they may continue to serve well for many years. Similarly, a given drug may have a proper function. If used in the furtherance of that end, it can preserve life and restore health. But if it is abused and employed for purposes for which it was never intended, it may cause serious harm and even death. The natural uses of things are good and proper, but their unnatural uses are bad and harmful.

What we must do, then, is to find the proper use, or the true purpose, of each organ in our bodies. Once we have discovered that, we will know what constitutes the natural use of each organ and what constitutes an unnatural, abusive, and potentially harmful employment of the various parts of our bodies. If we are rational, we will be careful to confine behavior to the proper functions and to refrain from unnatural behavior. According to those philosophers who follow this line of reasoning, the way to discover the proper use of any organ is to determine what it is peculiarly suited to do. The eye is suited for seeing, the ear for hearing, the nerves for transmitting impulses from one part of the body to another, and so on.

What are the sex organs peculiarly suited to do? Obviously, they are peculiarly suited to enable men and women to reproduce their own kind. No other organ in the body is capable of fulfilling that function. It follows, according to those who follow the natural-law line, that the proper or natural function of the sex organs is reproduction, and that strictly speaking, any use of those organs for other purposes is unnatural, abusive, potentially harmful, and therefore wrong. The sex organs have been given to us in order to enable us to maintain the continued existence of mankind on this earth. All perversions—including masturbation, homosexual behavior, and heterosexual intercourse that deliberately frustrates the design of the sexual organs—are unnatural and bad. As Pope Pius XI once said, "Private individuals have no other power over the members of their bodies than that which pertains to their natural ends."

But the problem is not so easily resolved. Is it true that every organ has one and only one proper function? A hammer may have been designed to pound nails, and it may perform that particular job best. But it is not sinful to employ a hammer to crack nuts if you have no other more suitable tool immediately available. The hammer, being a relatively versatile tool, may be employed in a number of ways. It has no one proper or natural function. A woman's eyes are well adapted to seeing, it is true. But they seem also to be well adapted to flirting. Is a woman's use of her eyes for the latter purpose sinful merely because she is not using them, at that moment, for their "primary" purpose of seeing? Our sexual organs are uniquely adapted for procreation, but that is obviously not the only function for which they are adapted. Human beings may—and do—use those organs for a great many other purposes, and it is difficult to see why any *one* use should be considered to be the only proper one. The sex organs seem to be particularly well adapted to give their owners and others intense sensations of pleasure.

Unless one believes that pleasure itself is bad, there seems to be little reason to believe that the use of the sex organs for the production of pleasure in oneself or in others is evil. In view of the peculiar design of these organs, with their great concentration of nerve endings, it would seem that they were designed (if they *were* designed) with that very goal in mind, and that their use for such purposes would be no more unnatural than their use for the purpose of procreation.

Nor should we overlook the fact that human sex organs may be and are used to express, in the deepest and most intimate way open to man, the love of one person for another. Even the most ardent opponents of "unfruitful" intercourse admit that sex does serve this function. They have accordingly conceded that a man and his wife may have intercourse even though she is pregnant, or past the age of child bearing, or in the infertile period of her menstrual cycle.

Human beings are remarkably complex and adaptable creatures. Neither they nor their organs can properly be compared to hammers or to other tools. The analogy quickly breaks down. The generalization that a given organ or instrument has one and only one proper function does not hold up, even with regard to the simplest manufactured tools, for, as we have seen, a tool may be used for more than one purpose—less effectively than one especially designed for a given task, perhaps, but properly and certainly not *sinfully*. A woman may use her eyes not only to see and to flirt, but also to earn money—if she is, for example, an actress or a model. Though neither of the latter functions seems to have been a part of the original design, if one may speak sensibly of *design* in this context, of the eye, it is difficult to see why such a use of the eyes of a woman should be considered sinful, perverse, or unnatural. Her sex organs have the unique capacity of producing ova and nurturing human embryos, under the right conditions; but why should any other use of those organs, including their use to bring pleasure to their owner or to someone else, or to manifest love to another person, or even, perhaps, to earn money, be regarded as perverse, sinful, or unnatural? Similarly, a man's sexual organs possess the unique capacity of causing the generation of another human being, but if a man chooses to use them for pleasure, or for the expression of love, or for some other purpose—so long as he does not interfere with the rights of some other person—the fact that his sex organs do have their unique capabilities does not constitute a convincing justification for condemning their other uses as being perverse, sinful, unnatural, or criminal. If a man "perverts" himself by wiggling his ears for the entertainment of his neighbors instead of using them exclusively for their "natural" function of hearing, no one thinks of consigning him to prison. If he abuses his teeth by using them to pull staples from memos—a function for which teeth were clearly not designed—he is not accused of being immoral, degraded, and degenerate. The fact that people *are* condemned for using their sex organs for their own pleasure or profit, or for that of others, may be more revealing about the prejudices and taboos of our society than it is about our perception of the true nature or purpose of our bodies.

In this connection, it may be worthwhile to note that with the development of artificial means of reproduction (that is, test tube babies), the sex organs may become obsolete for reproductive purposes but would still contribute greatly to human pleasure. In addition, studies of animal behavior and anthropological reports indicate that such nonreproductive sex acts as masturbation, homosexual intercourse, and mutual fondling of genital organs are widespread, both among human beings and among lower animals. Under suitable circumstances, many animals reverse their sex roles, males assuming the posture of females and presenting themselves to others for intercourse, and females mounting other females and going through all the actions of a male engaged in intercourse. Many peoples all around the world have sanctioned and even ritualized homosexual relations. It would seem that an excessive readiness to insist that human sex organs are designed only for reproductive purposes and therefore ought to be used only for such purposes must be based upon a very narrow conception that is conditioned by our own society's peculiar history and taboos.

To sum up, then, the proposition that any use of an organ that is contrary to its principal purpose or function is unnatural assumes that organs *have* a principal purpose or function, but this may be denied on the ground that the purpose or function of a given organ may vary according to the needs or desires of its owner. It may be denied on the ground that a given organ may have more than one principal purpose or function, and any attempt to call one use or another the only natural one seems to be arbitrary, if not question-begging. Also, the proposition suggests that what is unnatural is evil or depraved. This goes beyond the pure description of things, and enters into the problem of the evaluation of human behavior, which leads us to the fifth meaning of *natural.*

   5. *That which is natural is good, and whatever is unnatural is bad.* When one condemns homosexuality or masturbation or the use of contraceptives on the ground that it is unnatural, one implies that whatever is unnatural is bad, wrongful, or perverse. But as we have seen, in some senses of the word, the unnatural (the artificial) is often

very good, whereas that which is natural (that which has not been subjected to human artifice or improvement) may be very bad indeed.
Of course, interference with nature may be bad. Ecologists have made
us more aware than we have ever been of the dangers of unplanned
and uninformed interference with nature. But this is not to say that *all*
interference with nature is bad. Every time a man cuts down a tree to
make room for a home for himself, or catches a fish to feed himself
or his family, he is interfering with nature. If men did not interfere
with nature, they would have no homes, they could eat no fish, and,
in fact, they could not survive. What, then, can be meant by those who
say that whatever is natural is good and whatever is unnatural is bad?
Clearly, they cannot have intended merely to reduce the word *natural*
to a synonym of *good, right,* and *proper,* and *unnatural* to a synonym
of *evil, wrong, improper, corrupt,* and *depraved.* If that were all they had
intended to do, there would be very little to discuss as to whether a
given form of behavior might be proper even though it is not in strict
conformity with someone's views of what is natural; for *good* and *natural* being synonyms, it would follow inevitably that whatever is good
must be natural, and vice versa, by definition. This is certainly not what
the opponents of homosexuality have been saying when they claim
that homosexuality, being unnatural, is evil. For if it were, their claim
would be quite empty. They would be saying merely that homosexuality, being evil, is evil—a redundancy that could as easily be reduced to
the simpler assertion that homosexuality is evil. This assertion, however, is not an argument. Those who oppose homosexuality and other
sexual "perversions" on the ground that they are "unnatural" are saying that there is some objectively identifiable quality in such behavior
that is unnatural; and that that quality, once it has been identified by
some kind of scientific observation, can be seen to be detrimental to
those who engage in such behavior, or to those around them; and that
because of the harm (physical, mental, moral, or spiritual) that results
from engaging in any behavior possessing the attribute of unnaturalness, such behavior must be considered to be wrongful, and should be
discouraged by society. "Unnaturalness" and "wrongfulness" are not
synonyms, then, but different concepts. The problem with which we
are wrestling is that we are unable to find a meaning for *unnatural* that
enables us to arrive at the conclusion that homosexuality is unnatural
or that if homosexuality is unnatural, it is therefore wrongful behavior.
We have examined four common meanings of *natural* and *unnatural,*
and have seen that none of them performs the task that it must perform if the advocates of this argument are to prevail.

CHAPTER 28

Monogamy: A Critique

John McMurtry

It is an almost unquestioned assumption in our culture: the good life involves getting married and living happily ever after, remaining forever faithful to your one true love. The institution of marriage, already so pervasive, may even be expanding, as gay couples seek the right to participate in its legally sanctioned bliss.

John McMurtry wonders why this vision of the good life goes unchallenged. Monogamous marriage, he thinks, is essentially a form of ownership over another human being's sexuality. Seen in that light, marriage does not seem right for everybody.

John McMurtry is Professor Emeritus at the University of Guelph in Ontario, Canada. He is the author of *Value Wars: The Global Market Versus the Life Economy* (2002).

> "Remove away that black'ning church
> Remove away that marriage hearse
> Remove away that man of blood
> You'll quite remove the ancient curse."
> WILLIAM BLAKE

I

Almost all of us have entered or will one day enter a specifically standardized form of monogamous marriage. This cultural requirement is so very basic to our existence that we accept it for most part as a kind of intractable given: dictated by the laws of God, Nature,

From *The Monist*, vol. 56, no. 4 (1972), pp. 587–599. Reprinted by permission.

Government and Good Sense all at once. Though it is perhaps unusual for a social practice to be so promiscuously underwritten, we generally find comfort rather than curiosity in this fact and seldom wonder how something could be divinely inspired, biologically determined, coerced and reasoned out all at the same time. We simply take for granted. . . .

Even those irreverent adulterers and unmarried couples who would seem to be challenging the institution in the most basic possible way, in practice, tend merely to mimic its basic structure in unofficial form. The coverings of sanctity, taboo and cultural habit continue to hold them with the grip of public clothes.

II

"Monogamy" means, literally, "one marriage." But it would be wrong to suppose that this phrase tells us much about our particular species of official wedlock. The greatest obstacle to the adequate understanding of our monogamy institution has been the failure to identify clearly and systematically the full complex of principles it involves. There are four such principles, each carrying enormous restrictive force and together constituting a massive social control mechanism that has never, so far as I know, been fully schematized.

To come straight to the point, the four principles in question are as follows:

1. *The partners are required to enter a formal contractual relation:* (*a*) whose establishment demands a specific official participant, certain conditions of the contractors (legal age, no blood ties, etc.) and a standard set of procedures; (*b*) whose governing terms are uniform for all and exactly prescribed by law; and (*c*) whose dissolution may only be legally effected by the decision of state representatives.

The ways in which this elaborate principle of contractual requirement are importantly restrictive are obvious. One may not enter into a marriage union without entering into a contract presided over by a state-investured official. One may not set any of the terms of the contractual relationship by which one is bound for life. And one cannot dissolve the contract without legal action and costs, court proceedings and in many places actual legislation. . . . The extent of control here—over the most intimate and putatively "loving" relationships in all social intercourse—is so great as to be difficult to catalogue without exciting in oneself a sense of disbelief. . . .

2. *The number of partners involved in the marriage must be two and only two* (as opposed to three, four, five or any of the almost countless other possibilities of intimate union).

This second principle of our specific form of monogamy (the concept of "one marriage," it should be pointed out, is consistent with any number of participating partners) is perhaps the most important and restrictive of the four principles we are considering. Not only does it confine us to just *one* possibility out of an enormous range, but it confines us to that single possibility which involves the *least* number of people, two. It is difficult to conceive of a more thorough-going mechanism for limiting extended social union and intimacy. The fact that this monolithic restriction seems so "natural" to us (if it were truly "natural" of course, there would be no need for its rigorous cultural prescription by everything from severe criminal law to ubiquitous housing regulations) simply indicates the extent to which its hold is implanted in our social structure. It is the institutional basis of what I will call the "binary frame of sexual consciousness," a frame through which all our heterosexual relationships are typically viewed ("two's company, three's a crowd") and in light of which all larger circles of intimacy seem almost inconceivable.

3. *No person may participate in more than one marriage at a time or during a lifetime* (unless the previous marriage has been officially dissolved by, normally, one partner's death or successful divorce).

Violation of this principle is, of course, a criminal offence (bigamy) which is punishable by a considerable term in prison. Of various general regulations of our marriage institution it has experienced the most significant modification: not indeed in principle, but in the extent of flexibility of its "escape hatch" of divorce. . . .

4. *No married person may engage in any sexual relationship with any person whatever other than the marriage partner.*

Although a consummated sexual act with another person alone constitutes an act of adultery, lesser forms of sexual and erotic relationships may also constitute grounds for divorce and are generally prescribed as well by informal social convention and taboo. In other words, the fourth and final principle of our marriage institution involves not only a prohibition of sexual intercourse per se outside one's wedlock (this term deserves pause) but a prohibition of all one's erotic relations whatever outside this bond. The penalties for violation here are as various as they are severe, ranging from permanent loss of spouse, children, chattel, and income to job dismissal and social ostracism. In this way, possibly the most compelling natural force towards expanded intimate relations with others is strictly confined within the narrowest possible circle for the whole of adult life. The sheer weight and totality of this restriction is surely one of the great wonders of all historical institutional control.

III

. . . Perhaps the most celebrated justification over the years has proceeded from a belief in a Supreme Deity who secretly utters sexual and other commands to privileged human representatives. Almost as well known a line of defence has issued from a conviction, similarly confident, that the need for some social regulation of sexuality demonstrates the need for our specific type of two-person wedlock. . . .

If we put aside such arguments, we are left I think with two major claims. The first is that our form of monogamous marriage promotes a profound affection between the partners which is not only of great worth in itself but invaluable as a sanctuary from the pressures of outside society. Since, however, there are no secure grounds whatever for supposing that such "profound affection" is not at least as easily achievable by any number of *other* marriage forms (i.e., forms which differ in one or more of the four principles), this justification conspicuously fails to perform the task required of it.

The second major claim for the defence is that monogamy provides a specially loving context for child upbringing. However here again there are no grounds at all for concluding that it does so as, or any more, effectively than other possible forms of marriage (the only alternative type of upbringing to which it has apparently been shown to be superior is nonfamily institutional upbringing, which of course is not relevant to the present discussion). Furthermore, the fact that at least half the span of a normal monogamous marriage *involves no child-upbringing at all* is disastrously overlooked here, as is the reinforcing fact that there is no reference to or mention of the quality of child-upbringing in any of the four principles connected with it. . . .

There is, it seems, little to recommend the view that monogamy specially promotes "profound affection" between the partners or a "loving context" for child-upbringing. Such claims are simply without force. On the other hand, there are several aspects to the logic and operation of the four principles of this institution which suggest that it actually *inhibits* the achievement of these desiderata. . . . In these ways:

1. Centralized official control of marriage (which the Church gradually achieved through the mechanism of Canon Law after the Fall of the Roman Empire in one of the greatest seizures of social power in history) necessarily alienates the partners from full responsibility for and freedom in their relationship. "Profound closeness" between the partners—or least an area of it—is thereby expropriated rather than promoted, and "sanctuary" from the pressures of outside society prohibited rather than fostered.

2. Limitation of the marriage bond to two people necessarily restricts, in perhaps the most unilateral possible way consistent with offspring survival, the number of adult sources of affection, interest, material support and instruction for the young. The "loving context for child-upbringing" is thereby dessicated rather than nourished: providing the structural conditions for such notorious and far-reaching problems as (*a*) sibling rivalry for scarce adult attention and (*b*) parental oppression through exclusive monopoly of the child's means of life.

3. Formal exclusion of all others from erotic contact with the marriage partner systematically promotes conjugal insecurity, jealousy and alienation by:

(*a*) Officially underwriting a literally totalitarian expectation of sexual confinement on the part of one's husband or wife: which expectation is . . . more subject to anxiety and disappointment than one less extreme in its demand and/or cultural-juridical backing;

(*b*) Requiring so complete a sexual isolation of the marriage partners that should one violate the fidelity code the other is left alone and susceptible to a sense of fundamental deprivation and resentment;

(*c*) Stipulating such a strict restraint of sexual energies that there are habitual violations of the regulation: which violations are frequently if not always attended by (i) wilful deception and reciprocal suspicion about the occurrence or quality of the extramarital relationship, (ii) anxiety and fear on both sides of permanent estrangement from partner and family, and/or (iii) overt and covert antagonism over the prohibited act in both offender (who feels "trapped") and offended (who feels "betrayed").

The disadvantages of the four principles of monogamous marriage do not, however, end with inhibiting the very effects they are said to promote. There are further shortcomings:

1. The restriction of marriage union to two partners necessarily prevents the strengths of larger groupings. Such advantages as the following are thereby usually ruled out.

(*a*) The security, range and power of larger socioeconomic units;
(*b*) The epistemological and emotional substance, variety and scope of more pluralist interactions;
(*c*) The possibility of extra-domestic freedom founded on more adult providers and upbringers as well as more broadly based circles of intimacy.

2. The sexual containment and isolation which the four principles together require variously stimulates such social malaises as:

(*a*) Destructive aggression (which notoriously results from sexual frustration);
(*b*) Apathy, frustration and dependence within the marriage bond;
(*c*) Lack of spontaneity, bad faith and distance in relationships without the marriage bond;
(*d*) Sexual fantasizing, perversion, fetishism, prostitution and pornography in the adult population as a whole. . . .

IV

The ground of our marriage institution, the essential principle that underwrites all four restrictions, is this: *the maintenance by one man or woman of the effective right to exclude indefinitely all others from erotic access to the conjugal partner.*

The first restriction creates, elaborates on, and provides for the enforcement of this right to exclude. And the second, third and fourth restrictions together ensure that the said right to exclude is—respectively—not cooperative, not simultaneously or sequentially distributed, and not permissive of even casual exception.

In other words, the four restrictions of our form of monogamous marriage together constitute a state-regulated, indefinite and exclusive ownership by two individuals of one another's sexual powers. Marriage is simply a form of private property.

. . . The history of the institution is so full of suggestive indicators—dowries, inheritance, property alliances, daughter sales (of which women's wedding rings are a carry-over), bride exchanges, legitimacy and illegitimacy—that it is difficult not to see some intimate connections between marital and ownership ties. We are better able still to apprehend the ownership essence of our marriage institution, when in addition we consider:

(a) That until recently almost the only way to secure official dissolution of consummated marriage was to be able to demonstrate violation of one or both partner's sexual ownership (i.e., adultery);

(b) That the imperative of premarital chastity is tantamount to a demand for retrospective sexual ownership by the eventual marriage partner; . . .

(c) That the language of the marriage ceremony is the language of exclusive possession ("take," "to have and to hold," "forsaking all others and keeping you only unto him/her," etc.), not to mention the proprietary locutions associated with the marital relationship (e.g., "he's mine," "she belongs to him," "keep to your own husband," "wife stealer," "possessive husband," etc.). . . .

V

If our marriage institution is a linchpin of our present social structure, then a breakdown in this institution would seem to indicate a breakdown in our social structure. On the face of it, the marriage institution is breaking down—enormously increased divorce rates, nonmarital sexual relationships. . . . Therefore one might be led by the appearance of things to anticipate a profound alteration in the social system.

But it would be a mistake to underestimate the tenacity of an established order or to overestimate the extent of change in our marriage institution. Increased divorce rates merely indicate the widening of a traditional escape hatch. Nonmarital relationships imitate and culminate in the marital mold. . . . It may be changing. But history, as the old man puts it, weighs like a nightmare on the brains of the living.

CHAPTER **29**

*O*ur Sexual Ethics

Bertrand Russell

Bertrand Russell (1872–1970), who won the Nobel Prize for Literature, wrote on almost every philosophical subject. Many consider him to have been the greatest philosopher of the 20th century. "Bertie," as his friends called him, was certainly ahead of his time. In this essay, first published in 1936, Lord Russell advocates a rational approach to sexual ethics. He endorses such ideas as economic equality for women, sexual relations outside of marriage, and honest communication with one's children. Russell does not, however, offer a solution to what he sees as the greatest cause of sexual conflict, namely, the tension between wanting a variety of partners and wanting one's own partners to be monogamous.

I

Sex, more than any other element in human life, is still viewed by many, perhaps by most, in an irrational way. Homicide, pestilence, insanity, gold and precious stones—all the things, in fact, that are the objects of passionate hopes or fears—have been seen, in the past, through a mist of magic or mythology; but the sun of reason has now dispelled the mist, except here and there. The densest cloud that remains is in the territory of sex, as is perhaps natural since sex is concerned in the most passionate part of most people's lives.

From Bertrand Russell, *Why I Am Not a Christian,* edited by Paul Edwards (New York: Simon and Schuster, 1957, 1985), pp. 168–178, originally published in *The American Mercury* 38 (May 1936). Reprinted by permission.

It is becoming apparent, however, that conditions in the modern world are working to effect a change in the public attitude toward sex. As to what change, or changes, this will bring about, no one can speak with any certainty; but it is possible to note some of the forces now at work, and to discuss what their results are likely to be upon the structure of society.

In so far as human nature is concerned, it cannot be said to be *impossible* to produce a society in which there is very little sexual intercourse outside of marriage. The conditions necessary for this result, however, are such as are made almost unattainable by modern life. Let us, then, consider what they are.

The greatest influence toward monogamy is immobility in a region containing few inhabitants. If a man hardly ever has occasion to leave home and seldom sees any woman but his wife, it is easy for him to be faithful; but if he travels without her or lives in a crowded urban community, the problem is proportionately more difficult. The next greatest assistance to monogamy is superstition: those who genuinely believe that "sin" leads to eternal punishment might be expected to avoid it, and to some extent they do so, although not to so great an extent as might be expected. The third support of virtue is public opinion. Where, as in agricultural societies, all that a man does is known to his neighbors, he has powerful motives for avoiding whatever convention condemns. But all these causes of correct behavior are much less potent than they used to be. Fewer people live in isolation; the belief in hell-fire is dying out; and in large towns no one knows what his neighbor does. It is, therefore, not surprising that both men and women are less monogamous than they were before the rise of modern industrialism.

Of course, it may be said that, while an increasing number of people fail to observe the moral law, that is no reason for altering our standards. Those who sin, we are sometimes told, should know and recognize that they sin, and an ethical code is none the worse for being difficult to live up to. But I should reply that the question whether a code is good or bad is the same as the question whether or not it promotes human happiness. . . .

The difficulty of arriving at a workable sexual ethic arises from the conflict between the impulse to jealousy and the impulse to polygamy. There is no doubt that jealousy, while in part instinctive, is to a very large degree conventional. In societies in which a man is considered a fit object for ridicule if his wife is unfaithful, he will be jealous where she is concerned, even if he no longer has any affection for her. Thus jealousy is intimately connected with the sense of property and is much less where this sense is absent. If faithfulness is no part of what is conventionally expected, jealousy is much diminished. But although there is more possibility of lessening jealousy than many people suppose, there are very definite limits so long as fathers have rights and duties. So long as this is the case, it is inevitable that men should desire some assurance that they are the fathers of their wives' children. If women are to have sexual freedom, fathers must fade out, and wives must no longer expect to be supported by their husbands. This may come about in time, but it will be a profound social change, and its effects, for good or ill, are incalculable.

In the meantime, if marriage and paternity are to survive as social institutions, some compromise is necessary between complete promiscuity and lifelong monogamy. To decide on the best compromise at any given moment is not easy; and the decision should vary from time to time, according to the habits of the population and the reliability of birth-control methods. Some things, however, can be said with some definiteness.

In the first place, it is undesirable, both physiologically and educationally, that women should have children before the age of twenty. Our ethics should, therefore, be such as to make this a rare occurrence.

In the second place, it is unlikely that a person without previous sexual experience, whether man or woman, will be able to distinguish between mere physical attraction and the sort of congeniality that is necessary in order to make marriage a success. Moreover, economic causes compel men, as a rule, to postpone marriage, and it is neither likely that they will remain chaste in the years from twenty to thirty nor desirable psychologically that they should do so; but it is much better that, if they have temporary relations, that they should be not with prostitutes but with girls of their own class, whose motive is affection rather than money. For both these reasons, young unmarried people should have considerable freedom as long as children are avoided.

In the third place, divorce should be possible without blame to either party and should not be regarded as in any way disgraceful. A childless marriage should be terminable at the wish of one of the partners, and any marriage should be terminable by mutual consent—a year's notice being necessary in either case. Divorce should, of course, be possible on a number of other grounds—insanity, desertion, cruelty, and so on; but mutual consent should be the most usual ground.

In the fourth place, everything possible should be done to free sexual relations from the economic taint. At present, wives, just as much as prostitutes, live by the sale of their sexual charms; and even in temporary free relations the man is usually expected to bear all the joint expenses. The result is that there is a sordid entanglement of money with sex, and that women's motives not infrequently have a mercenary element. Sex, even when blessed by the church, ought not to be a profession. It is right that a woman should be paid for house-keeping or cooking or the care of children, but not merely for having sexual relations with a man. Nor should a woman who has once loved and been loved by a man be able to live ever after on alimony when his love and hers have ceased. A woman, like a man, should work for her living, and an idle wife is no more intrinsically worthy of respect than a gigolo.

II

Two very primitive impulses have contributed, though in very different degrees, to the rise of the currently accepted code of sexual behavior. One of these is modesty and the other, as mentioned above, is jealousy. Modesty, in some form and to some degree, is almost universal in the human race and constitutes a taboo which must only be broken through in accordance with certain forms and ceremonies, or, at the least, in conformity with some recognized etiquette. Not everything may be seen, and not all facts may be mentioned. This is not, as some moderns suppose, an invention of the Victorian age; on the contrary, anthropologists have found the most elaborate forms of prudery among primitive savages. The conception of the obscene has its roots deep in human nature. We may go against it from a love of rebellion, or from loyalty to the scientific spirit, or from a wish to feel wicked, such as existed in Byron; but we do not thereby eradicate it from among our natural impulses. No doubt convention determines, in a given community, exactly what is to be considered indecent, but the universal existence of *some* convention of the kind is conclusive evidence of a source which is not merely conventional. In almost every human society, pornography and exhibitionism are reckoned as offenses, except when, as not infrequently occurs, they form part of religious ceremonies. . . .

But jealousy, I believe, has been the most potent single factor in the genesis of sexual morality. Jealousy instinctively rouses anger; and anger, rationalized, becomes moral disapproval. The purely instinctive motive must have been reinforced, at an early stage in the development of civilization, by the desire of males to be certain of paternity. Without security in this respect the patriarchal family would have been impossible, and fatherhood, with all its economic implications, could not have become the basis of social institutions. It was, accordingly, wicked to have relations with another man's wife but not even mildly reprehensible to have relations with an unmarried woman. . . . It is the claim of women to equality with men that has done most to make a new system necessary in the world today. Equality can be secured in two ways: either by exacting from men the same strict monogamy as was, in the past, exacted from women; or by allowing women, equally with men, a certain relaxation of the traditional code. The first of these ways was preferred by most of the pioneers of women's rights and is still preferred by the churches; but the second has many more adherents in practice, although most of them are in doubt as to the theoretical justifiability of their own behavior. And those who recognize that *some* new ethic is required find it difficult to know just what its precepts should be.

There is another source of novelty, and that is the effect of the scientific outlook in weakening the taboo on sexual knowledge. It has come to be understood that various evils—for example, venereal disease—cannot be effectively combated unless they are spoken of much more openly than was formerly thought permissible; and it has also been found that reticence and ignorance are apt to have injurious effects upon the psychology of the individual. Both sociology and psychoanalysis have led serious students to reject the policy of silence in regard to sexual matters, and many practical educators, from experience with children, have adopted the same position. Those who have a scientific outlook on human behavior, moreover, find it impossible to label any action as "sin"; they realize that what we do has its origin in our heredity, our education, and our environment, and that it is by control of these causes, rather than by denunciation, that conduct injurious to society is to be prevented.

In seeking a new ethic of sexual behavior, therefore, we must not ourselves be dominated by the ancient irrational passions which gave rise to the old ethic, though we should recognize that they may, by accident, have led to some sound maxims, and that, since they still exist, though perhaps in a weakened form, they are still among the data of our problem. What we have to do positively is to ask ourselves what moral rules are most likely to promote human happiness, remembering always that, whatever the rules may be, they are not likely to be universally observed. That is to say, we have to consider the effect which the rules will in fact have, not that which they would have if they were completely effective.

III

Let us look next at the question of knowledge on sexual subjects, which arises at the earliest age and is the least difficult and doubtful of the various problems with which we are concerned. There is no sound reason, of any sort or kind, for concealing facts when talking to children. Their questions should be answered and their curiosity satisfied in exactly the same way in regard to sex as in regard to the habits of fishes, or any other subject that interests them. There should be no sentiment, because young children cannot feel as adults do and see no occasion for high-flown talk. It is a mistake to begin with the loves of the bees and the flowers; there is no point in leading up to the facts of life by devious routes. The child who is told what he wants to know and allowed to see his parents naked will have no pruriency and no obsession of a sexual kind. Boys who are brought up in official ignorance think and talk much more about sex than boys who have always heard this topic treated on a level with any other. Official ignorance and actual knowledge teach them to be deceitful and hypocritical with their elders. On the other hand, real ignorance, when it is achieved, is likely to be a source of shock and anxiety, and to make adaptation to real life difficult. All ignorance is regrettable, but ignorance on so important a matter as sex is a serious danger.

When I say that children should be told about sex, I do not mean that they should be told only the bare physiological facts; they should be told whatever they wish to know. There should be no attempt to represent adults as more virtuous than they are, or sex as occurring only in marriage. There is no excuse for deceiving children. And when, as must happen in conventional families, they find that their parents have lied, they lose confidence in them and feel justified in lying to them. There are facts which I should not obtrude upon a child, but I would tell him anything sooner than say what is not true. Virtue which is based upon a false view of the facts is not real virtue. Speaking not only from theory but from practical experience, I am convinced that complete openness on sexual subjects is the best way to prevent children from thinking about them excessively, nastily, or unwholesomely, and also the almost indispensable preliminary to an enlightened sexual morality.

Where adult sexual behavior is concerned, it is by no means easy to arrive at a rational compromise between the antagonistic considerations that have each their own validity. The fundamental difficulty is, of course, the conflict between the impulse to jealousy and the impulse to sexual variety. Neither impulse, it is true, is universal: there are those (though they are few) who are never jealous, and there are those (among men as well as among women) whose affections never wander from the chosen partner. If either of these types could be made universal, it would be easy to devise a satisfactory code. It must be admitted, however, that either type can be made more common by conventions designed to that end.

Much ground remains to be covered by a complete sexual ethic, but I do not think we can say anything very positive until we have more experience, both of the effects of various systems and of the changes resulting from a rational education in matters of sex. . . .

In the meantime, it would be well if men and women could remember, in sexual relations, in marriage, and in divorce, to practice the ordinary virtues of tolerance, kindness, truthfulness, and justice. Those who, by conventional standards, are sexually virtuous too often consider themselves thereby absolved from behaving like decent human beings. Most moralists have been so obsessed by sex that they have laid much too little emphasis on other more socially useful kinds of ethically commendable conduct.

CHAPTER 30

A lcohol and Rape

Nicholas Dixon

The black-and-white cases are easy: if a man has consensual sex with a woman who is slightly tipsy, it is not rape; if he has sex with a woman who has passed out from drunkenness, it is rape. Real life, however, contains a lot of gray. What if a woman slurs her words, is unsteady on her feet, and remembers almost nothing of the encounter the next day? Was it sexual assault? This kind of case is hard to assess, for all sorts of reasons.

Nicholas Dixon is a professor of philosophy at Alma College in Michigan.

Many date or acquaintance rapes, especially those that occur in a college setting, involve the use of alcohol by both rapist and victim. To what extent, if any, should the fact that a woman has been drinking alcohol before she has sexual relations affect our determination of whether or not she has been raped? I will consider the impact of the woman's intake of alcohol on both the *actus reus* ("guilty act") and *mens rea* ("guilty mind") elements of rape. A man is guilty of rape only if he not only commits the *actus reus* of rape—sex without his partner's consent—but does so with the requisite guilty mind, that is, intentionally, knowingly, recklessly, or negligently. I will take for granted that, regardless of a woman's alcoholic intake, she has been raped whenever a man forces himself on her after she says "no" or otherwise resists. I will focus instead on situations when women who have been drinking provide varying levels of acquiescence to sex. Let us begin

From *Public Affairs Quarterly*, vol. 15, no. 4 (October 2001), pp. 241–354. Reprinted by permission.

by considering two relatively straightforward examples, which we can use as limiting cases, of sexual encounters involving alcohol.

I. Two Limiting Cases

A. Fraternity Gang Rape. In 1988 four Florida State University fraternity members allegedly had sex with an 18-year-old female student after she had passed out with an almost lethal blood alcohol level of .349 percent. Afterwards, she was allegedly "dumped" in a different fraternity house.

If these events, which led to a five-year ban on the fraternity chapter, really happened, the woman was certainly raped. Since a woman who is unconscious after heavy drinking is unable to consent, the fraternity members committed the *actus reus* of rape. Moreover, any claim that they were unaware of her lack of consent, thus potentially negating the *mens rea* requirement, would ring hollow. We may extrapolate beyond this extreme case to situations where a person is so drunk that, while she is conscious, she is barely aware of where she is and who her partner is, and she has no recollection of what has happened the following day. She may acquiesce and give the physiological responses that indicate consent, and she may even say "yes" when asked whether she wants to have sex, but her mental state is so impaired by alcohol that she cannot give a sufficiently meaningful level of consent to rebut rape charges against the man with whom she has sexual relations.

B. A Regretted Sexual Encounter. A male and female college student go on a dinner date, and both drink a relatively small amount of alcohol, say a glass of wine or beer. The conversation flows freely, and she agrees to go back to his place to continue the evening. They have one more drink there, start kissing and making out, and he asks her to spend the night. She is not drunk and, impressed by his gentle and communicative manner, accepts his offer. However, she is not used to drinking, and, although she is not significantly cognitively impaired—her speech is not slurred and her conversation is lucid—her inhibitions have been markedly lowered by the alcohol. When she wakes up alongside him the following morning, she bitterly regrets their lovemaking.

No rape has occurred. While she now regrets having spent the night with her date, and would quite likely not have agreed to do so had she not drunk any alcohol, her consent at the time was sufficiently voluntary to rule out any question of rape. While their sexual encounter violated her more lasting values, this no more entails that she did not "really" consent than the fact that my overeating at dinner violates my long-term plan to diet entails that my indulgence was not an autonomous action. Moreover, even if we granted for the sake of argument the far fetched claim that the *actus reus* of rape occurred, his belief that she did consent was perfectly reasonable, so he would still fail to exhibit the requisite *mens rea*. . . . A distinction exists between rape and bad sex. Unwisely having sex after unwisely drinking alcohol is not necessarily rape. We do a lot of unwise things when drinking, like *continuing* to drink too long and getting a bad hangover, and staying up too late when we have to work the next day. In neither case would we question our consent to our act of continuing to drink or staying up late. Why should a person's consent to sex after moderate amounts of drinking be any more suspect?

II. Problematic Intermediate Cases: Impaired Sex

Real sexual encounters involving alcohol tend to fall in between these two limiting cases. Imagine, for instance, a college student who gets very drunk at a party. Her blood alcohol level is well above the legal limit for driving. She is slurring her words and is unsteady on her feet, but she knows where she is and with whom she is speaking or dancing. She ends up spending the night with a guy at the party—perhaps someone she has just met, perhaps an acquaintance, but no one with whom she is in an ongoing relationship. She willingly responds to his sexual advances, but, like the woman in case IB, horribly regrets her sexual encounter the next day. Although she remembers going home with the guy from the party, she cannot recall much else from the evening and night. Let us call this intermediate case, in which the woman's judgment is significantly impaired by alcohol, "impaired sex." Has she been raped?

In the next two subsections I will examine two competing analyses of impaired sex, each one suggested by one of the limiting cases in section I. First, though, I pause to consider how relevant the degree to which the man has helped to bring about the woman's impaired state is to the question of whether rape has occurred. Suppose that he has deliberately got her drunk, cajoling her to down drink after drink, with the intention of lowering her resistance to his planned sexual advances? The very fact that he uses such a strategy implies that he doubts that she would agree to have sex with him if she were sober. Should she bring rape charges, on the ground that her acquiescence to sex when she was drunk was invalid, his claim that he believed that she voluntarily consented would appear disingenuous. His recklessness

in disregarding doubts about the voluntariness of her consent arguably meets the *mens rea* requirement. (Remember that in this section
we are discussing women who are very drunk to the point of slurring
their words and being unsteady on their feet, not those who are less
inhibited after drinking a moderate amount of alcohol.)

For the remainder of this paper, I will focus instead on the more
difficult variant of impaired sex in which the man does not use alcohol as a tool for seduction. Instead, he meets the woman when she is
already drunk, or else he drinks with her with no designs on getting
her drunk. In either case, he spontaneously takes advantage of the
situation in which he finds himself. Is he guilty of rape?

A. Women's Responsibility for Their Own Actions. Few would deny
that the woman in section IB is responsible for her own unwise decision to engage in a sexual encounter that she now regrets. Katie
Roiphe and Camille Paglia would extend this approach to impaired
sex, involving a woman who is very drunk but not incoherent. Roiphe
insists that women are autonomous adults who are responsible for the
consequences of their use of alcohol and other drugs.[1] And Paglia
argues that sex is an inherently risky business, in which rape is an ever-
present danger. Rather than complain about sexual assault, women
who desire to be sexually active should take steps to minimize its danger, by being alert to warning signs, learning self-defense, and avoiding
getting drunk when doing so would put them at risk for rape.[2] . . .

Both Roiphe and Paglia are vulnerable to powerful criticisms.
. . . However, we can isolate from their more dubious views a relatively
uncontroversial underlying principle, which is surely congenial to
liberal and most other types of feminists: namely, that we should
respect women's status as agents, and we should not degrade them
by treating them as incapable of making autonomous decisions about
alcohol and sexuality. We should, instead, hold women at least partly
responsible for the consequences of their voluntary decision to drink
large amounts of alcohol, made in full knowledge that it may result in
choices that they will later regret. This principle would count against
regarding impaired sex as rape. A plausible corollary of this principle
is that women, as autonomous beings, have a duty to make their wishes
about sex clear to their partners. When a woman drinks heavily and
ends up having a sexual encounter that she later regrets, she has failed
to exercise this positive duty of autonomous people. Her actions have
sent the wrong message to her partner, and to blame him for the sex
in which she willingly engages but that she later regrets seems unfair.
Even if we allow that her consent is so impaired that the *actus reus* of

rape has occurred, on this view he does not fulfill the *mens rea* element of the crime of rape. The onus is on the woman to communicate her lack of consent and, in the absence of such communication, his belief in her consent is quite reasonable. In sum, proponents of this approach hesitate to regard impaired sex as rape, because doing so suggests that women are unable to make autonomous decisions about alcohol and sexuality, and because it ignores women's positive duty to exercise their autonomy by clearly communicating their considered preferences (and not just their momentary passion) about sex.

B. Communicative Sexuality: Men's Duty to Ensure That Women Consent. The "women's responsibility for sex" approach is very plausible in case IB, where a woman later regrets sex in which she willingly engaged after moderate drinking. However, men's accountability for unwanted sex becomes unavoidable in the gang rape described in subsection IA. Granted, the female student may have voluntarily and very unwisely chosen to drink massive amounts of alcohol, but once she had passed out, the four fraternity members who allegedly had intercourse with her had absolutely no reason to believe that she consented to sex. Regardless of whether they deliberately got her drunk or, on the other hand, took advantage of her after finding her in this condition, they are guilty of recklessly ignoring the evident risk that she did not consent, and hence fulfill the *mens rea* requirement for rape.

In cases such as this, Lois Pineau's model of "communicative sexuality" becomes enormously plausible.[3] . . . Its central tenet is that men too are responsible for ensuring that effective communication occurs. In particular, the burden is on men to ensure that their female partners really do consent to sexual intimacy, and they should refrain from sexual activity if they are not sure of this consent. A reasonable belief that a woman consented to sex will still count as a defense against rape, but the reasonableness of this belief will itself be judged on whether it would have been reasonable, from the woman's point of view, to consent to sex. Since virtually no woman would want four men to have sex with her after she has passed into an alcoholic coma, in the absence of some miraculous evidence that the female student actually wanted sex in such unpleasant circumstances, the four fraternity members blatantly violated their duty to be sure of the woman's consent, and are indeed guilty of rape.

More generally, Pineau argues that it is never reasonable to assume that a woman consents to "aggressive noncommunicative sex." Not only does her approach regard the extreme case of sex with an unconscious person as rape, but it would put any man who fails to take reasonable precautions to ensure that a woman consents to sex at risk for a rape conviction should she later declare that she did not consent. When doubt exists about consent, the burden is on the man to *ask*. The much-discussed Antioch University "Sexual Offense Policy," which requires explicit consent to each new level of sexual intimacy every time it occurs, is a quasi-legal enactment of Pineau's model of communicative sexuality.

Pineau's approach entails a very different analysis of our central case of impaired sex than the "women's responsibility for sex" model discussed in the previous section. At first blush, one might think that all that Pineau would require of a man would be to ask the woman whether she is really sure that she wants to continue with sexual intimacy. If he boldly forges ahead without even asking the woman this question, and if the woman later claims that she was too drunk for her acquiescence to sex to constitute genuine consent, he risks being found guilty of Pineau's proposed category of "nonaggravated sexual assault," which would carry a lighter penalty than "standard" rape when a woman communicates her lack of consent by saying "no" or otherwise resisting.

But even explicitly asking the woman for consent may be insufficient to protect him from blame and liability under the communicative sexuality model. The issue is precisely whether the word "yes," when spoken by a woman who is very drunk, is sufficient evidence of her consent. Being very drunk means that her judgment is impaired, as is evident from her horror and regret the following morning when she realizes what she has done. Given that we are only too aware of our propensity to do things that we later regret when we are very drunk, the man in this situation has good reason to doubt whether the woman's acquiescence to his advances and her "yes" to his explicit question is a fully autonomous reflection of lasting values and desires. Since he cannot be reasonably sure that the woman consents, he should refrain from sexual intercourse. Even if he is unaware of the danger that she does not consent, he *should* be aware and is, therefore, guilty of negligence. His belief that she consents may be sincere, but it is unreasonable and does not provide a defense to charges of nonaggravated sexual assault. On Pineau's "communicative sexuality" model, then, the man who proceeds with impaired sex meets both the *actus reus* and *mens rea* requirements of nonaggravated sexual assault.

III. Should We Punish Men for Impaired Sex?

Pineau's claim that men have a *moral obligation* to ensure that their partners consent to sex is very plausible. Given alcohol's tendency to cloud people's judgment, men should be especially careful to ensure that a woman consents to sex when she is very drunk. In most circumstances, this requires simply refraining from sexual activity. Imposing this relatively minor restriction on men's sexual freedom seems amply justified by the goal of preventing the enormous harm of rape. However, whether we should find men who fail to meet this duty and proceed to have sex with very drunk women guilty of rape—or even of nonaggravated sexual assault or a similar felony carrying a lighter penalty than "standard" rape—is much more controversial.

A. The Importance of Context. Alan Soble criticizes the Antioch University policy on the ground that it fails to distinguish between different types of sexual encounter.[4] Its demand that people obtain explicit verbal consent to each new level of sexual activity during each sexual encounter may be appropriate for one-night stands with strangers. However, it seems unduly intrusive in the context of an ongoing, committed relationship, when the partners may be sufficiently well attuned to one another's body language to be reasonably sure that both people consent to sex. Under Antioch's policy, "[t]he history of the relationship, let alone the history of the evening, counts for nothing."[5]

A similar criticism applies to the demand that men always refrain from impaired sex. While the existence of a long-term, committed relationship does not provide a man with immunity from charges of sexual misconduct—marital rape, after all, can occur—men may reasonably proceed with sexual intimacy with long-term partners who are very drunk when doing so with a stranger would be wrong. In the case of a stranger, the only clue to her wishes that he has is her current, drunken acquiescence, whereas his history of consenting lovemaking with his partner, presumably often when both are sober, gives him every reason to believe that her current consent is fully voluntary and reflective of her ongoing desires. Another exception that could apply even in the case of one-night stands would be when a woman, while sober, gives her advance consent to consuming large amounts of alcohol followed by sexual activity. So if we do criminalize sex with women whose judgment is impaired by large amounts of alcohol, we need to build in exceptions for ongoing relationships and advance consent. . . .

B. Imprecise Distinctions and Fairness to Men. Because of the risk of the substantial harm of sex without a woman's fully voluntary consent, men should normally not have impaired sex. And, provided that we widely publicize the change in rape law and allow exceptions for established relationships and advance consent, criminalizing impaired sex would not be inherently unfair to men. The strongest reason against doing so is that implementing such a law would be a logistical nightmare that would indeed create the risk of unjustly convicting men.

Distinctions that are morally significant are difficult to translate into law. For instance, whether a man deliberately encourages a woman to drink large amounts of alcohol in order to make her more responsive to his sexual advances or, on the other hand, encounters her when she is already drunk or else innocently drinks with her with no intention of taking advantage of her, is relevant to our judgment of his actions. However, proving such subtle differences in intention would be extremely difficult, especially when the prosecution's star witness, the woman who was allegedly assaulted, was drunk at the crucial time.

The biggest logistical problem of all concerns drawing boundaries. The only clear cases are of the type discussed in section I: sex with a woman who is unconscious or incoherent due to alcohol (rape), and communicative sex with a lucid, slightly tipsy woman who later regrets it (no rape). In between these limiting cases is a vast array of situations, whose diversity is concealed by my use of the blanket category of impaired sex. Just how impaired does a woman's judgment have to be to fall into this category? At what point does a woman progress from being merely tipsy, and responsible for any poor judgments that she makes as a result of her condition, to being so impaired that a man who proceeds to have sex with her recklessly or negligently runs the risk of sex without her fully voluntary consent? . . . But the vagueness of the meaning of "significantly impaired" does indeed create doubts about whether men would have fair warning about how to conform their behavior to this new law. Saying that when in doubt, men should err on the side of caution is fair enough, but the only way to be completely sure of avoiding conviction for this felony would be to completely abstain from sex with women who have drunk any alcohol, and this would be an unreasonable restriction on sexual freedom. A law that gives fair warning requires a certain amount of precision about forbidden behavior, and this is hard to come by in matters of impairment due to alcohol. Setting a certain blood alcohol level as the cutoff point seems arbitrary, and requiring a man to be aware of his partner's reading on this scale seems unreasonable and even absurd.

In defense of criminalizing impaired sex, one might argue that making judgment calls about how a legal rule applies to a particular case is precisely what courts are supposed to do. This approach works well when courts are asked to determine how a clear-cut rule applies to the often messy details of a case. The problem here, though, is that the distinction on which impaired sex is based is itself fuzzy, making judgments about whether rape has occurred doubly difficult.

Those who would make impaired sex a felony might point out the analogy with drunk driving laws, in which we set a more or less arbitrary blood alcohol level as the legally acceptable limit, in full knowledge that this limit corresponds only approximately with drivers' level of impairment. The overwhelmingly good overall consequences of a law that deters drunk driving help us to accept the occasional minor injustice of convicting a person whose driving ability was, despite his or her illegal blood alcohol level, not significantly affected. In this light, my dismissal of a blood alcohol level as a cutoff point for impaired sex may have been premature. Such a law would give men a strong incentive to refrain from sex when they have any doubts that their potential partner may be too impaired to give fully voluntary consent.

However, criminalizing impaired sex when the woman's blood alcohol level is above a certain limit is unacceptable for several reasons. First, it places an onerous burden on the man to know his partner's blood alcohol level, in contrast to drunk driving laws, which require us to monitor our *own* intake of intoxicants. Even a man who accompanies his partner throughout her drinking may be unaware of her tolerance level, which may be unusually low. Men who meet women who have already been drinking would have even less reason to be sure that their blood alcohol level is within the legal limit. To be sure of escaping conviction for rape, men in these circumstances would have to either administer portable breathalyzer tests to their partners or else simply abstain from sex. Now showing such restraint may be precisely the kind of caring, thoughtful behavior that we, following Pineau's communicative sexuality model, want to encourage. But to require men to do so, on pain of criminal sanctions (typically imprisonment), seems to be an unduly heavy-handed intrusion into the sex lives of two adults.

Second, measuring a woman's blood alcohol level in order to secure convictions for rape will very likely not be feasible in most cases. Courts need to know her level of impairment at the time of the alleged rape, but in very few cases will a woman be available for a blood test immediately after the sexual encounter. Even an hour afterwards may be too late, in that her blood alcohol level may have dropped below the legal limit for her partner to be at risk for impaired sex.

Due to the emotional trauma or the effects of alcohol, many women will not report the incident until several hours afterwards or even the next day, by which time most or all of the alcohol will have worked its way through her system.

In sum, making impaired sex a felony would be unfair to men, in that the concept "significantly impaired" is too vague for (1) courts to be able to make non-arbitrary judgments to distinguish the guilty from the innocent or (2) men to have fair warning to enable them to conform their behavior to the law. If, on the other hand, we make the law more precise and objective by specifying a blood alcohol content above which a woman's sexual partner would be liable for prosecution for impaired sex, we are placing an undue burden on men whose potential sexual partners have been drinking. Moreover, few women who believe that they have been raped will submit to blood alcohol tests early enough to secure convictions for impaired sex.

One way we might soften the blow of concerns with fair warning would be to make impaired sex a misdemeanor rather than a felony. Such a law would protect women, while the occasional injustice done to men who are convicted though they reasonably believe that their partners consent would result only in such minimal penalties as suspended sentences, fines, or community service. Granted, these minimal penalties might provide little deterrence to men, but they would at least send the desired message that men should exercise care in sexual intimacy when alcohol is involved. And the fact that the penalties are light would minimize whatever danger might exist of frivolous or vindictive complaints against men. However, even if we reduce it to a misdemeanor, we would be hard pressed to rid impaired sex of the connotations of moral turpitude that currently attach to rape and other sexual offenses, so the issue of fair warning would remain significant. Moreover, even though the penalties for a misdemeanor would be slight, we should hesitate to involve courts in prosecuting cases that are very difficult to prove and that people may well sometimes justly perceive as unfair to defendants.

IV. Conclusion

Existing rape laws probably suffice to convict men for clear cases of sexual misconduct involving alcohol, such as sex with unconscious women or with women who are drunk to the point of incoherence. In jurisdictions where such laws do not exist, we should create a category of rape—on the lines of "sex with a partner who is incapable of consent"—that would criminalize such cases. Granted, complications would arise. We would probably have to allow for exceptions for advance consent and for ongoing relationships. And, as in all rape cases, proving guilt may often be difficult, often reducing to "her word against his." But the harm done by men who take advantage of women in such circumstances is great enough to justify taking on these problems.

However, we would do better to deal with impaired sex by means of moral disapproval and educational measures rather than legal sanctions. The dangers of unjustly convicting men on the basis of unworkable distinctions, and of simultaneously degrading women (however inadvertently) and being unfair to men by underestimating women's ability to take responsibility for their alcohol intake and sexuality, are too great. Instead, we should regard impaired sex as a moral wrong on the lines of obtaining sexual gratification by means of trickery, such as concealing the fact that one has a spouse or significant other, or declaring one's undying love when all one wants is a brief fling. In the case of both impaired sex and trickery, one's partner is prevented from making a fully autonomous decision about her sexual activity: either because her judgment is clouded by alcohol, or because she has been denied vital information. Both are wrong, and both are better dealt with by informal sanctions than by inevitably heavy-handed and sometimes unfair legal interventions.

Notes

1. Katie Roiphe, *The Morning After*, in Robert Trevas, Arthur Zucker, and Donald Borchert (eds.), *Philosophy of Sex and Love: A Reader* (Upper Saddle River, NJ: Prentice Hall, 1997), p. 365.

2. Camille Paglia, "Date Rape: Another Perspective," in William H. Shaw (ed.), *Social and Personal Ethics*, 2nd edition (Belmont, CA: Wadsworth Publishing Co., 1996).

3. Lois Pineau, "Date Rape: A Feminist Analysis," *Law and Philosophy* 8 (1989).

4. Alan Soble, "Antioch's 'Sexual Offense Policy': A Philosophical Exploration," *Journal of Social Philosophy*, vol. 28, no. 1 (Spring 1997), pp. 30–32.

5. Ibid., p. 30.

CHAPTER 31

*L*etter from the Birmingham City Jail

Martin Luther King, Jr.

Born in 1929, Martin Luther King, Jr., followed in his father's footsteps and became a Baptist minister. In 1956, while he was pastor of the Dexter Avenue Baptist Church in Montgomery, Alabama, he led a boycott of that city's segregated public buses, and then went on to become the leading voice in the American civil rights movement. Dr. King was awarded the Nobel Peace Prize in 1964. He was murdered in 1968, two months after calling the United States "the world's greatest purveyor of violence."

In 1963, while incarcerated in an Alabama jail, he read a statement that had been issued by some of his fellow clergymen. The statement sympathized with the goals of his movement but questioned the wisdom of his tactics. King advocated—and practiced—nonviolent civil disobedience, while these critics argued that we should follow laws even when they are unjust. Using a pen his lawyers smuggled in and some tattered scraps of paper that were lying about, King wrote an "open letter" replying to them. This "Letter from the Birmingham City Jail" was printed in many liberal magazines and newspapers until almost a million copies were in circulation. It became the single most famous document of the movement.

MY DEAR FELLOW CLERGYMEN,

While confined here in the Birmingham city jail, I came across your recent statement calling our present activities "unwise and untimely." Seldom, if ever, do I pause to answer criticism of my work and ideas. If I sought to answer all of the criticisms that cross my desk, my secretaries would be engaged in little else in the course of the day, and I would have no time for constructive work. But since I feel that you are men of genuine good will and your criticisms are sincerely set forth, I would like to answer your statement in what I hope will be patient and reasonable terms.

You may well ask, "Why direct action? Why sit-ins, marches, etc.? Isn't negotiation a better path?" You are exactly right in your call for negotiation. Indeed, this is the purpose of direct action. Nonviolent direct action seeks to create such a crisis and establish such creative tension that a community that has constantly refused to negotiate is forced to confront the issue. It seeks so to dramatize the issue that it can no longer be ignored. I just referred to the creation of tension as a part of the work of the nonviolent resister. This may sound rather shocking. But I must confess that I am not afraid of the word *tension*. I have earnestly worked and preached against violent tension, but there is a type of constructive nonviolent tension that is necessary for growth. Just as Socrates felt that it was necessary to create a tension in the mind so that individuals could rise from the bondage of myths and half-truths to the unfettered realm of creative analysis and objective appraisal, we must see the need of having nonviolent gadflies to create the kind of tension in society that will help men to rise from the dark depths of prejudice and racism to the majestic heights of understanding and brotherhood. So the purpose of the direct action is to create a situation so crisis-packed that it will inevitably open the door to negotiation. We, therefore, concur with you in your call for negotiation. Too long has our beloved Southland been bogged down in the tragic attempt to live in monologue rather than dialogue.

One of the basic points in your statement is that our acts are untimely. Some have asked, "Why didn't you give the new administration time to act?" The only answer that I can give to this inquiry is that the new administration must be prodded about as much as the outgoing one before it acts. We will be sadly mistaken if we feel that the election of Mr. Boutwell will bring the millennium to Birmingham. While Mr. Boutwell is much more articulate and gentle than Mr. Connor, they are both segregationists, dedicated to the task of maintaining the status quo. The hope I see in Mr. Boutwell is that he will be reasonable enough to see the futility of massive resistance to desegregation. But he will not see this without pressure from the devotees of civil rights. My friends, I must say to you that we have not made a single gain in civil rights without determined legal and nonviolent pressure. History is the long and tragic story of the fact that privileged groups seldom give up their privileges voluntarily. Individuals may see the moral light and voluntarily give up their unjust posture; but as Reinhold Niebuhr has reminded us, groups are more immoral than individuals.

We know through painful experience that freedom is never voluntarily given by the oppressor; it must be demanded by the oppressed. Frankly, I have never yet engaged in a direct action movement that was "well-timed," according to the timetable of those who have not suffered unduly from the disease of segregation. For years now I have heard the word "Wait!" It rings in the ear of every Negro with a piercing familiarity. This "Wait" has almost always meant "Never." It has been a tranquilizing thalidomide, relieving the emotional stress for a moment, only to give birth to an ill-formed infant of frustration. We must come to see with the distinguished jurist of yesterday that "justice too long delayed is justice denied." We have waited for more than 340 years for our constitutional and God-given rights. The nations of Asia and Africa are moving with jetlike speed toward the goal of political independence, and we still creep at horse and buggy pace toward the gaining of a cup of coffee at a lunch counter. I guess it is easy for those who have never felt the stinging darts of segregation to say, "Wait." But when you have seen vicious mobs lynch your mothers and fathers at will and drown your sisters and brothers at whim; when you have seen hate-filled policemen curse, kick, brutalize and even kill your black brothers and sisters with impunity; when you see the vast majority of your twenty million Negro brothers smothering in an airtight cage of poverty in the midst of an affluent society; when you suddenly find your tongue twisted and your speech stammering as you seek to explain to your six-year-old daughter why she can't go to the public amusement park that has just been advertised on television, and see tears welling up in her little eyes when she is told that Funtown is closed to colored children, and see the depressing clouds of inferiority begin to form in her little mental sky, and see her begin to distort her little personality by unconsciously developing a bitterness toward white people; when you have to concoct an answer for a five-year-old son asking in agonizing pathos: "Daddy, why do white people treat colored people so mean?"; when you take a cross-country drive and find it necessary to sleep night after night in the uncomfortable corners of your automobile because no motel will accept you; when you are humiliated day in and day out by nagging signs reading "white" and "colored"; when your first name becomes "nigger" and your middle name becomes "boy" (however old you are) and your last name becomes "John," and when your wife and mother are never given the respected title "Mrs."; when you are harried by day and haunted by night by the fact that you are a Negro, living constantly at tiptoe stance never quite knowing what to expect next, and plagued with inner fears and outer resentments; when you are forever fighting a degenerating sense of "nobodiness"; then you will understand why we find it difficult to wait. There comes a time when the cup of endurance runs over, and men are no longer willing to be plunged into an abyss of injustice where they experience the blackness of corroding despair. I hope, sirs, you can understand our legitimate and unavoidable impatience.

You express a great deal of anxiety over our willingness to break laws. This is certainly a legitimate concern. Since we so diligently urge people to obey the Supreme Court's decision of 1954 outlawing segregation in the public schools, it is rather strange and paradoxical to find us consciously breaking laws. One may well ask, "How can you advocate breaking some laws and obeying others?" The answer is found in the fact that there are two types of laws: there are *just* and there are *unjust* laws. I would agree with Saint Augustine that "An unjust law is no law at all."

Now what is the difference between the two? How does one determine when a law is just or unjust? A just law is a man-made code that squares with the moral law or the law of God. An unjust law is a code that is out of harmony with the moral law. To put it in the terms of Saint Thomas Aquinas, an unjust law is a human law that is not rooted in eternal and natural law. Any law that uplifts human personality is just. Any law that degrades human personality is unjust. All segregation statutes are unjust because segregation distorts the soul and damages the personality. It gives the segregator a false sense of superiority, and the segregated a false sense of inferiority. To use the words of Martin Buber, the great Jewish philosopher, segregation substitutes an "I-it" relationship for the "I-thou" relationship, and ends up relegating persons to the status of things. So segregation is not only politically, economically and sociologically unsound, but it is morally wrong and sinful. Paul Tillich has said that sin is separation. Isn't segregation an existential expression of man's tragic separation, an expression of his awful estrangement, his terrible sinfulness? So I can urge men to disobey segregation ordinances because they are morally wrong.

Let us turn to a more concrete example of just and unjust laws. An unjust law is a code that a majority inflicts on a minority that is not binding on itself. This is difference made legal. On the other hand a just law is a code that a majority compels a minority to follow that it is willing to follow itself. This is sameness made legal.

Let me give another explanation. An unjust law is a code inflicted upon a minority which that minority had no part in enacting or creating because they did not have the unhampered right to vote. Who can say that the legislature of Alabama which set up the segregation laws was democratically elected? Throughout the state of Alabama all types of conniving methods are used to prevent Negroes from becoming registered voters and there are some counties without a single Negro registered to vote despite the fact that the Negro constitutes a majority of the population. Can any law set up in such a state be considered democratically structured?

These are just a few examples of unjust and just laws. There are some instances when a law is just on its face and unjust in its application. For instance, I was arrested Friday on a charge of parading without a permit. Now there is nothing wrong with an ordinance which requires a permit for a parade, but when the ordinance is used to preserve segregation and to deny citizens the First Amendment privilege of peaceful assembly and peaceful protest, then it becomes unjust.

I hope you can see the distinction I am trying to point out. In no sense do I advocate evading or defying the law as the rabid segregationist would do. This would lead to anarchy. One who breaks an unjust law must do it *openly, lovingly* (not hatefully as the white mothers did in New Orleans when they were seen on television screaming, "nigger, nigger, nigger"), and with a willingness to accept the penalty. I submit that an individual who breaks a law that conscience tells him is unjust, and willingly accepts the penalty by staying in jail to arouse the conscience of the community over its injustice, is in reality expressing the very highest respect for law.

Of course, there is nothing new about this kind of civil disobedience. It was seen sublimely in the refusal of Shadrach, Meshach and Abednego to obey the laws of Nebuchadnezzar because a higher moral law was involved. It was practiced superbly by the early Christians who were willing to face hungry lions and the excruciating pain of chopping blocks, before submitting to certain unjust laws of the Roman Empire. To a degree academic freedom is a reality today because Socrates practiced civil disobedience.

We can never forget that everything Hitler did in Germany was "legal" and everything the Hungarian freedom fighters did in Hungary was "illegal." It was "illegal" to aid and comfort a Jew in Hitler's Germany. But I am sure that if I had lived in Germany during that time I would have aided and comforted my Jewish brothers even though it was illegal. If I lived in a Communist country today where certain principles dear to the Christian faith are suppressed, I believe I would openly advocate disobeying these anti-religious laws. I must make two honest confessions to you, my Christian and Jewish brothers. First, I must confess that over the last few years I have been gravely disappointed with the white moderate. I have almost reached the regrettable conclusion that the Negro's great stumbling block in the stride toward freedom is not the White Citizens Counciler or the Ku Klux Klanner, but the white moderate who is more devoted to "order" than to justice; who prefers a negative peace which is the absence of tension to a positive peace which is the presence of justice; who constantly says, "I agree with you in the goal you seek, but I can't agree with your methods of direct action"; who paternalistically feels that he can set the timetable for another man's freedom; who lives by the myth of time and who constantly advises the Negro to wait until a "more convenient season." Shallow understanding from people of good will is more frustrating than absolute misunderstanding from people of ill will. Lukewarm acceptance is much more bewildering than outright rejection.

I had hoped that the white moderate would understand that law and order exist for the purpose of establishing justice, and that when they fail to do this they become dangerously structured dams that block the flow of social progress. I had hoped that the white moderate would understand that the present tension of the South is merely a necessary phase of the transition from an obnoxious negative peace, where the Negro passively accepted his unjust plight, to a substance-filled positive peace, where all men will respect the dignity and worth of human personality. Actually, we who engage in nonviolent direct action are not the creators of tension. We merely bring to the surface the hidden tension that is already alive. We bring it out in the open where it can be seen and dealt with. Like a boil that can never be cured as long as it is covered up but must be opened with all its pus-flowing ugliness to the natural medicines of air and light, injustice must likewise be exposed, with all of the tension its exposing creates, to the light of human conscience and the air of national opinion before it can be cured.

In your statement you asserted that our actions, even though peaceful, must be condemned because they precipitate violence. But can this assertion be logically made? Isn't this like condemning the robbed man because his possession of money precipitated the evil act of robbery? Isn't this like condemning Socrates because his unswerving commitment to truth and his philosophical delvings precipitated the misguided popular mind to make him drink the hemlock? Isn't this like condemning Jesus because His unique God-consciousness and never-ceasing devotion to His will precipitated the evil act of crucifixion? We must come to see, as federal courts have consistently affirmed, that it is immoral to urge an individual to withdraw his efforts to gain his basic constitutional rights because the quest precipitates violence. Society must protect the robbed and punish the robber. . . .

I must close now. But before closing I am impelled to mention one other point in your statement that troubled me profoundly. You warmly commended the Birmingham police force for keeping "order" and "preventing violence." I don't believe you would have so warmly commended the police force if you had seen its angry violent dogs literally biting six unarmed, nonviolent Negroes. I don't believe you would so quickly commend the policemen if you would observe their ugly and inhuman treatment of Negroes here in the city jail; if you would watch them push and curse old Negro women and young Negro girls; if you would see them slap and kick old Negro men and young boys; if you will observe them, as they did on two occasions, refuse to give us food because we wanted to sing our grace together. I'm sorry that I can't join you in your praise for the police department.

It is true that they have been rather disciplined in their public handling of the demonstrators. In this sense they have been rather publicly "nonviolent." But for what purpose? To preserve the evil system of segregation. Over the last few years I have consistently preached that nonviolence demands that the means we use must be as pure as the ends we seek. So I have tried to make it clear that it is wrong to use immoral means to attain moral ends. But now I must affirm that it is just as wrong, or even more so, to use moral means to preserve immoral ends. Maybe Mr. Connor and his policemen have been rather publicly nonviolent, as Chief Pritchett was in Albany, Georgia, but they have used the moral means of nonviolence to maintain the immoral end of flagrant racial injustice. T. S. Eliot has said that there is no greater treason than to do the right deed for the wrong reason.

I wish you had commended the Negro sit-inners and demon-strators of Birmingham for their sublime courage, their willingness to suffer and their amazing discipline in the midst of the most inhu-man provocation. One day the South will recognize its real heroes. They will be the James Merediths, courageously and with a majestic sense of purpose facing jeering and hostile mobs and the agonizing loneliness that characterizes the life of the pioneer. They will be old, oppressed, battered Negro women, symbolized in a seventy-two-year-old woman of Montgomery, Alabama, who rose up with a sense of dignity and with her people decided not to ride the segregated buses, and responded to one who inquired about her tiredness with ungram-matical profundity: "My feet is tired, but my soul is rested." They will be the young high school and college students, young ministers of the gospel and a host of their elders courageously and nonviolently sitting-in at lunch counters and willingly going to jail for conscience's sake. One day the South will know that when these disinherited chil-dren of God sat down at lunch counters they were in reality standing up for the best in the American dream and the most sacred values in our Judeo-Christian heritage, and thusly, carrying our whole nation back to those great wells of democracy which were dug deep by the Founding Fathers in the formulation of the Constitution and the Dec-laration of Independence. . . .

I hope this letter finds you strong in the faith. I also hope that cir-cumstances will soon make it possible for me to meet each of you, not as an integrationist or a civil rights leader, but as a fellow clergyman and a Christian brother. Let us all hope that the dark clouds of racial prejudice will soon pass away and the deep fog of misunderstanding will be lifted from our fear-drenched communities and in some not too distant tomorrow the radiant stars of love and brotherhood will shine over our great nation with all of their scintillating beauty.

Yours for the cause of Peace and Brotherhood,
MARTIN LUTHER KING, JR.

CHAPTER 32

*I*s Racial Discrimination Arbitrary?

Peter Singer

When the Major League Baseball season ended in 1973, Atlanta Braves slugger Hank Aaron was just one swing away from the greatest prize in baseball: Babe Ruth's record of 714 career home runs. History was in the making; the Bambino was about to get hammered. Aaron's first at bat of the '74 season saw number 714. Number 715 came on April 8, 1974, before a sellout crowd in Atlanta. Today, outside the Braves' stadium, there is a statue of Hank Aaron, and though the stadium has moved, a sign in the outfield still commemorates the spot where home run 715 cleared the fence.

There is, however, an unpleasant side to this story. Aaron now recalls those "glory" days as being the worst days of his life. Why? Because Aaron is African-American, and for daring to break Babe Ruth's record, he had to endure a torrent of hatred. In 1973, he received 930,000 pieces of mail, most of it filled with racial slurs. As he got near Ruth's record, Aaron holed up in his apartment, afraid to go outside. The FBI uncovered a plot to kill his daughter, who lived in Nashville. And when he actually hit number 715, Aaron's mother, Estella, jumped out of the stands and rushed onto the field, not out of joy, but because she believed that her son was about to be murdered.

Racial discrimination violates one of our most deeply held moral beliefs: that people should not be treated badly for arbitrary reasons like the color of their skin. The hatred Hank Aaron had to endure was clearly vile. However, other cases of differential treatment are less clear. Peter Singer discusses three such cases in this selection.

From *Philosophia,* vol. 8, no. 1, October 1978. Reprinted by permission.

1. Introduction

There is nowadays wide agreement that racism is wrong. To describe a policy, law, movement, or nation as "racist" is to condemn it. It may be thought that since we all agree that racism is wrong, it is unnecessary to speculate on exactly what it is and why it is wrong. This indifference to moral fundamentals could, however, prove dangerous. For one thing, the fact that most people agree today that racism is wrong does not mean that this attitude will always be so widely shared. Even if we had no fears for the future, though, we need to have some understanding of what it is about racism that is wrong if we are to handle satisfactorily all the problems we face today. For instance, there is the contentious issue of "reverse discrimination" or discrimination in favor of members of oppressed minority groups. It must be granted that a university which admits members of minority groups who do not achieve the minimum standard that others must reach in order to be admitted is discriminating on racial lines. Is such discrimination therefore wrong?

Or, to take another issue, the efforts of Arab nations to have the United Nations declare Zionism a form of racism provoked an extremely hostile reaction in nations friendly to Israel, particularly the United States, but it led to virtually no discussion of whether Zionism is a form of racism. Yet the charge is not altogether without plausibility, for if Jews are a race, then Zionism promotes the idea of a state dominated by one race, and this has practical consequences in, for instance, Israel's immigration laws. Again, to consider whether this makes Zionism a form of racism we need to understand what it is that makes a policy racist and wrong. . . .

If we ask those who regard racial discrimination as wrong to say why it is wrong, it is commonly said that it is wrong to pick on race as a reason for treating one person differently from others, because race is irrelevant to whether a person should be given a job, the vote, higher education, or any benefits or burdens of this sort. The irrelevance of race, it is said, makes it quite arbitrary to give these things to people of one race while withholding them from those of another race. I shall refer to this account of what is wrong with racial discrimination as the "standard objection" to racial discrimination.

A sophisticated theory of justice can be invoked in support of this standard objection to racial discrimination. Justice requires, as Aristotle so plausibly said, that equals be treated equally and unequals be treated unequally. To this we must add the obvious proviso that the equalities or inequalities should be relevant to the treatment in question. Now when we consider things like employment, it becomes clear that the relevant inequalities between candidates for a vacant position are inequalities in their ability to carry out the duties of the position and, perhaps, inequalities in the extent to which they will benefit through being offered the position. Race does not seem to be relevant at all. Similarly with the vote, capacity for rational choice between candidates or policies might be held a relevant characteristic, but race should not be; and so on for other goods. It is hard to think of anything for which race in itself is a relevant characteristic, and hence to use race as a basis for discrimination is arbitrarily to single out an irrelevant factor, no doubt because of a bias or prejudice against those of a different race.

As we shall see, this account of why racial discrimination is wrong is inadequate because there are many situations in which, from at least one point of view, the racial factor is by no means irrelevant, and therefore it can be denied that racial discrimination in these situations is arbitrary.

One type of situation in which race must be admitted to be relevant to the purposes of the person discriminating need not delay us at this stage; this is the situation in which those purposes themselves favor a particular race. Thus if the purpose of Hitler and the other Nazi leaders was, among other things, to produce a world in which there were no Jews, it was certainly not irrelevant to their purposes that those rounded up and murdered by the SS were Jews rather than so-called "Aryans." But the fundamental wrongness of the aims of the Nazis makes the "relevance" of race to those aims totally inefficacious so far as justifying Nazi racial discrimination is concerned. While their type of racial discrimination may not have been arbitrary discrimination in the usual sense, it was no less wrong for that. *Why* it was wrong is something that I hope will become clearer later in this article. Meanwhile I shall look at some less cataclysmic forms of racial discrimination, for too much contemporary discussion of racial discrimination has focused on the most blatant instances: Nazi Germany, [the former situation in] South Africa, and the American "Deep South" during the period of legally enforced racial segregation. These forms of racism are not the type that face us now in our own societies . . . and to discuss racial discrimination in terms of these examples today is to present an oversimplified picture of the problem of racial discrimination. By looking at some of the reasons for racial discrimination that might actually be offered today in countries all over the world I hope to show that the real situation is usually much more complex than consideration of the more blatant instances of racial discrimination would lead us to believe.

2. Examples

I shall start by describing an example of racial discrimination which may at first glance seem to be an allowable exception to a general rule that racial discrimination is arbitrary and therefore wrong; and I shall then suggest that this case has parallels with other cases we may not be so willing to allow as exceptions.

Case 1. A film director is making a film about the lives of blacks living in New York's Harlem. He advertises for black actors. A white actor turns up, but the director refuses to allow him to audition, saying that the film is about blacks and there are no roles for whites. The actor replies that, with the appropriate wig and make-up, he can look just like a black; moreover he can imitate the mannerisms, gestures, and speech of Harlem blacks. Nevertheless the director refuses to consider him for the role, because it is essential to the director's conception of the film that the black experience be authentically portrayed, and however good a white actor might be, the director would not be satisfied with the authenticity of the portrayal.

   The film director is discriminating along racial lines, yet he cannot be said to be discriminating arbitrarily. His discrimination is apt for his purpose. Moreover his purpose is a legitimate one. So the standard objection to racial discrimination cannot be made in this instance.

   Racial discrimination may be acceptable in an area like casting for films or the theater, when the race of a character in the film or play is important, because this is one of the seemingly few areas in which a person's race is directly relevant to his capacity to perform a given task. As such, it may be thought, these areas can easily be distinguished from other areas of employment, as well as from areas like housing, education, the right to vote, and so on, where race has no relevance at all. Unfortunately there are many other situations in which race is not as totally irrelevant as this view assumes.

Case 2. The owner of a cake shop with a largely white and racially prejudiced clientele wishes to hire an assistant. The owner has no prejudice against blacks himself, but is reluctant to employ one, for fear that his customers will go elsewhere. If his fears are well-founded (and this is not impossible) then the race of a candidate for the position is, again, relevant to the purpose of the employer, which in this case is to maintain the profitability of his business.

What can we say about this case? We cannot deny the connection between race and the owner's purposes, and so we must recognize that the owner's discrimination is not arbitrary, and does not necessarily indicate a bias or prejudice on his part. Nor can we say that the owner's purpose is an illegitimate one, for making a profit from the sale of cakes is not generally regarded as wrong, at least if the amount of profit made is modest.

We can, of course, look at other aspects of the matter. We can object to the racial discrimination shown by customers who will search out shops staffed by whites only—such people do discriminate arbitrarily, for race is irrelevant to the quality of the goods and the proficiency of service in a shop—but is this not simply a fact that the shop-owner must live with, however much he may wish he could change it? We might argue that by pandering to the prejudices of his customers, the owner is allowing those prejudices to continue unchallenged; whereas if he and other shopkeepers took no notice of them, people would eventually become used to mixing with those of another race, and prejudices would be eroded. Yet it is surely too much to ask an individual shop-owner to risk his livelihood in a lone and probably vain effort to break down prejudice. Few of the most dedicated opponents of racism do as much. If there were national legislation which distributed the burden more evenly, by a general prohibition of discrimination on racial grounds (with some recognized exceptions for cases like casting for a film or play) the situation would be different. Then we could reasonably ask every shop-owner to play his part. Whether there should be such legislation is a different question from whether the shop-owner may be blamed for discriminating in the absence of legislation. I shall discuss the issue of legislation shortly, after we consider a different kind of racial discrimination that, again, is not arbitrary.

Case 3. A landlord discriminates against blacks in renting the accommodation he owns. Let us say that he is not so rigid as never to rent an apartment to a black, but if a black person and a white person appear to be equally suitable as tenants, with equally good references and so on, the landlord invariably prefers the white. He defends his policy along the following lines:

> If more than a very small proportion of my tenants get behind in their rent and then disappear without paying the arrears, I will be out of business. Over the years, I have found that more blacks do this than whites. I admit that there are many honest blacks (some of my best tenants have been black) and many dishonest whites, but, for some reason I do not claim to understand, the odds on a white tenant defaulting are longer than on a black doing so, even when their references and other credentials appear equally good. In this business you can't run a full-scale probe of every prospective tenant—and if I tried I would be abused for invading privacy—so you have to go by the average rather than the individual. That is why blacks have to have better indications of reliability than whites before I will rent to them.

Now the landlord's impression of a higher rate of default among blacks than among comparable whites may itself be the result of prejudice on his part. Perhaps in most cases when landlords say this kind of thing, there is no real factual basis to their allegations. People have grown up with racial stereotypes, and these stereotypes are reinforced by a tendency to notice occurrences which conform to the stereotype and to disregard those which conflict with it. So if unreliability is part of the stereotype of blacks held by many whites, they may take more notice of blacks who abscond without paying the rent than of blacks who are reliable tenants; and conversely they will take less notice of absconding whites and more of those whites who conform to their ideas of normal white behaviour.

If it is prejudice that is responsible for the landlord's views about black and white tenants, and there is no factual basis for his claims, then the problem becomes one of eliminating this prejudice and getting the landlord to see his mistake. This is by no means an easy task, but it is not a task for philosophers, and it does not concern us here, for we are interested in attempts to justify racial discrimination, and an attempted justification based on an inaccurate description of a situation can be rejected without raising the deeper issue of justification.

On the other hand, the landlord's impression of a higher rate of default among black tenants *could* be entirely accurate. (It might be explicable in terms of the different cultural and economic circumstances in which blacks are brought up.) Whether or not we think this likely, we need to ask what its implications would be for the justifiability of the racial discrimination exercised by the landlord. To refuse even to consider this question would be to rest all one's objections to the landlord's practice on the falsity of his claims, and thereby to fail to examine the possibility that the landlord's practice could be open to objection even if his impressions on tenant reliability are accurate.

If the landlord's impressions were accurate, we would have to concede, once again, that racial discrimination in this situation is not arbitrary; that it is, instead, relevant to the purposes of the landlord. We must also admit that these purposes—making a living from letting property that one owns—are not themselves objectionable, provided the rents are reasonable, and so on. Nor can we, this time, locate the origin of the problem in the prejudices of others, except insofar as the problem has its origin in the prejudices of those responsible for the conditions of deprivation in which many of the present generation of blacks grew up—but it is too late to do anything to alter those prejudices anyway, since they belong to previous generations.

We have now looked at three examples of racial discrimination, and can begin to examine the parallels and differences between them. Many people, as I have already said, would make no objection to the discriminatory hiring practice of the film director in the first of these cases. But we can now see that if we try to justify the actions of the film director in this case on the grounds that his purpose is a legitimate one and the discrimination he uses is relevant for his purpose, we will have to accept the actions of the cake-shop owner and the landlord as well. I suspect that many of those ready to accept the discriminatory practice in the first case will be much more reluctant about the other two cases. But what morally significant difference is there between them?

It might be suggested that the difference between them lies in the nature of what blacks are being deprived of, and their title to it. The argument would run like this: No one has a right to be selected to act in a film; the director must have absolute discretion to hire whomsoever he wishes to hire. After all, no one can force the director to make the film at all, and if he didn't make it, no one would be hired to play in it; if he does decide to make it, therefore, he must be allowed to make it on his own terms. Moreover, since so few people ever get the chance to appear in a film, it would be absurd to hold that the director violates someone's rights by not giving him something which most people will never have anyway. On the other hand, people do have a right to employment, and to housing. To discriminate against blacks in an ordinary employment situation, or in the letting of accommodation, threatens their basic rights and therefore should not be tolerated.

Plausible as it appears, this way of distinguishing the first case from the other two will not do. Consider the first and second cases: almost everything that we have said about the film director applies to the cake-shop owner as well. No one can force the cake-shop owner to keep his shop open, and if he didn't, no one would be hired to work in it. If in the film director's case this was a reason for allowing him to make the film on his own terms, it must be a reason for allowing the shop-owner to run his shop on his own terms. In fact, such reasoning, which would allow unlimited discrimination in restaurants, hotels, and shops, is invalid. There are plenty of examples where we would not agree that the fact that someone did not have to make an offer or provide an opportunity at all means that if he does do it he must be allowed to make the offer or provide the opportunity on his own terms. The United States Civil Rights Act of 1965 certainly does not recognize this line of argument, for it prohibits those offering food and lodgings to the public from excluding customers on racial grounds. We may, as a society, decide that we shall not allow people to make certain offers, if the way in which the offers are made will cause hardship or offense to others. In so doing we are balancing people's freedom to do as they please against the harm this may do to others, and coming down on the side of preventing harm rather than enlarging freedom. This is a perfectly defensible position, if the harm is sufficiently serious and the restriction of freedom not grave.

Nor does it seem possible to distinguish the first and second cases by the claim that since so few people ever get the chance to appear in a film, no one's rights are violated if they are not given something that most people will never have anyway. For if the number of jobs in cake-shops was small, and the demand for such jobs high, it would also be true that few people would ever have the chance to work in a cake-shop. It would be odd if such an increase in competition for the job justified an otherwise unjustifiable policy of hiring whites only. Moreover, this argument would allow a film director to discriminate on racial lines even if race was irrelevant to the roles he was casting; and that is quite a different situation from the one we have been discussing.

The best way to distinguish the situations of the film director and the shop-owner is by reference to the nature of the employment offered, and to the reasons why racial discrimination in these cases is not arbitrary. In casting for a film about blacks, the race of the actor auditioning is intrinsically significant, independently of the attitudes of those connected with the film. In the case of hiring a shop assistant, race is relevant only because of the attitudes of those connected (as customers) with the shop; it has nothing to do with the selling of cakes in itself, but only with the selling of cakes to racially prejudiced customers. This means that in the case of the shop assistant we could eliminate the relevance of race if we could eliminate the prejudices of the customers; by contrast there is no way in which we could eliminate the relevance of the race of an actor auditioning for a role in a film about blacks, without altering the nature of the film. Moreover, in the case of the shop-owner racial discrimination probably serves to perpetuate the very prejudices that make such discrimination relevant and (from the point of view of the owner seeking to maintain his profits) necessary. Thus people who can buy all their cakes and other necessities in shops staffed only by whites will never come into the kind of contact with comparable blacks which might break down their aversion to being served by blacks; whereas if shop-owners were to hire more blacks, their customers would no doubt become used to it and in time might wonder why they ever opposed the idea. . . .

Hence if we are opposed to arbitrary discrimination we have reason to take steps against racial discrimination in situations like Case 2, because such discrimination, while not itself arbitrary, both feeds on and gives support to discrimination by others which is arbitrary. In prohibiting it we would, admittedly, be preventing the employer from discriminating in a way that is relevant to his purposes; but if the causal hypothesis suggested in the previous paragraph is correct, this situation would only be temporary, and after some time the circumstances inducing the employer to discriminate racially would have been eliminated.

The case of the landlord presents a more difficult problem. If the facts he alleges are true his nonarbitrary reasons for discrimination against blacks are real enough. They do not depend on present arbitrary discrimination by others, and they may persist beyond an interval in which there is no discrimination. Whatever the roots of hypothetical racial differences in reliability as tenants might be, they would probably go too deep to be eradicated solely by a short period in which there was no racial discrimination.

We should recognize, then, that if the facts are as alleged, to legislate against the landlord's racially discriminatory practice is to impose a long-term disadvantage upon him. At the very least, he will have to take greater care in ascertaining the suitability of prospective tenants. Perhaps he will turn to data-collecting agencies for assistance, thus contributing to the growth of institutions that are threats, potential or actual, to our privacy. Perhaps, if these methods are unavailable or unavailing, the landlord will have to take greater losses than he otherwise would have, and perhaps this will lead to increased rents or even to a reduction in the amount of rentable housing available.

None of this forces us to conclude that we should not legislate against the landlord's racial discrimination. There are good reasons why we should seek to eliminate racial discrimination even when such discrimination is neither arbitrary in itself nor relevant only because of the arbitrary prejudices of others. These reasons may be so important as to make the disadvantage imposed on the landlord comparatively insignificant.

An obvious point that can be made against the landlord is that he is judging people, at least in part, as members of a race rather than as individuals. The landlord does not deny that some black prospective tenants he turns away would make better tenants than some white prospective tenants he accepts. Some highly eligible black prospective tenants are refused accommodation simply because they are black. If the landlord assessed every prospective tenant as an individual this would not happen. . . .

There are plenty of reasons why in situations like admitting people to higher education or providing them with employment or other benefits we should regard people as individuals and not as members of some larger group. For one thing we will be able to make a selection better suited for our own purposes, for selecting or discarding whole groups of people will generally result in, at best, a crude approximation to the results we hope to achieve. This is certainly true in an area like education. On the other hand it must be admitted that in some situations a crude approximation is all that can be achieved anyway. The landlord claims that his situation is one of these, and that as he cannot reliably tell which individuals will make suitable tenants, he is justified in resorting to so crude a means of selection as race. Here we need to turn our attention from the landlord to the prospective black tenant.

To be judged merely as a member of a group when it is one's individual qualities on which the verdict should be given is to be treated as less than the unique individual that we see ourselves as. Even where our individual qualities would merit less than we receive as a member of a group—if we are promoted over better-qualified people because we went to the "right" private school—the benefit is usually less welcome than it would be if it had been merited by our own attributes. Of course in this case qualms are easily stilled by the fact that a benefit has been received, never mind how. In the contrary case, however, when something of value has been lost, the sense of loss will be compounded by the feeling that one was not assessed on one's own merits, but merely as a member of a group.

To this general preference for individual as against group assessment must be added a consideration arising from the nature of the group. To be denied a benefit because one was, say, a member of the Communist Party, would be unjust and a violation of basic principles of political liberty, but if one has chosen to join the Communist Party, then one is, after all, being assessed for what one has done, and one can choose between living with the consequences of continued party membership or leaving the party. Race, of course, is not something that one chooses to adopt or that one can ever choose to give up. The person who is denied advantages because of his race is totally unable to alter this particular circumstance of his existence and so may feel with added sharpness that his life is clouded, not merely because he is not being judged as an individual, but because of something over which he has no control at all. This makes racial discrimination peculiarly invidious.

So we have the viewpoint of the victim of racial discrimination to offset against the landlord's argument in favor, and it seems that the victim has more at stake and hence should be given preference, even if the landlord's reason for discriminating is nonarbitrary and hence in a sense legitimate. The case against racial discrimination becomes stronger still when we consider the long-term social effects of discrimination.

When members of a racial minority are overwhelmingly among the poorest members of a society, living in a deprived area, holding jobs low in pay and status, or no jobs at all, and less well educated than the average member of the community, racial discrimination serves to perpetuate a divided society in which race becomes a badge of a much broader inferiority. It is the association of race with economic status and educational disadvantages which in turn gives rise to the situation in which there could be a coloring of truth to the claim that race is a relevant ground for discriminating between prospective tenants, applicants for employment, and so on. Thus there is, in the end, a parallel between the situation of the landlord and the cake-shop owner, for both, by their discrimination, contribute to the maintenance of the grounds for claiming that this discrimination is nonarbitrary. Hence prohibition of such discrimination can be justified as breaking this circle of deprivation and discrimination. The difference between the situations, as I have already said, is that in the case of the cake-shop owner it is only a prejudice against contact with blacks that needs to be broken down, and experience has shown that such prejudices do evaporate in a relatively short period of time. In the case of the landlord, however, it is the whole social and economic position of blacks that needs to be changed, and while overcoming discrimination would be an essential part of this process it may not be sufficient. That is why, if the facts are as the landlord alleges them to be, prohibition of racial discrimination is likely to impose more of a long-term disadvantage on the landlord than on the shop-owner—a disadvantage which is, however, outweighed by the costs of continuing the circle of racial discrimination and deprivation for those discriminated against; and the costs of greater social inequality and racial divisiveness for the community as a whole. . . .

CHAPTER 33

In Defense of Quotas

James Rachels

Affirmative action programs began in the 1960s as a way of redressing past and present discrimination against African-Americans. Later, these programs were expanded to include other groups, such as women, Hispanics, and people with disabilities.

There are two kinds of affirmative action: quotas and racially sensitive policies. *Quotas* set numerical requirements for admissions, hirings, or promotions. For example, a quota would be imposed on a country club if it were told to admit at least five members of a specific minority group within a year's time. *Racially sensitive policies* merely consider race as one factor in making a decision; no quota is imposed. For instance, some universities have policies to promote "diversity," where one kind of diversity is racial diversity. In *California v. Bakke* (1978), the U.S. Supreme Court ruled that quotas are unconstitutional but that racially sensitive policies are permitted.

In this selection, James Rachels specifies some conditions under which quotas seem justified. He begins by discussing an unfamiliar type of prejudice: "heightism," or prejudice against short males. An important study on height and salary came out in 2004, after this essay was written. It confirmed Rachels' belief that heightism is a serious problem— heightism, it found, affects earning power as much as racism and sexism do. However, it suggested that the problem is not prejudice against short *men*, as Rachels argues, but prejudice against short *adolescents*. Discrimination against short boys seems to permanently affect their self-esteem and economic prospects. Rachels does cite evidence for

Published as "Coping with Prejudice" in James Rachels, *Can Ethics Provide Answers? And Other Essays in Moral Philosophy* (Rowman & Littlefield, 1997), pp. 199–212. Reprinted by permission.

prejudice against short men, however, so the empirical issues may not be entirely clear.

James Rachels (1941–2003) wrote and edited thirteen books, including *The Legacy of Socrates: Essays in Moral Philosophy* (2007) and *Problems from Philosophy* (second edition, 2009), an introduction to philosophy.

"Good sense," said Descartes, "is of all things in the world the most equally distributed, for everybody thinks himself so abundantly provided with it, that even those most difficult to please in all other matters do not commonly desire more of it than they already possess."[1] Much the same might be said about prejudice: everyone believes himself or herself to be objective and free of bias. We recognize that other people may be prejudiced, but we imagine that we ourselves see things as they really are.

But of course this is a mistake. We feel that we are unprejudiced only because we are unaware of our biases and how they work. This is true not only of bigots but of relatively open-minded people as well. It is a mistake for any of us to think that we are free of bias. Even when we are striving hardest to be objective, prejudices of all sorts can creep into our thinking without our noticing it.

To illustrate this, we may consider a type of example that does not often occur to us. We are familiar enough with prejudice based on race or gender. But those are not the only ways in which we discriminate. There is an impressive body of evidence that we are also prejudiced against people because of their height. I do not mean abnormally short or tall people—dwarfs or giants. That sort of prejudice is familiar enough. The less widely-recognized form of prejudice is against shorter people whose height falls within the normal range. Let me briefly mention some of the investigations that show this.[2]

In one study, 140 job-placement officers were asked to choose between two applicants with exactly the same qualifications, but one was described, parenthetically, as being 6'1" while the other candidate was listed as 5'5". 102 of the recruiters judged the taller candidate to be better qualified, while only one preferred the shorter candidate. The rest of them—a mere 27 percent—recognized that the two were equally qualified.

Other studies have shown that a person's earning potential is affected more by height than by, say, educational performance. One study compared the starting salaries of male librarians between 6'1" and 6'3" with the starting salaries of male librarians less than 6'. The same comparison was then made between those who had been in the top half of their classes academically and those in the bottom half. The average difference in starting salary between the taller and shorter graduates was found to be more than three times greater than the difference between the salaries of the more and less academically gifted. Another study using a sample of over five thousand men found that after twenty-five years of pursuing their varied careers, those who were 5'6" or 5'7" were earning on average $2,500 per year less than those who were 6'0" or 6'1".

The moral seems to be: if you could choose between being tall and being smart, from a crass economic standpoint, it's better to be tall.

The same sort of prejudice influences the way we vote. Of all U.S. presidents, only two—James Madison and Benjamin Harrison—were shorter than the average height for American males at the time of their election. And since 1904, the taller candidate has emerged victorious in 80 percent of presidential elections. Another moral might be drawn: if you are trying to predict the outcome of such an election, forget the other factors and put your money on the taller man.

Prejudice against short people seems importantly different from racist or sexist prejudice, because the latter sorts of prejudice seem to be motivated, at least in part, by the fact that members of the dominant group derive advantages from the discriminatory practices. These advantages are often economic. However, this seems much less plausible where height is concerned. It seems more likely that prejudice regarding height has some other, deeper psychological source. John S. Gillis, a psychologist who has written at length about this, has speculated that the source of our association of height with ability is to be found in childhood experiences:

> All of us experience a real association between height and power throughout our childhood. Adults tower over us physically as children, and they are the ones who control every single important thing in our lives. This may be the fountainhead of heightism. Each of us begins life with a dozen years or so of learning that the bigger person is more powerful and intelligent. This learning takes place not so much on an intellectual level but, more importantly, on the emotional level. Our attitudes and feelings are shaped in ways of which we are unaware.[3]

Whatever the source of these feelings, it is clear that they have deep and long-lasting effects.

The facts about "heightism" are quite remarkable. They suggest a number of points that should be of interest to anyone who is thinking about the philosophical problem of equality, especially as it relates to the formulation and assessment of social policies. First, the studies I have cited show that prejudice can have its influence quite unconsciously. No one—or so nearly no one as makes no difference—realizes that he thinks less well of shorter people. Yet the available evidence shows that this prejudice exists, and that it is widespread. The people who are affected by it are simply unaware of it.

Second, this evidence also suggests that people are very good at rationalizing their prejudiced judgments. The men and women whose actions were studied in these investigations—those who hired, promoted, and gave pay raises to the taller candidates—were, no doubt, reasonable people who could "explain" each decision by reference to the lucky employee's objective qualifications. No one believed that he was simply rewarding height. Yet the evidence shows that this is what was happening much of the time. The behavior induced by prejudice includes, importantly, the verbal behavior that "justifies" the prejudiced judgments.

These points, taken together, have a discouraging implication. They suggest that it is difficult even for people of good will to prevent such prejudice from influencing their deliberations. If I am prejudiced in ways that I do not fully realize, and if I am skilled at coming up with reasons to "justify" the decisions that such prejudice leads me to make, then my good intention to "think objectively"—no matter how sincerely I want to do this—may be depressingly ineffective.

The Justification of Quotas

People ought to be treated fairly. Yet we know that our assessments of people are often corrupted by prejudice. Does this make any difference in the sorts of policies that should be adopted?

Choosing Widgets. Suppose you are the president of a manufacturing company and each year in the course of your business you need a supply of widgets. Widgets vary greatly in quality, and from among the hundreds available you need to get the ten best you can find. You are not able to devote much of your own time to this task, but luckily you have an assistant who is one of the most astute widget evaluators in the land. "Examine all the available widgets," you tell her, "and bring me the ten best."

In the fullness of time your assistant brings you ten good widgets, and all seems well. But then you notice that all ten were made at the Buffalo Widget Works. This is odd, because you know that the Albany Widget Works makes an equally good product; and moreover, you know that the pool from which your assistant made her selection contained equal numbers of Albany widgets and Buffalo widgets. So why should the ten best all come from Buffalo? One would expect that, on average, five would come from Buffalo and five from Albany. But perhaps this was just a statistical fluke, and it will all average out over time.

The next year, however, much the same thing happens. You need ten widgets; you assign your assistant to identify the best; and she brings you nine made in Buffalo and only one made in Albany. "Why?" you ask, and in response she assures you that, even though the Albany company does make excellent widgets, most of the best ones available this year happened to be from Buffalo. To prove the point she gives you quite an intelligent and persuasive analysis of the merits of the widgets in this year's pool. You are so impressed that you name her Vice President for Widget Procurement (VPWP).

In subsequent years the story is repeated again and again, with only slight variations. Each year you are told that almost all the best available widgets are from Buffalo. You begin to feel sure that something peculiar is going on. Briefly, you wonder whether your VPWP is accepting bribes from the Buffalo company, but you reject that hypothesis. She is an honest woman, and you cannot help but believe that she is using her best judgment. Then you consider whether, in fact, the Buffalo widgets are simply better than the Albany widgets. But you reject this possibility also; other experts testify that they are equally good.

Finally, you make a discovery that explains everything. It turns out that your vice president was raised in Buffalo, where there is a strong sense of civic pride, and an even stronger sense of rivalry with Albany. Children in Buffalo, it seems, have it drilled into them that everything about Buffalo is better than anything about Albany. Moreover, before coming to work for you, your VPWP worked for the Buffalo Chamber of Commerce and was in charge of promoting Buffalo products. Obviously, then, she is prejudiced, and that explains why she almost always judges Buffalo widgets to be superior.

What are you to do? You could forget about it; after all, the widgets you are getting from Buffalo are pretty good. But you don't want to do that; it is important to you to have the very best widgets you can get. So you talk to your VPWP, you confront her with your suspicion that she is prejudiced, and you stress the importance of getting the best widgets regardless of whether they are from Buffalo or Albany. She is a bit offended by this because she is a good woman and believes herself to be impartial. Again, she assures you that she is selecting the best widgets available, and if they happen to be from Buffalo, she can't help it. And as time passes, nothing changes; she continues to select mostly Buffalo widgets.

Now what? You are certain she is prejudiced, but because the prejudice is entirely unconscious, your VPWP seems unable to overcome it or even to recognize it. You could get a new VPWP. But you don't want to do that, because this woman is an excellent judge of widgets, except for this one problem. Then an obvious solution occurs to you. You could simply change your instructions. Instead of saying, each year, "Bring me the ten best widgets," you could say, "Bring me the five best Buffalo widgets and the five best Albany widgets." She might not like that—she might take it as an insult to her ability to judge widgets impartially—but, if it is true that Albany widgets are equally as good as Buffalo widgets, this would result in your getting a better overall quality of widget, on average, year in and year out. . . .

The VPWP might, however, offer an interesting objection. She might point out that, in carrying out your new instructions, she would sometimes have to include in the total of ten an Albany widget that is inferior to a Buffalo widget that was also available. You will have to admit that this is so. But your problem is a practical one. You can trust the VPWP to judge which are the best Albany widgets, and you can trust her to judge which are the best Buffalo widgets. But you cannot trust her to compare objectively the relative merits of a widget from one city with a widget from the other city. In these circumstances, your new instructions give you a better chance of ending up with the best overall supply. Or to put it another way: you want the best-qualified widgets to get the jobs, and the quota system you have established will see to that more effectively than the alternative method of simply allowing your VPWP to exercise her judgment.

Hiring People. In the workplace, people ought to be treated equally, but often they are not. Among the important reasons is prejudice; after all, somebody has to decide who is to be hired, or promoted, or given a pay raise, and those who get to make such decisions are only human and might be prejudiced. Social policies ought to be devised with this in mind. Such policies should contain provisions to ensure that people are given equal treatment, insofar as this is possible, despite the fact that those policies must be administered by imperfect human beings.

Of all the kinds of policies that have been devised to combat discrimination, quotas are the most despised. Almost no one has a good word to say about them. Yet the widget example suggests that, under certain circumstances, quotas can be defensible. Can a similar argument be constructed, not for choosing widgets, but for hiring people?

Suppose you are the dean of a college, and you are concerned that only the best-qualified scholars are hired for your faculty. You notice, however, that your philosophy department never hires any women. (They did hire one woman, years ago, so they have a token female. But that's as far as it has gone.) So you investigate. You discover that there are, indeed, lots of women philosophers looking for jobs each year. And you have no reason to think that these women are, on average, any less capable than their male colleagues. So you talk to the (male) chairperson of the department and you urge him to be careful to give full and fair consideration to the female applicants. Being a good liberal fellow, he finds this agreeable enough—although he may be a little offended by the suggestion that he is not already giving the women due consideration. But the talk has little apparent effect. Whenever candidates are being considered, he continues to report, with evident sincerity, that in the particular group under review a male has emerged as the best qualified. And so, he says each year, if we want to hire the best-qualified applicant we have to hire the male, at least this time.

This is repeated annually, with minor variations. One variation is that the best female philosopher in the pool may be listed as the department's top choice. But when, predictably enough, she turns out to be unavailable (having been snapped up by a more prestigious university), no women in the second tier are considered to be good alternatives. Here you notice a disturbing asymmetry: although the very best males are also going to other universities, the males in the second tier are considered good alternatives. Momentarily, then, you consider whether the problem could be that philosophical talent is distributed in a funny way: while the very best women are equal to the very best men, at the next level down, the men suddenly dominate. But that seems unlikely.

After further efforts have been made along these lines, without result, you might eventually conclude that there is an unconscious prejudice at work. Your department, despite its good intentions and its one female member, is biased. It isn't hard to understand why this could be so. In addition to the usual sources of prejudice against women—the stereotypes, the picture of women as less rational than men, and so forth—an all-male or mostly male group enjoys a kind of camaraderie that might seem impossible if females were significantly included. In choosing a new colleague, the matter of how someone would "fit in" with the existing group will always have some influence. This will work against females, no matter their talents as teachers and scholars.

Finally, then, you may conclude that the existing prejudice cannot be countered by any measure short of issuing a new instruction, and you tell the philosophy department that it must hire some additional women, in numbers at least in proportion to the number of women in the applicant pool. The reply, of course, will be that this policy could result in hiring a less qualified woman over a better qualified man. But the answer is the same as in the example about the widgets. You are not trying to give women a special break, any more than you were trying to give Albany widgets a special break. Nor are you trying to redress the injustices that women have suffered in the past; nor are you trying to provide "role models" for female students. You may be pleased if your policy has these effects, but the purpose of your policy is not to achieve them. Your only purpose is to get the best-qualified scholars for your faculty, regardless of their gender. The fact of unconscious prejudice makes the usual system of simply allowing your experts—the philosophy department—to exercise their judgment an imperfect system for accomplishing that purpose. Allowing them to exercise their judgment within the limits of a quota system, on the other hand, may be more effective, because it reduces the influence of unconscious prejudice.

It is sure to be objected that people are not widgets, and so the two cases are not analogous. But they do seem to be analogous in the relevant respects. The features of the widget example that justified imposing a quota were: (1) There was a selection process that involved human judgment. (2) The result of the process was that individuals from a certain group were regularly rated higher than members of another group. (3) There was no reason to think that the members of the former group were in fact better than the members of the latter group. (4) There was reason to think that the human beings who were judging these individuals might have been prejudiced against members of the latter group. The case of hiring women faculty also has these four features. That is what permits the construction of a similar argument.

This argument takes into account a feature of the selection process that is often ignored when quotas (or "affirmative action," or "reverse discrimination") are discussed. Often, the question is put like this: assuming that X is better qualified than Y, is it justifiable to adopt a policy that would permit hiring or promoting Y rather than X? Then various reasons are produced that might justify this, such as that a preferential policy redresses wrongs, or that it helps to combat racism or sexism. The debate then focuses on whether such reasons are sufficient. But when the issue is approached in this way, a critical point is overlooked. People do not come prelabeled as better or worse qualified. Before we can say that X is better qualified than Y, someone has to have made that judgment. And this is where prejudice is most likely to enter the picture. A male philosopher, judging other philosophers, might very well rate women lower, without even realizing he is doing so. The argument we are considering is intended to address this problem, which arises before the terms of the conventional discussion are even set.

Of course, this argument does not purport to show that *any* system of quotas, applied in any circumstances, is fair. The argument is only a defense of quotas used in a certain way in certain circumstances. But the circumstances I have described are not uncommon. Actual quota systems, of the sort that have been established and tested in the courts during the past three decades, often have just this character: they are instituted to counter the prejudice, conscious or otherwise, that corrupts judgments of merit. Here is a real case that illustrates this.

In 1972 there were no blacks in the Alabama State Police. In the 37-year history of the force, there had never been any. Then the NAACP brought suit to end this vestige of segregation. They won their case in the trial court when federal district Judge Frank Johnson condemned what he termed a "blatant and continuous pattern and practice of discrimination." Judge Johnson did not, however, simply order the Alabama authorities to stop discriminating and start making their decisions impartially. He knew that such an order would be treated with amused contempt; the authorities would have been only too happy to continue as before, "impartially" finding that no blacks were qualified. So in order to prevent this and to ensure that the Alabamians could not avoid hiring qualified blacks, Johnson ordered that the state hire and promote one qualified black for every white trooper hired or promoted, until 25 percent of the force was black.

Judge Johnson's order was appealed to the Eleventh Circuit Court, where it was upheld. Time went by while the state was supposed to be carrying out his instructions. In 1984, twelve years later, the district court reviewed the situation to see what progress had been made. Forced by the court to do so, the department had hired some blacks. But virtually none had been promoted. The court found that, among the six majors on the force, none was black. Of the 25 captains, none was black. Of the 35 lieutenants, none was black. Of the 65 sergeants, none was black. Of the 66 corporals, however, there were four blacks. The court declared: "This is intolerable and must not continue."

The state of Alabama's last hope was the U.S. Supreme Court, which heard the case and rendered its decision in 1987. By a five-to-four vote, the Supreme Court upheld Judge Johnson's orders, and the *Birmingham News* ran a front-page story describing the "bitter feelings" of the white troopers, who viewed the ruling as a "setback." A spokesman for the Alabama Department of Public Safety assured the newspaper, "The department will comply with this ruling." It was clear enough from the official statements, however, that "complying with the ruling" would force the department to take steps—actually promoting blacks—that it would never take voluntarily.[4]

The Circumstances in Which Quotas Are Justified. The imposition of a quota may be justified as a way of countering the effects of prejudice. As I have said, this argument does not justify just any old quota. Our argument envisions the imposition of a quota as a corrective to a "normal" decision-making process that has gone wrong. For present purposes we may define a normal process as follows: (1) The goal of the process is to identify the best-qualified individuals for the purpose at hand. (2) The nature of the qualifications is specified. (3) A pool of candidates is assembled. (4) The qualifications of the individuals in the pool are assessed, using the specified criteria, and the individuals are ranked from best to worst. (5) The jobs, promotions, or whatever are awarded to the best-qualified individuals.

This process may go wrong in any number of ways, of course, some of them not involving prejudice. We are not concerned here with all the ways in which things can go wrong. We are concerned only with the following set of circumstances: First, we notice that, as the selection process is carried out, individuals from a certain group are regularly rated higher than members of another group. Second, we can find no reason to think that the members of the former group are in fact better than the members of the latter group; on the contrary, there is reason to think the members of the two groups are, on average, equally well qualified. And third, there is reason to think that the people performing the assessments are prejudiced against members of the latter group. These are the circumstances in which our argument says the imposition of a quota may be justified.

Even in these circumstances, however, the use of a quota does not eliminate human judgment, and so it does not guarantee that prejudice will disappear from the equation. Prejudice is eliminated from one part of the process, but it may reappear at a different point.

Consider again the male philosophy professors who always recommended the hiring of other males. In our example, the dean concluded that the male philosophers were prejudiced. In order to reach this conclusion, however, the dean had to make the judgment that female philosophers are equally as talented as males. (Otherwise, there would have been no grounds for thinking that the philosophy department's preference for hiring males was the result of bias.) An analogous judgment had to be made by Judge Johnson. He had to assume that black people were as qualified as whites for employment and promotion in the Alabama State Police. But prejudice can infect these general assessments just as it can influence the specific judgments that were being made by the philosophy professors and the highway patrol officials.

Therefore, our argument seems to require the assumption that some people—the hypothetical dean and, more to the point, actual federal court judges—are less prejudiced than others.

This assumption, however, seems correct. Some people are in fact less prejudiced than others; that is why prejudiced decisions can sometimes be successfully appealed. In general, people who are a step removed from a decision-making process are in a better position to be unbiased, or at least to recognize their biases and act to correct them, than those who are close to the "front lines." Part of the reason is that they have less at stake personally. The dean does not have to live in the philosophy department, and the judge does not have to work in the highway patrol. Another part of the reason is that in many instances the officials who impose the quotas are better educated and are more practiced in dealing with prejudice than those on whom the quotas are imposed. Judge Johnson was one of the most distinguished southern jurists with long experience in handling civil rights cases. The argument that I have presented does indeed assume that he was more capable of thinking objectively about what was going on, as well as about the likely qualifications of blacks, than the officials of the Alabama highway patrol. If that assumption is false, then our argument in defense of his action collapses. But I do not think that assumption is false.

Our argument has one other limitation that should be mentioned. It does not apply in the case of decisions made solely on the basis of "objective" criteria—test scores and the like—assuming, of course, that the tests really are objective and do not contain hidden bias. We can imagine procedures that, by using only such objective criteria, leave no room for the operation of prejudice. So in such cases the "normal" procedure will work well enough. The best-qualified will win out, and quotas will be unnecessary.

But such cases will be rare. Consider the range of cases that must be dealt with in the real world. Is there any decision procedure that a rational person would adopt for hiring teachers that would not disclose that an applicant for a teaching job was female? Should we be willing to hire teachers without an interview? Is there any imaginable multiple-choice test that one would be willing to use as the sole criterion for promotion in a police department? Would we want to eliminate the use of the assessments of those who have observed the officer's performance?

Moreover, it should also be remembered that so-called objective criteria often involve the use of tainted evidence. Suppose, in order to be perfectly impartial, I resolve to make a hiring decision using only objective criteria such as college grades. In this way I prevent any prejudices that I might have from coming into play. So far, so good. But the grades themselves were handed out by teachers whose prejudices could have come into play during the grading process.

Objections and Replies. The quota policy mandated by Judge Johnson continues to cause controversy. Newspaper columnist James J. Kilpatrick summed up the case against the judge's order succinctly. In the process of complying with the judge's ruling, he wrote, "white troopers with higher test scores and objectively better qualifications lost out. They themselves had engaged in no discrimination. They were the innocent victims of a remedial process addressed to blacks as a group. Were those whites denied equal protection of the law?"[5] These familiar objections are often taken to vitiate the whole idea of quotas as such. Do they undercut the argument presented here? In the time-honored way, we may consider these objections one by one.

Objection: People ought to be hired or promoted on the basis of their qualifications, and not on the basis of their race or sex. To give preference to a black merely because he is black, or to a woman merely because she is a woman, is no more defensible than to prefer a white man because he is white or male.

Reply: The whole point of the argument is that quotas may be justified as part of a plan to make sure that people *are* hired or promoted on the basis of their qualifications. The sort of policy that I have discussed does not involve hiring or promoting on the basis of race or gender, but only on the basis of qualifications. Quota policies are being defended, in some circumstances, because they are the most effective policies for achieving that goal.

Objection: The white male who is passed over is not responsible for the injustices that were done to blacks in the past; therefore it is unfair to make him pay the price for it. As Kilpatrick pointed out, the Alabama state troopers who were not promoted were not responsible for the injustices that were done to blacks, so why should they now be penalized?

Reply: Again, this misses the point. The argument does not envision the use of quotas as a response to past discrimination, but as a way of preventing, or at least minimizing, *present* discrimination. Sometimes people who defend the use of quotas or other such policies defend them as only temporary measures to be used reluctantly until racism and sexism have been eliminated. It may be agreed that if racist and sexist prejudice were eliminated, there would be no need for race- or gender-based quotas. But unfortunately, despite the progress that has been made, there is little reason to expect this to happen anytime soon.

Objection: To repeat the most obvious objection: Wouldn't there be some instances of injustice (that is, instances in which a less well qualified individual is preferred to a better-qualified individual) under a policy of quotas that otherwise wouldn't occur? And isn't this inherently unfair?

Reply: Of course this will inevitably happen. But the question is whether there would be fewer injustices under this policy than under the alternative of "hiring strictly according to qualifications," which means, in practice, hiring according to assessments of qualifications made by biased judges. Some philosophers have also urged that it is not acceptable to treat someone unjustly for the purpose of preventing other injustices, but that point, even if it is correct, doesn't apply here. The choice here is between two policies neither of which is perfect and each of which would inevitably involve some injustices. The relevant question is, which policy would involve more?

Objection: Finally, there is an objection that will surely have occurred to many readers. If our argument were accepted, wouldn't it lead to all sorts of quotas—not only to quotas favoring blacks and women, but also to quotas favoring short people, for example? After all, as has been pointed out here, short people are also the victims of bias.

Reply: If it were possible to devise practical policies that would ensure fair treatment for short people, I can see no reason to object. However, I do not know whether there are particular circumstances in which quotas would be practicable and effective, so I do not know whether such a policy would be defensible. The problem is that prejudice against short people has never been perceived as a serious social issue; consequently it has received little study, and it is less well understood and its effects are less well documented than, say, racist or sexist prejudice. But I know of no reason to rule out in advance the adoption of policies that would counter this sort of bias.

This admission might be taken to show the absurdity of our argument. The very idea of quotas in favor of short people may seem so silly that if the argument leads to this, then the argument may be thought absurd. But why? One might well fear the intrusion of the heavy hand of government in still another area. Yet, if in fact short people are being treated unfairly—if they are singled out for unfavorable treatment because of an irrelevant characteristic—this seems, on its face, just as objectionable as any other form of discrimination and just as good a cause for corrective action. "Heightism" is not now a social issue. But it could become one.

In the meantime, those who have studied the subject have made some modest suggestions. John S. Gillis, the psychologist I quoted above, has made this form of prejudice his special concern. Here are a few of the things he proposes we do:[6] Employers should become aware of height bias and try to ensure that it does not influence personnel decisions. (The effects of such individual efforts might be small and imperfect, but they are better than nothing.) To help break the psychological connection between height and worth, we should avoid using the word "stature" to refer to status, caliber, and prestige. Teachers should stop the common practice of lining up schoolchildren according to height, which suggests to the children that this correlates with something important. Gillis also urges that metric measurements be used to indicate height. This, he says, would help to break "the mystique of the six-footer"—being 6 feet tall is perceived as a grand thing for a man, but being 183 centimeters tall doesn't have the same ring. These are all modest and reasonable proposals. The imposition of quotas in hiring and the like would be a much more drastic measure, which probably would not be wise until such time as heightism is established as a more pressing social concern.

Notes

1. Elizabeth S. Haldane and G. R. T. Ross, *The Philosophical Works of Descartes* (New York: Dover Books, 1955), 1:81.

2. The following information is drawn from John S. Gillis, *Too Tall, Too Small* (Champaign, IL: Institute for Personality and Ability Testing, 1982).

3. Gillis, *Too Tall*, 125.

4. *Birmingham News*, 26 February 1987, sec. A, p. 1.

5. James J. Kilpatrick, "Reverse Discrimination Is Still Discrimination," *Birmingham News*, 5 November 1986, sec. A, p. 9.

6. Gillis, *Too Tall*, chap. 7.

CHAPTER 34

The Morality of Euthanasia

James Rachels

James Rachels wrote *The End of Life: Euthanasia and Morality* (1986).
Here he defends the "argument from mercy." Euthanasia, he thinks, is
justified when death is the only way to escape awful pain. In Rachels'
main example, the pain is suffered by someone dying from cancer.

James Rachels himself died of cancer in 2003. At the end of
his life, nothing persuaded him to change his view of euthanasia. But
he did wonder whether the argument from mercy would require less
intentional killing than he had thought. Often a humane death occurs
when a patient is given more and more pain medication, administered
in order to relieve pain. Under such circumstances, the intention to
kill is unnecessary.

The single most powerful argument in support of euthanasia is the
argument from mercy. It is also an exceptionally simple argument,
at least in its main idea, which makes one uncomplicated point. Terminally ill patients sometimes suffer pain so horrible that it is beyond
the comprehension of those who have not actually experienced it.
Their suffering can be so terrible that we do not even like to read
about it or think about it; we recoil even from the description of such
agony. The argument from mercy says euthanasia is justified because
it provides an end to *that*.

The great Irish satirist Jonathan Swift took eight years to die,
while, in the words of Joseph Fletcher, "His mind crumbled to pieces."
At times the pain in his blinded eyes was so intense he had to be

From James Rachels, "Euthanasia," in *Matters of Life and Death,* 2nd ed., ed. Tom Regan, pp. 49–52. Copyright © 1986.

restrained from tearing them out with his own hands. Knives and other potential instruments of suicide had to be kept from him. For the last three years of his life, he could do nothing but sit and drool: and when he finally died it was only after convulsions that lasted thirty-six hours.

Swift died in 1745. Since then, doctors have learned how to eliminate much of the pain that accompanies terminal illness, but the victory has been far from complete. So, here is a more modern example.

Stewart Alsop was a respected journalist who died in 1975 of a rare form of cancer. Before he died, he wrote movingly of his experiences as a terminal patient. Although he had not thought much about euthanasia before, he came to approve of it after rooming briefly with someone he called Jack:

> The third night that I roomed with Jack in our tiny double room in the solid-tumor ward of the cancer clinic of the National Institutes of Health in Bethesda, Md., a terrible thought occurred to me.
>
> Jack had a melanoma in his belly, a malignant solid tumor that the doctors guessed was about the size of a softball. The cancer had started a few months before with a small tumor in his left shoulder, and there had been several operations since. The doctors planned to remove the softball-sized tumor, but they knew Jack would soon die. The cancer had metastasized—it had spread beyond control.
>
> Jack was good-looking, about 28, and brave. He was in constant pain, and his doctor had prescribed an intravenous shot of a synthetic opiate—a pain-killer, or analgesic—every four hours. His wife spent many of the daylight hours with him, and she would sit or lie on his bed and pat him all over, as one pats a child, only more methodically, and this seemed to help control the pain. But at night, when his pretty wife had left (wives cannot stay overnight at the NIH clinic) and darkness fell, the pain would attack without pity.
>
> At the prescribed hour, a nurse would give Jack a shot of the synthetic analgesic, and this would control the pain for perhaps two hours or a bit more. Then he would begin to moan, or whimper, very low, as though he didn't want to wake me. Then he would begin to howl, like a dog.
>
> When this happened, either he or I would ring for a nurse, and ask for a pain-killer. She would give him some codeine or the like by mouth, but it never did any real good—it affected him no more than half an aspirin might affect a man who had just broken his arm. Always the nurse would explain as encouragingly as she could that there was not long to go before the next

intravenous shot—"Only about 50 minutes now." And always poor Jack's whimpers and howls would become more loud and frequent until at last the blessed relief came.

The third night of this routine, the terrible thought occurred to me. "If Jack were a dog," I thought, "what would be done with him?" The answer was obvious: the pound, and chloroform. No human being with a spark of pity could let a living thing suffer so, to no good end.

The NIH clinic is, of course, one of the most modern and best-equipped hospitals we have. Jack's suffering was not the result of poor treatment in some backward rural facility; it was the inevitable product of his disease, which medical science was powerless to prevent.

I have quoted Alsop at length not for the sake of indulging in gory details but to give a clear idea of the kind of suffering we are talking about. We should not gloss over these facts with euphemistic language or squeamishly avert our eyes from them. For only by keeping them firmly and vividly in mind can we appreciate the full force of the argument from mercy: If a person prefers—and even begs for—death as the only alternative to lingering on *in this kind of torment,* only to die anyway after a while, then surely it is not immoral to help this person die sooner. As Alsop put it, "No human being with a spark of pity could let a living thing suffer so, to no good end."

The Utilitarian Version of the Argument

In connection with this argument, the utilitarians deserve special mention. They argued that actions and social policies should be judged right or wrong *exclusively* according to whether they cause happiness or misery; and they argued that when judged by this standard, euthanasia turns out to be morally acceptable. The utilitarian argument may be elaborated as follows:

(1) Any action or social policy is morally right if it serves to increase the amount of happiness in the world or to decrease the amount of misery. Conversely, an action or social policy is morally wrong if it serves to decrease happiness or to increase misery.

(2) The policy of killing, at their own request, hopelessly ill patients who are suffering great pain would decrease the amount of misery in the world. (An example could be Alsop's friend Jack.)

(3) Therefore, such a policy would be morally right.

The first premise of this argument, (1), states the Principle of Utility, which is the basic utilitarian assumption. Today most philosophers think that this principle is wrong, because they think that the promotion of happiness and the avoidance of misery are not the *only* morally important things. Happiness, they say, is only one among many values that should be promoted: freedom, justice, and a respect for people's rights are also important. To take one example: people *might* be happier if there were no freedom of religion, for if everyone adhered to the same religious beliefs, there would be greater harmony among people. There would be no unhappiness caused within families by Jewish girls marrying Catholic boys, and so forth. Moreover, if people were brainwashed well enough, no one would mind not having freedom of choice. Thus happiness would be increased. But, the argument continues, even if happiness *could* be increased this way, it would not be right to deny people freedom of religion, because people have a right to make their own choices. Therefore, the first premise of the utilitarian argument is unacceptable.

There is a related difficulty for utilitarianism, which connects more directly with the topic of euthanasia. Suppose a person is leading a miserable life—full of more unhappiness than happiness—but does *not* want to die. This person thinks that a miserable life is better than none at all. Now I assume that we would all agree that the person should not be killed; that would be plain, unjustifiable murder. Yet it *would* decrease the amount of misery in the world if we killed this person—it would lead to an increase in the balance of happiness over unhappiness—and so it is hard to see how, on strictly utilitarian grounds, it could be wrong. Again, the Principle of Utility seems to be an inadequate guide for determining right and wrong. So we are on shaky ground if we rely on *this* version of the argument from mercy for a defense of euthanasia.

Doing What Is in Everyone's Best Interests

Although the foregoing utilitarian argument is faulty, it is nevertheless based on a sound idea. For even if the promotion of happiness and avoidance of misery are not the *only* morally important things, they are still very important. So, when an action or a social policy would decrease misery, that is *a* very strong reason in its favor. In the cases of voluntary euthanasia we are now considering, great suffering is eliminated, and since the patient requests it, there is no question of violating individual rights. That is why, regardless of the difficulties of the Principle of Utility, the utilitarian version of the argument still retains considerable force.

I want now to present a somewhat different version of the argument from mercy, which is inspired by utilitarianism but which avoids the difficulties of the foregoing version by not making the Principle of Utility a premise of the argument. I believe that the following argument is sound and proves that euthanasia *can* be justified:

(1) If an action promotes the best interests of *everyone* concerned and violates *no one's* rights, then that action is morally acceptable.

(2) In at least some cases, active euthanasia promotes the best interests of everyone concerned and violates no one's rights.

(3) Therefore, in at least some cases, active euthanasia is morally acceptable.

It would have been in everyone's best interests if active euthanasia had been employed in the case of Stewart Alsop's friend Jack. First, and most important, it would have been in Jack's own interests, since it would have provided him with an easier, better death, without pain. (Who among us would choose Jack's death, if we had a choice, rather than a quick painless death?) Second, it would have been in the best interests of Jack's wife. Her misery, helplessly watching him suffer, must have been almost unbearable. Third, the hospital staff's best interests would have been served, since if Jack's dying had not been prolonged, they could have turned their attention to other patients whom they could have helped. Fourth, other patients would have benefited, since medical resources would no longer have been used in the sad, pointless maintenance of Jack's physical existence. Finally, if Jack himself requested to be killed, the act would not have violated his rights. Considering all this, how can active euthanasia in this case be wrong? How can it be wrong to do an action that is merciful, that benefits everyone concerned, and that violates no one's rights?

CHAPTER **35**

A ssisted Suicide: Pro-Choice or Anti-Life?

Richard Doerflinger

In the 1990s, Dr. Jack Kevorkian of Pontiac, Michigan, helped over 100 people commit suicide. These people suffered from a variety of diseases, and their prognoses were grim, but for many of them, death was not imminent. They came to Kevorkian from around the country, since they felt they could not get what they wanted from their doctors at home. Kevorkian considered himself a crusader for the individual's right to die, and his activities got a lot of press. In 1997, Oregon passed a law allowing physician-assisted suicide, but no other states followed suit until Washington passed a similar law in 2008. Kevorkian was convicted of second-degree murder in Michigan in 1999 and was released on parole in 2007.

Richard Doerflinger works at the Secretariat for Pro-Life Activities of the National Conference of Catholic Bishops. In this essay, he argues against physician-assisted suicide. The act of suicide, he says, robs an individual of his freedom to choose. Moreover, Doerflinger fears that physician-assisted suicide, if it becomes accepted, will be used too often.

The intrinsic wrongness of directly killing the innocent, even with the victim's consent, is all but axiomatic in the Jewish and Christian world-views that have shaped the laws and mores of Western civilization and the self-concept of its medical practitioners. This norm grew

From *Hastings Center Report,* Special Supplement (January/February 1989), pp. 16–19. Reprinted by permission of The Hastings Center.

out of the conviction that human life is sacred because it is created in the image and likeness of God, and called to fulfillment in love of God and neighbor.

With the pervasive secularization of Western culture, norms against euthanasia and suicide have to a great extent been cut loose from their religious roots to fend for themselves. Because these norms seem abstract and unconvincing to many, debate tends to dwell not on the wrongness of the act as such but on what may follow from its acceptance. Such arguments are often described as claims about a "slippery slope," and debate then shifts to the validity of slippery slope arguments in general.

Since it is sometimes argued that acceptance of assisted suicide is an outgrowth of respect for personal autonomy, and not lack of respect for the inherent worth of human life, I will outline how autonomy-based arguments in favor of assisting suicide do entail a statement about the value of life. I will also distinguish two kinds of slippery slope argument often confused with each other, and argue that those who favor social and legal acceptance of assisted suicide have not adequately responded to the slippery slope claims of their opponents.

Assisted Suicide versus Respect for Life

Some advocates of socially sanctioned assisted suicide admit (and a few boast) that their proposal is incompatible with the conviction that human life is of intrinsic worth. Attorney Robert Risley has said that he and his allies in the Hemlock Society are "so bold" as to seek to "overturn the sanctity of life principle" in American society. A life of suffering, "racked with pain," is "not the kind of life we cherish."[1]

Others eschew Risley's approach, perhaps recognizing that it creates a slippery slope toward practices almost universally condemned. If society is to help terminally ill patients to commit suicide because it agrees that death is objectively preferable to a life of hardship, it will be difficult to draw the line at the seriously ill or even at circumstances where the victim requests death.

Some advocates of assisted suicide therefore take a different course, arguing that it is precisely respect for the dignity of the human person that demands respect for individual freedom as the noblest feature of that person. On this rationale a decision as to when and how to die deserves the respect and even the assistance of others because it is the ultimate exercise of self-determination—"ultimate" both in the sense that it is the last decision one will ever make and in the sense that through it one takes control of one's entire self. What makes such decisions worthy of respect is not the fact that death is chosen over life but that it is the individual's own free decision about his or her future.

Thus Derek Humphry, director of the Hemlock Society, describes his organization as "pro-choice" on this issue. Such groups favor the establishment of a constitutional "right to die" modeled on the right to abortion delineated by the U.S. Supreme Court in 1973. This would be a right to choose *whether or not* to end one's own life, free of outside government interference. In theory, the recognition of such a right would betray no bias toward choosing death.

Life versus Freedom

This autonomy-based approach is more appealing than the straight-forward claim that some lives are not worth living, especially to Americans accustomed to valuing individual liberty above virtually all else. But the argument departs from American traditions on liberty in one fundamental respect.

When the Declaration of Independence proclaimed the inalienable human rights to be "life, liberty, and the pursuit of happiness," this ordering reflected a long-standing judgment about their relative priorities. Life, a human being's very earthly existence, is the most fundamental right because it is the necessary condition for all other worldly goods including freedom; freedom in turn makes it possible to pursue (without guaranteeing that one will attain) happiness. Safeguards against the deliberate destruction of life are thus seen as necessary to protect freedom and all other human goods. This line of thought is not explicitly religious but is endorsed by some modern religious groups:

> The first right of the human person is his life. He has other goods and some are more precious, but this one is fundamental—the condition of all the others. Hence it must be protected above all others.[2]

On this view suicide is not the ultimate exercise of freedom but its ultimate self-contradiction: A free act that by destroying life, destroys all the individual's future earthly freedom. If life is more basic than freedom, society best serves freedom by discouraging rather than assisting self-destruction. Sometimes one must limit particular choices to safeguard freedom itself, as when American society chose over a century ago to prevent people from selling themselves into slavery even of their own volition.

It may be argued in objection that the person who ends his life has not truly suffered loss of freedom, because unlike the slave he need not continue to exist under the constraints of a loss of freedom. But the slave does have some freedom, including the freedom to seek various means of liberation or at least the freedom to choose what attitude to take regarding his plight. To claim that a slave is worse off than a corpse is to value a situation of limited freedom less than one of no freedom whatsoever, which seems inconsistent with the premise of the "pro-choice" position. Such a claim also seems tantamount to saying that some lives (such as those with less than absolute freedom) are objectively not worth living, a position that "pro-choice" advocates claim not to hold.

It may further be argued in objection that assistance in suicide is only being offered to those who can no longer meaningfully exercise other freedoms due to increased suffering and reduced capabilities and lifespan. To be sure, the suffering of terminally ill patients who can no longer pursue the simplest everyday tasks should call for sympathy and support from everyone in contact with them. But even these hardships do not constitute total loss of freedom of choice. If they did, one could hardly claim that the patient is in a position to make the ultimate free choice about suicide. A dying person capable of making a choice of that kind is also capable of making less monumental free choices about coping with his or her condition. This person generally faces a bewildering array of choices regarding the assessment of his or her past life and the resolution of relationships with family and friends. He or she must finally choose at this time what stance to take regarding the eternal questions about God, personal responsibility, and the prospects of a destiny after death.

In fact proponents of assisted suicide do *not* consistently place freedom of choice as their highest priority. They often defend the moderate nature of their project by stating, with Derek Humphry, that "we do not encourage suicide for any reason except to relieve unremitting suffering." It seems their highest priority is the "pursuit of happiness" (or avoidance of suffering) and not "liberty" as such. Liberty or freedom of choice loses its value if one's choices cannot relieve suffering and lead to happiness; life is of instrumental value insofar as it makes possible choices that can bring happiness.

In this value system, choice as such does not warrant unqualified respect. In difficult circumstances, as when care of a suffering and dying patient is a great burden on family and society, the individual who chooses life despite suffering will not easily be seen as rational, and thus will not easily receive understanding and assistance for this choice.

In short, an unqualified "pro-choice" defense of assisted suicide lacks coherence because corpses have no choices. A particular choice, that of death, is given priority over all the other choices it makes impossible, so the value of choice as such is not central to the argument.

A restriction of this rationale to cases of terminal illness also lacks logical force. For if ending a brief life of suffering can be good, it would seem that ending a long life of suffering may be better. Surely the approach of the California "Humane and Dignified Death Act"—where consensual killing of a patient expected to die in six months is presumably good medical practice, but killing the same patient a month or two earlier is still punishable as homicide—is completely arbitrary.

Slippery Slopes, Loose Cannons

Many arguments against sanctioning assisted suicide concern a different kind of "slippery slope": Contingent factors in the contemporary situation may make it virtually inevitable in practice, if not compelling at the level of abstract theory, that removal of the taboo against assisted suicide will lead to destructive expansions of the right to kill the innocent. Such factors may not be part of euthanasia advocates' own agenda; but if they exist and are beyond the control of these advocates, they must be taken into account in judging the moral and social wisdom of opening what may be a Pandora's box of social evils.

To distinguish this sociological argument from our dissection of the conceptual *logic* of the rationale for assisted suicide, we might call it a "loose cannon" argument. The basic claim is that the socially accepted killing of innocent persons will interact with other social factors to threaten lives that advocates of assisted suicide would agree should be protected. These factors at present include the following:

The psychological vulnerability of elderly and dying patients. Theorists may present voluntary and involuntary euthanasia as polar opposites;

in practice there are many steps on the road from dispassionate, autonomous choice to subtle coercion. Elderly and disabled patients are often invited by our achievement-oriented society to see themselves as useless burdens on younger, more vital generations. In this climate, simply offering the *option* of "self-deliverance" shifts a burden of proof, so that helpless patients must ask themselves why they are *not* availing themselves of it. Society's offer of death communicates the message to certain patients that they *may* continue to live if they wish but the rest of us have no strong interest in their survival. Indeed, once the choice of a quick and painless death is officially accepted as rational, resistance to this choice may be seen as eccentric or even selfish.[3]

The crisis in health care costs. The growing incentives for physicians, hospitals, families, and insurance companies to control the cost of health care will bring additional pressures to bear on patients. Curt Garbesi, the Hemlock Society's legal consultant, argues that autonomy-based groups like Hemlock must "control the public debate" so assisted suicide will not be seized upon by public officials as a cost-cutting device. But simply basing one's own defense of assisted suicide on individual autonomy does not solve the problem. For in the economic sphere also, offering the option of suicide would subtly shift burdens of proof.

Adequate health care is now seen by at least some policymakers as a human right, as something a society owes to all its members. Acceptance of assisted suicide as an option for those requiring expensive care would not only offer health care providers an incentive to make that option seem attractive—it would also demote all other options to the status of strictly private choices by the individual. As such they may lose their moral and legal claim to public support—in much the same way that the U.S. Supreme Court, having protected abortion under a constitutional "right of privacy," has quite logically denied any government obligation to provide public funds for this strictly private choice. As life-extending care of the terminally ill is increasingly seen as strictly elective, society may become less willing to appropriate funds for such care, and economic pressures to choose death will grow accordingly.

Legal doctrines on "substituted judgment." American courts recognizing a fundamental right to refuse life-sustaining treatment have concluded that it is unjust to deny this right to the mentally incompetent. In such cases the right is exercised on the patient's behalf by others, who seek either to interpret what the patient's own wishes might have been or to serve his or her best interests. Once assisted suicide is established as a fundamental right, courts will almost certainly find that it is unjust not to extend this right to those unable to express their wishes. Hemlock's political arm, Americans Against Human Suffering, has underscored continuity between "passive" and "active" euthanasia by offering the Humane and Dignified Death Act as an amendment to California's "living will" law, and by including a provision for appointment of a proxy to choose the time and manner of the patient's death. By such extensions our legal system would accommodate nonvoluntary, if not involuntary, active euthanasia.

Expanded definitions of terminal illness. The Hemlock Society wishes to offer assisted suicide only to those suffering from terminal illnesses. But some Hemlock officials have in mind a rather broad definition of "terminal illness." Derek Humphry says "two and a half million people alone are dying of Alzheimer's disease."[4] At Hemlock's 1986 convention, Dutch physician Pieter Admiraal boasted that he had recently broadened the meaning of terminal illness in his country by giving a lethal injection to a young quadriplegic woman—a Dutch court found that he acted within judicial guidelines allowing euthanasia for the terminally ill, because paralyzed patients have difficulty swallowing and could die from aspirating their food at any time.

The medical and legal meaning of terminal illness has already been expanded in the United States by professional societies, legislatures, and courts in the context of so-called passive euthanasia. A Uniform Rights of the Terminally Ill Act proposed by the National Conference of Commissioners on Uniform State Laws in 1986 defines a terminal illness as one that would cause the patient's death in a relatively short time if life-preserving treatment is *not* provided—prompting critics to ask if all diabetics, for example, are "terminal" by definition. Some courts already see comatose and vegetative states as "terminal" because they involve an inability to swallow that will lead to death unless artificial feeding is instituted. In the *Hilda Peter* case, the New Jersey Supreme Court declared that the traditional state interest in "preserving life" referred only to "cognitive and sapient life" and not to mere "biological" existence, implying that unconscious patients are terminal, or perhaps as good as dead, so far as state interests are concerned. Is there any reason to think that American law would suddenly resurrect the older, narrower meaning of "terminal illness" in the context of *active* euthanasia?

Prejudice against citizens with disabilities. If definitions of ter-minal illness expand to encompass states of severe physical or mental disability, another social reality will increase the pressure on patients to choose death: long-standing prejudice, sometimes bordering on revulsion, against people with disabilities. While it is seldom baldly claimed that disabled people have "lives not worth living," able-bodied people often say they could not live in a severely disabled state or would prefer death. In granting Elizabeth Bouvia a right to refuse a feeding tube that preserved her life, the California Appeals Court bluntly stated that her physical handicaps led her to "consider her existence meaningless" and that "she can-not be faulted for so concluding." According to disability rights expert Paul Longmore, in a society with such attitudes toward the disabled, "talk of their 'rational' or 'voluntary' suicide is simply Orwellian newspeak."[5]

Character of the medical profession. Advocates of assisted suicide realize that most physicians will resist giving lethal injections because they are trained, in Garbesi's words, to be "enemies of death." The California Medical Association firmly opposed the Humane and Dig-nified Death Act, seeing it as an attack on the ethical foundation of the medical profession.

Yet California appeals judge Lynn Compton was surely cor-rect in his concurring opinion in the *Bouvia* case, when he said that a sufficient number of willing physicians can be found once legal sanctions against assisted suicide are dropped. Judge Comp-ton said this had clearly been the case with abortion, despite the fact that the Hippocratic Oath condemns abortion as strongly as it condemns euthanasia. Opinion polls of physicians bear out the judgment that a significant number would perform lethal injections if they were legal.

Some might think this division or ambivalence about assisted suicide in the medical profession will restrain broad expansions of the practice. But if anything, Judge Compton's analogy to our experience with abortion suggests the opposite. Most physicians still have qualms about abortion, and those who perform abortions on a full-time basis are not readily accepted by their colleagues as paragons of the healing art. Consequently they tend to form their own professional societies, bolstering each other's positive self-image and developing euphe-misms to blunt the moral edge of their work.

Once physicians abandon the traditional medical self-image, which rejects direct killing of patients in all circumstances, their new substitute self-image may require ever more aggressive efforts to make this killing more widely practiced and favorably received. To allow killing by physicians in certain circumstances may create a new lobby of physicians in favor of expanding medical killing.

The human will to power. The most deeply buried yet most power-ful driving force toward widespread medical killing is a fact of human nature: Human beings are tempted to enjoy exercising power over others; ending another person's life is the ultimate exercise of that power. Once the taboo against killing has been set aside, it becomes progressively easier to channel one's aggressive instincts into the destruction of life in other contexts. Or as James Burtchaell has said: "There is a sort of virginity about murder; once one has violated it, it is awkward to refuse other invitations by saying, 'But that would be murder!'"[6]

Some will say assisted suicide for the terminally ill is morally dis-tinguishable from murder and does not logically require termination of life in other circumstances. But my point is that the skill and the instinct to kill are more easily turned to other lethal tasks once they have an opportunity to exercise themselves. Thus Robert Jay Lifton has perceived differences between the German "mercy killings" of the 1930s and the later campaign to annihilate the Jews of Europe, yet still says that "at the heart of the Nazi enterprise . . . is the destruction of the boundary between healing and killing."[7] No other boundary separat-ing these two situations was as fundamental as this one, and thus none was effective once it was crossed. As a matter of historical fact, person-nel who had conducted the "mercy killing" program were quickly and readily recruited to operate the killing chambers of the death camps.[8] While the contemporary United States fortunately lacks the anti-Semitic and totalitarian attitudes that made the Holocaust possible, it has its own trends and pressures that may combine with acceptance of medical killing to produce a distinctively American catastrophe in the name of individual freedom.

These "loose cannon" arguments are not conclusive. All such arguments by their nature rest upon a reading and extrapolation of certain contingent factors in society. But their combined force pro-vides a serious case against taking the irreversible step of sanctioning assisted suicide for any class of persons, so long as those who advocate this step fail to demonstrate why these predictions are wrong. If the strict philosophical case on behalf of "rational suicide" lacks coherence, the pragmatic claim that its acceptance would be a social benefit lacks grounding in history or common sense.

Notes

1. Presentation at the Hemlock Society's Third National Voluntary Euthanasia Conference, "A Humane and Dignified Death," September 25–27, 1986, Washington, DC. All quotations from Hemlock Society officials are from the proceedings of this conference unless otherwise noted.

2. Vatican Congregation for the Doctrine of the Faith, *Declaration on Procured Abortion* (1974), para. 11.

3. I am indebted for this line of argument to Dr. Eric Chevlen.

4. Denis Herbstein, "Campaigning for the Right to Die," *International Herald Tribune,* September 11, 1986.

5. Paul K. Longmore, "Elizabeth Bouvia, Assisted Suicide, and Social Prejudice," *Issues in Law & Medicine* 3, no. 2 (1987), 168.

6. James T. Burtchaell, *Rachel Weeping and Other Essays on Abortion* (Kansas City: Andrews & McMeel, 1982), 188.

7. Robert Jay Lifton, *The Nazi Doctors: Medical Killing and the Psychology of Genocide* (New York: Basic Books, 1986), 14.

8. Yitzhak Rad, *Belzec, Sobibor, Treblinka* (Bloomington, IN: Indiana University Press, 1987), 11, 16–17.

CHAPTER 36

The New Eugenics

Matt Ridley

Charles Darwin (1809–1882), the greatest biologist in history, knew almost nothing about genetics. The first real achievement in this field was made by the monk Gregor Mendel (1822–1884), whose laws of inheritance became widely known around 1900. Biologists understood very little about the mechanisms of inheritance until James D. Watson and Francis Crick accurately described the structure of DNA in 1953. Knowledge has advanced since then at a lightning clip. In the last twenty years, technological advances have made it possible to rapidly sequence genes and to store and share the large amount of resulting data. By 2003, scientists working on the Human Genome Project had mapped out the human DNA—a sequence of three billion pairs of nucleotides—and had identified most of the 20,000 to 25,000 genes encoded in that sequence.

New technology often creates new moral questions. The better we understand inheritance, the better we can control it. Soon we'll be able to determine many of our children's genetic traits with scientific precision. This technology will have beneficial applications, at least in reducing genetic disease. However, many people worry that this technology will also be misused.

Matt Ridley is not worried. Mr. Ridley is a science writer who holds a doctorate degree in zoology from Oxford University.

From *National Review*, vol. 52, no. 14 (July 31, 2000), pp. 34–60. Reprinted by permission.

The entire human genome has been read. Even ten years ago, that seemed a distant goal; but last month, scientists announced that they have completed reading a "rough draft" of the complete recipe for a human being. It will soon be available on compact disc for anybody to read: a book 800 times longer than the Bible. This breakthrough will open an amazing world of possibilities for medicine—including the prediction, prevention, and treatment of many diseases, from kidney stones to cancer.

But why stop at disease? Instead of merely eliminating the negative, why not accentuate the positive—by tinkering with the text to improve it? After all, in pursuit of the perfect human being, we have willingly tried every weapon that falls into our hands, from prayer to psychoanalysis to breast implants. Will we—and should we—do the same with genes?

It is fashionable to answer that we *should* not, that we probably nonetheless *will*, and that that would be a disaster; I am more sanguine. Genetically modified people will not pose a great threat to society, even if we choose to create them; but we will, on the whole, not choose to create them, so there is little to worry about on this score.

A Sad Legacy

Discussions of these issues are burdened by a complicated history. A century ago, progressive social reformers were obsessed by the new agenda of "eugenics." There was a sense of urgency in their desire to improve the human race by selective breeding. It had worked well enough in cattle and chickens, but we human beings were not only failing to breed from the best specimens; we were allowing the worst to have the most children.

"Some day," said Theodore Roosevelt in 1910, "we will realize that the prime duty, the inescapable duty, of the good citizen of the right type is to leave his or her blood behind him in the world." In the same year. Winston Churchill lobbied for compulsory sterilization of the mentally handicapped: "I feel that the source from which the stream of madness is fed should be cut off and sealed up before another year has passed."

Britain never did pass such a law, thanks to determined opposition from a libertarian member of parliament named Josiah Wedgwood. In America, however, states began to pass laws allowing mandatory sterilization. In 1927, the Supreme Court upheld Virginia's eugenic-sterilization law in *Buck v. Bell.* Carrie Buck, whom the state wished to sterilize, lived in a colony for "epileptics and the feeble minded" in Lynchburg, with her mother Emma and her daughter Vivian. After a cursory examination, Vivian was declared an imbecile—she was six months old at the time!—and Carrie was ordered sterilized to prevent her from bringing more imbeciles into the world. Supreme Court Justice Oliver Wendell Holmes thundered that "Three generations of imbeciles are enough!" Compulsory-sterilization laws were thenceforth upheld in many states; more than 100,000 Americans were sterilized under them.

The tragedy of that story lies not in the science behind eugenics, but in the politics: It is the *coercion* that was wrong. An individual who volunteers for sterilization is doing no harm, whatever his or her motives; one who orders another to be sterilized against his or her will is doing wrong. It is that simple.

The eugenic movement began with the best of intentions. Many of its most strident advocates were socialists, who saw eugenics as enlightened state planning of reproduction. But what it actually achieved, when translated into policies, was a human-rights catastrophe: the rejection of many immigrants, the sterilization of many people whose only crime was to have below-average intelligence, and eventually, in Germany, the murder of millions of people.

But now, a century later, we are once again practicing a sort of eugenics: We abort fetuses that would be born with Down syndrome or inherited disorders. In New York, Ashkenazi Jews who carry the Tay-Sachs mutation can avoid marrying each other through blood testing organized by the Committee for the Prevention of Jewish Genetic Disease. We also stand on the brink of cosmetic genetic engineering.

Are we simply repeating the mistakes of the past? No. The principal difference is that whereas eugenics, as conceived in the early part of the 20th century, was a public project, modern genetic screening is a private matter. Only China still preaches eugenics for the good of society; everywhere else, modern eugenics is about individuals applying private criteria to improve their own offspring by screening their genes. The benefits are individual, and any drawbacks are social—exactly the opposite of the old eugenics.

Another difference is precision: The selective breeding of the past worked slowly and unpredictably—but today, we can insert a gene into an organism and be all but certain what the effect will be: For example, inserting the genetic phrase "Make insulin!" into a bacterium transforms the life of a diabetic.

Genetic engineering of plants and animals is now routine. Only the genetic engineering of human beings is forbidden.

It would work: Of this, there is no doubt. Take a simple example: the gene on chromosome 4 that is associated with Huntington's disease, a terrible mental affliction of middle age. You could go into the gene in a fertilized egg, find the crucial phrase "CAG"—which, in affected people, is repeated more than 39 times in the middle of the gene—and remove about half of the repeats. It would not be easy, but it could probably be done. The result would be a healthy person with no risk of Huntington's, and no risk of passing it on to her children.

This procedure might become a neater and less intrusive option than the three now available: 1) *screening followed by abortion*—the course of action followed by many couples who find themselves carrying a child with a devastating disease; 2) *pre-implantation genetic diagnosis,* which is in vitro fertilization followed by implantation of a healthy embryo and rejection of one that carries the faulty gene; and 3) *gene therapy,* the immensely difficult and dangerous procedure of trying to infect sufficient cells in your body with a gene-carrying virus to correct the faulty gene.

It is not just medical genetic engineering that is feasible; cosmetic genetic engineering could also begin tomorrow, though it would still be very primitive. There is a gene on chromosome 17 called the ACE gene, which comes in two equally common varieties, long and short. On average, people who inherit two long ACE genes (one from each parent) are better athletes than people who inherit two short versions. For instance, of 123 British-army recruits, the long-gened ones improved their weight-lifting ability much faster during training than the short-gened ones.

It would be comparatively trivial to engineer a human embryo so that it had two long ACE genes. The result would be a child slightly more likely to win long-distance running races. There would be no risk of unpredictable consequences, because about one in four of us have two long ACE genes already; it is not unnatural. It would not be cruel to the child, and it would have no consequences for society. But should it be allowed?

Everybody—from scientists to theologians—seems to agree that human genetic engineering is wrong. Their reasons are a mixture of respect for the sanctity of life and fear of the unpredictable. But if they were ever to relent and allow it, it would be for medical, not cosmetic purposes. To correct a cruel inherited disease—like Huntington's—is one thing. To use the same technology to correct a subjective defect—non-blue eyes or short stature—would be quite another.

No Nightmare Scenarios

Yet even at this "easy" end of the spectrum, there are uncomfortable questions. Cures might seem uncontroversial, but they are not. My colleague, the sociologist Tom Shakespeare, is achondroplasic, but he regards his inherited short stature as a disability only to the extent that society imposes that prejudice on him. With a first-class degree from Cambridge University and a good career, he does not see his genetic disorder as a reason for eliminating future people like him.

He sees genetic engineering as undermining society's respect for people like him, because it sends the message that disability could be—and therefore perhaps *should* be—eliminated. In a genetically engineered society, the parents of a genetically disabled child would feel social opprobrium for not having "done something about it."

I see his point, but I do not fully agree with it, for the following reason: I see nothing in history to suggest that the ability to cure a condition lessens compassion or respect towards its sufferers. Indeed, society's respect for people with "preventable" disabilities has surely never been greater than now: People with Down syndrome, for example, were once abandoned or shunned; they are now treated with much more respect.

I suspect it will prove impossible in practice to draw a line between cure and enhancement, between medical and cosmetic genetic engineering. One person's cure is another person's enhancement. Is an inherited weight problem a disease? Would it be a cosmetic enhancement to "cure" dyslexia?

Assume that one day, genetic alleles that predict homosexuality are discovered—a wild assumption, but not inconceivable. To a heterosexual couple, disabling the "gay genes" in their potentially homosexual child might seem like a "cure" that prevents an "abnormal" life. But if so, then for a homosexual couple trying to procreate through a surrogate mother, disabling the "straight genes" in their child might also seem to be a "cure." . . .

Another objection to genetic engineering is that it would drive out diversity, as people converge on the "ideal." Again, I think this argument is mistaken. Far from threatening diversity, genetic engineering may actually increase it. Supposing cosmetic genetic engineering became accepted, musical people might seek out musical genes for their children; athletes might seek athletic genes; etc. It is very unlikely that everybody would choose the same priority.

If diversity is not threatened by genetic engineering, then another argument—that in a genetically engineered world, there would be an underclass of those who could not afford the procedure—also evaporates. In this scare scenario, the rich might buy themselves an even better start in life with the best genes. But this argument applies only if genetic engineering becomes commonplace, and it is at least partly undermined if everybody is using different criteria of perfection. After all, just by choosing our marriage partners we have been practicing private eugenics ever since we became human: Dark good looks, a slender figure, a winning personality, or a quick mind—in considering these attributes in potential mates, we are, at least partly, selecting genes. Yet diversity is not threatened, because each of us has different criteria.

When artificial insemination was first thought of, in the 1930s, a prominent Nobel-prize-winning American geneticist, H. J. Muller, wrote a book speculating about the uses to which such a technique would be put. "How many women," he wrote, "in an enlightened community devoid of superstitious taboos and of sex slavery, would be eager and proud to bear and rear a child of Lenin or of Darwin! Is it not obvious that restraint, rather than compulsion, would be called for?"

Well, no, it is not obvious. Attempts to make test-tube babies "engenic" by establishing banks of sperm from clever men, or of eggs from beautiful women, have largely failed. People use in vitro fertilization (IVF) to have their own children, not to have other people's—let alone Lenin's. IVF is actually an instructive precedent for the current debate: When it was invented in the 1970s, society as a whole largely disapproved, finding the procedure unnatural and abhorrent. It gained acceptance because mild disapproval by the many was matched by fierce demand from the few; it took off because infertile individuals demanded it, not because society as a whole decided they could have it. It was an individual decision, not a collective one.

Just as infertile people demanded access to IVF, even before it had been fully tested for safety, it is possible that people who carry fatal genes will demand access to genetic engineering; but this is not very likely. Unlike infertile people, they already have an alternative: pre-implantation genetic diagnosis, which can spot and discard affected embryos in favor of unaffected ones. And if these people, for whom a "bad" gene is the difference between misery and happiness, do not need genetic engineering, why would anybody else need it? It is true that a few people might wish for a blue-eyed boy, but would they really be prepared to abandon the easy business of natural conception for a painful and exhausting test-tube conception instead?

My point is that cosmetic genetic engineering would attract a very small—and probably half-hearted—clientele, even if it were made legal and safe. I simply cannot think of a single feature of my own children that I would have liked to fix in advance. People do not want particular types of children; they just want their own children, and they want them to be a bit like themselves.

When faced with a mediocre hand at poker, you change some cards and start again. But when faced with perhaps 40,000 human genes, any of which you could change for what may or may not be a slightly better version, which would you change? Looks, intelligence, talents, skin color? It doesn't sound so tempting, does it?

The history of eugenics teaches that nobody should be forced to engineer her children's genes—but, by implication, neither should anyone be forced *not* to. To regulate such decisions with heavy-handed state intervention would be to fall into the very trap that caught the do-gooder eugenicists of 1910. I am not against all regulation: At the very least, governments can step in to ensure standards among practitioners (something they are quite good at). But they would be unwise to try to specify in detail what people can and cannot decide to do for themselves. As Thomas Jefferson said: "I know no safe depository of the ultimate powers of the society but the people themselves; and if we think them not enlightened enough to exercise their control with a wholesome discretion, the remedy is not to take it from them, but to inform their discretion."